COMMENTARY

ON THE

BOOK OF THE PROPHET ISAIAH

BY JOHN CALVIN

TRANSLATED FROM THE ORIGINAL LATIN, AND COLLATED WITH
THE LATEST FRENCH VERSION,

BY THE REV. WILLIAM PRINGLE

VOLUME SECOND

WIPF & STOCK · Eugene, Oregon

Wipf and Stock Publishers
199 W 8th Ave, Suite 3
Eugene, OR 97401

Commentary on the Book of the Prophet Isaiah, Volume 2
By Calvin, John and Pringle, William
Softcover ISBN-13: 979-8-3852-1702-1
Hardcover ISBN-13: 979-8-3852-1703-8
eBook ISBN-13: 979-8-3852-1704-5
Publication date 2/15/2024
Previously published by Baker Book House, 2005

This edition is a scanned facsimile of the original edition published in 2005.

TRANSLATOR'S PREFACE

IN preparing the First Volume of the COMMENTARY ON ISAIAH, many attempts were made, but without success, to procure the FRENCH TRANSLATION. After much fruitless labour, and some expense, a copy of that rare work, which happens to be in the possession of the Parker Society, has been kindly lent to the Translator, who takes this opportunity of conveying his warmest thanks for this favour. The references in the foot-notes of the present and future Volumes will give some idea of the assistance derived from that source. But it has also supplied materials for a history, more complete than we could formerly give, of this Commentary, and of the forms in which it was successively brought before the public.

Various scribes, on some occasions, united their efforts to obtain a perfect record of what had been uttered by the Reformer in his private Lessons, as they were called, which he delivered to students of theology. But, in the present instance, we are indebted almost exclusively to the earnest, judicious, and unwearied labours of one man, *Mr. Nicolas Des Gallars*, a minister of Geneva, from whose notes, after having been revised by the Author, the first Latin edition was printed in 1550. He appears to have executed, under the Author's eye, a French Translation, which came forth almost simultaneously with the Latin copy, and enjoyed the advantage of being known to be well authenticated. After the lapse of several years, CALVIN availed himself of a season of leisure for re-writing this Commentary, added more than a third to its original size,[1] and made such extensive altera-

---
[1] See page xvii.

tions, that he ventured to call it "a new work.[1]" It bears the date of 15th January 1559. The third edition, which is dated 1583, lays claim to still greater accuracy; for it professes to have received corrections from the Author's Manuscript.

While the COMMENTARY was thus extensively circulated,[2] the benefits of it were chiefly confined to those who were acquainted with the Latin language; for even the French reader was left to struggle with all the imperfections which belonged to the first edition. At least, it was only eleven years before the last mentioned date, and eight years after the Author's death, that a new French translation appeared, which was printed at Geneva by *François Perrin*, in 1572. There is reason to believe that the first French translation would be treated by the second translator with great deference, and that he would scarcely consider himself to be at liberty to depart from it, except for the purpose of introducing the extensive alterations and additions which had been made to the original work. Let us hope that some future editor, having obtained access to copies now slumbering in the shelves of our continental neighbours, or perhaps of our own countrymen, will enjoy the satisfaction of collating the earlier and later editions in both languages, and will be enabled to reveal the steps by which this valuable Commentary passed from the first rough notes of the laborious scribe to the form which was imparted to it by the fastidious corrections of the Author.

This Volume contains an "Address to the Readers" by *Nicolas des Gallars*, Latinized *Gallasius*, (which appears to have been prefixed to his French translation of the Commentary,) his Epistolary Dedication of the Latin edition of 1583 to a learned author and eminent printer, John Crispin, and a short "Address to the Readers" by the latest French trans-

---

[1] See Com. on Isaiah, vol. i. p. xvi.   [2] See page xv.

lator, all of which, it is hoped, will be perused with deep interest. The relation in which *Gallars* stood to CALVIN, and to his published writings, has thrown around him many pleasing associations ; and his style, both Latin and French, displays such judgment, and taste, and scholarship, as justifies the marked preference given to him by the Reformer, and assures the reader that the responsible office which he held could not have been committed to abler hands.

The NOTES added to these Volumes shew that it is the aim of the CALVIN SOCIETY not only to give exact Translations, but to aid the investigation of dark passages by the labours of modern critics. Among the works which have been consulted with greatest advantage may be named " The Prophecies of Isaiah, Earlier and Later, by *Joseph Addison Alexander*, Professor in the Theological Seminary, Princeton, New Jersey," an exceedingly valuable addition to the stores of exegetical theology, and not a little enhanced by the care with which the learned editor, Dr. Eadie, has superintended the British edition. Yet we are again and again constrained to remark the extent to which the critical researches of our own age have been anticipated by the sagacity of the Reformer, to whom our greatest men delight in acknowledging their obligations. " CALVIN," says Professor Alexander, " still towers above all interpreters in large commanding views of revelation, in its whole connection, with extraordinary insight into the logical relations of a passage, even where its individual expressions were not fully understood. These qualities, together with his fixed belief of fundamental doctrines, his eminent soundness of judgment, and his freedom from all tendency to paradox, pedantic affectation, or fanciful conceit, place him more completely on a level with the very best interpreters of our day than almost any intervening writer."

AUCHTERARDER, 3d *September*, 1851.

PREFATORY ADVERTISEMENT

BY

NICOLAS DES GALLARS

TO THE READERS.

THOUGH in collecting these COMMENTARIES I was astonished, first, at the labour and difficulty, and next at the various opinions of men, yet I thought, Christian Readers, that I must not refuse to labour or shrink from anything, provided that I can be of any service. With respect to the difficulties, I quickly surmounted them, through the clear method of instruction which the Author has been accustomed to employ, as may be seen in his writings, but still more in his speaking. And if some obscure passages, of which there are many in that Prophet, made me pause, it was not because I had not the benefit of his judgment and advice in clearly explaining and revising the whole; for, in consequence of the familiar and daily intercourse which I had with him, those intricacies which might have retarded or perplexed me were easily disentangled and removed. Besides, at any hour when one could go by stealth, that is, when he had any relaxation from the weighty affairs which almost overwhelmed him, I read to him all that I had written, in order that, if he could not closely examine the whole, he might at least add, or take away, or give me directions, as far as was necessary. All this he did carefully, though hardly ever did I read to him two or three verses when he was not immediately called away, either by persons who wanted his advice, or by his friends. Yet reviewing these things with all the fidelity and diligence that I could, I still returned, and frequently put questions to him.

As to my labour, it was partly relieved by some expository remarks which I had collected from his own mouth, while he was preaching; for it is now four years and more since he explained that Prophet to us, in a highly profitable manner, in public Discourses, before giving us the interpretation in the school. At that time, recording not only the faithful exhortations which relate to the correction of vices, to the condition of that age, and to the restoration of the purity of doctrine and of the Church, but also the exact interpretations on which he dwelt largely, in order to draw from them a solid doctrine to be applied to the use of the people, when I returned to the house, I wrote them down in Latin, so far as I remembered and had leisure. That was of great use to me in collecting these Commentaries; not that I put into them everything that I then wrote, or in the same order and method, but so far as I already understood the sentiments, and had been habituated, by some practice, to that mode of interpretation, I had not so much trouble as if I had come quite raw and ill-prepared to that way of writing.

So far as relates to the judgments of men, who must have very various opinions about this labour of mine, I soon foresaw that there would be many of them who would take no great pleasure in that which cost me pain, because they would have preferred to have this written by the Author himself instead of being collected and arranged by me. And indeed I am very much of their opinion; for the whole would have been sent forth by him in a more complete and finished state. But as he was employed in preparing other works, the advantage of which is so evident that it is unnecessary for me to proclaim it; and as he was harassed by so much business that he scarcely had leisure to read, it would hardly have been possible for him to put his hand to that work.

Accordingly, having been for a long time attached to that Prophet, and wishing clearer expositions of many passages, and now enjoying them, I thought that I would do what was good and profitable, if, while I promoted my own benefit, I had regard also to others whose desire might not be less than mine, and whose minds, even supposing that they had not so strong a desire, might be aroused by reading this Commentary, and might receive from it an increase of knowledge. In order, therefore, that you, believing Reader, might enjoy along with me the explanation of that Prophet, I suddenly undertook this labour, lest if we waited longer for these Commentaries, they might be taken from us by some injury or calamity in these wretched times. For we see every day what snares are laid by Satan for the Church, which is newly born, and for her faithful teachers. We meet with treachery in some, from whom we had expected better things; in others we find fickleness and lightness, and others are blinded by the glimmering of this age. There are very few of them who, in defence of the kingdom of Christ, oppose the tyrannical laws of Antichrist.

Let us therefore welcome those who, through the unspeakable mercy of God, are left to us; or rather let us welcome the gifts which God has given them, that hereafter, as far as we shall have opportunity, we may provide for the Church. While we can enjoy their doctrine, let us seize it eagerly as the armour fitted for repelling our enemies; for there is great reason to believe that the Lord will take vengeance on the malice of men by such punishments as they deserve, and will deprive us of the excellent gifts with which in the present day he has adorned his Church. Many have great gifts of tongues, while others excel in interpretations, and undoubtedly they have strong claims on our attention; but this gift of prophecy, which surpasses all others, and to which we ought to be especially devoted, is generally despised. Hence it arises that many persons are more addicted to ostentation than eager to promote the salvation of the Church, and take more pleasure in vaunting before the people than in edifying the Church of Christ. St. Paul, already perceiving in his time that imminent danger, said, "Desire to pursue spiritual gifts, but still more that you may prophesy." (1 Cor. xiv. 1.) For in the Christian Church the most important point, and that which we ought above all things to desire, is that the hidden meanings and divine mysteries of Scripture may be explained to us with some advantage. If that is wanting, the rest must gradually be thrown down, as we have found it to be in past ages, to the great injury of the whole Church.

We must therefore devote ourselves to this gift above all others, for fear of abusing those passages of Scripture which have been turned to a wrong purpose, or of being ourselves guilty of torturing those passages to a meaning which is foreign to them. And especially we must throw ourselves on the doctrine of the prophets; for they who are faithfully employed in them open up a road for easily going higher, and lay a firm and solid foundation for salvation. Now, if that exercise was ever necessary, it is at the present time, when we must make war not only against Papists or Jews, but against dreadful monsters which, concealed under the appearance of men, endeavour to overturn all religion and humanity.

Among all the prophets ISAIAH justly holds the chief place, because he gives very clear testimonies concerning Christ, and places before our eyes the state and condition of his Church, that is, of his kingdom, as the reading will alone clearly shew, so that it will be unnecessary for me to make a long preface. He who shall have understood him well will be abundantly prepared for reading the other Prophets. The perusal of these Commentaries will enable you better to understand how well adapted the doctrine of Isaiah is to the present time; and if you are diligent and attentive, I am not afraid that you will think that I have laboured in vain.

Yet if you compared this work with the Sermons which the Author preached on that Prophet, you might well exclaim, as Æschines did with regard to Demosthenes, "What would you have thought if you had heard him speak it?" He adjusted his sentences so admirably, touched the hearts of his hearers, explained every thing by familiar and obvious examples, and treated his subjects in so popular a manner, that he seemed actually to place it before their eyes. Very frequently, too, an opportunity presented itself of discoursing on some passage, when it would have been impossible purposely to select out of the whole Scripture a passage better adapted to the place, the persons, and the occasion;

so that all were astonished at it, and clearly understood that it had not been directed by the wisdom of a man, but by the Spirit of God; and the advantage which afterwards resulted from it fully verified that conclusion.

If these Sermons can ever be published, (which I should earnestly desire,) you will know these things better, though the truth of what has been said cannot be so clearly perceived by any as by those who have seen them with their eyes. Here you have the substance, however, both of the Sermons and of the Lessons, from which I shall reckon myself to have derived great benefit, if you partake of it as you ought. It was my study, it was the object which I proposed to myself, not to have any favour from men, but to be of advantage to believers; and, so far as my conscience bears me witness, I see not why I ought to dread the judgment of men. I hold it to be certain that they who shall carefully weigh the whole will judge of me with candour; and that, if there be any fault or omission in what I have done, they will cheerfully lay in the balance the benefit which they shall have derived from the work.

GENEVA, *December* 27, 1551

EPISTOLARY DEDICATION

BY

NICOLAS DES GALLARS

TO HIS ANCIENT FRIEND,

JOHN CRISPIN.

WHENEVER I call to remembrance, my dear CRISPIN, (as I cannot but often do,) that eminent and godly pastor of the Church, JOHN CALVIN, I have a feeling of deep grief, and at the same time of joy. For when I bring before my mind the candour and uprightness of that man, his kind disposition towards me, and the pleasant and intimate friendship which I enjoyed with him for sixteen years, it is impossible that I should not be deeply affected by the loss of such a friend, or, I ought rather to say, of such a parent. Nor is it only on my own account that I grieve, but rather on account of the whole Church, which has been deprived of so great a man, and has thus sustained a heavy loss by his death.

What labours, what watchings and solicitudes he endured, with what faithfulness and wisdom he attended to the interests of all, with what frankness and courtesy he received those who visited him, how ready and clear were his replies to those who consulted him even on the weightiest matters, how learnedly, both in private and in public, he solved the difficult and perplexing questions which were proposed to him, with what gentleness he comforted the afflicted and cheered those who were faint and sorrowful, with what firmness he resisted adversaries, and with what energy he was wont to restrain the haughty and obstinate, with what strength of mind he bore adversity, what moderation he exercised in prosperity, and, in short, with what ability and cheerfulness he performed all the duties of a true and faithful servant of God, I certainly cannot find words to express! Lest any one should think that the ardour of my regard for him prompts me to make these statements, let him consider the actual facts, which truly exceed the power both of speech and of thought. Besides the writings and records which convey a stupendous testimony of his virtues, many things were done and many were spoken by him which cannot be made known to all, as they are known to those who were present when he did or uttered them.

When I recall those remarkable events, my grief is alleviated; and the advantage which is derived from them, and which is shared with me by so many godly men, gives me consolation. My joy is of such a nature, and is so steady and full, that it swallows up all my sorrow and lamentation however great. And on this ground also do I congratulate you, my dear CRISPIN, that you not only peruse with the highest delight the works and writings of that man whom you ardently loved, but labour to impart them to others. Those treasures of wisdom are thus enlarged, and return with high interest to those from whom they come. You thus cause the regret for the loss of so great a man to be alleviated, and the grief produced by his lamented and early death to be diminished.

For the third time, after having been wrought and polished on your anvil, this book now comes forth, which I may truly call a treasure, because it contains vast riches of heavenly grace, and opens up the path to what is greater. Whoever shall give to it a cheerful and laborious perusal, let him know with certainty that he will not return empty; for he will gather what shall be advantageous with regard not only to this Prophet but to all the other Prophets, and to the whole of Scripture, and if he attend to the directions which are scattered throughout the book, he will undoubtedly possess a strong light for beholding and enjoying those things which were hidden and concealed from many. By frequently applying your hand, therefore, to this work, you not only gratify me, who first sent it forth after long and severe toil, but you gratify all those who have perused or even tasted the work. You might have sufficiently perceived and actually known this from the numerous copies which have been already circulated.

I have not been disappointed in the expectation which I at that time formed, when during the whole period of four years, with unwearied toil, having first heard the public Sermons and afterwards the private Lectures, but employing my own judgment and style, I returned home and committed these things to writing. And whenever I recollect that period, during which this Church, which formerly was small and feeble, received wonderful accessions, I cannot but feel the utmost joy. You also may well remember what was its condition when, banished from your native country, you first came hither; and likewise what large additions had been made to it when you brought your family, and settled down permanently here for the express purpose of assisting the efforts of the godly by your skill and industry.

These things I take pleasure in relating, in order that, by calling to remembrance what you have experienced, I may quicken your zeal, and may stimulate you to perform those things which you have undertaken, and of which it will be impossible for you ever to repent, and may give a fresh impulse even to your cheerful and willing exertions. Proceed then, my dear CRISPIN, in assisting by your diligence the efforts of those who are devoted to Sacred Literature, and labour not only to promote this work, but also to publish others. You see that many things, though useful in the highest degree, are passed by and almost neglected by those who aim at immediate gain rather than at public usefulness.

The smaller Treatises of this Author were edited by me fifteen years ago; and although since that time he wrote many other Treatises, yet no one put his hand to that work, so as to bring out a uniform edition, (I speak of the Latin copies,) either of those or of others which were afterwards added. I therefore earnestly and repeatedly urge my request, that you will take charge of those works, and also of others with which you are well acquainted, and that you will not allow any of the writings of so great a man to be lost; and, in short, that you will grant the request made to you by godly and studious persons, and that you will fulfil and go beyond those expectations respecting you which you have already excited. May God favour your undertakings, and make you prosperous and happy!

GENEVA, *January* 1, 1570.

THE FRENCH TRANSLATOR'S
PREFATORY ADDRESS

TO THE READERS.

It is upwards of twenty years, my dear Readers, since the Lessons of Mr. John Calvin, having been collected by *Mr. Nicolas Des Gallars*, were published under the title of a Commentary, and dedicated to that illustrious Prince, of blessed memory, Edward VI., King of England. Long afterwards, the Author himself, revising that collection printed in Latin and in French, was not satisfied with merely revising it, so as to elucidate what might be obscure on account of its brevity, and to arrange better what was confused, but laboured so diligently and so successfully, that he enlarged it in Latin, by more than a third, with excellent and necessary matter for understanding the text, putting everything so completely in its proper order, that if any person will take the trouble of comparing the first Commentary, or Collection of Lessons, with this second edition, he will find that what we have said is true.

What is more, it was not in the school that this Commentary was collected for the second time, but it was written in the house, and word for word, under the eye of the Author, who has so skilfully arranged and digested the whole, that when you read it, you will perceive that in this book, as in others which have already come forth from him, he did much good service to the Church of God, and faithfully pointed out the road to those who wish to make progress in the study of theology, especially by these Commentaries, which, when they are read attentively, will not only be very useful for explaining the true meaning of the prophet Isaiah, but will not less contribute to throw light on many passages of the other books of the Holy Scripture. This has induced me to translate them anew into French, in order that those of you who do not understand the Latin tongue may not be deprived of such an advantage. Read, and profit in the fear of the Lord.

COMMENTARY

ON THE BOOK OF

THE PROPHET ISAIAH.

CHAPTER XVII.

1. The burden of Damascus. Behold, Damascus is taken away from *being* a city, and it shall be a ruinous heap.

2. The cities of Aroer *are* forsaken; they shall be for flocks, which shall lie down, and none shall make *them* afraid.

3. The fortress also shall cease from Ephraim, and the kingdom from Damascus, and the remnant of Syria: they shall be as the glory of the children of Israel, saith the Lord of hosts.

4. And in that day it shall come to pass, *that* the glory of Jacob shall be made thin, and the fatness of his flesh shall wax lean.

5. And it shall be as when the harvest-man gathereth the corn, and reapeth the ears with his arm; and it shall be as he that gathereth ears in the valley of Rephaim.

6. Yet gleaning grapes shall be left in it, as the shaking of an olive-tree, two *or* three berries in the top of the uppermost bough, four *or* five in the outmost fruitful branches thereof, saith the Lord God of Israel.

7. At that day shall a man look to his Maker, and his eyes shall have respect to the Holy One of Israel.

8. And he shall not look to the altars, the work of his hands, neither

1. Onus Damasci. Ecce Damascus ablata est, ne sit civitas; nam erit acervus ruinæ.

2. Derelictæ sunt urbes Aroer, in caulas vertentur; accubabunt, nec erit qui exterreat.

3. Et cessabit præsidium ab Ephraim, et regnum a Damasco. Et reliquiæ Syriæ, quasi gloriæ filiorum Israel erunt, dicit Iehova exercituum.

4. Et erit in die illa, attenuabitur gloria Iacob, et pinguedo carnis ejus macrescet.

5. Et erit sicut qui colligit messem segetis, qui brachio suo spicas metit; similiter ut quis colligit spicas in valle Rephaim.

6. Et relinquetur in ea racematio, sicut excussio oleæ; duæ illic aut tres baccæ restant in cacumine altioris rami, quatuor aut quinque in expansis ramis fructus ejus, dicit Iehova Deus Israel.

7. In die illa respiciet homo ad factorem suum, et oculi ejus ad sanctum Israelis intuebuntur.

8. Nec respiciet ad altaria opus manuum suarum, non aspiciet quæ

shall respect *that* which his fingers have made, either the groves or the images.

9. In that day shall his strong cities be as a forsaken bough, and an uppermost branch, which they left because of the children of Israel: and there shall be desolation.

10. Because thou hast forgotten the God of thy salvation, and hast not been mindful of the Rock of thy strength, therefore shalt thou plant pleasant plants, and shalt set it with strange slips:

11. In the day shalt thou make thy plant to grow, and in the morning shalt thou make thy seed to flourish; *but* the harvest *shall be* a heap in the day of grief and of desperate sorrow.

12. Woe to the multitude of many people, *which* make a noise like the noise of the seas; and to the rushing of nations, *that* make a rushing like the rushing of mighty waters!

13. The nations shall rush like the rushing of many waters: but *God* shall rebuke them, and they shall flee far off, and shall be chased as the chaff of the mountains before the wind; and like a rolling thing before the whirlwind.

14. And behold at evening-tide trouble; *and* before the morning he *is* not. This *is* the portion of them that spoil us, and the lot of them that rob us.

fecerunt digiti ejus, nec lucos, nec simulachra.

9. In die illa erunt urbes fortitudinis ejus, quasi derelictio virgulti et frondis, quemadmodum reliquerunt coram filiis Israel; et erit desolatio.

10. Quoniam oblita es Dei salutis tuæ, nec memor fuisti Dei fortitudinis; idcirco plantabis plantas amœnas, et palmitem alienum conseres.

11. Die plantationis tuæ crescere facies eam, et mane germinare facies semen tuum; sed recedet messis in die fruendi, et erit dolor desperatus.

12. Hei multitudo populorum multorum; instar sonitus maris sonabunt, et strepitus nationum; instar strepitus aquarum ingentium tumultuabuntur.

13. Strepent populi instar strepitus aquarum ingentium, et increpabit eum, et fugiet procul; fugabitur quasi stipula montium coram vento, et quasi globus coram turbine.

14. Tempore vespertino ecce turbatio; antequam sit mane, nusquam erit. Hæc est pars conculcantium nos, et sors eorum qui nos diripiunt.

1. *The burden of Damascus.* Here he prophesies against the kingdom of Syria, and mentions the chief city in which the seat of the kingdom lay. It was proper that this calamity, like others which came before it, should be described, that the righteous might confidently believe that God would one day assist them, and would not always permit them to be oppressed by the wicked without end. The king of Syria had formed an alliance with Israel against Judah, as we saw formerly in the seventh chapter; and as the Jews were not able to contend with him, and were deprived of other aids, they might also entertain doubts about God's assistance, as if he had utterly abandoned them. To free them, therefore,

from these doubts, he threatens the destruction of that kingdom, from which they would readily conclude that God fought in defence of his people.

It is uncertain at what time Isaiah uttered this prophecy, for, as I have already remarked, he does not follow the order of time in threatening against each nation the punishment which it deserved. But, as far as I am able to conjecture, he foretold those events at the time when those two kings, that is, the kings of Israel and Syria, invaded Judea, and entered into a league to destroy it and the whole Church, (Isaiah vii. 1, 2 ;) for, by joining together the Israelites and the Syrians, he summons them to a mutual judgment, in order to show that the only advantage which they had derived from the wicked and disgraceful conspiracy was, to be involved in the same destruction. In this manner Isaiah intended to comfort godly persons who were of the tribe of Judah; for he has his eye chiefly on them, that they may not be discouraged, and not on the Syrians, or even the Israelites, whose destruction he foretells.

Behold, Damascus is taken away. The demonstrative particle, *Behold,* seals the certainty of the prophecy. When he expressly mentions *Damascus,* it does not follow from this that the other parts of the kingdom are exempted, but it was customary with the prophets to take a part for the whole, so as to include under the destruction of the metropolis the fate of the whole nation; for what must ordinary towns expect when the citadel of the kingdom has been stormed? Yet there is another reason why the Prophets pronounce heavier threatenings on the chief and royal cities, and especially direct their discourse against them. It is, because a polluted flood of crimes overflows from them into the whole country.

2. *The cities of Aroer are forsaken.* It is not probable that *Aroer* here denotes the city which is mentioned elsewhere, (Num. xxxii. 34 ; Deut. ii. 36 ; and iii. 12 ; and iv. 48 ;) but it is rather the name of a country. He draws the picture of a country which has been ruined; for he shews that those places in which cities had been built will be devoted to pasture, and that no habitation will be left there but huts and

shepherds' tents ; for if any inhabitants remained, the shepherds would drive their flocks to some other place.

3. *The fortress shall cease.*[1] He points out the reason why the Lord determines to cut off the kingdom of Syria. Amos (i. 3) enumerates additional reasons, but the most important was that which the Prophet mentions, namely, that they had drawn the kingdom of Israel to their side for the purpose of making war against the Jews. The Israelites were undoubtedly allured, by the blandishments of the Syrians, to form an alliance with them against their brethren. It was a pretext exceedingly fitted to impose upon them, that the Syrians would aid them against all their enemies ; and hence also the Israelites placed confidence in the forces and power of the Syrians to such an extent, that they reckoned themselves able to oppose any adversary. All Israel is here, as in many other passages, denoted by the name *Ephraim,* which was the chief tribe of that people. Now, "the assistance and kingdom" are said to "cease" from any place, when its strength is broken and its rank is thrown down.

And the remnant of Syria. That is, both of these nations, the Syrians and the Israelites, shall be brought to nothing ; and, for the purpose of giving additional weight to the prophecy, he states that it is God who declares it ; for he immediately adds these words, *saith Jehovah of hosts.* Now, when the Lord punished so severely those two kingdoms, he unquestionably promoted in this way the benefit of his Church, delivering it by the destruction of its enemies. And, indeed, in destroying both nations, he employed as his agents the Assyrians, to whom even the Jews had applied ; and although in this respect they had heinously sinned, yet their offence did not hinder the Lord from promoting the benefit of his Church, or from delivering it by bringing its enemies into conflict with each other. Hence we perceive how great is the care which God exercises over us, since he does not spare even the greatest kingdoms in order to preserve us. We ought also to observe, that though all the wicked enter into a league, and join hands to destroy us, yet

[1] " Le secours venant d'Ephraim cessera ;"—" The assistance coming from Ephraim shall cease."

the Lord will easily rescue us from their jaws. Besides, we ought to remark that it is advantageous to us to be deprived of earthly aids, on which it is in vain for us to rely in opposition to God; for when we are blinded by our prosperity, we flatter ourselves, and cannot hear the voice of God. It therefore becomes necessary to remove these obstructions, that we may perceive our helplessness, as was the case with the Israelites, who were bereft of their aid after Syria had been destroyed.

4. *The glory of Jacob shall be diminished.*[1] Although he had undertaken to speak of Syria and Damascus, he takes occasion to join Israel with the Syrians, because they were bound by a mutual league, and were united in the same cause. The Syrians, indeed, whom Isaiah chiefly addresses, were like a torch to inflame the Israelites, as we have already said. But the Israelites themselves were equally in fault, and therefore they were justly drawn, by what might be called a mutual bond, to endure the same punishment.

It is not easy to say whether under the name *Jacob* he speaks of the whole elect people, so as to include also the tribe of Judah. But it is probable that he refers only to the ten tribes, who laid claim to the name of the nation, and that it is in mockery that he describes them as *glorious*, because, being puffed up with their power and multitude and allies, they despised the Jews their brethren.

And the fatness of his flesh shall wax lean. When he next threatens them with *leanness*, his object is to reprove their indolence, as the Prophets frequently reprove them for their fatness. (Jer. v. 28; and l. 11.) On account of their prosperity and of the fertility of the country, they became proud, as horses that are fat and excessively pampered grow restive. Hence also they are elsewhere called "fat cows." (Amos iv. 1.) But however fierce and stubborn they might be, God threatens that he will take away their fatness with which they were puffed up.

5. *And it shall be as when the harvest-man gathereth the corn.* He shews by a comparison how great will be the desolation. "As the reapers," he says, "gather the corn in

"Sera diminué;"—" Shall be made thin."—Eng. Ver.

armfuls, so this multitude, though large and extended, will be mowed down by the enemies." Now that he may not leave a remainder, he adds that at the conclusion of the harvest *the ears will be gleaned,* as if he had said, that when the multitude shall have been destroyed and the country laid bare like a field which has been reaped, even the shaken and scattered ears will not be left. Besides, he employs the metaphor of a harvest because the people, trusting to their great number, dreaded nothing ; but as the reapers are not terrified by the large quantity of the corn, so he declares that their vast number will not prevent God from utterly destroying them. This may also refer to the Assyrians, but the meaning will be the same, for they were God's servants in executing this vengeance.

We need not spend much time in explaining the word *gather,* for it means nothing else than that the slaughter will resemble a harvest, the conclusion of which has been followed by the gleaning of the ears. When the ten tribes had been carried away, the Assyrians, having learned that they were meditating a revolution, destroyed them also. (2 Kings xvii. 4.) He especially mentions *the valley of Rephaim,* because its fertility was well known to the Israelites.

6. *Yet gleaning grapes shall be left in it.* This metaphor has a different meaning from the former; for as if the name of the nation were to be entirely blotted out, he had expressly foretold that nothing would be left after the slaughter. He now adds a consolation, and thus abates the severity of the destruction ; for he declares that, although the enemies had resolved to consume and destroy everything, still some remnant would be left. In like manner the gleaning of grapes is never made so completely as not to allow some grapes or even clusters to remain, which were concealed under the leaves, and the olive tree is never so thoroughly shaken as not to leave at least some olives on the tops of the trees. Consequently, to whatever extent the enemies may rage, and even the vengeance of God may be kindled, still he foretells that the Judge, notwithstanding his severity, will reserve for himself a small number, and will not allow the attacks of enemies to fall upon his own elect.

Hence it follows, that amidst the heaviest vengeance there will still be room for mercy. The present discourse relates to the posterity of Abraham; and though they had revolted from God so as to deserve to be cast off, yet the goodness of God rose above their wickedness. They had indeed rendered themselves unworthy of such goodness, but the covenant of God must remain firm and impregnable, and a proof of that firmness must be given by him in some remnant, though the nation entirely set it aside as far as lay in their power. This ought to be carefully observed, so that when we perceive no traces of the Church, and when the godly appear to be destroyed, still we may not think that the Church has perished; for the promise of the Lord stands, that it will continue for ever. (Gen. xvii. 7.) Some remnant, therefore, will always remain, though frequently it is not visible to our eyes.

7. *At that day shall a man look to his Maker.* He now shews the fruit of this chastisement, and this is the second consolation with which the godly ought to fortify themselves amidst their afflictions. Although they perceive nothing but the wrath of God, yet they ought to reflect that the Lord, who never forgets himself, will continually preserve his Church, and not only so, but that the chastisements will be advantageous to them. After having spoken, therefore, about the continual existence of the Church, he next adds, that *men will look to God.* This is the most desirable of all, for when men betake themselves to God, the world, which was formerly disordered, is restored to its proper order; but when we have been estranged from him, no one repents of his own accord, and therefore there is no other way in which we can be brought back than to be driven by the scourge of chastisements. We are thus reminded that we ought not to be so impatient in enduring chastisements, which cure us of the fearfully dangerous disease of apostasy.

To look to God means nothing else than that, when we have turned away, we return to a state of favour with him, betake ourselves and are converted to him. For how comes it that men abandon themselves to every kind of wickedness but because they forget God? Where the knowledge of God exists, there reverence dwells; where forgetfulness of God is found, there contempt of him also prevails. Yet this relates properly to faith, as if he had said, "When chastisements so severe shall have tamed the Israelites, they will then perceive that there is no help for them but in God. For this reason he immediately adds the expression, *To his Maker*. It was indeed a proof of abominable indolence that they did not rely on God alone, who had bestowed on them so many precious gifts. The Prophet therefore says, that when they had been subdued by distresses and afflictions, they would afterwards return to a sound mind, so as to begin to hope in him who had bound them to himself by so many acts of kindness. And indeed he calls God their *Maker*, not as having created the whole human race, but in the same sense in which he likewise calls him *The Holy One of Israel*. Although therefore all men were created after the image of God, (Gen. i. 27,) yet Israel was peculiarly his workmanship, because he was his heritage, and his holy and chosen people. (Exodus xix. 6.) This repetition, in accordance with the ordinary custom of the Hebrew language, is employed to denote the same thing. He therefore calls God *Holy*, not only as viewed in himself, but from the effect produced, because he has sanctified or separated to himself the children of Abraham. Hence it follows, that the creation which he speaks of must be understood to relate to spiritual reformation, in reference to which he is especially called *the Maker of Israel*. (Isaiah xlv. 11; Hosea viii. 14.)

8. *And he shall not look to the altars.* This contrast shews more clearly that the *looking* which he spoke of in the former verse relates strictly to hope and confidence, for he says that every kind of sinful confidence will vanish away when men have learned to hope in God; and indeed in no other manner can any one obtain clear views of God than by driving far from him all superstitions. We are thus taught that obstacles of this kind ought to be removed if we wish to approach to God. It is vain to think of making a union between God and idols, as the Papists do, and as the Jews formerly did; for that vice is not peculiar to our age, but has prevailed in all ages. Every obstruction ought there-

fore to be removed, that we may look to God with such earnestness as to have just and clear views of him, and to put our trust in him.

The work of his hands. It is for the purpose of exciting abhorrence that he calls the false gods *the work of their hands*, that the Israelites, being ashamed of their folly, may shake off and drive away from them such a disgraceful reproach. On this vice, however, he dwells the more largely, because they were more chargeable with it than with any other, and because none can be more abominable in the sight of God. There were innumerable superstitions among them, and in places without number they had set up both idols and altars, so that Isaiah had good reason for reproving and expostulating with them at great length on account of these crimes.

It might be objected that the altar at Jerusalem was also built by men, and therefore they ought to forsake it in order to approach to God. (Exodus xxvii. 1.) I reply, that altar was widely different from others, for although it consisted of stone and mortar, silver and gold, and was made like others by the agency of men, yet we ought not to look at the materials or the workmanship, but at God himself who was the maker, for by his command it was built. We ought therefore to consider the essential form, so to speak, which it received from the word of God; other matters ought not to be taken into view, since God alone is the architect. (Exodus xx. 24, 25; Deut. xxvii. 5, 6.) Other altars, though they bore some resemblance to it, should be abhorred, because they had not the authority of the word. Such is the estimate which we ought to form of every kind of false worship, whatever appearance of sanctity it may assume; for God cannot approve of anything that is not supported by his word.

9. *In that day shall his strong cities be as a forsaken bough.* He follows out what he had begun to say about driving out the inhabitants of the country; and as the Israelites, trusting to their fortified cities and to their bulwarks, thought that they were in safety, he threatens that they will be of no more use than if enemies were marching

through desert places. The view entertained by some, that חוֹרֶשׁ (chōrĕsh) and עֲזוּבַת (ăzūbăth[1]) are proper names of towns, is a forced interpretation. I understand them rather to denote unpleasant and disagreeable places, or that the walls and ditches will contribute no more to their defence than if the Israelites dwelt amidst thickets and bushes.

As they left.[2] Here the particle אֲשֶׁר, (asher,) I have no doubt, denotes comparison; and therefore I have rendered it *in like manner as,* which makes the statement of the Prophet to be, in connection with what had been already said, that the people would tremble and flee and be scattered, in the same manner as God had formerly driven out the ancient inhabitants. Those who think that אֲשֶׁר, (asher,) is a relative are constrained to supply something, and to break up the thread of the discourse. But it simply brings to their remembrance an ancient example, that the Israelites may perceive how vain and deceitful is every kind of defence that is opposed to the arm of God. It is a severe reproach; for the Israelites did not consider that the Lord gave to them that land, as it were, by hereditary right, in order that they might worship him, and that he drove out their enemies to put them in possession of it. And now, by their ingratitude, they rendered themselves unworthy of so great a benefit; and, consequently, when they had been deprived of it, there was good reason why they should feel distresses which were the reverse of their former blessings.

This passage will be made more plain by the writings of Moses, whom the prophets follow; for in the promises he employs this mode of expression, "One of you shall chase a thousand," (Lev. xxvi. 8; Joshua xxiii. 10,) and in the threatenings, on the other hand, he says, "One shall chase a thousand of you." (Deut. xxxii. 30.) Accordingly, as he struck such terror into the Canaanites, that at the sight of

---

[1] "'Like the leaving of the ploughed field, or on the topmost bough.' I adopt with pleasure the interpretation of this disputed passage proposed in the excellent Lexicon of Parkhurst, v. חרשׁ, as being most natural, and in strict conformity with the Jewish law, Lev. xix. 9, 10; Deut. xxiv. 19-21; which commanded 'a leaving of the ploughman, and of the branches of the vine and olive,' to be given up to the use of the poor in harvest. Avarice would be apt to make these leavings very scanty."—*Bishop Stock.*

[2] *Whom they left.*—Eng. Ver.

the Israelites they immediately fled, so he punished the ingratitude of the people in such a manner that they had no power to resist. Thus the Lord gave a display of his power in two ways, both in driving out the Canaanites and in punishing his people. The Prophet, therefore, by mentioning that ancient kindness, reproaches the people with ingratitude, forgetfulness, and treachery, that they may acknowledge that they are justly punished, and may perceive that it proceeds from the Lord, that they are thus chased by the enemies to whom they were formerly a terror.

10. *Because thou hast forgotten the God of thy salvation.* He shews the reason why the Lord exercises such severity against the Ten Tribes, that they may not complain of being unjustly afflicted or too harshly treated. The sum of what is stated is, that all those evils come to them because they have wickedly despised God. It was excessively base and altogether inexcusable ingratitude, after having received so many favours, to prostitute their hopes to heathen nations and to idols, as if they had never in any respect experienced the love of God. Indeed, no unbelievers, when they are called to account, will vindicate themselves from the charge of offering an insult to God by wandering after creatures. But the argument was applicable, in a special manner, to the people of Israel, to whom God had revealed himself in such a manner that they ought to have left off all the impostures of the world and relied on his grace alone. They are therefore justly accused of ingratitude, for having buried in forgetfulness the object of true faith; and indeed, when God has once allowed us to taste the delight of his goodness, if it gain a place in our hearts, we shall never be drawn away from it to anything else. Hence it follows that they are convicted of ingratitude who, not being satisfied with the true God, are unsteady and driven about in all directions; for in this manner they despise his invaluable grace.

Accordingly, the Prophet expressly calls him *the God of salvation* and the *God* or *Rock of strength.* צוּר (*tsūr*) has both significations; for it was a monstrous thing that they were not kept in fidelity to God, who had so often preserved them, and, as it were, with an outstretched hand. When he adds that they *had not been mindful*, this is an amplification; for he indirectly charges them with base slothfulness in not considering in how many ways they had formerly been made to know the kindness of God.

Therefore thou shalt plant. Next follows the punishment, that they might not think that this ingratitude would remain unpunished. That is, because they forsook the fountain of all good, though they labour to obtain food, yet they will be consumed by famine and hunger; for all that shall be obtained with great labour the enemy will either carry away or destroy. This passage is taken from Moses; for it is a curse pronounced amidst other curses. "The fruit of thy land, and all thy labours, shall a nation which thou knowest not eat up." (Deut. xxviii. 33.) Hence we see what I have often mentioned before, that the prophets borrow many things from Moses, and are the true interpreters of the law. He speaks of choice vines and branches taken from them; because the greatness of the loss aggravates the sorrow.

11. *In the day.* This denotes the incessant labour which is bestowed on plants and seeds. Yet we might understand by it the fruit which is yielded, as if a vine newly planted would immediately produce wine. And this agrees with the next clause, in which *the morning* is put for *the day.* This appears to denote sudden maturity, unless perhaps this also be supposed to denote carefulness, because from the very earliest dawn they will devote themselves to labour.

The words are somewhat ambiguous; for some render them, "the removing of the branch on the day of affliction." But as נחלה (năchălāh) means "an inheritance," here, in my opinion, it literally denotes produce. It is not derived from חלה (chālāh,) and I do not see how the word "Branch" agrees with it. I grant, indeed, that as vines are mentioned, the word *Harvest* is employed (καταχρηστικῶς) differently from its natural meaning.

It might also be rendered a Collector; and yet I do not choose to dispute keenly about those two significations, for the meaning will be the same, provided that נחלה (năchălāh) be understood to denote "the gathering of the fruits." In this way the passage will flow easily enough. "Though you labour hard in dressing the vines, and though you begin your toil at the earliest dawn, you will gain nothing; for by the mere shaking of the branches the fruit will fall off of its own accord, or your vines will be plundered." Thus, by a figure of speech in which a part is taken for the whole, the word *plant* denotes that unwearied toil which husbandmen and vine-dressers are wont to bestow on plants and vines.

This is a very severe punishment, and undoubtedly proceeds from the curse of God; for if he who has no possession be driven out and banished from a country, he will not be rendered so uneasy as the man who has well cultivated fields, and particularly if he has bestowed his labour on them for a long time. In this manner the Lord determined to punish the Israelites, because they abused the fertility of the country and grew wanton amidst their abundance. A similar punishment is also threatened against the wicked in general terms, that "in vain do they rise early, and vex themselves with unremitted toil;" for they gain nothing by it. (Psalm cxxvii. 2.) On the other hand, it is declared that they who trust in the Lord will undoubtedly receive the reward of their toil, for the blessing of God will accompany their labours. (Psalm cxxviii. 2, 4.)

12. *Alas*[1] *for the multitude!* Some render it *Woe*, making it to denote execration. Sometimes, as we have seen elsewhere, it is employed in calling to a person; but on the present occasion I rather think that it betokens sorrow,[2] for he groans on account of the calamity which he foresees will befall Israel, and he does so either out of brotherly affection, or in order that the prophecy may make a more powerful impression on the minds of a sluggish and indolent people. It is certain, that the prophets regarded with greater horror than other men the vengeance of God, of which they were the heralds; and although, in sustaining the character assigned to them, they threatened severely, still they never laid aside human feelings, so as not to have compassion on those who perished. But the chief reason was a consideration

---

[1] *Woe to the multitude.*—Eng. Ver.
[2] "Mais il me semble plustost qu'il se prend ici pour Helas."—"But I rather think that here it stands for *Alas!*"

of the covenant which God had made with the seed of Abraham; and we see that Paul also had this feeling to such an extent, that he "wished to be accursed for his brethren." (Rom. ix. 3.) When therefore Isaiah brings the fact before his mind, he cannot but be deeply affected with grief; and yet, as I have hinted, it tends to make the fact more certain, when he places it before his eyes as if he actually saw it.

The word *multitude* is here employed, because the army had been collected out of many and various nations, of which the Assyrian monarchy was composed. The metaphors which he adds are intended for no other purpose than to exhibit more forcibly what has been already stated; for he compares them to a sea or a deluge, which overflows a whole country.

13. *The nations shall rush.* Although he appears to follow out that threatening which he formerly uttered, yet he begins to comfort believers by repeating the same statement, as if we should say, "They who were unmindful of God must be punished for their wicked revolt, and must be, as it were, overwhelmed by a deluge; but the Lord will restrain this savage disposition of the enemies, for, when they have exercised their cruelty, he will find a method of casting them out and driving them away." This is a remarkable consolation, by which he intended to support the remnant of the godly. Nor does he speak of the Jews only, as is commonly supposed, for hitherto he has addressed his discourse to the ten tribes, and it is certain that there were still left in Israel some who actually feared God, and who would have despaired if they had not been upheld by some promise.

By these metaphors he describes dreadful storms and tempests. When the Holy Spirit intends to bring comfort to the godly, he holds out those objects which are wont to terrify and discourage the minds of men, that we may learn that God will easily allay all tempests, however violent and dreadful. As the winds and seas and storms are at his command, so it is easy for him to restrain enemies and their violence; and therefore immediately afterwards he compares the Assyrians to *chaff*.

As the chaff of the mountains before the wind. Although with regard to the Israelites their attack was terrible, yet he shews that before God they will be like *chaff*, for without any effort he will scatter all their forces. Hence it follows that we ought not to judge of their resources and strength by our senses. Whenever therefore we see the restraints laid on the wicked withdrawn,[1] that they may rush forward for our destruction, let us indeed consider that, so far as lies in ourselves, we are ruined, but that God can easily frustrate their attacks. גַּלְגַּל (*galgal*) means *a rolling thing*,[2] which is easily driven by the wind.

14. *And, behold, at evening tide trouble.* The meaning is, "As when a storm has been raised in the *evening*, and soon afterwards allayed, no trace of it is found in the *morning*, so will cheerful prosperity suddenly arise, contrary to expectation." The Prophet intended to state two things—first, that the attack of the enemy will be sudden; and secondly, that the ravages which they shall commit will not be of long duration. As the Assyrians rose suddenly against the Israelites, so their fall was sudden.

From this passage all the godly ought to draw wonderful consolation, whenever they see that everything is in disorder, and when dreadful changes are at hand; for what is it but a sudden storm which the Lord will allay? Tyrants rush upon us like storms and whirlwinds, but the Lord will easily dispel their rage. Let us therefore patiently wait for his assistance; for though he permit us to be tossed about, yet through the midst of the tempests he will at length conduct us "to the haven." (Psalm cvii. 30.) And if the Prophet comforted a small remnant, who appeared to be almost none at all, this promise undoubtedly belongs to us also. True, we are almost none, and a wretched church is concealed in a few corners; but if we look at the condition of the kingdom of Israel, how few were the servants of God in it! And these hardly ventured to mutter, such was the universal hatred of religion and godliness. Although therefore the

---

[1] "Toutes les fois donc que nous voyous les meschans avoir la bride sur le col pour nous ruiner." "Whenever then we see the wicked have the bridle on their neck to ruin us."

[2] "And like the gossamer before the whirlwind."—*Lowth.* "And like thistle-down before the storm."—*Stock.*

Lord destroy the multitude of the wicked, yet to the small number of the godly, who may be said to be tossed about in the same ship with them, he will hold out a plank to rescue them from shipwreck, and will guide them safely and comfortably into the harbour.

This is the portion. He addresses the believers who were concealed in the kingdom of Israel, and joins them with the Church, although, as is frequently the case with the children of God, the members were scattered in every direction. We see here what will be the end of the wicked who have persecuted us. Though we are exposed to their rage, so that they tear and plunder and trample upon us, and inflict on us every kind of insult, yet they will be like storms which are subdued by their own violence and quickly disappear. We ought to expect that this will be the lot of all the tyrants who at the present day wretchedly harass the Church, and treat cruelly the children of God. Let this consolation be engraved on our minds, that we may know that the same thing will happen to them.

CHAPTER XVIII.

1. Woe to the land shadowing with wings, which *is* beyond the rivers of Ethiopia:
2. That sendeth ambassadors by the sea, even in vessels of bulrushes upon the waters, *saying*, Go, ye swift messengers, to a nation scattered and peeled, to a people terrible from their beginning hitherto; a nation meted out and trodden down, whose land the rivers have spoiled!
3. All ye inhabitants of the world, and dwellers on the earth, see ye, when he lifteth up an ensign on the mountains; and when he bloweth a trumpet, hear ye.
4. For so the Lord said unto me, I will take my rest, and I will consider in my dwelling-place like a clear heat upon herbs, *and* like a cloud of dew in the heat of harvest.
5. For afore the harvest, when

1. Heus terra inumbrans alis, quæ est trans flumina Æthiopiæ.

2. Mittens per mare legatos, in vasis junceis super aquas. Ite nuntii celeres ad gentem distractam et expilatam, ad populum formidabilem ab eo et deinceps, gentem undique conculcatam, cujus terram flumina diripuerunt.

3. Omnes habitatores orbis, et incolæ terræ, cum signum sustulerit in montibus, videbitis; cum tuba clanxerit, audietis.

4. Porro sic mihi dixit Iehova, Quiescam, et videbo in tabernaculo meo, sicut calor siccans pluviam, et sicut nubes roscida in calore messis.

5. Quia dum adfuerit messis, per-

the bud is perfect, and the sour grape is ripening in the flower, he shall both cut off the sprigs with pruning-hooks, and take away *and* cut down the branches.

6. They shall be left together unto the fowls of the mountains, and to the beasts of the earth: and the fowls shall summer upon them, and all the beasts of the earth shall winter upon them.

7. In that time shall the present be brought unto the Lord of hosts of a people scattered and peeled, and from a people terrible from their beginning hitherto; a nation meted out and trodden under foot, whose land the rivers have spoiled, to the place of the name of the Lord of hosts, the mount Zion.

fectum erit germen, et ex flore fructus erit maturescens; tum amputabit ipsos palmites falcibus, et propagines auferendo exscindet.

6. Derelinquentur pariter volatili montium et animalibus terræ. Æstivabit super illud volatile, et omnia animalia terræ hyemabunt.

7. Tempore illo adducetur Iehovæ exercituum munus, populus laceratus et expilatus, et de populo terribili, ex quo esse cœpit et deinceps; gente undique conculcata, cujus terram flumina diripuerunt, ad locum nominis Iehovæ exercituum, ad montem Sion.

1. *Woe to the land.* I cannot determine with certainty what is the nation of which Isaiah speaks, though he shews plainly that it bordered on *Ethiopia.* Some consider it to refer to the whole of Egypt; but this is a mistake, for in the next chapter he treats of Egypt separately, from which it is evident that the people here meant were distinct from the Egyptians. Some think that the Troglodytes are here meant, which does not appear to me to be probable, for they had no intercourse with other nations, because their language, as geographers tell us, was hissing and not speech;[1] but those who are mentioned evidently had intercourse and leagues with other nations.

Still it is uncertain whether they leagued against the Jews or joined with the Egyptians in driving out the Assyrians. If they were avowed enemies to the Jews, Isaiah threatens punishment; but if they deceived them by false promises, he shews that nothing is to be expected from them, because by idle messages they will only protract the time. However that may be, from the neighbouring nations to be mentioned in the next chapter, we may in part ascer-

[1] "The Ethiopian Troglodytes," says Herodotus, "are the swiftest of foot of all men of whom we have received any accounts. The Troglodytes feed on serpents, and lizards, and reptiles of that sort, and the language which they have adopted has no resemblance to any other, but they screech like bats.—*Herod.* iv. 183.

tain where they were situated, that is, not far from Egypt and Ethiopia: yet some may be disposed to view it as a description of that part of Ethiopia which lay on the sea-coast; for we shall afterwards see that the Assyrians were at war with the king of the Ethiopians. (Isaiah xxxvii. 9.)

When he says that that *land shadows with wings,* we learn from it that its sea was well supplied with harbours, so that it had many vessels sailing to it and was wealthy; for small and poor states could not maintain intercourse or traffic with foreign countries. He therefore means that they performed many voyages.

2. *Sending ambassadors by the sea.* This relates strictly to the state of those times. It would appear that this nation solicited the Egyptians or Syrians to harass the Jews, or that the Assyrians employed them for the purpose of harassing the Jews, or that they had formed an alliance with the Egyptians, in order that, by their united force, they might prevent the power of the Assyrians from increasing beyond bounds; for nothing more than conjectures can be offered, because we have no histories that give any account of it, and where historical evidence is wanting, we must resort to probable conjectures. These voyages, there is reason to believe, were not made to any place near at hand, but to a distant country.

In ships of reeds.[1] We ought not to think it strange that he calls them *ships of reeds,* for it is evident from the ancient histories that these were commonly used by the Egyptians, because the channel of the Nile is in some places very steep and dangerous to navigators on account of the cataracts, which the Greeks call Καταδουπα, so that ships of wood cannot be used at those places without being broken and dashed to pieces on the rocks; and therefore it is necessary to employ ships of pliant materials. That the ships might not admit water and thus be sunk, historians tell us that they were daubed within with pitch.

Go, ye swift messengers. This passage is obscure, but I shall follow what I consider to be probable. The Prophet shews the design of his prediction, or the reason why he

[1] " In vessels of bulrushes."—Eng. Ver.

foretold the destruction of that nation. If we believe them to have been avowed enemies of the Jews, the design was to afford some consolation to believers who were wretchedly broken up and scattered, that having received this message they might rejoice and give thanks to God. But if we rather think that the Jews were led by this nation into an unlawful league, we must then consider that this exhortation is ironical, and that the Prophet intended to reprove the folly of the chosen people, in forsaking God and relying on useless aid. Some think that these words were spoken by God, as if he commanded those nations who inhabited the seacoast to destroy the Jews; but I am not at all of that opinion.

To a nation scattered and plundered.[1] I do not agree with those who think that these words describe the destruction of that unknown or obscure nation; for by "a plundered nation" he means the Jews who were to be grievously harassed and scattered, so that no part of them escaped injury.

To a people terrible from their beginning hitherto. He calls it *terrible*, because so great calamities would disfigure it in such a manner that all who beheld it would be struck with terror. I cannot approve of the exposition given by some, that this relates to the signs and miracles which the Lord performed amongst them, so as to render them an object of dread to all men; for the allusion is rather to that passage in the writings of Moses, "The Lord will make thee an astonishment and a terror." Deut. xxviii. 37. In like manner it is said elsewhere, "for the shaking of the head and mockery." (Jer. xviii. 16, and xix. 8, and xxv. 9, 13, 18.) He therefore means that they are a nation so dreadful to behold as to fill all men with astonishment, and we know that this was foretold and that it also happened to the Jews.

A nation trodden down on every side.[2] קו קו, (*kav-kav,*) that is, *on every side,* as if one drew lines and joined them so closely that no space was left between them, or as if one

[1] "Scattered and peeled, or, outspread and polished."—Eng. Ver.
[2] "A nation meted out and trodden down." Heb. "A nation of line, and line, and treading under foot."—Eng. Ver.

drew furrows in a field so as to break every clod; for in this manner was the nation thrown down and trampled under foot.[1]

Whose land the rivers have spoiled. By *the rivers* he means the vast army of the enemies, that is, of the Assyrians. He alludes to what he had formerly said, that the nation, not satisfied with its own little stream, longed for rapid and boisterous rivers. (Isaiah viii. 6.) After having applied to them for assistance, they were overwhelmed by them as by a deluge; and the reason of the whole evil was this, that they were not satisfied with the promises of God, and sought assistance in another quarter. Now, if this command is understood to be given to the *swift messengers* in the name of God, we infer from it that he does not immediately assist his own people, but delays his aid till they are brought to a state of despair. He does not send to them a cheerful and prosperous message while they are still uninjured, or when they have received a light stroke, but he sends a message to a nation altogether trodden down and trampled under foot. Yet when he commands them to make haste, he means that the judgment will be sudden and unexpected, so that light will suddenly burst forth amidst the darkness.

3. *All ye inhabitants of the world.* He shews that this work of God will be so manifestly excellent as to draw the attention not only of the Jews but of all nations.

When he shall lift up an ensign on the mountains, you will see it.[2] These words, which are in the future tense, are rendered by some, agreeably to the custom of Scripture, in the imperative mood;[3] but it is better to view them as denoting what is future. It is as if he had said that the most distant nations will be witnesses of this destruction, because not only will the *ensign* be beheld by all, but the sound of

---

[1] "A nation *meted out by line,* that is, utterly subdued. Heb. *Put under line and line,* to decide what part of them should be destroyed, and what saved by the conquerors. In this manner David is described, (2 Sam. viii. 2,) as having dealt with the children of Moab. See Lam. ii. 8. Such a nation might well deserve to be called *drawn out and pilled,* that is drawn through the fingers (or an instrument) like a willow, in order to be peeled and made fit for wicker work."—*Stock.*

[2] "Videbitis." "Vous le verrez."

[3] "See ye." "Hear ye."—Eng. Ver.

the trumpets will be heard throughout the whole world. This will plainly shew that the war did not originate with men, but with God himself, who will prove himself to be the author of it by remarkable tokens. When wars are carried on, every one sees clearly what is done; but the greater part of men ascribe the beginning and end of them to chance. On the other hand, Isaiah shews that all these things ought to be ascribed to God, because he will display his power in a new and extraordinary manner; for sometimes he works so as to conceal his hand and to prevent his work from being perceived by men, but sometimes he displays his hand in such a manner that all are constrained to acknowledge it; and that is what the Prophet meant.

4. *But thus said Jehovah unto me.* After having threatened a slaughter of the Ethiopians or their neighbours, and at the same time shewn that comfort will arise from it to the Jews, or ironically reproved the foolish confidence with which the Jews had been deceived, he now adds that God will regulate these confused changes in such a manner as to gather to him at length his chosen people. The particle כִּי, (*ki,*) which I have translated *but,* sometimes means *for* and sometimes *but.* The latter meaning appears to be more appropriate in this passage, for the Prophet replies to a doubt which otherwise might grievously perplex weak minds; because when confusion arises, there may be said to be a veil which conceals from us the providence of God. Such also was the state of that nation whose destruction he foretells, that this prediction might be reckoned fabulous and worthy of ridicule; for, as we may gather from it, there was no danger or change to be dreaded.

I will rest. Some consider this as referring to the person of Isaiah, as if, relying on what God had revealed, he *rested,* that is, was in a state of composure, as we ought to be when we have heard the word of God, and fully expect what has been foretold. In like manner Habakkuk also says, *On my watch-tower will I stand.* (Hab. ii. 1.) But unquestionably he relates what the Lord had foretold to him, and the Lord himself, by the mouth of the Prophet, makes this declaration, *I will rest,* that is, I will remain unemployed.

And I will look in my tabernacle.[1] The phrase, *I will look*, has the same import with the former; for a spectator takes no part in doing, but rests satisfied with *looking*. Such is likewise the force of the term *tabernacle*, as if the Lord betook himself to rest under a roof; while, on the contrary, he says that he ascends the judgment-seat, when he avenges the transgressions of the wicked; for these modes of expression are adapted to our capacity. But perhaps it may be thought more probable that the Prophet alludes to the sanctuary; because, although the majesty of God will remain concealed for a time among an afflicted people, yet his rest will not be without effect. It amounts to this, that though everything be turned upside down, so as to awaken a suspicion that God takes no further concern in the government of the world, yet he *rests* for an express purpose, as if he shut himself up unemployed in a chamber, and the effect of this rest will in due time appear.

As the heat that drieth up the rain.[2] By this beautiful metaphor the Prophet expresses more fully what he had formerly said. Yet there are two ways in which it may be shewn to agree with the Prophet's meaning; either that God, aroused, as it were, from his rest, will shew a smiling countenance to gladden believers, or will water them by a refreshing shower; and in this way the Prophet would describe their varied success. Or there is an implied contrast, by which he reminds us that, while God appears to remain unemployed and to look at what is going on, still he can execute his judgments as if it were in sport. And yet, as the two following verses are closely connected with this verse, Isaiah appears to mean, that though God does not act in a bustling manner like men, or proceed with undue eagerness and haste, still he has in his power concealed methods of executing his judgments without moving a finger. Perhaps also he intended to shew, that in destroying this nation, God will act in an extraordinary manner. But we ought to be satisfied with what I lately suggested, that when

---

[1] " And I will consider in my dwelling-place."—Eng. Ver. " I will rest, and look round in my dwelling-place."—*Stock*.

[2] " Like a clear heat upon herbs," or " after rain."—Eng. Ver.

men carelessly resign themselves to sleep in the midst of prosperity, and, intoxicated by their pleasures, imagine that they have nothing to do with God, " sudden destruction is at hand," because God, by a look, frustrates all the designs or preparations of the world. (1 Thes. v. 3.) He therefore declares that he will be like a clear and calm sky,[1] and *like the heat that drieth up the rain.*

And as a cloud of dew in the heat of harvest.[2] Now we know that this rain is exceedingly adapted to ripen the fruits, and likewise that the heat which follows the rain penetrates the fruits with its force, and drives the moisture more inward, by which it hastens their maturity and renders them more productive. Now the Prophet meant, that though calamities and distresses await the reprobate, still everything proceeds so much to their wish, that they appear to be supremely happy, as if the Lord intended to load them with every kind of blessings; but that they are fattened like oxen destined for slaughter, for when they appear to have reached the highest happiness, they suddenly perish.

Hence it follows, that we ought not to form an estimate of the judgments of God according to outward appearances; for when men imagine themselves to be exceedingly safe, they are not far from destruction and from utter ruin. Thus he speedily comforts believers, that they may not suppose that it fares better with the reprobate so long as God forbears to strike; for though he appears to cherish in his bosom those whom he sustains, he will quickly reduce them to nothing. These statements ought to be applied to those wretched and disastrous times when the tyrants who oppress the Church are the only persons that are prosperous, and

---

[1] *Like the clear heat at the coming of daylight.* The resting of Jehovah, hovering over the enemy till they are ripe for destruction, is here beautifully compared to the condensed gloom before daylight, which is wont to usher in a hot summer's day, and to the sheet of dew that appears to hang over the ground in harvest time presently after sunset. עֲלֵי, (*ălĕ,*) is here used for near the time of, as we say, against such a time. עֲלֵי אוֹר, (*ălĕ ōr,*) prope lucem, adventante luce.—*Stock.*

[2] Rosenmüller takes notice of another reading supported by the Septuagint, Syriac, and Vulgate, ביום קציר, (*bĕyōm kātzīr,*) "*at* the time of harvest," instead of, בהם קציר, (*bĕhōm kātzīr,*) "in the heat of harvest." but justly remarks that it makes no difference as to the meaning.—*Ed.*

abound in all kinds of wealth, and contrive in such a manner as if everything were in their power, because they surpass other men in power, and skill, and cunning. But let us know that all these things are done by the appointment of God, who promotes their endeavours and renders them successful, that he may at length slay and destroy them in a moment. I am aware that a widely different meaning is given by some to these words of the Prophet; but any one who takes a judicious view of the whole passage will have little difficulty, I trust, in assenting to my interpretation.

5. *For when the harvest shall be at hand.* Literally it is, "in presence of the harvest;" but we must soften the harshness of the expressions; and it cannot be doubted that the meaning of the Prophet is, that when the harvest is close at hand, and when the grapes are nearly ripe, the whole produce, in the expectation of which wicked men had rejoiced, will suddenly be snatched from them. The Prophet continues the same subject, and confirms by these metaphors what he had formerly uttered, that the wicked are not immediately cut off, but flourish for a time, and the Lord spares them; but that when the harvest shall be at hand, when the vines shall put forth their buds and blossoms, so that the *sour grapes* make their appearance, the branches themselves shall be cut down. Thus when the wicked shall be nearly ripe, not only will they be deprived of their fruit, but they and their offspring shall be rooted out. Such is the end which the Lord will make to the wicked, after having permitted them for a time to enjoy prosperity; for they shall be rooted out, so that they cannot revive or spring up again in any way.

Hence we obtain this great consolation, that when God conceals himself, he tries our faith, and does not suffer everything to be carried along by the blind violence of fortune, as heathens imagine; for God is in heaven, as in his tabernacle, dwelling in his Church as in a mean habitation; but at the proper season he will come forth. Let us thus enter into our consciences, and ponder everything, that we may sustain our minds by such a promise as this, which alone will enable us to overcome and subdue temptations. Let us also consider that the Lord declares that he advances and promotes the happiness of wicked men, which tends to exhibit and to display more illustriously the mercy of God. If he instantly cut down and took them away like a sprouting blade of corn, his power would not be so manifest, nor would his goodness be so fully ascertained as when he permits them to grow to a vast height, to swell and blossom, that they may afterwards fall by their own weight, or, like large and fat ears of corn, cuts them down with pruning-knives.

6. *They shall be left together.*[1] He means that they will be cast aside as a thing of no value, as John the Baptist also compares them to chaff, which is thrown on the dunghill. (Matt. iii. 12; Luke iii. 17.) Thus Isaiah shews that they will be exposed to the wild beasts and to the fowls, so that the fowls will nestle in them in summer, and the wild beasts will make their lairs in them in winter; as if he had said, that not only men, but the wild beasts themselves will disdain them. Such therefore is the end of wicked men, who, situated in a lofty place, and thinking that they are beyond all danger, despise every one but themselves. The fowls and the beasts of prey will make use of them for nests and for food. They will be thrown down, I say, not only beneath all men, but even beneath the beasts themselves, and, being exposed to every kind of insult and dishonour, they will be a proof of the wonderful providence of God.[2]

7. *In that time.* The Prophet again shews why he threatened the destruction of a heathen nation; for when almost all the nations had leagued together against the Church, it appeared as if the Church were utterly ruined, and therefore Jehovah declares that in due time he will render assistance. Had he not opposed such designs, and seasonably restrained the attacks of enemies, the Jews would have despaired; and on this account he shews that he takes care of the Church, and that though he determines to chastise it, still he comes forward at the proper season to hinder it from perishing, and

[1] " That is, their dead bodies."—*Jarchi.*
[2] " To quit the metaphor, the flourishing leaders of a people, devoted by Jehovah to destruction, shall be cut off and trampled on. The people here spoken of are the Assyrians under Sennacherib."—*Stock.*

displays his power in opposition to tyrants and other enemies, that they may not overthrow it or succeed in accomplishing what they imagined to be in their power. In order therefore to excite them to patience, he not only distinguishes them from the Ethiopians, but likewise reminds them that God mitigates his judgments for their preservation.

A present shall be brought. He alludes to the second verse of this chapter, in which we have seen the same names and descriptions applied to the Jewish nation, and he employs the word *brought* because they would first of all be led into captivity, so that it would not be more practicable for them than for foreign nations to go up into the temple.

From a people. This expression deserves notice, for מעם, (*mĕgnăm,*) means that it will not be an entire nation; as if he had said, though you must be reduced to a small number, so as to be a feeble remnant, yet those few who are left will be offered in sacrifice to God. Hence we ought to learn a doctrine highly useful and exceedingly adapted to our times, for at the present day the Church is not far from despair, being plundered, scattered, and every where crushed and trodden under foot. What must be done in straits so numerous and so distressing? We ought to lay hold of these promises, so as to believe that still God will preserve the Church. To whatever extent the body may be torn, shivered into fragments and scattered, still by his Spirit he will easily unite the members, and will never allow the remembering and the calling on his name to perish. Out of those fragments which are now broken and scattered, the Lord will unite and assemble the people. Those whom he joins together in one spirit, though widely separated from each other, he can easily collect into one body. Although therefore we see the nation diminished in numbers, and some of its members cut off, yet some present will be offered by it to the Lord.

To the place of the name. This mode of expression is customary with the prophets. When they speak of the worship of God they describe it by outward acts, such as altars, sacrifices, washings, and such like; and, indeed, the worship of God being within the soul, there is no way in which it can be described but by outward signs, by which men declare that they worship and adore God. But he chiefly calls it *Mount Zion,* because that place was consecrated to God, and God commanded that sacrifices should be offered there. The chief honour which he bestowed upon it was when he caused the doctrine of his word (Isaiah ii. 3) to go forth from it, as we have formerly seen ;[1] so that the name of *Mount Zion* may be properly understood to denote the pure and uncorrupted worship of God. In short, the prophets do not describe the worship of God as it would be after the coming of Christ, but as it was in their own time, because they found it necessary to accommodate themselves to the people to whom they ministered. Hence it ought to be inferred that there is no other way in which we can belong to the Church than by being offered to God in sacrifice. Let every one therefore who wishes to belong to God present himself for such an oblation, and let him no longer live to himself, but be wholly dedicated to God. (Rom. xii. 1 ; 2 Cor. v. 15.) Now we know that it is by this sword of the word, that is, by the gospel, that Paul boasts of offering and sacrificing men to God. (Rom. xv. 16.)

By *the place of the name of the Lord,* he does not mean that his essence, of which we ought not to form any gross or earthly conception, is confined to it, as if God were limited to a place, but because it was a place in which the Lord commanded that his power should be acknowledged, and that men should worship and call upon him where he manifested his presence by his benefits and by his power, and that on account of the ignorance of the people, who could not otherwise comprehend his majesty. Yet it ought to be observed, that we cannot become acceptable to God without being united in one and the same faith, that is, without being members of the Church ; for it is not necessary for us to run to Jerusalem, or to *Mount Zion,* because in the present day *Zion* is as wide and extensive as the whole world, which is entirely devoted to God. All that is necessary therefore is, that the same faith dwell in us, and that we be joined together by the bond of love. If this be want-

[1] See vol. i. p. 96.

ing, every thing about us is heathen, and we have nothing that is sacred or holy.

CHAPTER XIX.

1. The burden of Egypt. Behold, the Lord rideth upon a swift cloud, and shall come into Egypt: and the idols of Egypt shall be moved at his presence, and the heart of Egypt shall melt in the midst of it.
2. And I will set the Egyptians against the Egyptians: and they shall fight every one against his brother, and every one against his neighbour; city against city, *and* kingdom against kingdom.
3. And the spirit of Egypt shall fail in the midst thereof; and I will destroy the counsel thereof: and they shall seek to the idols, and to the charmers, and to them that have familiar spirits, and to the wizards.
4. And the Egyptians will I give over into the hand of a cruel lord; and a fierce king shall rule over them, saith the Lord, the Lord of hosts.
5. And the waters shall fail from the sea, and the river shall be wasted and dried up.
6. And they shall turn the rivers far away; *and* the brooks of defence shall be emptied and dried up: the reeds and flags shall wither.
7. The paper reeds by the brooks, by the mouth of the brooks, and every thing sown by the brooks, shall wither, be driven away, and be no *more*.
8. The fishers also shall mourn, and all they that cast angle into the brooks shall lament, and they that spread nets upon the waters shall languish.
9. Moreover, they that work in fine flax, and they that weave networks, shall be confounded.
10. And they shall be broken in the purposes thereof, all that make sluices *and* ponds for fish.

1. Onus Ægypti. Ecce Iehova equitat super nubem celerem, et veniet in Ægyptum; et commovebuntur idola Ægypti a facie ejus, et cor Ægypti dissolvetur in medio ejus.
2. Et committam Ægyptios cum Ægyptiis, pugnabit quisque tunc contra fratrem suum; quisque, inquam, contra proximum suum; civitas contra civitatem, et regnum contra regnum.
3. Et exinanietur spiritus Ægypti in medio ejus: et consilium ejus destruam, etiamsi quærant illud apud idola, apud magos, apud pythones, apud divinos.
4. Et tradam Ægyptios in manum domini sævi, et rex fortis dominabitur eis, dicit Dominus Iehova exercituum.
5. Tunc deficient aquæ a mari, et fluvius exsiccabitur atque arescet.
6. Elongabuntur flumina; exhaurientur et siccabuntur rivi munitionis, arundo et carectum succidentur.
7. Herbæ ad rivum et super os rivi, et omnis sementis rivi arescet, et propelletur, ut non sit.
8. Et mœrebunt piscatores, et lugebunt omnes qui hamum projiciunt in rivum; qui expandunt rete super faciem aquarum debilitabuntur.
9. Qui in lino optimo operantur erubescent, et qui texunt plagas foratas, (*vel, pellucidas.*)
10. Erunt enim retia ejus dissipata; et omnes architecti retis (*vel, mercedis*) tristes erunt anima.

11. Surely the princes of Zoan *are* fools, the counsel of the wise counsellors of Pharaoh is become brutish: how say ye unto Pharaoh, I *am* the son of the wise, the son of ancient kings?

12. Where *are* they? where *are* thy wise *men?* and let them tell thee now, and let them know what the Lord of hosts hath purposed upon Egypt.

13. The princes of Zoan are become fools, the princes of Noph are deceived; they have also seduced Egypt, *even they that are* the stay of the tribes thereof.

14. The Lord hath mingled a perverse spirit in the midst thereof; and they have caused Egypt to err in every work thereof, as a drunken *man* staggereth in his vomit.

15. Neither shall there be *any* work for Egypt, which the head or tail, branch or rush, may do.

16. In that day shall Egypt be like unto women; and it shall be afraid and fear, because of the shaking of the hand of the Lord of hosts, which he shaketh over it.

17. And the land of Judah shall be a terror unto Egypt; every one that maketh mention thereof shall be afraid in himself, because of the counsel of the Lord of hosts, which he hath determined against it.

18. In that day shall five cities in the land of Egypt speak the language of Canaan, and swear to the Lord of hosts: one shall be called, The city of destruction.

19. In that day shall there be an altar to the Lord in the midst of the land of Egypt, and a pillar at the border thereof to the Lord.

20. And it shall be for a sign and for a witness unto the Lord of hosts in the land of Egypt: for they shall cry unto the Lord because of the oppressors, and he shall send them a saviour, and a great one, and he shall deliver them.

21. And the Lord shall be known to Egypt, and the Egyptians shall know the Lord in that day, and shall do sacrifice and oblation; yea,

11. Certe stulti principes Zoan; prudentum consiliariorum Pharaonis consilium infatuatum est. Quomodo dicitis Pharaoni, Filius sapientum ego, et filius regum antiquorum?

12. Ubi nunc prudentes tui? ut annuntient tibi, aut etiam sciant quid decreverit Iehova exercituum super Ægyptum.

13. Infatuati sunt principes Zoan, decepti sunt principes Noph, seduxerunt Ægyptum angulus tribuum ejus.

14. Iehova miscuit in medio ejus spiritum perversitatis; et seduxerunt Ægyptum in omni opere ejus, quemadmodum circumagitur ebrius in vomitu suo.

15. Nec erit Ægypto opus quod faciat caput vel cauda, ramus aut juncus.

16. In die illa erit Ægyptus instar mulierum; horrebit enim et pavebit a facie agitationis manus Iehovæ exercituum, quam agitabit ipse super eam.

17. Et erit terra Iuda Ægyptiis in tremorem. Omnis qui recordatus fuerit illius pavebit super ipsam, propter consilium Iehovæ exercituum, quod decrevit super eam.

18. In die illa erunt quinque civitates in terra Ægypti loquentes labio Canaan, et jurantes per Iehovam exercituum. Civitas desolationis una vocabitur.

19. In die illa erit altare Iehovæ in medio terræ Ægypti, statua item juxta terminum ejus Iehovæ.

20. Eritque in signum et in testem Iehovæ exercituum, in terra Ægypti; quia clamabunt ad Iehovam propter oppressores, et mittet eis servatorem et principem, ut liberet eos.

21. Et cognoscetur Iehova ab Ægyptiis, cognoscent, inquam, Ægyptii Iehovam in illo die; et facient sacrificium et oblationem,

they shall vow a vow unto the Lord, and perform *it*.

22. And the Lord shall smite Egypt; he shall smite and heal *it:* and they shall return *even* to the Lord, and he shall be entreated of them, and shall heal them.

23. In that day shall there be a highway out of Egypt to Assyria, and the Assyrian shall come into Egypt, and the Egyptian into Assyria; and the Egyptians shall serve with the Assyrians.

24. In that day shall Israel be the third with Egypt and with Assyria, *even* a blessing in the midst of the land:

25. Whom the Lord of hosts shall bless, saying, Blessed *be* Egypt my people, and Assyria the work of my hands, and Israel mine inheritance.

vovebuntque vota Iehovæ et reddent.

22. Itaque percutiet Iehova Ægyptum, percutiens et sanans; convertentur enim ad Iehovam, et exorabitur ab eis, et sanabit eos.

23. In die illa erit via ab Ægypto in Assyriam; commeabunt Assyrii in Ægyptum, et Ægyptii in Assyriam; et colent Ægyptii Assyrios (*vel, cum Assyriis.*)

24. In die illa erit Israel tertia cum Ægypto, et Assyria benedictio in medio terræ.

25. Quia benedicet illi Iehova exercituum, dicens: Benedictus populus meus Ægyptius, et opus manus meæ Assyrius, et hæreditas mea Israel.

1. *The burden of Egypt.* The Prophet here prophesies against *Egypt*, because it was a kind of refuge to the Jews, whenever they saw any danger approaching them; for when they had forsaken God, to whom they ought to have had recourse, they thought that they had no help left to them but in the Egyptians. It was therefore necessary that that kingdom should be overthrown, that its wealth or its forces might no longer deceive the Jews; for so long as Egypt was prosperous, the Jews thought that, on account of its being exceedingly populous and highly fortified, they were far removed from danger, and therefore despised God, or at least paid scarcely any regard to his promises. This led to evil consequences in two respects; first, because when they ought to have relied on God alone, they were puffed up with that vain confidence in Egypt; and secondly, because whenever the Lord punished them, they defended themselves against his chastisements by the power of the Egyptians, as if by human resources they could make void his judgments, when they ought to have been turned to God altogether. On this subject Isaiah speaks more fully in a later portion of this book. (Isaiah xxx. 2.)

Behold, the Lord rideth on a swift cloud. This mode of expression is found also in other passages of Scripture, but in a general form. (Psalm civ. 3.) The Prophet applies it to this prediction, because the Egyptians thought that they were so well fortified on all sides, that there was no way by which God could approach them. He therefore ridicules their foolish confidence, and exhibits the exalted power of God, when he *rideth on a swift cloud,* by which he will easily make a descent upon them, and neither walls nor bulwarks shall hinder his progress. Again, because in addition to earthly aid the Jews were likewise bewitched by a false religion, on this ground also the Prophet ridicules their madness, because God will dash to the ground all the assistance which they expected to obtain from idols. I pass by the foolish notion which many have entertained, as to the idols which Christ overthrew in Egypt, when he was carried thither in infancy; for it does not deserve a refutation. (Matt. ii. 14.) This passage has been perverted to prove it, and to prove many conjectures of the same kind. But the Prophet's meaning is totally different; for he speaks of the defeat of the Egyptians by the Assyrians, and shews that it ought to be ascribed to God, and not, as irreligious men commonly do, to fortune. He shews it to be a judgment of God, by whose hand all things are governed.

And the idols of Egypt shall be moved at his presence. He declares that *the idols* shall fall; that is, that they shall be of no avail to the Egyptians, though they rely on their assistance, and think that they are under their protection. No nation ever was so much addicted to superstitions; for they worshipped cats, and oxen, and crocodiles, and even onions, and plants of every sort, and there was nothing to which they did not ascribe some kind of divinity. He means that the power of all those false gods, whom the Egyptians had taken for their protectors, will be overthrown. Having declared that the Egyptians rely in vain on their superstitions, he likewise casts down the pride which they cherished as to their earthly resources.

And the heart of Egypt shall melt in the midst of her. By the word *heart* he means the courage which sometimes fails even the bravest men, so that they do not attempt any action, even when their strength and forces are abundant; and in this manner he declares that they will be at war with God, who will *melt their hearts* within them, before they are called to contend with their enemies. Not only does he threaten that they will be terrified, but he likewise adds *in the midst* of the whole kingdom, where they had an exceedingly safe and peaceful dwelling, because they were far removed from every attack. It was the duty of all believers to consider this, when war was waged against the Egyptians; and we also ought to behold the same thing exemplified in all revolutions of kingdoms, which proceed solely from the hand of God. If *the heart melts*, if the strength fails, in men who are usually brave, and who had formerly displayed great courage, this ought to be ascribed to the vengeance of God.

2. *And I will set the Egyptians against the Egyptians.* Here he describes more particularly the calamity which the Lord had determined to bring on Egypt. By the expression, *I will set*, he means the internal struggles, in which those who ought to be mutual defenders cut down one another; and no evil can be more destructive than this to a state or a people. It was of importance also to convince the Jews that God, in whose hands are the hearts of men, (Prov. xxi. 1,) could by his unseen influence inflame the Jews to mutual animosities, that they might slay each other, though they were victorious over foreign enemies. Hence we learn that nations never rise in a seditious manner, unless the Lord *set them* against each other, as when one brings forward gladiators to the place of combat. He inflames their minds for battle, and prompts them to slay each other by mutual wounds; and therefore, as we ought to reckon it an evidence of God's favour, when friendship is cherished among citizens, so we ought to ascribe it to his vengeance, when they rage against and slay and injure one another.

And they shall fight every one against his brother. For the sake of heightening the picture, he adds what was still more monstrous, that those who were related to them by blood would take up arms to destroy each other; for if men are worse than beasts when, forgetting their common nature, they engage in battle, how much more shocking is it to nature that brethren or allies should fight with each other!

But the more monstrous it is, the more ought we to acknowledge the judgment of God and his terrible vengeance.

City against city, and kingdom against kingdom. Isaiah appears to advance by degrees; for he mentions, first, *a brother;* secondly, a *neighbour;* thirdly, *cities;* and, fourthly, *kingdoms.* By *kingdoms* he means *provinces,* into which Egypt was divided, which the Greeks called νομοὶ, the term by which the Greek translators have rendered it in this passage.[1]

3. *And the spirit of Egypt shall be emptied.*[2] As Isaiah had, a little before, deprived the Egyptians of courage, so he now takes away their understanding, both of which are exceedingly necessary for the defence of kingdoms; for when these have been taken away, there is no possibility of transacting national affairs. Now, the Egyptians had so high an opinion of their own wisdom, that they reckoned themselves superior to other nations; and it is well known that they haughtily despised all other nations as barbarians, as if there had been no civilisation, refinement, learning, or skill, but in Egypt alone. They boasted that they were the inventors of learning, that philosophy and astronomy came from them, and, in short, that Egypt was the workshop of all the liberal arts; and therefore they would never have thought it possible that they should fail in wisdom and prudence, and unquestionably, if this prediction had come to their knowledge, they would have laughed at it in disdain, and would have thought, that sooner would the waters of the sea be dried up, and everything be overturned, than this should befall those who imagined that prudence was their birthright. But Isaiah declares it boldly, for he did not speak from himself.

Again, since he had predicted that they would be deprived of courage, in which they excelled, the context requires us to understand the meaning to be, that they would be struck

---

[1] Καὶ νομὸς ἐπὶ νομόν. The reader will observe the distinction between the *paroxytone* νόμος, *a law,* and the *oxytone* νομός, a *field* or a *dwelling;* for it is the latter that is employed by Herodotus to denote a *district* or province. Herod. ii. 164.—*Ed.*

[2] "And the spirit of Egypt shall fail. Heb. *shall be emptied.*"—Eng. Ver.

with blindness; for both faculties of the soul depend entirely on the favour of God. Consequently, רוּחַ (*rūăch*) means here understanding and sagacity, which ought to be carefully observed, for many are mistaken as to the meaning of this word. When he immediately adds, *I will destroy the counsel thereof*, this is a stronger expression of the former statement; for it shews what is the cause of that *emptiness*, namely, that God will take and carry away their *counsel*.

Even though they seek it. This is spoken by anticipation, for he meets the objections of the Egyptians, who might have said, "Have we not gods whom we can consult? Have we not magicians, diviners, and soothsayers? Do you reckon those to be of no value?" He threatens that all these things will be of no avail to them, to whatever extent they may rely on them, and be puffed up with the empty name of wisdom. I shall not spend much time on these names, though it is probable that Isaiah's enumeration proceeds by gradual advancement. First, he mentions *gods*, next *magicians*, and afterwards *diviners* and *fortune-tellers*. They had their oracles, in which they placed the highest confidence. Next after them came the *magicians*, though these too had great influence. In matters of smaller moment they consulted the soothsayers. Superstitious men are so restless that nothing can satisfy them; for they are fickle and unsteady, and sometimes resort to one remedy and sometimes to another; and indeed Satan deceives them in such a manner, that at first he holds out to them the appearance of peace and quietness, which they think that they have fully obtained, but afterwards shews them that they have not reached it, and distresses and harasses them more and more, and compels them to seek new grounds of confidence. Thus our minds cannot obtain rest and peace but in God alone. And undoubtedly the Prophet condemns those arts as contrary to reason; for God has revealed all that is necessary to be known by means of the arts and sciences, which he intended to be used, and of which he approves. If any man shall wish to be wise in any other manner, he must have Satan for his teacher.

4. *And I will deliver the Egyptians into the hand of a cruel*

master.[1] He now shews what will happen to the Egyptians, after having lost courage and been deprived of understanding. Nothing will be left for them but to be reduced to slavery; for a nation destitute of these must fall of its own accord, even though it were not violently attacked by any enemy. Of such aids, therefore, God deprives those on whom he determines to take vengeance, and shuts them out from every method of upholding their liberty. Yet the Prophet threatens what is still more shocking, that not only will the empire of which the Egyptians proudly vaunted fall down, but the inhabitants also will undergo hard bondage. Though the adjective קָשֶׁה, (*kāshĕh,*) *cruel,* is in the singular number, yet he says, in the plural number, that they shall be subject to *lords,* which is harder to endure than if there had been but one lord to whom they were subject.

And a powerful king[2] *shall rule over them.* He means that the power of the tyrant to whom he will subject them shall be so great, that it will not be easy to restore them to liberty. Historians shew that various changes occurred in many countries, which they who subdued them were unable to hold and retain; for to keep what has been obtained is often more difficult than to conquer. But the Prophet intimates that this condition will not be easily changed, and that the bondage of the Egyptians shall be of long duration, because no one will dare to enter the lists with an exceedingly powerful conqueror. We may also understand the meaning to be, that the princes of smaller nations will deal more gently with their people than more powerful monarchs, who, relying on their greatness, allow themselves to do whatever they please; for, reckoning their power to be unlimited, they set no bounds to their freedom of action, and rush forward, without restraint, wherever their passions drive them. Whether the one view or the other be adopted, it will amount to this, that the Egyptians, who consider themselves to be the highest and most distinguished of all men, shall fall under the power of another, and shall be oppressed by hard

---

[1] " And the Egyptians will I give over, *or, shut up.*"—Eng. Ver. " And I will shut up Egypt in the hand of cruel lords."—*Stock.*
[2] " A fierce king."—Eng. Ver.

bondage, that is, by the bondage of *a powerful king,* whom no one will dare to oppose. Hence we see how great is the folly of men who are desirous to have a powerful and wealthy king reigning over them, and how justly they are punished for their ambition, though it cannot be corrected by the experience of every day, which is everywhere to be seen in the world. France and Spain, at the present day, boast that they are governed by mighty princes, but feel to their cost how little advantage they derive from that which dazzles them by a false pretence of honour. But on this subject we have spoken formerly in another place.[1] (Isaiah viii. 6, 7.)

5. *Then the waters shall fail from the sea.* He follows out the subject which he had already begun, that the fortifications, by which the Egyptians thought that they were admirably defended, will be of no avail to them. They reckoned themselves to be invincible, because they were surrounded by the sea, and by the Nile, and by fortifications; and historians tell us that it was difficult to gain entrance to them, because the Nile had no mouth, by which they could not easily prevent ships from landing. They therefore boasted that their situation was excellent, and that they were strongly fortified by nature, in like manner as the inhabitants of Venice, at the present day, think that, in consequence of being surrounded by deep ditches, they are impregnable; but fortresses are useless, when God has determined to punish us.

6. *And the brooks of defence shall be emptied and dried up.*[2] What he adds about fortifications is to the same purpose with what he had stated immediately before. He alludes to the embankments, which not only restrained the overflowings of the Nile, but protected the whole country; as if he had said that the embankments will not be needed, because the Nile will be dried up. Now, it is certain that the Nile was not laid dry, and yet the Prophet did not foretell what was not accomplished. We must therefore call to remembrance what we have already said, that on account of

[1] See vol. i. p. 266.
[2] "*Embanked canals.* Rivi aggerum, as the Vulgate has it. The canals by which the waters of the Nile were distributed were fortified by mounds or banks, מָצוֹר, (*mātzōr,*) which word Rosenmüller vainly endeavours to shew to be another name for Egypt or Mizraim."—*Stock.*

our stupidity those calamities are represented to us in a lively manner, which places them as it were before our eyes; for we need to have a representation made to us which is fitted to impress our minds, and to arouse us to consider the judgments of God, which otherwise we despise. We ought to observe the haughtiness of the Egyptians, whose resources were so various and abundant, and who thought that it was impossible for them to be overtaken by such a calamity.

7. *And the reed and the rush shall wither.* He mentions *the reed* and *the rush*, because they had abundance of them, and employed them for various purposes; or, it may be thought to mean that the marshes will be dried up.

By the mouth of the brooks. Some render it *embankments*, but it rather means the fountain itself, which seldom is dried up, though torrents or rivers fail. By *the mouth*, therefore, he means the source of the river, which shall be dried up in such a manner that no part of the country can be watered. Though the source of the Nile was at a great distance, yet not without reason did the Prophet threaten that that river, on whose waters the fertility almost of the whole land depended, shall be dried up at its very source; for in that country rain seldom falls, but its place is supplied every year by the Nile. If that river overflow but scantily, it threatens scarcity and famine; and therefore, when the Prophet threatens that it will be dried up, he means that the whole country will be barren. For this reason he says also, that, even at its very *mouth*, from which the waters spring up, there will be a lack of waters, so that in that place the herbs will be withered.

8. *And the fishers shall mourn.* Isaiah still keeps in his eye the condition of Egypt. We have formerly mentioned[1] that the prophets made use of those figures of speech by which, when any country is mentioned, they chiefly name those things which abound in that country, and for which it is celebrated. Thus, when a vinebearing country is spoken of, they mention vines; if it abound in gold, they speak of gold; and if it abound in silver, they speak of silver. Ac-

---

[1] See vol. i. p. 492.

cordingly, when he speaks of Egypt, which was well watered, and contained abundance of streams, he mentions *fishing.*

They who spread a net on the face of the waters shall languish. Some translate the word אָמְלָלוּ, (*ămlālū,*) "they shall be cut off," but the more correct rendering is, "they shall be weakened;" for this corresponds to the mourning and lamentation which was formerly mentioned. Now, we know that in that country there was a great number of fishers, and that these formed a great part of the wealth of Egypt. When fishers were taken away, of whom there were vast numbers among the Egyptians, and of whom their wealth chiefly consisted, they must have been *weakened.* Now, if the nation be deprived of that which is its ordinary food, great poverty will follow. He therefore describes an astonishing change that shall pass on the whole country.

9. *And they who work in the finest flax.* As he spoke of mourning, so he now speaks of shame; for they who formerly earned an abundant livelihood by this trade will have no gains. Now, the two occupations are closely connected, to weave nets and to fish. Yet it is doubtful if he speaks of those only who manufactured nets; for if we understand שְׂרִיקוֹת, (*sĕrīkōth*) to mean certain very fine linens, it is probable that the latter clause relates to other productions of the loom, manufactured out of small fine thread, and of the most elegant workmanship. We know that linens of very great value were woven in Egypt, and there may be good reason for interpreting the phrase *white nets,* or, as we have rendered it, "perforated," to mean also linen garments, which were more costly in proportion to the greater delicacy of their texture.

It will thus be a metaphorical expression, by which the Prophet indirectly taunts them with their unbecoming luxury, alleging that the Egyptians cover themselves with linen garments in the same manner as if they clothed themselves with a net. If this meaning be adopted, it will agree with the following verse; and indeed I do not see how such exquisite skill in weaving can be applied to fishing. But if it be thought better to understand the whole as relating to fishes, the meaning will be, that they who had been much employed in fishing, and had found it to be a profitable occupation, will be overwhelmed with sorrow.[1]

10. *And all that make ponds.* As to the word שֶׂכֶר, (*secher*,) there is no absolute necessity, in my opinion, for translating it *a net;* for the derivation shews it, on the contrary, to denote a lucrative occupation.[2]

Where fishes are very abundant, they are also preserved in pools and ponds; because the fishers would otherwise be constrained to sell them at a very low price. Besides, when they throw a net, they are not always successful. He therefore follows out the same subject, " It will not be possible either to take or to preserve fishes. Pools will be of no use."

11. *Surely the princes of Zoan are fools.* Here he joins wisdom with folly, and not without reason; for it is impossible to take away from men a conviction of their wisdom, which leads them to believe, in opposition to God himself, that they are wise. It is therefore a kind of acknowledgment, when he calls those persons wise whom he at the same time accuses of folly or stupidity. Though the Hebrew particle אַךְ, (*ăch*,) sometimes means *but*, yet as the Prophet appears to attack the Egyptians, I choose rather to render it " surely," or " truly," or " now at least;" for he scoffs at *the counsellors of Pharaoh* for wishing to be regarded, and believing themselves to be, exceedingly wise, though they are the most foolish of all men. Thus it is an exclamation: " Where is that wisdom of Egypt? Where are the counsellors who held all men in contempt? Why do they

[1] " And ashamed (disappointed or confounded) are the workers of combed (or hatchelled) flax, and the weavers of white (stuffs.) The older writers supposed the class of persons here described to be the manufacturers of nets for fishing, and took הוֹרִי, (*hōrai*,) in the sense of perforated open work or net-work. The moderns understand the verse as having reference to the working of flax and manufacture of linen. Knobel supposes הוֹרִי, (*hōrai*,) to mean *cotton*, as being white by nature, and before it is wrought. Some of the older writers identified שְׂרִיקוֹת, (*sĕrīkōth*,) with *sericum*, the Latin word for silk. CALVIN supposes an allusion in the last clause to the diaphanous garments of luxurious women."—*Professor Alexander*.

[2] Our author is puzzled about this word. In his version he follows the old rendering, " all that make a net," but his marginal reading is, " all that make gain," and to the latter he adheres in his commentary. Bishops Lowth and Stock render it, " all that make a gain," and Professor Alexander, " all labourers for hire."—*Ed.*

not preserve their kingdom?" Now, at least, it is evident what kind of wisdom they had. This tends to confirm and seal the prophecy, in which the Prophet obviously does not speak of things unknown, but has before his eyes, as it were, the destruction of Egypt. "Armed therefore with the authority of God, I venture to pronounce all those princes to be fools, though they think that they are wise."

Finally, the Prophet shews that vain is the glory of men who, without God, claim for themselves even a spark of wisdom; because their folly is at length exposed, and when the actual trial comes, they shew that they are children. The Lord permits them, indeed, to achieve many exploits, that they may obtain reputation among men, but in the end he infatuates them, so that, notwithstanding their sagacity and long experience, they act more foolishly than children. Let us therefore learn to seek from the Lord the spirit of wisdom and counsel, and if he shall bestow it upon us, let us use it with propriety and moderation; for God opposes the wisdom of men when they claim more than they have a right to claim, and those who are too ambitious to exalt themselves, must be punished for their folly; and therefore he often puts them to shame, that it may be made manifest that their wisdom is nothing but empty smoke. There is no wisdom but that which is founded on the fear of God, which Solomon also declares to be the chief part of wisdom. (Prov. i. 7; ix. 10.)

How say ye to Pharaoh, I am the son of the wise, the son of ancient kings? He reproves the counsellors of Pharaoh for flattering him, as courtiers are wont to flatter princes; for they utter nothing but what is intended to soothe and gratify the ears of princes, because this is the way by which they succeed and obtain favour. Thus, amidst many flatteries and lies, there is no room for truth. Though this vice is commonly found in the courts of great princes, yet at that time it abounded chiefly among the Egyptians. They boasted that they were the most ancient of all nations, and that they were the inventors of the arts, and of all liberal education; and if such a conviction existed even among the common people, how much stronger must it have been in the kings themselves?

The boasting related to two points, antiquity and knowledge; and Isaiah reproves both, or at least says that they will be of no value. Pharaoh boasted both of the antiquity and of the wisdom of his nation; and indeed this was common among the whole people; but he speaks chiefly of the king as the head, in whom this haughtiness was more conspicuous than among ordinary persons. Now, we ought not to boast of the wisdom of our ancestors, as if it belonged to us by hereditary right, but we must look to heaven and ask it from its Author. So far as relates to antiquity, it is a foolish and idle boast; and yet princes are so deeply infected by this vice, that they would willingly seek their birth and descent out of the world, and cannot easily be drawn away from that vanity. This madness is heightened by flatterers, who have contrived, as we perceive, many things about the genealogy of certain princes. No song is more delightful to them than when they are separated from the common herd of men, like demigods or heroes. But it frequently happens, that when they carry their curiosity to excess in inquiring about their grandfathers and great-grandfathers, they lay themselves open to ridicule, because it is found that they are descended from one of the common people.

I have heard an amusing anecdote, related by persons worthy of credit, about the Emperor Maximilian, who was very eager to inquire into his descent, and was induced by a silly trifler to believe that he had traced his lineage to Noah's ark. This subject made so powerful an impression on his mind, that he left off all business, applied himself earnestly to this single investigation, and would allow no one to draw him away from it, not even the ambassadors who came to treat with him about important matters. All were astonished at this folly, and silently blamed him for it, but no one had power or courage to suggest a remedy. At length his cook, who was likewise his jester, and often entertained him with his sayings, asked leave to speak, and, as one who was desirous to uphold the Emperor's dignity, told him that this eagerness to trace his descent would neither be useful nor honourable; for, said he, at present I revere your majesty, and worship you as a god; but if we must come to

Noah's ark, there we shall all be cousins, for we are all descended from it. Maximilian was so deeply affected by this saying of the jester, that he became ashamed of his undertaking, though formerly neither friends, nor counsellors, nor business could dissuade him from it; for he perceived that his name, which he wished to render more illustrious by inquiring into his remote ancestors, would be altogether degraded if they came to its earliest source, from which princes and peasants, nobles and artisans, are descended.

What is blamed even by jesters and fools must be great madness; and yet it is not a vice which has lately sprung up, but is deeply rooted in the minds of almost all men. In order to avoid it, let us learn to depend on God alone, and let us prefer the blessedness of adoption to all riches, and lineage, and nobility. So far as relates to the kings of Egypt being descended from very ancient kings, who had kept possession of the throne for many ages, they were as proud as if wisdom had been born with them.[1]

12. *Where are thy wise men? that they may tell thee.* Though literally it runs thus, "*And* they shall tell thee, and shall know," yet the word ought to be regarded as meaning, "that they may tell thee, and even that at length they may know;" for this mode of expression is frequently employed by the Hebrews. The Egyptians had their diviners from whom they thought that nothing, however secret, was concealed; for they consulted them about the smallest and greatest affairs, and held their replies to be oracles. The Prophet, mocking that vanity, says, "How shall they tell what they do not know? Have they been admitted to the counsel of God?" It is also probable that he condemns the art which they used in divination, because it was not only unlawful, but also made use of absolute tricks and deceptions.

There are three ways in which we may foresee or know

---

[1] קדם, (*kĕdĕm*,) has two meanings, "antiquity" and "the east;" and accordingly Bishop Stock renders this clause, "the son of the kings of the east," adding the following note:—"*Kings of the east.* A synonyme for *wise men*, μάγοι ἀπὸ ἀνατολῶν, the quarter of the world where the arts of divination originated, and to whose sovereigns Egyptian sages pretended kindred. Hence the magi, that came to worship Christ, are often denominated *the three kings.*"—*Ed.*

what is future. The first and chief way is, by the revelation of the Spirit, which alone can make us certain, as by the gift of prophecy, which is rare and uncommon. The second is, by astronomy. The third is, by a comparison of past events, from which prudence is commonly obtained.

As to a knowledge of the stars, from their position and conjunction, some things may occasionally be learned, such as famine, scarcity, pestilence, abundant harvests, and things of that sort; but even these cannot be certain, for they rest on mere conjecture. Now, we ought always to consider what relation the stars bear to these lower regions; for the actions of men are not regulated by them, as idle and false astrologers imagine, a vast number of whom, at the present day, endeavour to insinuate themselves into the minds of princes and subjects, as if they possessed a knowledge of everything, both present and future. Such men resemble the impostors of whom the Prophet speaks, who deceive men by their jugglery. Yet princes lend an attentive ear to such persons, and receive them as gods; and indeed they deserve to be thus imposed upon, and are justly punished for their curiosity.

They likewise boast of magic, in which those Egyptian diviners were skilled. But they add many things which are worse, and more abominable, exorcisms and calling on devils, than which nothing more destructive can be expressed or conceived. The Lord pronounces a curse on such conjectures and arts of divination, and the issue of them cannot but be disastrous and wretched. And if they were formerly condemned in the Egyptians, how much more do they deserve condemnation in those who use the name of God as a pretext? It is wonderful that men otherwise acute and sagacious should be so childishly deceived by such jugglery, so that they appear to be deprived of understanding and judgment; but it is the Lord's righteous vengeance, who punishes the wickedness of men.

Again, when from past events we calculate what is future, and judge by experience and observation what is most proper to be done, that cannot in itself be blamed; but neither can we by these means learn with certainty what is future, for the matter always lies in conjecture. Yet Isaiah directly attacks that sagacity which is universally applauded as something highly excellent, not because it is in itself sinful, but because we can scarcely find an acute or ingenious person who does not confidently believe that his skill places within his reach all that deserves or is necessary to be known. In this manner they despise the secret providence of God, as if nothing were hidden from them.

What the Lord of hosts hath decreed. There is still another vice, that craftiness and sleight of hand are preferred by them to true wisdom. But Isaiah expressly censures that pride which led men endued with great abilities to measure events by their own judgment, as if the government of the world were not in the hand of God; and therefore with their divinations he contrasts the heavenly decree. And hence learn how skilfully Isocrates says, Κράτιστον εἶναι παρὰ μὲν Θεοῦ εὐτυχίαν, παρὰ δὲ ἡμῶν αὐτῶν εὐβουλίαν, "that the best gift of God is success, and the best gift from ourselves is prudence." At first sight, this maxim of the elegant orator appears beautiful; but since he robs God of the spirit of prudence and bestows it on mortals, the distribution is both wicked and foolish, to ascribe to men sound counsel, and to leave nothing to God but prosperous fortune. Now, if any one neglect the methods by which God teaches us, and resort to Satan's impostures, he richly deserves to be deceived and involved in the greatest disgrace; for he seeks remedies that are nowhere to be found, and despises those which were offered by God.

13. *The princes of Zoan are become infatuated, the princes of Noph are deceived.* Zoan was one of the chief cities of Egypt; *Noph* also was highly celebrated;[1] but what cities they were we cannot with certainty determine. Some think that one of them was Alexandria, the antiquity and wealth of which may be inferred from many passages of Scripture, which serve also to refute the notion of those who think

[1] "Zoan, the Tanis of the Greeks, was one of the most ancient cities of Lower Egypt, (Num. xiii. 22,) and a royal residence. The name is of Egyptian origin, and signifies a low situation. *Noph* is the Memphis of the Greek geographers, called Moph, (Hos. ix. 6.) It was one of the chief cities of ancient Egypt, the royal seat of Psammetichus."—*Alexander*.

that it was founded by Alexander the Great; for although it had been frequently destroyed, yet he did not build it anew, but only repaired it. That at one time it was an independent state, and allied to the Egyptians, and that it was one of the most flourishing cities in the whole world, is evident from Nahum iii. 8. The Prophet justly represents the stupidity of the princes to be the forerunner of its destruction; because the chief strength of any commonwealth or kingdom consists in wisdom and prudence, without which neither great riches nor a numerous population can be of any avail.

A corner of its tribes have deceived Egypt.[1] I consider the word *corner* to be here used metaphorically for the chief part of a building on which the whole weight rests; and I choose rather to view it in the nominative than in the accusative case.[2] It ought, I think, to be viewed as referring to those wise men by whom the Egyptians supposed themselves to be so powerfully defended that no evil could befall them. But Isaiah says that this is too feeble a support, because, having been deceived in their counsels, they ruined Egypt; and therefore he holds up to mockery that pretended wisdom which, when it is not accompanied by the fear of God, ought to be called vanity and folly, and not wisdom. Not only do men abuse an excellent gift of God, but they are puffed up with vain ambition, and are more delighted with cunning than with real prudence. To this is added a devilish fury, which leads them to disregard the providence of God, and to bring down all events to the level of their own capacity. This is the reason why Scripture so frequently attacks wise men of that description, and declares that they are fools. They usurp what belongs to God, and claim it for themselves; which is shocking and intolerable sacrilege. We need not wonder if the Lord make fearful

---

[1] "The stay (Heb., corners) of the tribes thereof."—*Eng. Ver.*

[2] Instead of פִנַּת, (*pinnăth*,) the construct singular, Grotius, Lowth, and others, prefer the conjectural reading, פִנּוֹת, (*pinnōth*,) *corners*. But Rosenmüller removes the difficulty of the Syntax by remarking, that פִנָּה, (*pinnāh*,) a collective noun, and agreeably to the frequent usage of the Hebrew tongue, fitly agrees with a plural verb; and he quotes 2 Sam. xix. 41, as a parallel instance.—*Ed.*

displays against such wise men, so that with all their great acuteness and ingenuity they stumble and fall in the smallest matters, and run into great dangers which any peasant or artisan would have foreseen. Let these things be a warning to us, that we may not be elated or lay claim to the praise of wisdom. If we have any abilities or prudence, we ought to ascribe it wholly to God, and conform ourselves to the rule of sobriety and modesty; for if our wisdom rest on God he will truly be a steadfast corner-stone, which no one shall shake or overthrow.

14. *The* LORD *hath mingled a spirit of perverseness.* Because it was a thing unexpected and incredible that the leaders of a sagacious and prudent nation would destroy the country by their stupidity, the Prophet therefore ascribes it to the judgment of God, that the Jews may not shut their eyes against an example so striking and remarkable, as irreligious men usually attribute the judgments of God to chance when anything new or unexpected has happened. The expression is metaphorical, as if one were to mix wine in a cup, that the Lord thus intoxicates the wise men of this world so that they are stunned and amazed, and can neither think nor act aright. The consequence is, that they deceive Egypt, because, first, they were themselves deceived. That the Egyptians suffer themselves to be imposed on, and cannot guard against the deception, is the judgment of the Lord.

And yet Isaiah does not represent God to be the Author of this folly in such a manner that the Egyptians could impute blame to him, but we ought to view the matter in this light: " Men have in themselves no understanding or judgment, for whence comes wisdom but from the Spirit of God, who is the only fountain of light, understanding, and truth? Now, if the Lord withhold his Spirit from us, what right have we to dispute with him? He is under no obligations to us, and all that he bestows is actually a free gift." Yet when he strikes the minds of men with *a spirit of giddiness,* he does it always for good reasons, though they are sometimes concealed from us. But very frequently he punishes with blindness those wicked men who have risen up against him, as happened to those Egyptians who, puffed up with a conviction of their wisdom, swelled with pride and despised all other men. It is therefore superfluous to dispute here about predestination, for the Lord punishes them for open vice; and, accordingly, when God blinds men or gives them over to a reprobate mind, (Rom. i. 28,) he cannot be accused of cruelty; for it is the just punishment of their wickedness and licentiousness, and he who acts justly in punishing transgressions cannot be called the Author of sin.

Let us now attend to the manner of punishing. He delivers them up to Satan to be punished; for he it is, strictly speaking, that mingles the spirit of giddiness and perverseness; but as he does nothing but by the command of God, it is therefore said that God does what Satan does. The statement commonly made, that it is done by God's permission, is an excessively frivolous evasion; for the Prophet has expressed more than this, namely, that this punishment was inflicted by God, because he is a righteous judge. God therefore acts by means of Satan, as a judge by means of an executioner, and inflicts righteous punishment on those who have offended him. Thus in the book of Kings we read that Satan presented himself before God, and asked leave to deceive Ahab's prophets; and having obtained it, he then obeyed the command of God, for he could have done nothing by himself. It is unnecessary to produce a multitude of quotations in a matter so obvious.

And they have misled Egypt in all her work. When he adds that her counsellors *deceived* her, he points out a second judgment of God; for it might have happened that the princes were deprived of understanding, and resembled *drunkards,* and yet the common people continued to possess some judgment; but here he says, that the impostors obtained also the power of leading astray so as to deceive the people. This is a two-fold vengeance of God, both on them that lead astray, and on those who are led astray by them.

As a drunken man staggereth in his vomit. By a *vomit* he means shameful drunkenness. This is added ($\pi\rho\grave{o}s$ $a\ddot{v}\xi\eta\sigma\iota\nu$) by way of amplification, in order to shew that they were not ordinary drunkards, who have still some understanding left, but that they resembled swine.

15. *Neither shall Egypt have any work to do.* This is the conclusion of the former statement, for it means that all the Egyptians shall be stupified to such a degree that whatever they undertake shall be fruitless. This must happen where there is no counsel, and it is the righteous punishment of our pride and rashness. He therefore intended to describe the result and effect, so as to shew that it will be unhappy and miserable.

Head or tail, branch or rush. When he threatens both the *head* and the *tail,* he means, that all ranks, from the highest to the lowest, all without exception, shall be deprived of counsel, so that they will not succeed in anything. Or perhaps it will be thought rather to mean the order which they observe in their actions. Hence we learn, that both the beginning and the end of everything depend on God ; for we ought to ask from him counsel, and prudence, and success, if we do not wish that the same thing should happen to us which happened to the Egyptians.

16. *In that day shall Egypt be like women.* He again repeats what he had formerly said, that the Egyptians will have nothing that is manly. Some think that he alludes to an effeminate custom, on account of which the ancient historians censured the Egyptians, namely, that, by inverting the order of things, women appeared in public and transacted the affairs of state, and men performed the occupations of women. It is possible that the Prophet may have had this in his eye, but when I take a more careful view of the whole passage, this conjecture cannot be admitted ; for here he threatens a judgment of God, which will hold up men to astonishment. If he were speaking of an ordinary custom, this would not apply to the matter in hand, for he does not charge the hearts of the Egyptians with being effeminate, but, on the contrary, threatens that they shall be struck with such dread that in no respect will they differ from women. The Egyptians not only thought that they were able to maintain war, but attacked without provocation, and gave aid to other nations. We see that heathen writers re-

late many of the exploits of the Egyptians, and expatiate largely on their praises ; and, therefore, although the Egyptians were feeble and effeminate in comparison with other nations, yet they wished to retain the praise and renown of warlike men.

Because of the shaking of the hand of Jehovah of hosts.[1] The sudden change which is now effected is a striking display of the judgment of heaven, and therefore he adds, that *the shaking of the hand of God* will be the cause of the terror. By these words he shews that this war will be entirely carried on by the Lord, and therefore that the Egyptians cannot stand against it, because they have not to do with men. What Isaiah declares concerning Egypt ought to be likewise applied to other nations ; for if wars arise and insurrections spring up, we ought to acknowledge it to be a judgment of God when men lose courage and are overwhelmed with terror. We see how the most warlike nations give way, and shew themselves to be less courageous than women, and are vanquished without any preparations of war, whenever the Lord strikes their minds with dread.

17. *And the land of Judah shall be a terror to the Egyptians.* Some explain it simply to mean, that the land of Judah will be an astonishment to the Egyptians as well as to other nations, and compare this passage with the saying which has formerly come under our observation, " You shall be an astonishment."[2] But I think that the meaning of the Prophet here is different, for he intended to point out the reason why the Lord would make such a display against the Egyptians. It was because they had brought destruction on the Jews, for they had turned them aside from the

---

[1] Professor Alexander prefers the literal rendering, "from before the shaking of the hand," and thus explains the passage : " מִפְּנֵי, (*mippĕnē,*) may be rendered, *on account of,* which idea is certainly included, but the true force of the original expression is best retained by a literal translation. תְּנוּפַת יָד, (*tĕnūphăth yăd,*) is not the act of beckoning for the enemy, but that of threatening or preparing to strike. The reference is not to the slaughter of Sennacherib's army, but more generally to the indications of Divine displeasure."

[2] The only passage which occurs to my remembrance as likely to be in the author's eye is, " And thou shalt become an astonishment, a proverb, and a bye-word, among all the nations whither the Lord shall lead thee." (Deut. xxviii. 37.)—*Ed.*

confidence which they ought to have placed in God, as princes frequently solicit their neighbours, and offer them their aid, that they may afterwards make use of them for their own advantage. Now the Lord had forbidden them (Deut. xvii. 16) to resort to the Egyptians for the purpose of asking assistance from them; but those wretched people, instead of obeying God, listened to the solicitation of unbelievers who made offers to them, and on this account they were justly punished.

But the Egyptians also, who had given occasion to their unbelief and distrust, did not pass unpunished, for they were so sharply chastised that whenever they remembered the Jews they were overwhelmed with terror. Hence we ought to draw a profitable doctrine, that they who have turned aside the Church from obeying and trusting in God, and who, by fear, or counsel, or any enticements, have given occasion for offence, will be severely punished. The meaning of the Prophet's words is as if we should say, that the look of a woman will bring a blush on him who has seduced her, when the disgrace of the uncleanness shall have been laid open, and when God shall come forth as the avenger of conjugal fidelity.

18. *In that day there shall be five cities.* After having threatened the Egyptians, and at the same time explained the reason of the divine judgment, he comforts them, and promises the mercy of God. He declares that they will be in part restored, and will regain a prosperous and flourishing condition; for he says that out of six *cities five* will be saved, and only one will perish. He had already foretold a frightful destruction to the whole kingdom, so that no one who examines the former prediction can think of anything else than a condition that is past remedy. He therefore promises that this restoration will be accomplished by the extraordinary kindness of God, so that it will be a kind of addition to the redemption of the Church, or a large measure of the grace of God, when the Redeemer shall be sent.

The manner of expression is somewhat obscure, but if we observe it carefully, there is no difficulty about the meaning; for the Prophet means that only the sixth part of the cities will be destroyed, and that the rest will be saved. The difficulty lies in the word הֶהָרֶס, (hăhĕrĕs.) Some read it הַחֶרֶס, (hăchĕrĕs,) that is, *of the sun*, but they have mistaken the letter ה (*he*) for ח, (*cheth*,) which resembles it. Those who explain it "*of the sun*," think that the Prophet spoke of Heliopolis;[1] but this does not agree with the context; and he does not merely promise that *five cities* would be restored, (for how inconsiderable would such a restoration have been!) but generally, that *five* cities out of six would be saved. We know that the cities in Egypt were very numerous. I do not mention the fables of the ancients, and those who have assigned to them twenty thousand cities. But still, there must have been a vast number of cities in a country so highly celebrated, in a kingdom so flourishing and populous, with a climate so mild and temperate. Let us then suppose that there were a thousand cities in it, or somewhat more. He says that only the sixth part will perish, that the rest will be restored, so that but few will be destroyed. From what follows it is evident that this restoration must be understood to relate to the worship.

Speaking with the lip of Canaan. By the word *lip* he means the *tongue*, (συνεκδοχικῶς,) taking a part for the whole. He expresses their agreement with the people of God, and the faith by which they will make profession of the name of God; for by the *tongue* he metaphorically describes confession. Since there was but one language which acknowledged and professed the true God, that is, the language of that nation which inhabited the land of Canaan, it is evident that by such a language must be meant agreement in religion. It is customary enough to employ these modes of expression, "to speak the same language," or, "to speak a different language," when we intend to describe agreement or diversity of opinion. But at the same time it must be remembered that it is not every kind of agreement that is sufficient, as if men were to form a conspiracy about the worship which they preferred, but if they agree in the truth

---

[1] *Heliopolis* is a Greek word, and signifies "the city of the sun." It is the name of a famous city of Lower Egypt, in which there was a temple dedicated to the sun.— *Ed.*

which was revealed to the fathers. He does not merely say that the Egyptians will speak the same language, but that they will speak the language *of Canaan.* They must have changed their language, and adopted that which God had sanctified; not that the dialect was more holy, but it is commended on account of its containing the doctrine of truth.

This ought to be carefully observed, that we may understand what is the true method of agreement. We must by all means seek harmony, but we must see on what conditions we obtain it; for we must not seek any middle course, as is done by those who overturn religion, and yet who wish to be regarded as peace-makers. Away with such fickle and changeful tongues! Let the truth itself be preserved, which cannot be contained but in the word. Whosoever shall determine to agree to it, let him talk with us, but away with every one who shall corrupt it, choose what language he may. Let us abide firmly by this. It will therefore be impossible for the Egyptians to speak the language of Canaan till they have first relinquished their own language, that is, till they have relinquished all superstitions. Some refer this to the age of Ptolemy, but it is absurd, and we may infer from what follows that the Prophet speaks of piety and of the true worship of God.

And swearing by Jehovah of hosts. First, employing a figure of speech in which a part is taken for the whole, he shews that their conversation will be holy, by exhibiting a single class of them, for in *swearing* they will make profession that they worship the true God. It may also be read, *swearing to the* LORD, or, *by the* LORD, for ל (*lamed*) often signifies *by.* If we read, "to the Lord," the meaning will be, that they will promise obedience to him, and that by a solemn oath, as when any nation promises fidelity to its prince; as if he had said, "They will acknowledge the authority of God, and submit to his government." But since another reading has been more generally approved, I willingly adopt it; for since one part of the worship of God is *swearing,* by taking a part for the whole, as I have said, it fitly describes the whole of the worship of God. Again, to "swear by the Lord" often means to testify that he is the true God.

(Deut. vi. 13.) In a word, it denotes a perfect agreement with the Church of God.

Hence we ought to learn that outward confession is a necessary part of the true worship of God; for if any person wish to keep his faith shut up in his heart, he will have but a cold regard for it. (Rom. x. 9, 10.) True faith breaks out into confession, and kindles us to such a degree that we actually profess what we inwardly feel. "To me," says the Lord in another passage, "every knee shall bow, and every tongue shall swear." (Isaiah xlv. 23.) Accordingly, there ought to be an outward worship and outward profession wherever faith dwells. It ought also to be observed, that those things which belong to the worship of God ought not to be applied to any other purpose, and therefore it is a profanation of an oath if we swear by any other. It is written, "Thou shalt swear by my name." (Deut. vi. 13.) Accordingly, he is insulted and robbed of his honour, if the name of saints, or of any creature, be employed in an oath. Let it likewise be observed with what solemnity oaths should be made; for if by swearing we profess to worship God, we ought never to engage in it but with fear and reverence.

One shall be called the city of desolation. When he devotes to destruction every sixth city, he means that all who are not converted to God, so as to worship him, perish without hope of salvation; for he contrasts the cities of Egypt which shall begin to acknowledge God with those which are destined to destruction. Where the worship of God is wanting, nothing but destruction can remain behind. הרס (*hĕrĕs*) denotes execration and curse, which is followed by ruin and eternal death.

19. *In that day shall there be an altar in the midst of the land of Egypt.* He continues what he had said in the former verse, and states more clearly that the aspect of Egypt will be renewed, because there true religion will flourish, the pure worship of God will be set up, and all superstitions will fall to the ground. He employs the word *altar* to denote, as by a sign, the worship of God; for sacrifices and oblations were the outward acts of piety. By *the midst of Egypt* he means the chief part of the whole kingdom, as if he had

said, " in the very metropolis," or, " in the very heart of the kingdom."

And a statue[1] *to the Lord.* Let it not be supposed that by *statue* are meant images which carry the resemblance of men or of saints; but memorials (μνημόσυνα) of piety; for he means that they will be marks similar to those which point out the boundaries of kingdoms, and that in this manner signs will be evident, to make known to all men that God rules over this nation. And indeed it usually happens that a nation truly converted to God, after having laid aside idols and superstitions, openly sets up signs of the true religion, that all may know that the worship of God is purely observed in it.

Josephus relates (Ant. XIII. iii. 1,) that Onias perverted this passage, when he fled to Ptolemy Philometor,[2] whom he persuaded that it would be advantageous to erect an altar there, on which the Jews who dwelt in that country might sacrifice; and he brought forward this passage, alleging that what the Prophet had foretold ought to be accomplished. The wicked and ambitious priest persuaded the king to do this, though it was openly opposed by the Jews; for the king looked to his own advantage, and that scoundrel, who had been deprived of his rank, sought to obtain additional honour and advancement; so that no entreaty could prevent the execution of that wicked counsel. But Isaiah simply describes the pure worship of God under the figure of signs which were then in use; for he has his eye upon his own age and the men with whom he had to do. This passage, therefore, was wickedly and maliciously perverted by Onias.

But not less impudently do the Popish doctors of the present day torture a passage in Malachi to defend the sacrifice of the Mass. When he says that " a pure oblation will everywhere be offered to God," (Mal. i. 11,) they infer that it is some sacrifice different from the ancient sacrifices, because oxen and sheep must no longer be sacrificed, and there-

---

[1] "*Pillar.*"—Eng. Ver.
[2] The name " Philometor," which means " loving his mother," was ironically given to him on account of his known hatred of his mother Cleopatra.— *Ed.*

fore that it is the Mass. A witty and ingenious argument truly! Now, it is evident that under the legal figure Malachi describes nothing else than the pure worship of God, as Isaiah does here; and we ought carefully to observe such forms of expression, which are frequently employed by the prophets.

This will be clearly explained by a passage in Joel, which we shall quote as an example. "Your sons and your daughters," says he, "shall prophesy, and your young men shall see visions, and your old men shall dream dreams." (Joel ii. 28.) Peter shows (Acts ii. 16) that this prediction was fulfilled, when the apostles spoke various languages through the inspiration of the Holy Spirit. Having formerly been uneducated men, they began to be qualified for declaring the mysteries of God. On that occasion we perceive no "dreams," so that it might be thought that Peter quoted that passage inappropriately; but it is evident that Joel there describes nothing else than prophecy, and for the purpose of adorning it, he mentioned "visions and dreams," by means of which the Lord anciently held communication with the prophets. (Num. xii. 6.) He kept in view the ordinary custom of that age; for otherwise the Jews would have found it difficult to comprehend the gifts of the Spirit which at that time were unknown. Having been reared under that preparatory instruction of the Law,[1] they could rise no higher than where they were conducted by sacrifices, ceremonies, sacraments, and signs.[2] So then the prophets addressed them as children, who ought to have nothing set before them beyond what they can learn in a homely style ($\pi\alpha\chi\nu\mu\epsilon\rho\acute{\epsilon}\sigma\tau\epsilon\rho o\nu$) by custom and experience.

This doctrine will unfold to us various passages, the obscurity of which might lead to much hesitation. It is plain that the Prophet speaks of the kingdom of Christ, and that these things were not fulfilled before his coming. We must therefore take away the shadows and look at the reality of things, in order that by the *altar* we may understand a true and sincere calling on God. But by these signs the Prophet likewise shews that the worship of God cannot be maintained

[1] "Sous ceste pedagogie de la Loy."   [2] "Les signes et sacramens."

without external acts of devotion, though we have no right to lay down rules for them. Away with the inventions of men, that we may listen to God alone on this subject.

20. *And he will send them a Saviour.* We cannot serve God unless he first bestow his grace upon us; for no one will dedicate himself to God, till he be drawn by his goodness, and embrace him with all his heart. He must therefore call us to him before we call upon him; we can have no access till he first invite us. Formerly he shewed that they must be subdued by various afflictions in order that they may submit to God, and now he repeats the same thing; for men never deny themselves and forsake idle follies any farther than the scourge compels them to yield obedience. But he likewise adds another kind of invitation, that, having experienced the kindness of God, they will freely approach to him.

They will cry unto the Lord. The *cry* of which he speaks proceeds from faith, for they would never resort to this refuge till they had been allured and delighted by the goodness of God. When the Lord promises that he will send a *Saviour,* by whose hand the Egyptians will be delivered, this can mean no other than Christ; for Egypt was not delivered from its distresses before the doctrine of Christ reached it. We read of various changes which that country suffered for four hundred years, foreign and civil wars by which it was wasted and almost destroyed; but when we would be ready to think that it is utterly ruined, lo! it is converted to the Lord, and is rescued from the hand of enemies and tyrants. Thus Christ delivered that country, when it had begun to know him. In like manner, we must be brought to the knowledge and worship of God, that, where we have suffered various afflictions, we may learn that salvation is found in him alone. Would that the world would now learn this lesson, having suffered so many calamities that it appears to be on the brink of ruin! For what can be the issue but that it shall either perish or by repentance acknowledge that it has been justly punished for so great wickedness?

That he may deliver them. When he adds these words, we ought to draw from them a profitable doctrine, that God assists us through Christ, by whose agency he gave deliverance to his own people from the beginning. He has always been the Mediator, by whose intercession all blessings were obtained from God the Father; and now that he has been revealed, let us learn that nothing can be obtained from God but through him.[1]

21. *And the Lord shall be known by the Egyptians.* Isaiah now adds what was most important; for we cannot worship the Lord, or call upon him, till we have first acknowledged him to be our Father. "How," says Paul, "shall they call on him whom they know not?"[2] (Rom. x. 14.) We cannot be partakers of the gifts of God for our salvation without previously having true knowledge, which is by faith. He therefore properly adds, the knowledge of God, as the foundation of all religion, or the key that opens to us the gate of the heavenly kingdom. Now, there cannot be knowledge without doctrine; and hence infer, that God disapproves of all kinds of false worship; for he cannot approve of anything that is not guided by knowledge, which springs from hearing

[1] Of one clause in this verse, rendered by our translators "and a great one," CALVIN takes no notice. Rosenmüller considers רב (*rāb*) to be the participle Kal of רוב, (*rūb*,) and assigns to Cocceius the honour of having discovered that the punctuation, which the Masoretic annotators have set aside, in the parallel passage of Deuteronomy, as a peculiarity for which they could not account, was the key to the true interpretation. "Almost all the commentators, Cocceius excepted, render רב (*rāb*) "a great one," some of them supposing that Ptolemy the Great, the son of Lagus, and others that Alexander the Great, was meant. But Cocceius was the first to perceive that the signification "Great" does not agree with the context, and has justly remarked that the word רב (*rāb*,) with a Kametz, ought not to be confounded with רב (*rāb*,) with a Pathach, but that its meaning should be sought from the verb רוב (*rūb*) or ריב (*rīb*,) "to contend, to argue, to defend one's cause in a court of justice;" and he quotes a parallel passage, in which Moses, while he blesses Judah, speaking of God, says, ידיו רב לו (*yādaiv rāb lō*) "his hands shall be his protector." (Deut. xxxiii. 7.) See Robertson's Clavis Pentateuchi, p. 561. The ancients appear to have taken a similar view. The Septuagint renders it thus. Καὶ ἀποστελεῖ αὐτοῖς ἄνθρωπον ὃς σώσει αὐτούς, κρίνων σώσει αὐτούς. The Chaldee and Syriac render it, "a deliverer and a judge," and Jerome's rendering is, *propugnatorem*, "a defender or champion." Rosenmüller Scholia. "A saviour and a vindicator." Lowth. "An advocate." Stock. "The explanation of רב, (*rab*) as a participle," says Professor Alexander, "is found in all the ancient versions, and is adopted by most modern writers. —*Ed.*

[2] The words of the Apostle are, "How shall they call on him in whom they have not *believed?*" But CALVIN's remark, which immediately follows, vindicates the appropriateness, though not the verbal accuracy, of the quotation.—*Ed.*

true and pure doctrine. Whatever contrivance therefore men may make out of their own minds, they will never attain by it the true worship of God. We ought carefully to observe passages like this, in which the Spirit of God shews what is the true worship and calling of God, that, having abandoned the inventions to which men are too obstinately attached, we may allow ourselves to be taught by the pure word of God, and, relying on his authority, may freely and boldly condemn all that the world applauds and admires.

The Egyptians shall know. It is not without good reason that he twice mentions this *knowledge.* A matter of so great importance ought not to be slightly passed by; for it holds the chief place, and without it there is nothing that can properly be called worship.

And shall make sacrifice and oblation. This passage must be explained in the same manner as the former, in which he mentioned an *altar.* What would have been the use of sacrifices after the manifestation of Christ? He therefore describes metaphorically confession of faith and calling on God, which followed the preaching of the gospel. Here he includes everything that was offered to God—slain beasts, bread, fruits of every description, and all that was fitted to express gratitude. But we must attend to the difference between the Old and New Testaments, and under the shadows of ceremonies we must understand to be meant that "reasonable worship" of which Paul speaks. (Rom. xii. 1.)

And shall vow vows to the Lord and perform them. What he adds about *vows* is likewise a part of the worship of God. The Jews were accustomed to express their gratitude to God by *vows,* and especially they rendered thanksgiving by a solemn vow, when they had received from God any extraordinary blessing. Of their own accord also, when any one chose to do so, they made *vows* on various occasions. (Deut. xii. 6; xxiii. 21-23.) And yet every person was not at liberty to make this or that vow according to his own pleasure; but a rule was laid down. (Num. xxx. 3.) Whatever may be in that respect, it is evident that by the word *vows* the Prophet means nothing else than the worship of God, to which the Egyptians devoted themselves after having learned it from the word of God; but he mentions the acts of devotion by which the Jews made profession of the true worship and religion.

Hence the Papists draw an argument to prove, that whatever we vow to God ought to be performed; but since they make vows at random, and without any exercise of judgment, this passage lends no aid to defend their error. Isaiah foretells what the Egyptians will do, after having embraced and followed the instruction given by God.[1] In like manner, when David exhorts the people to vow and to perform their vows, (Psalm lxxvi. 11,) they think that he is on their side; but he does not therefore exhort them to make unlawful and rash vows. (Eccl. v. 2.) There always remains in force the law of vows, which we are not at liberty to transgress, namely, the word of God, by which we learn what he requires from us, and what he wishes us to vow and perform. We never received permission to vow whatever we please, because we are too much disposed to go to excess, and to take every kind of liberty with regard to God, and because we act more imprudently towards him than if we had to deal with men. It was therefore necessary that men should be laid under some restraint to prevent them from taking so great liberties in the worship of God and religion.

This being the case, it is evident that God permits nothing but what is agreeable to his law, and that he rejects everything else as unacceptable and superstitious. What a man has vowed of his own accord, and without the support of the word, cannot be binding. If he perform it, he offends doubly; first, in vowing rashly, as if he were sporting with God; and secondly, in executing his resolutions wickedly and rashly, when he ought rather to have set them aside and repented. So far, therefore, is any man from being bound by vows, that he ought, on the contrary, to turn back and acknowledge his sinful rashness.

Now, if any one inquire about the vows of Papists, it will be easy to shew that they derive no support from the word of God. If those things which they highly applaud and reckon to be lawful, such as the vows of monks, are unlawful and

---

[1] " La doctrine de salut;"—" The doctrine of salvation."

wicked, what opinion must we form of the rest? They vow perpetual celibacy, as if it were indiscriminately permitted to all; but we know that the gift of continence is not an ordinary gift, and is not promised to every one, not even to those who in other respects are endued with extraordinary graces. Abraham was eminent for faith, steadfastness, meekness, and holiness, and yet he did not possess this gift. (Gen. xi. 29; xxv. 1.) Christ himself, when the apostles loudly commended this state of celibacy, testified that it is not given to all. (Matt. xix. 11, 12.) Paul states the same thing. (1 Cor. vii. 7, 9, 26.) Whosoever, therefore, does not possess this gift of continence, if he vow it, does wrong, and will be justly punished for his rashness. Hence have arisen dreadful instances of want of chastity, by which God has justly punished Popery for this presumption.

They likewise vow poverty, as if they would have nothing of their own, though they have abundance of everything beyond other men. Is not this an open mockery of God? The obedience which they vow is full of deceit; for they shake off the yoke of Christ, that they may become the slaves of men. Others vow pilgrimages, to abstain from eating flesh, to observe days, and other things full of superstition. Others promise to God toys and trinkets, as if they were dealing with a child. We would be ashamed to act thus, or to pursue such a line of conduct towards men, among whom nothing is settled till it has been agreed to on both sides by mutual consent. Much less is it lawful to attempt anything in the worship of God but what has been declared by his word. What kind of worship will it be, if the judgment of God has no weight with us, and if we yield only to the will of men? Will it be possible that it can please God? Will it not be ($\dot{\epsilon}\theta\epsilon\lambda o\theta\rho\eta\sigma\kappa\epsilon\acute{\iota}a$) "will-worship," which Paul so severely censures? (Col. ii. 23.) In vain, therefore, do they who make such vows boast that they serve God; and in vain do they endeavour to find support in this passage; for the Lord abhors that kind of worship.

22. *Therefore Jehovah will smite Egypt.* From what has been already said the Prophet draws the conclusion, that the chastisement which he has mentioned will be advantageous

to the Egyptians, because it will be a preparation for their conversion;[1] as if he had said, that it will be for the good of Egypt that the Lord will punish her. Those who translate the words, " he will strike with a wound that may be healed," misinterpret this passage, and greatly weaken the Prophet's meaning; for it means that the wounds will be advantageous to them, and that by means of these wounds the Lord will bring them back. Hence we ought to conclude, that we must not refuse to be chastised by God, for it is done for our benefit. (Prov. iii. 11, 12; Heb. xii. 5-7.) Exemption from punishment would cherish a disposition to sin with less control. As men are exceedingly prone to give way to their own inclinations, whenever God spares them for a little, it is necessary on this account that the Lord should prevent this danger, which he does by chastisements and stripes, which excite and arouse us to repentance. A remarkable instance of this is here exhibited in Egypt, which abounded in superstitions and wickedness, and went beyond all nations in idolatry, and yet experienced the mercy of God.

For they shall be turned to Jehovah. We must attend to the manner of its accomplishment, which is, their conversion to God. It is the explanation of the former clause; as if he had said, " God will heal the Egyptians, because they shall be converted." The copulative ו (*vau*) signifies *for*. Hence we infer that conversion may be said to be a resurrection from eternal death. We are utterly ruined so long as we are turned away from God; but when we are converted, we return to his favour, and are delivered from death; not that we deserve the favour of God by our repentance, but because in this manner God raises us up, as it were, from death to life. To repentance is added a promise, from which we conclude, that when we sincerely repent,[2] we do not in vain implore forgiveness. Now, when the Prophet says that the Lord will be gracious and reconciled to the Egyptians, he at the same time shews, that as soon as they have been converted, they will obtain forgiveness. It will therefore be a

[1] " Ce sera un preparatif pour les amener à repentance;"—" It will be a preparation to lead them to repentance."
[2] " Pourvenu que notre repentance ne soit hypocritique;"—" Provided that our repentance be not hypocritical."

true conversion when it is followed by a calling on God. But without faith (Rom. x. 14) it is impossible to call on God; for even the ungodly may acknowledge sin; but no man will have recourse to the mercy of God, or obtain reconciliation, till he be moved by a true feeling of repentance, which is likewise accompanied by faith.

And will heal them. He does not repeat what he had said, that God strikes in order to *heal;* but he promises *healing* in another sense, that is, that God will cease to inflict punishments. The former healing, which he mentioned a little before, was internal; but the latter relates to stripes and wounds. In short, he means that it will be a speedy remedy for all their distresses. After having been reconciled to God, there is nothing in us that calls for punishment; for whence comes punishment but on account of guilt? and when guilt is pardoned, exemption from punishment will quickly follow.[1] And if we be chastised, it is an evidence that we are not yet sufficiently prepared for repentance.

In a word, let us remember this order, which the Prophet points out to us; first, that stripes prepare men for repentance; secondly, that they are healed, because they are delivered from eternal destruction; thirdly, that when they have been brought to the knowledge of their guilt, they obtain pardon; fourthly, that God is gracious and reconciled to them; fifthly, that chastisements cease after they have obtained pardon from God. There is no man who ought not to acknowledge in himself what Isaiah here declares concerning the Egyptians, in whom the Lord holds out an example to the whole world.

23. *In that day.* The Prophet now foretells that the Lord will diffuse his goodness throughout the whole world; as if he had said, "It will not be shut up in a corner, or exclusively known, as it formerly was, by a single nation." Here he speaks of two nations that were the most inveterate enemies of the Church, and that appeared to be farther removed than any other from the kingdom of God; for much more

[1] " D'où viennent les chastimens, si non de nos pechez? S'ils sont pardonnez, aussi le sont les chastimens meritez a cause d'iceux."—" Whence come chastisements but from our sins? If they are remitted, so are also the chastisements deserved on account of them."

might have been expected from distant nations, because the nations here mentioned openly made war with God and persecuted his Church. And if the Lord is so gracious to the deadly enemies of the Church, that he pardons and adopts them to be his children, what shall be the case with other nations? This prophecy thus includes the calling of all nations.

There shall be a highway. Now, when he says that, in consequence of a *highway* having been opened up, there will be mutual access that they may visit each other, he describes brotherly intercourse. We know that the Egyptians carried on almost incessant wars with the Assyrians, and cherished an inveterate hatred towards each other. He now foretells that the Lord will change their dispositions, and will reconcile them to each other, so that they will have mutual communications, mutual coming in and going out, in consequence of laying open the *highways* which were formerly shut. Here we ought to observe what we formerly remarked at the fourth verse of the second chapter,[1] namely, that when men have been reconciled to God, it is likewise proper that they should cherish brotherly kindness towards each other. Strife, quarrelling, disputes, hatred, and malice, ought to cease when God has been pacified. We need not wonder, therefore, that he says that a highway to Egypt is opened up for the Assyrians; but this ought undoubtedly to be referred to the reign of Christ, for we do not read that the Egyptians were on a friendly footing with the Assyrians till after they had known Christ.

And the Egyptians shall serve the Assyrians, (or, with the Assyrians.)[2] This clause may be rendered, "shall serve God;" but as the name of God is not expressed here, it may refer to the Assyrians, which is also pointed out by the particle את (*ĕth.*)[3] It may therefore be explained thus. They

---

[1] See vol. i. p. 101.   [2] This is the Author's version. See p. 48.

[3] The particle את (*ĕth*) does not decide the question, for it may either be the sign of the accusative case, or a preposition signifying *with*. Professor Alexander adopts the latter view, and argues powerfully in favour of the rendering, "they shall serve God," in which he concurs with Lowth, "And the Egyptian shall worship with the Assyrian," and with Stock, "And Egypt shall serve [God] with Assyria."—*Ed.*

who formerly burned with a desire to injure one another will be changed in their dispositions, and will desire to shew kindness. In short, the fruit of true repentance will be made evident, for they who formerly distressed each other in mutual wars will lend mutual aid. And this opinion will agree very well with those words of the Prophet with which they stand connected. Yet I do not set aside another interpretation which is almost universally adopted, namely, "They who formerly worshipped other gods will henceforth acknowledge one God, and will assent to the same confession of faith." I leave every one to adopt that interpretation which he thinks best. If the latter interpretation be preferred, the Prophet makes brotherly love to flow from godliness,[1] as from its source.

24. *In that day shall Israel.* Isaiah concludes the promise which he had briefly glanced at, that the Egyptians and Assyrians, as well as Israel, shall be *blessed.* Formerly the grace of God was in some measure confined to Israel, because with that nation only had the Lord entered into covenant. The Lord had stretched out " his cord" over Jacob, (Deut. xxxii. 9,) as Moses speaks;[2] and David says, "He hath not done so to any nation, and hath not made known to them his judgments." (Psalm cxlvii. 20.) In a word, the blessing of God dwelt solely in Judea, but he says that it will be shared with the Egyptians and Assyrians, under whose name he includes also the rest of the nations. He does not mention them for the purpose of shewing respect, but because they were the constant enemies of God, and appeared to be more estranged from him and farther removed from the hope of favour than all others. Accordingly, though he had formerly adopted none but the children of Abraham, he now wished to be called, without distinction, "The father of all nations." (Gen. xvii. 7; Ex. xix. 5, 6; Deut. vii. 6, and xiv. 2.)

Israel shall be the third blessing. Some render it, *Israel shall be the third.*[3] I do not approve of that rendering; for

[1] " De la crainte de Dieu,"—" from the fear of God."

[2] " Jacob is the lot (Heb. cord) of his inheritance."—Eng. Ver.

[3] " The meaning obviously is," says Professor Alexander, " that Israel should be one of three, or a party to a triple union." By an analogous

the adjective being in the feminine gender, ought to be construed with the noun ברכה, *(berachah,) blessing*, and *blessing* means here a form or pattern of blessing.

25. *Because the Lord of hosts will bless him.*[1] He assigns a reason, and explains the former statement; for he shews that, through the undeserved goodness of God, the Assyrians and Egyptians shall be admitted to fellowship with the chosen people of God. As if he had said, "Though these titles belonged exclusively to Israel, they shall likewise be conferred on other nations, which the Lord hath adopted to be his own." There is a mutual relation between God and his people, so that they who are called by his mouth " a holy people," (Ex. xix. 6,) may justly, in return, call him their God. Yet this designation is bestowed indiscriminately on Egyptians and Assyrians.

Blessed be Egypt my people, and Assyria the work of my hands. Though the Prophet intended to describe foreign nations as associated with the Jews who had belonged to God's household, yet he employs most appropriate marks to describe the degrees. By calling the Egyptians "the people of God," he means that they will share in the honour which God deigned to bestow in a peculiar manner on the Jews alone. When he calls Assyrians *the work of his hands*, he distinguishes them by the title peculiar to his Church. We have elsewhere remarked[2] that the Church is called " the workmanship" (τὸ ποίημα) of God, (Eph. ii. 10,) because by the spirit of regeneration believers are created anew, so as to bear the image of God. Thus, he means that we are "the work of God's hands," not so far as we are created to be men, but so far as they who are separated from the world, and become new creatures, are created anew to a new life. Hence we acknowledge that in "newness of life" nothing ought to be claimed as our own, for we are wholly " the work of God."

idiom of the Greek language, Peter calls Noah ὄγδοον, " the eighth," that is, " one of eight persons." (2 Pet. ii. 5.) From classical writers other instances might be given, such as εἰς οἰκίαν δωδέκατος, " he went to his house the twelfth," or, " one of twelve," that is, " along with eleven other persons."—*Ed.*

[1] " Whom the Lord of hosts shall bless."—Eng. Ver.

[2] Our Author perhaps refers to his expository remarks on Eph. ii. 10 and on Isa. xvii. 7, and lxiv. 7. See p. 26.

And Israel my inheritance. When he comes to *Israel,* he invests him with his prerogative, which is, that he is *the inheritance of God,* so that among the new brethren he still holds the rank and honour of the first-born. The word *inheritance* suggests the idea of some kind of superiority; and indeed that covenant which the Lord first made with them, bestowed on them the privilege which cannot be made void by their ingratitude; for "the gifts and calling of God are without repentance," as Paul declares, (Rom. xi. 29,) who shews that in the house of God they are the first-born. (Eph. ii. 12.) Although therefore the grace of God is now more widely spread, yet they still hold the highest rank, not by their own merit, but by the firmness of the promises.

CHAPTER XX.

1. In the year that Tartan came unto Ashdod, (when Sargon the king of Assyria sent him,) and fought against Ashdod, and took it;
2. At the same time spake the Lord by Isaiah the son of Amoz, saying, Go and loose the sackcloth from off thy loins, and put off thy shoe from thy foot. And he did so, walking naked and barefoot.
3. And the Lord said, Like as my servant Isaiah hath walked naked and barefoot three years *for* a sign and wonder upon Egypt and upon Ethiopia;
4. So shall the king of Assyria lead away the Egyptians prisoners, and the Ethiopians captives, young and old, naked and barefoot, even with *their* buttocks uncovered, to the shame of Egypt.
5. And they shall be afraid and ashamed of Ethiopia their expectation, and of Egypt their glory.
6. And the inhabitant of this isle shall say in that day, Behold, such *is* our expectation, whither we flee for help to be delivered from the king of Assyria: and how shall we escape?

1. Anno quo venit Thartan in Asdod, cùm misisset eum Sargon rex Assyriæ, oppugnassetque Asdod, et cepisset;
2. Tempore illo, inquam, loquutus est Iehova in manu Isaiæ filii Amoz, dicendo: Vade et solve saccum de lumbis tuis, et calceamentum tuum extrahe de pede tuo; fecitque sic, ambulans nudus et discalceatus.
3. Et dixit Iehova: Sicut ambulavit servus meus Isaias nudus et discalceatus tribus annis, signum et portentum super Ægypto et Ethiopia;
4. Ita abducet rex Assur captivitatem Ægypti, et transmigrationem Æthiopiæ juvenum et senum, nudam et discalceatam, et discoopertos natibus in ignominiam Ægypti.
5. Et timebunt, et pudefient ab Æthiopia respectu suo, et ab Ægypto gloriatione (*vel, pulchritudine*) sua.
6. Dicetque incola insulæ hujus in die illa; Ecce, quomodo habeat respectus noster, quò confugimus auxilii causa, ut liberemur a facie regis Assur; et quomodo effugiemus nos?

1. *In the year that Tartan came to Ashdod.* In the preceding chapter Isaiah prophesied about the calamity which threatened Egypt, and at the same time promised to it the mercy of God. He now introduces the same subject, and shews that Israel will be put to shame by this chastisement of the Egyptians, because they placed their confidence in Egypt. He now joins Ethiopia, which makes it probable that the Ethiopians were leagued with the Egyptians, as I have formerly remarked, and as we shall see again at the thirty-seventh chapter.

First, we must observe the time of this prediction. It was when the Jews were pressed hard by necessity to resort, even against their will, to foreign nations for assistance. Sacred history informs us (2 Kings xviii. 17) that *Tartan* was one of Sennacherib's captains, which constrains us to acknowledge that this *Sargon* was Sennacherib, who had two names, as may be easily learned from this passage. We must also consider what was the condition of Israel, for the ten tribes had been led into captivity. Judea appeared almost to be utterly ruined, for nearly the whole country was conquered, except Jerusalem, which was besieged by Rabshakeh. (2 Kings xviii. 13.) Tartan, on the other hand, was besieging Ashdod. Sacred history (2 Kings xviii. 17) mentions three captains;[1] and this makes it probable that Sennacherib's forces were at that time divided into three parts, that at the same instant he might strike terror on all, and might throw them into such perplexity and confusion that they could not render assistance to each other. Nothing was now left for the Jews but to call foreign nations to their aid. In the mean time, Isaiah is sent by God to declare that their expectation is vain in relying on the Egyptians, against whom the arm of the Lord was now lifted up, and who were so far from assisting them, that they were unable to defend themselves against their enemies. Hence the Jews ought to acknowledge that they are justly punished for their unbelief, because they had forsaken God and fled to the Egyptians.

We must consider the end which is here proposed, for the

[1] "Tartan, and Rabsaris, and Rabshakeh."

design of God was not to forewarn the Egyptians, but to correct the unbelief of the people, which incessantly carried them away to false and wicked hopes. In order therefore to teach them that they ought to rely on God alone, the Prophet here foretells what awaits their useless helpers. The warning was highly seasonable, for the Ethiopians had begun to repel the Assyrians, and had forced them to retire, and no event could have occurred which would have been more gladly hailed by the Jews. Lest those successful beginnings should make them wanton, he foretells that this aid will be of short duration, because both the Ethiopians and the Egyptians will soon be most disgracefully vanquished.

2. *Go and loose the sackcloth from thy loins.* In order to confirm this prophecy by the use of a symbol, the Lord commanded Isaiah to walk naked. If Isaiah had done this of his own accord, he would have been justly ridiculed; but when he does it by the command of the Lord, we perceive nothing but what is fitted to excite admiration and to strike awe. In this nakedness, and in the signs of a similar kind, something weighty is implied. Besides, the Lord does nothing either by himself or by his servants without likewise explaining the reason; and therefore the Prophet does not merely walk naked, but points out the design which the Lord had in view in ordering him to do so. In other respects false prophets imitate the true servants of God, and put on varied and imposing shapes, to dazzle the eyes of the multitude, and gain credit to themselves; but those symbols are worthless, because God is not the author of them.

This ought to be carefully observed in opposition to the Papists, who bring forward empty ceremonies instead of true sacraments. This is the rule with which we ought to meet them. If they proceed from God, we ought to embrace them, but if not, we may boldly reject them; and, indeed, they cannot be adopted without offering an insult to God, because in such cases men usurp his authority. Besides, God does not bring forward signs without the word, for what would a sacrament be if we beheld nothing but the sign? It is the doctrine alone that makes the sacrament, and therefore let us know that it is mere hypocrisy where no doctrine is taught, and that Papists act wickedly when they lay aside doctrine, and give the name of sacrament to empty ceremonies; for the Lord has connected them in such a manner that no man can separate them without infringing that order which he has enjoined.

When the Lord commands him to *loose the sackcloth;* almost all the commentators infer from it that Isaiah at that time wore a garment of mourning, because he bewailed the distressed condition of Israel; for sackcloth was a mourning dress, as is evident from Joel (i. 13.) Their interpretation is, that this was done in order that, in the dress of culprits, he might supplicate pardon from God, or that it was impossible for his countenance or his dress to be cheerful when his heart was sad, and he could not but be affected with the deepest grief when he beheld so great a calamity. Some think that it was his ordinary dress, because the Prophets, as Zechariah informs us, commonly wore a mantle. (Zech. xiii. 4.) But that conjecture rests on exceedingly slight grounds, and has no great probability. It is more probable that he wore sackcloth as expressive of mourning. Judea was at that time sunk into such a state of indifference, that when men saw their brethren wretchedly distressed and wasted, still they were not affected by it, and did not think that the affliction of their brethren was a matter which at all concerned them. They still thought that they were beyond the reach of danger, and mocked at the Prophets when they threatened and foretold destruction. Hence Micah also complains that no man bewails the distresses of Israel. (Micah i. 11.)

A question arises, Was this actually done, or was it merely and simply a vision which he told to the people? The general opinion is, that the Prophet never went naked, but that this was exhibited to him in a vision, and only once. They allege as a reason, that on account of heat and cold, and other inconveniences of the weather, he could not have walked naked during the whole period of three years. What if we should say that the Prophet wore clothes at home, and also in public, unless when he wished to come forth to teach, and that on such occasions he was accustomed to present to the people a spectacle of nakedness? I pay little attention to the argument, that he was unable to endure heat and cold; for God, who commanded him to do this, could easily strengthen and protect him. But they assign another reason, that nakedness would have been unbecoming in a Prophet. I answer, this nakedness was not more unbecoming than circumcision, which irreligious men might consider to be the most absurd of all sights, because it made an exposure of the uncomely parts. Yet it must not be thought that the Prophet went entirely naked, or without covering those parts which would present a revolting aspect. It was enough that the people understood what the Lord was doing, and were affected by it as something extraordinary.

I am led to form this opinion by what is here said, "*By the hand* of Isaiah;" for although this mode of expression frequently occurs elsewhere, still we never find it where it does not imply something emphatic, to describe the effect produced. He places himself in the midst between God and his countrymen, so as to be the herald of a future calamity, not only in words, but likewise by a visible symbol. Nor is it superfluous that it is immediately added, *He did so.* I am therefore of opinion that Isaiah walked naked whenever he discharged the office of a prophet, and that he uncovered those parts which could be beheld without shame.

So far as relates to *sackcloth,* although it was customary for men in private stations of life to express their guilt in this manner in adversity, yet it is probable that it was with a view to his office that Isaiah made use of this symbol to confirm his doctrine, that he might the better arouse the people from their sluggishness. If at any time the Lord chastise ourselves or our brethren, he does not enjoin us to change our raiment, but we are cruel and (ἄστοργοι) without natural affection, if we are not moved by the afflictions of brethren and the ruin of the Church. If we have any feeling towards God, we ought to be in sadness and tears; and if it be our duty to mourn, we ought also to exhort others and stimulate them by our example to feel the calamities of the Church, and to be touched with some (συμπαθεία) compassion.

3. *Three years.* Why for such a period? Because that was the time granted to the Egyptians and Ethiopians, during which the Lord gave them a truce for repentance, and at the same time wished to make trial of the obedience of his people, that without delay they might relinquish unlawful aid, and that, though the Egyptians and Ethiopians appeared to be secure, they might know that they were not far from ruin. The Lord intended also to expose the rebellion of wicked men; for undoubtedly many persons made an open display of their impiety when they despised the nakedness of the prophet, and the godly, on the other hand, moved by the sight of his nakedness, though the prosperity of the Ethiopians was delightfully attractive, still did not hesitate to fix their attention on the word. What they were bound to consider was not the nakedness itself, but the mark which the Lord had put upon it; in the same manner as, in the visible sacraments, we ought to behold those things which are invisible.

4. *The captivity of Egypt and the removal of Ethiopia.*[1] The words "captivity" and "removal" are taken collectively, to denote the multitude of captives and emigrants. Next, he shews that there will be no distinction of age, declaring that the *old,* as well as the *young,* shall be led into captivity.

5. *And they shall be afraid.* He now shews for whose benefit he had foretold these things about the Egyptians and Ethiopians. It was in order that the Jews might learn amidst their afflictions to hope in God, and might not have recourse to foreign aid, which the Lord had forbidden.

6. *Lo, what is become of our expectation?* He calls them *expectation,* or *lurking,* because the Jews turned towards them, whenever they were oppressed by any calamity, and placed their hope in them. We are accustomed to turn our eyes to that quarter from which we expect any assistance.

---

[1] "The Egyptians prisoners (Heb. the captivity of Egypt) and Ethiopians captives."—*Eng. Ver.* "The captives of Egypt and the exiles of Cush."—*Lowth.*

Hence also, to "look" often signifies, in the Hebrew language, to "hope." (Psalm xxxiv. 5; Job vi. 19.) Now, they ought to have looked to God alone. Their wandering levity is therefore censured. And the same thing must happen to us, and deservedly, that when we have been invited by God, and refuse the sure refuge which he offers to us, and allow ourselves to be captivated by the delusions of Satan, we may lie down naked and destitute with shame and disgrace.

And the inhabitants of the island shall say. He gives the name *island* not only to Jerusalem, but to the whole of Judea; and it is generally thought that the name is given because its shores are washed by the Mediterranean sea. But I think that there is a different reason for this metaphor, for it is but a small portion of the sea that washes it; but as an *island* is separated from other lands, so the Lord separated Judea from other countries. It was kept apart from all the nations, which cherished a mortal hatred towards the Jews; for there was a "wall" between them, as Paul says, (Eph. ii. 14,) which Christ at length threw down. Here again Isaiah confirms his prophecy. If you are not now moved by my nakedness, you shall one day be taught by the event, that these words were not spoken to you in vain. Thus, at a late hour, obstinate and rebellious men are constrained by God to confess their guilt, so that they are struck with amazement, and argue within themselves how they could be so greatly blinded by their own stubbornness.

CHAPTER XXI.

1. The burden of the desert of the sea. As whirlwinds in the south pass through; *so* it cometh from the desert, from a terrible land.
2. A grievous vision is declared unto me: The treacherous dealer dealeth treacherously, and the spoiler spoileth. Go up, O Elam; besiege, O Media: all the sighing thereof have I made to cease.
3. Therefore are my loins filled

1. Onus deserti maris. Sicut tempestates in australi regione, transiturae a deserto, veniet a terra horribili.
2. Visio dura indicata est mihi: transgressor transgressori, et vastator vastatori. Ascende, Persa; obside, Mede; omnem gemitum ejus cessare feci.
3. Propterea impleti sunt lumbi

with pain: pangs have taken hold upon me, as the pangs of a woman that travaileth: I was bowed down at the hearing *of it;* I was dismayed at the seeing *of it.*

4. My heart panted, fearfulness affrighted me: the night of my pleasure hath he turned into fear unto me.

5. Prepare the table, watch in the watch-tower, eat, drink: arise, ye princes, *and* anoint the shield.

6. For thus hath the Lord said unto me, Go, set a watchman, let him declare what he seeth.

7. And he saw a chariot *with* a couple of horsemen, a chariot of asses, *and* a chariot of camels; and he hearkened diligently with much heed.

8. And he cried, A lion: My lord, I stand continually upon the watchtower in the day-time, and I am set in my ward whole nights;

9. And, behold, here cometh a chariot of men, *with* a couple of horsemen. And he answered and said, Babylon is fallen, is fallen; and all the graven images of her gods he hath broken unto the ground.

10. O my thrashing, and the corn of my floor: that which I have heard of the Lord of hosts, the God of Israel, have I declared unto you.

11. The burden of Dumah. He calleth to me out of Seir, Watchman, what of the night? Watchman, what of the night?

12. The watchman said, The morning cometh, and also the night: if ye will enquire, enquire ye; return, come.

13. The burden upon Arabia. In the forest in Arabia shall ye lodge, O ye travelling companies of Dedanim.

14. The inhabitants of the land of Tema brought water to him that was thirsty, they prevented with their bread him that fled.

15. For they fled from the swords, from the drawn sword, and from the bent bow, and from the grievousness of war.

16. For thus hath the Lord said

mei dolore; angustiæ corripuerunt me, sicut angustiæ parturientis; incurvatus sum audiendo, et videndo obstupui.

4. Concussum est cor meum; horror perterruit me; noctem deliciarum mearum posuit mihi in horrorem.

5. Adorna mensam, speculare in specula, comede, bibe; surgite, Principes, et ungite clypeum.

6. Quoniam sic dixit ad me Dominus: Vade, constitue vigilem, qui annuntiet quod viderit.

7. Et vidit currum paris equitum, currum asini, et currum cameli; deinde attentius speculatus est, multum, inquam, speculatus est.

8. Tum clamavit, Leo. In specula mea, Domine mi, jugiter sto interdiu, et totis noctibus in custodia mea locatus sum.

9. Et ecce, hic venit currus hominis, par equitum. Et loquutus est, ac dixit, Cecidit, cecidit Babel, et omnia sculptilia deorum ejus contrivit ad terram.

10. Tritura mea, et filius areæ meæ. Quæ audivi a Iehova exercituum Deo Israel, nuntiavi vobis.

11. Onus Duma. Clamat ad me ex Seir: Custos, quid de nocte? Custos, quid de nocte?

12. Dixit custos: Venit mane, postea nox. Si interrogaveris, interrogate. Revertimini, venite.

13. Onus in Arabia. In nemore in Arabia pernoctabitis, in viis Dedanim.

14. In occursum ferte aquas sitienti, incolæ terræ Tema, pane suo succurrite profugo.

15. Quia a facie gladiorum fugiunt, a facie gladii extenti, a facie arcus intenti, a facie gravitatis belli.

16. Nam sic dixit mihi Dominus:

unto me, Within a year, according to the years of an hireling, and all the glory of Kedar shall fail:	Adhuc annus, secundum annos mercenarii, tum deficiet omnis gloria Cedar;
17. And the residue of the number of archers, the mighty men of the children of Kedar, shall be diminished: for the Lord God of Israel hath spoken it.	17. Et residuum arcus, quod numerabitur fortium filiorum Cedar, imminuetur; quoniam Iehova Deus Israel loquutus est.

1. *The burden of the desert of the sea.* The Prophet, after having taught that their hope ought to be placed, not on the Egyptians, but on the mercy of God alone, and after having foretold that calamities would come on the nations on whose favour they relied, adds a consolation in order to encourage the hearts of the godly. He declares, that for the Chaldeans, to whom they will be captives, a reward is prepared; from which it follows, that God takes account of the injuries which they endure. By *the desert*[1] he means Chaldea, not that it was deserted or thinly inhabited, but because the Jews had a desert on that side of them; just as if, instead of Italy, we should name "the Alps," because they are nearer to us, and because we must cross them on our road to Italy. This reason ought to be kept in view; for he does not describe the nature of the country, but forewarns the Jews that the destruction of the enemies, which he foretells, is near at hand, and is as certain as if the event had been before their eyes, as that desert was. Besides, the prophets sometimes spoke ambiguously about Babylon, that believers alone might understand the hidden mysteries, as Jeremiah changes the king's name.[2]

As storms from the south. He says *from the south*, because that wind is tempestuous, and produces storms and whirlwinds.[3] When he adds that "it cometh from the desert,"

---

[1] "This plainly means Babylon, which is the subject of the prophecy. The country about Babylon, and especially below it towards the sea, was a great flat morass, often overflowed by the Euphrates and Tigris. It became habitable by being drained by the many canals that were made in it." —*Lowth.*

[2] The allusion appears to be to the use of the name "Coniah" instead of "Jehoiachin." "Though Coniah . . . . . were the signet upon my right hand. Is this man Coniah a despised broken idol?" (Jer. xxii. 24, 28.)—*Ed.*

[3] Lowth remarks, and quotes Job i. 19, and xxxvii. 9, and Zech. ix. 14, in support of the statement, that "the most vehement storms to which

this tends to heighten the picture; for if any storm arise in a habitable and populous region, it excites less terror than those which spring up in deserts. In order to express the shocking nature of this calamity, he compares it to storms, which begin in the desert, and afterwards take a more impetuous course, and rush with greater violence.

Yet the Prophet appears to mean something else, namely, that as they burst forth like storms from that direction to lay Judea desolate, so another storm would soon afterwards arise to destroy them; and therefore he says that this burden will come *from a terrible land*. By this designation I understand Judea to be meant, for it was not enough to speak of the ruin of Babylon, if the Jews did not likewise understand that it came from God. Why he calls it "a terrible land" we have seen in our exposition of the eighteenth chapter.[1] It was because, in consequence of so many displays of the wrath of God, its disfigured appearance might strike terror on all. The occasion on which the words are spoken does not allow us to suppose that it is called "terrible" on account of the astonishing power of God by which it was protected. Although therefore Babylon was taken and plundered by the Persians and Medes, Isaiah declares that its destruction will come from Judea; because in this manner God will revenge the injuries done to that nation of which he had promised to be the guardian.

2. *A harsh vision.* As the object was to soothe the grief of the people, it may be thought not to be appropriate to call a vision, which is the occasion of joy, *a harsh vision.* But this refers to the Babylonians, who, puffed up with their prosperity, dreaded no danger; for wealth commonly produces pride and indifference. As if he had said, "It is useless to hold out the riches and power of the Babylonians, and when a stone is hard, there will be found a hard hammer to break it."

The spoiler. As Babylon had gained its power by plundering and laying waste other nations, it seemed to be free from all danger. Although they had been a terror to others,

Judea was subject came from the great desert country to the south of it."
—*Ed.* [1] See p. 37.

and had practised every kind of barbarity and cruelty, yet they could not avoid becoming a prey and enduring injuries similar to those which they had inflicted on others. The Prophet goes farther, and, in order to obtain credit to his statements, pronounces it to be a righteous retaliation, that violence should correspond to violence.

Go up, O Elam. *Elam* is a part of Persia; but is taken for the whole of Persia, and on this account also the Persians are called Elamites. It is worthy of observation, that, when Isaiah foretold these things, there was no probability of war, and that he was dead a hundred years before there was any apprehension of this calamity. Hence it is sufficiently evident that he could not have derived his information on this subject from any other than the Spirit of God; and this contributes greatly to confirm the truth and certainty of the prediction.

Besiege, O Mede. By commanding the Medes and Persians, he declares that this will not befall the Babylonians at random or by chance, but by the sure decree of God, in whose name, and not in that of any private individual, he makes the announcement. Coming forward therefore in the name of God, he may, like a captain or general, command his soldiers to assemble to give battle. In what manner God employs the agency of robbers and wicked men, has been formerly explained at the tenth chapter.[1]

I have made all his groaning to cease. Some understand it to mean, that the groaning, to which the Babylonians had given occasion, ceased after they were subdued by the Medes and Persians; for by their tyrannical measures they had caused many to groan, which must happen when wicked and ungodly men possess rank and power. Others approach more closely, perhaps, to the real meaning of the Prophet, when they say, that "the groaning ceased," because the Babylonians experienced no compassion, having formerly shewn none to others. But I explain it more simply to mean, that the Lord was deaf to their groanings; as if he had said, that there would be no room for their groanings and lamentations, because, having been cruel and barbarous,

[1] See vol. i. p. 341.

it was just that they should receive back the same measure which they had meted out to others. (Matt. vii. 2.)

3. *Therefore are my loins filled with pain.* Here the Prophet represents the people as actually present, for it was not enough to have simply foretold the destruction of Babylon, if he had not confirmed the belief of the godly in such a manner that they felt as if the actual event were placed before their eyes. Such a representation was necessary, and the Prophet does not here describe the feelings of his own heart, as if he had compassion on the Babylonians, but, on the contrary, as we have formerly said,[1] he assumes, for the time, the character of a Babylonian.[2] It ought undoubtedly to satisfy our minds that the hidden judgments of God are held out to us, as in a mirror, that they may arouse the sluggishness of our faith; and therefore the Prophets describe with greater beauty and copiousness, and paint in lively colours, those things which exceed the capacity of our reason. The Prophet, thus expressing his grief, informs believers how awful is the vengeance of God which awaits the Chaldeans, and how dreadfully they will be punished, as we are struck with surprise and horror when any sad intelligence is brought to us.

As the pangs of a woman that travaileth. He adds a stronger expression of grief, when he compares it to that of a woman in labour, as when a person under fearful anguish turns every way, and writhes in every part of his body. Such modes of expression are employed by the Prophets on account of our sluggishness, for we do not perceive the judgments of God till they be pointed at, as it were, with the finger, and affect our senses. We are warned to be on our guard before they arrive.

4. *My heart was shaken.* Others render it not amiss, " my heart wandered ;" for excessive terror moves the heart, as it were, out of its place. He declares how sudden and unlooked for will be the destruction of Babylon, for a sudden calamity makes us tremble more than one which has been

[1] See vol. i. p. 494.
[2] " Vivacity is here imparted to the description by the Prophet's speaking of himself as of a Babylonian present at Belshazzar's feast, on the night when the town was surprised by Cyrus."—*Stock*.

long foreseen and expected. Daniel relates, that what Isaiah here foretells was accomplished, and that he was an eye-witness. Belshazzar had that night prepared a magnificent banquet, when the Persians suddenly rushed upon him, and nothing was farther from his expectation than that he would be slain. High delight was thus suddenly changed into terror. (Daniel v. 30.)

5. *Prepare the table.* These verbs may be taken for participles; as if he had said, " While they were preparing the table and appointing a guard, while they were eating and drinking, sudden terror arose; there was a call to arms, Arise ye princes," &c. But Isaiah presents lively descriptions, so as to place the actual event, as it were, before our eyes. Certainly Xenophon does not describe so historically the storming of the city; and this makes it evident that it was not natural sagacity, but heavenly inspiration, that taught Isaiah to describe so vividly events that were unknown. Besides, we ought to observe the time when these predictions were uttered; for at that time the kingdom of Babylon was in its most flourishing condition, and appeared to have invincible power, and dreaded no danger. Isaiah ridicules this vain confidence, and shews that this power will speedily be laid in ruins.

Let it not be thought absurd that he introduces the watchmen as speaking; for although the siege had not shaken off the slothfulness of a proud and foolish tyrant so as to hinder him from indulging in gaiety and feasting, still there is no room to doubt that men were appointed to keep watch. It is customary indeed with princes to defend themselves by guards, that they may more freely and without any disturbance abandon themselves to every kind of pleasure; but the Prophet expressly mixes up the sentinels with the delicacies of the table, to make it more evident that the wicked tyrant was seized with a spirit of giddiness before he sunk down to drunken revelling. The king of Babylon was thus feasting and indulging in mirth with his courtiers, when he was overtaken by a sudden and unexpected calamity, not that he was out of danger, but because he disregarded and scorned the enemy. The day before it happened, it might have been thought incredible, for the conspiracy of Gobryas, and of that party which betrayed him, had not yet been discovered. At the time when Isaiah spoke, none would have thought that an event so extraordinary would ever take place.

6. *For thus hath the Lord said to me.* The Prophet is commanded to set a *watchman* on the watchtower, to see these things at a distance; for they cannot be perceived by the eyes, or learned by conjecture. In order, therefore, that all may know that he did not speak at random, he declares that he foretells these things; for although they are unknown to men, and incredible, yet he clearly and distinctly knows them by the spirit of prophecy, because he is elevated above the judgment of men. This ought to be carefully observed; for we must not imagine that the prophets learned from men, or foresaw by their own sagacity, those things which they made known; and on this account also they were justly called "Seers." (1 Sam. ix. 9.) Though we also see them, yet our sight is dull, and we scarcely perceive what is at our feet; and even the most acute men are often in darkness, because they understand nothing but what they can gather by the use of reason. But the prophets speak by the Spirit of God, as from heaven. The amount of what is stated is, that whosoever shall attempt to measure this prophecy by their own judgment will do wrong, because it has proceeded from God, and therefore it goes far beyond our sense.

Go, appoint a watchman. It gives additional weight that he "appoints a watchman in the name of God." If it be objected, "You relate incredible things as if they had actually happened," he replies that he does not declare them at random; for he whom the prince has appointed to be a watchman, sees from a distance what others do not know. Thus Isaiah saw by the revelation of the Spirit what was unknown to others.

7. *And he saw a chariot.* What he now adds contains a lively description of that defeat. Some think that it is told by the king's messenger. This is a mistake; for the Prophet, on the contrary, foretells what he has learned from the

watchman whom he appointed by the command of God. Here he represents the watchman as looking and reporting what he saw. As if at the first glance he had not seen it clearly, he says that there is " a chariot," and afterwards observing more closely, he says that there is " a couple of horses" in the chariot. At first, on account of the novelty and great distance of the objects, the report given is ambiguous and confused; but afterwards, when a nearer view is obtained, they are better understood. There is no absurdity in applying to prophets or to divine visions what belongs to men; for we know that God, accommodating himself to our feeble capacity, takes upon himself human feelings.

8. *And he cried, A lion.* " Having hearkened diligently with much heed," at length he observes *a lion.* This is supposed to mean Darius who conquered and pillaged Babylon, as we learn from Daniel. (v. 28, 31.)

I stand continually. When the watchman says that he is continually on his watchtower by day and by night, this tends to confirm the prediction, as if he had said that nothing can be more certain than this vision; for they whom God has appointed to keep watch are neither drowsy nor dim-sighted. Meanwhile, by this example, he exhorts and stimulates believers to the same kind of attention, that by the help of the lamp of the word, they may obtain a distant view of the power of God.

9. *Babylon is fallen, is fallen.* This shews plainly that it is not king Belshazzar's watchman who is introduced, for this speech would be unsuitable to such a character. The Prophet therefore makes known, by the command of God, what would happen. Now, this may refer either to God or to Darius, as well as to the watchman; and it makes little difference as to the meaning, for Darius, being God's servant in this matter, is not inappropriately represented to be the herald of that judgment. There would be greater probability in referring it to God himself; for Darius had no such thoughts when he overthrew the idols of the Babylonians. But the speech agrees better with the character of a guardian, as if an angel added an interpretation to the prophecy.

And all the graven images of her gods. There is here an implied contrast between the living God and dead idols. This mode of expression, too, deserves notice, when he calls them " images of gods ;" for the Babylonians knew, as all idolaters loudly proclaim, that their images are not gods. Yet they ascribed to them divine power, and when this is done, " the truth of God is changed into a lie," (Rom. i. 25,) and not only so, but God himself is denied. But on this subject we shall afterwards speak more largely. Here we see, that by her destruction Babylon was punished for idolatry, for he assigns the reason why Babylon was destroyed. It was because the Lord could not endure that she should glory in her " graven images."

10. *My thrashing, and the son of my floor.*[1] The wealth of that powerful monarchy having dazzled the eyes of all men by its splendour, what Isaiah foretold about its destruction might be reckoned fabulous. He therefore leads their minds to God, in order to inform them that it was God who had undertaken to destroy Babylon, and that it is not by the will of men, but by divine power, that such loftiness will fall to the ground. The " thrashing," and " the son of the floor," mean the same thing ; for this mode of expression is frequently employed by Hebrew writers, who often repeat the same statement in different language.

This passage ought to be carefully observed, that we may correct a vice which is natural to us, that of measuring the power of God by our own standard. Not only does our feebleness place us far below the wisdom of God, but we are wicked and depraved judges of his works, and cannot be induced to take any other view of them than of what comes within the reach of the ability and wisdom of men. But we ought always to remember his almighty power, and especially when our own reason and judgment fail us. Thus, when the Church is oppressed by tyrants to such a degree that there appears to be no hope of deliverance, let us know that the Lord will lay them low, and, by trampling on their pride and abasing their strength, will shew that they are his " thrashing-floor ;" for the subject of this prediction

[1] " The corn (Heb. son) of my floor."—Eng. Ver.

was not a person of mean rank, but the most powerful and flourishing of all monarchies. The more they have exalted themselves, the more quickly will they be destroyed, and the Lord will execute his "thrashing" upon them. Let us learn that what the Lord has here given as a manifestation of inconceivable ruin, applies to persons of the same stamp.

That which I have heard from the LORD *of hosts.* When he says that he has "heard it from the Lord of hosts," he sets a seal, as it were, on his prophecy; for he declares that he has not brought forward his own conjectures, but has received it from the Lord himself. Here it is worthy of our notice, that the servants of God ought to be fortified by this boldness to speak in the name of God, as Peter also exhorts, "He that speaketh, let him speak as the oracles of God." (1 Peter iv. 11.) Impostors also boast of the name of God, but his faithful servants have the testimony of their conscience that they bring forward nothing but what God has enjoined. Observe, also, that this confirmation was highly necessary, for the whole world trembled at the resources of this powerful monarchy.

From the LORD *of hosts, the God of Israel.* It is not without reason that he gives to God these two appellations. As to the former, it is indeed a title which always applies to God; but here, undoubtedly, the Prophet had his eye on the matter in hand, in order to contrast the power of God with all the troops of the Babylonians; for God has not a single army, but innumerable armies, to subdue his enemies. Again, he calls him "the God of Israel," because by destroying Babylon he shewed himself to be the defender and guardian of his people; for the overthrow of that monarchy procured freedom for the Jews. In short, all these things were done for the sake of the Church, which the Prophet has here in view; for it is not the Babylonians, who undoubtedly laughed at these predictions, but believers, whom he exhorts to rest assured that, though they were oppressed by the Babylonians, and scattered and tossed about, still God would take care of them.

11. *The burden of Dumah.* It is evident from Gen. xxv. 14, that this nation was descended from a son of Ishmael, to

whom this name was given, and hence his posterity are called Dumeans.[1] The cause of their destruction, which is here foretold, cannot be known with certainty, and this prophecy is obscure on account of its brevity. Yet we ought always to remember what I have formerly remarked, that it was proper that the Jews should be fortified against the dreadful stumbling-blocks which were approaching. When so many changes take place, particularly if the world is turned upside down, and if there is a rapid succession of events, we are perplexed and entertain doubts whether all things happen at random and by chance, or are regulated by the providence of God. The Lord therefore shews that it is he who effects this revolution, and renews the state of the world, that we may learn that nothing here is of long duration, and may have our whole heart and our whole aim directed to the reign of Christ, which alone is everlasting.

Since therefore these changes were near at hand, it was proper that the Jews should be forewarned, that when the event followed, they should call them to remembrance, contemplate the wisdom of God, and strengthen their faith. Besides, there is no room to doubt that the Jews were harassed by various thoughts, when they saw the whole world shaken on all sides, and desired to have some means of avoiding those storms and tempests; for we always wish to be in safety and beyond the reach of danger. Some might have wished to find new abodes, that they might better provide for their own safety; but when storms raged on every hand, they were reminded to remain at home, and to believe that no safer habitation could anywhere be found than in the company of the godly.

[1] " Of *Dumah* there are two interpretations. J. D. Michaelis, Gesenius, Maurer, Hitzig, Ewald, and Umbreit understand it as the name of an Arabian tribe descended from Ishmael, (Gen. xxv. 14 ; 1 Chron. i. 30,) or of a place belonging to that tribe, perhaps the same now called *Dumah Eljandil*, on the confines of Arabia and Syria. In that case, Seir, which lay between Judah and the desert of Arabia, is mentioned merely to denote the quarter whence the sound proceeded. But as Seir was itself the residence of the Edomites or children of Esau, Vitringa, Rosenmüller, and Knobel follow the Septuagint and Jarchi in explaining דומה (*Dumah*) as a variation of אדום, (*Edom,*) intended at the same time to suggest the idea of *silence*, solitude, and desolation."—*Alexander*.

This example ought also to be a warning to many who separate themselves from the Church through fear of danger, and do not consider that a greater danger awaits them out of it. These thoughts might therefore distress the Jews, for we have seen in the eighth chapter that their minds were restless.[1] When they were thus tossed about in uncertainty, and fleeing to foreign nations, they would naturally lose heart; and this, I think, is the chief reason why the destruction of the Dumeans is foretold, namely, that the Jews might seek God with their whole heart, and that above all things they might commit to his care the safety of the Church. Let us therefore learn to keep ourselves within the Church, though she be afflicted by various calamities, and let us bear patiently the fatherly chastisements which are inflicted on children, instead of choosing to go astray, that we may drink the dregs which choke the wicked. (Psalm lxxv. 8; Isaiah li. 17.) What shall become of strangers and reprobates, if children are thus chastised? (1 Peter iv. 17, 18.) Yet it is possible that the chosen people suffered some molestation from the people of God, when their neighbours assailed them on every side.

Out of Seir. Mount Seir, as we learn from the book of Genesis, was a mountain of the Edomites. (Gen. xiv. 6; xxxii. 3; xxxvi. 8, 9.) Under the name of this mountain he includes the whole kingdom. In this place he represents, as in a picture, those things which called for an earnest address.

Watchman, what of the night? It is probable that the Edomites, who put the question, were not at a great distance from them, and that they were solicitous about the danger as one in which they were themselves involved. He introduces them as inquiring at the "watchman," not through curiosity, but with a view to their own advantage, what he had observed in "the night," just as when one has asked a question, a second and a third person follow him, asking the same thing. This is the meaning of the repetition, that the inquiry is made not by one individual only, but by many persons, as commonly happens in cases of doubt and per-

---

[1] See vol. i. p. 265.

plexity, when every man is afraid on his own account, and does not believe what is said by others.

12. *The morning cometh.* This means that the anxiety will not last merely for a single day, or for a short time, as if the watchman had replied, "What I tell you to-day, I will tell you again to-morrow; if you are afraid now, you will also be afraid to-morrow." It is a most wretched condition when men are tortured with anxiety, in such a manner that they hang in a state of doubt between death and life; and it is that dismal curse which the Lord threatens against wicked men by Moses, "Would that I lived till the evening; and in the evening, would that I saw the dawn!" (Deut. xxviii. 67.) The godly indeed are beset with many dangers, but they know that they and their life are committed to the hand of God, and even in the jaws of death they see life, or at least soothe their uneasy fears by hope and patience. But the wicked always tremble, and not only are tormented by alarm, but waste away in their sorrows.

Return, come. These words may be explained in two ways; either that if they run continually, they will lose their pains, or in this way, "If any among you be more careful, let them go to Dumah, and there let them tremble more than in their native country, for nowhere will they be safe." But since God always takes care of his Church, nowhere shall we find a safer retreat, even though we shall compass sea and land.

13. *The burden upon Arabia.* He now passes on to the Arabians, and foretells that they too, in their own turn, will be dragged to the judgment-seat of God; so that he does not leave unnoticed any of the nations which were known to the Jews. He declares that they will be seized with such fear that they will leave their houses and flee into the woods; and he states the direction in which they will flee, that is, to "Dedanim."

14. *To meet the thirsty bring waters.*[1] He heightens the description of that trembling with which the Lord had de-

[1] " Brought water (or, bring ye, or, prevent ye) to him that was thirsty." —Eng. Ver. CALVIN's version follows closely that of the Septuagint, *εἰς συνάντησιν ὕδωρ διψῶντι φέρετε,* and agrees with other ancient versions; but modern critics assign strong reasons for reading this verse in the preterite rather than in the imperative.— *Ed.*

termined to strike the Arabians in such a manner that they thought of nothing but flight, and did not take time even to collect those things which were necessary for the journey. Isaiah therefore declares that the Arabians will come into the country of Dedanim, empty and destitute of all things, and that they will not be provided with any food. On this account he exhorts the inhabitants to go out and meet them with bread and water, because otherwise they will faint through the want of the necessaries of life.

I am aware that this passage is explained differently by some commentators, who think that the Prophet mocks at the Arabians, who had been cruel and barbarous towards the Jews; as if he had said, "How gladly you would now bring water to the thirsty!" But that exposition is too constrained. And yet I do not deny that they received the reward of their cruelty, when they ran hither and thither in a state of hunger. But the meaning which I have given is twofold,[1] that the Arabians in their flight will be so wretched that they will not even have the necessary supply of water, and they will therefore faint with thirst, if they do not quickly receive assistance ; and he intimates that there will be a scarcity both of food and of drink. He calls on the neighbours to render assistance ; not to exhort them to do their duty, but to state the fact more clearly ; and he enjoins them to give their bread to them, not because it is deserved, but because they are suffering extreme want. Yet as it is founded on the common law of nature and humanity, the Prophet indirectly insinuates that the hungry and thirsty are defrauded of their bread, when food is denied to them.

15. *For they flee from the face of the swords.*[2] He means that the calamity will be dreadful, and that the Arabians will have good reason for betaking themselves to flight, because the enemies will pursue them with arms and with

---

[1] It would appear that, instead of "geminus est sensus," some copies had read, "genuinus est sensus;" for the French version gives " Cependant l'exposition que j'ay mise en avant est plus simple ;" " but the exposition which I have given is more simple."—*Ed.*

[2] "From the swords," or, for fear (Heb. from the face.)—Eng. Ver. "From before the swords."—*Stock.* "From the presence of swords."—*Alexander.*

swords, so that they will have no other way of providing for their safety than by flight. The reason why he foretells this defeat is plain enough; for it was necessary that the Jews should obtain early information of that which should happen long after, that they might learn that the world is governed by the providence of God and not by chance, and likewise that they should be taught by the example of others to behold God as the judge of all nations, wherever they turned their eyes. We do not know, and history does not inform us, whether or not the Arabians were enemies of the Jews. However that may be, it is certain that these things are spoken for the consolation of the godly, that they may behold the justice of God towards all nations, and may acknowledge that his judgment-seat is at Jerusalem, from which he will pronounce judgment on the whole world.

16. *For thus hath the Lord said to me.* He adds that this defeat of the Arabians, of which he prophesied, is close at hand; which tended greatly to comfort the godly. We are naturally fiery, and do not willingly allow the object of our desire to be delayed; and the Lord takes into account our weakness in this respect, when he says that he hastens his work. He therefore declares that he prophesies of things which shall happen, not after many ages, but immediately, that the Jews may bear more patiently their afflictions, from which they know that they will be delivered in a short time.

Yet a year according to the years of the hireling. Of the metaphor of " the year of the hireling," which he adds for the purpose of stating the matter more fully, we have already spoken.[1] It means that the time will not be delayed. The same comparison is used by heathen authors, where they intend to describe a day appointed and desired; as appears from that passage in Horace, " The day appears long to those who must render an account of their work."[2]

17. *And the residue of the archers.* He threatens that

[1] See vol. i. p. 496.
[2] " Diesque longa videtur opus debentibus."—Hor. Ep. I. 21. Another reading of this passage, which gives "lenta" instead of "longa," is not less apposite to the purpose for which the quotation is made. " To those who perform task-work the day appears to advance *slowly.*"—*Ed.*

this slaughter will not be the end of their evils, because if there be any residue in Arabia, they will gradually decrease; as if he had said, "The Lord will not merely impoverish the Arabians by a single battle, but will pursue to the very utmost, till all hope of relief is taken away, and they are utterly exterminated." Such is the vengeance which he executes against the ungodly, while he moderates the punishment which he inflicts on the godly, that they may not be entirely destroyed.

Of the mighty men. He means warlike men and those who were fit to carry arms, and says, that although they escaped that slaughter, still they will be cut off at their own time. He formerly threatened similar chastisements against the Jews, but always accompanied by a promise which was fitted to alleviate their grief or at least to guard them against despair. It frequently happens that the children of God are afflicted as severely as the reprobate, or even with greater severity; but the hope of favour which is held out distinguishes them from the whole world. Again, when we learn that God visits on the wicked deadly vengeance, this is no reason why we should be immoderately grieved even at the heaviest punishments; but, on the contrary, we ought to draw from it this consolation, that he chastises them gently, and " does not give them over to death." (Psalm cxviii. 18.)

The God of Israel hath spoken it. The Prophet shews, as we have frequently remarked on former occasions, that we ought not only to acknowledge that these things happened by divine appointment, but that they were appointed by that God whom Israel adores. All men are sometimes constrained to rise to the acknowledgment of God, though they are disposed to believe in chance, because the thought that there is a God in heaven comes into their minds, whether they will or not, and that both in prosperity and in adversity; but then they imagine a Deity according to their own fancy, either in heaven or on earth. Since therefore irreligious men idly and foolishly imagine a God according to their own pleasure, the Prophet directs the Jews to that God whom they adore, that they may know the distinguished privilege which they enjoy in being placed under his guardianship and protection.

Nor is it enough that we adore some God as governor of the world, but we must acknowledge the true God, who revealed himself to the fathers, and hath manifested himself to us in Christ. And this ought to be earnestly maintained, in opposition to the profane thoughts of many persons who contrive some strange and confused notion of a Deity, because they dare not openly deny God.

CHAPTER XXII.

1. The burden of the valley of vision. What aileth thee now, that thou art wholly gone up to the house-tops?

2. Thou that art full of stirs, a tumultuous city, a joyous city: thy slain *men are* not slain with the sword, nor dead in battle.

3. All thy rulers are fled together, they are bound by the archers: all that are found in thee are bound together, *which* have fled from far.

4. Therefore said I, Look away from me; I will weep bitterly, labour not to comfort me, because of the spoiling of the daughter of my people.

5. For *it is* a day of trouble, and of treading down, and of perplexity by the Lord God of hosts in the valley of vision, breaking down the walls, and of crying to the mountains.

6. And Elam bare the quiver with chariots of men *and* horsemen, and Kir uncovered the shield.

7. And it shall come to pass, *that* thy choicest valleys shall be full of chariots, and the horsemen shall set themselves in array at the gate.

8. And he discovered the covering of Judah, and thou didst look in that day to the armour of the house of the forest.

9. Ye have seen also the breaches of the city of David, that they are many; and ye gathered together the waters of the lower pool:

10. And ye have numbered the

1. Onus vallis visionis. Quid tibi hic, (*vel, nunc?*) quia tu universa conscendisti super tecta?

2. Strepituum plena, urbs turbulenta, civitas exultans; interfecti tui non interfecti gladio, et non mortui in prælio.

3. Cuncti principes tui profugerunt pariter ab arcu; vincti sunt. Omnes, inquam, in te reperti vincti sunt pariter, qui a longinquo fugerunt.

4. Propterea dixi, Desistite a me; amarus ero in fletu meo, ne contendatis me consolari super vastatione filiæ populi mei.

5. Quoniam dies perturbationis, et conculcationis, et anxietatis Domino Iehovæ exercituum in valle visionis, diruenti urbem, et clamor ad montem.

6. Atqui Elam portans pharetram in curru hominis, equitum, inquam, et Ceir nudans clypeum.

7. Et fuit ut electio vallium tuarum repleta sit curribus, et equites instruendo instruerent ad portam.

8. Et transtulit operimentum Iuda; et respexisti in die illa ad armaturam domus saltus.

9. Et interruptiones civitatis David vidistis, quæ multæ erant; et collegistis aquas piscinæ inferioris.

10. Et domos Ierusalem numer-

houses of Jerusalem, and the houses have ye broken down to fortify the wall.

11. Ye made also a ditch between the two walls for the water of the old pool: but ye have not looked unto the maker thereof, neither had respect unto him that fashioned it long ago.

12. And in that day did the Lord God of hosts call to weeping, and to mourning, and to baldness, and to girding with sackcloth:

13. And behold joy and gladness, slaying oxen and killing sheep, eating flesh and drinking wine: let us eat and drink, for to-morrow we shall die.

14. And it was revealed in mine ears by the Lord of hosts, Surely this iniquity shall not be purged from you till ye die, saith the Lord God of hosts.

15. Thus saith the Lord God of hosts, Go, get thee unto this treasurer, *even* unto Shebna, which *is* over the house, *and say*,

16. What hast thou here, and whom hast thou here, that thou hast hewed thee out a sepulchre here, *as* he that heweth him out a sepulchre on high, *and* that graveth an habitation for himself in a rock?

17. Behold, the Lord will carry thee away with a mighty captivity, and will surely cover thee.

18. He will surely violently turn and toss thee *like* a ball into a large country: there shalt thou die, and there the chariots of thy glory *shall be* the shame of thy lord's house.

19. And I will drive thee from thy station, and from thy state shall he pull thee down.

20. And it shall come to pass in that day, that I will call my servant Eliakim the son of Hilkiah;

21. And I will clothe him with thy robe, and strengthen him with thy girdle, and I will commit thy government into his hand; and he shall be a father to the inhabitants of Jerusalem, and to the house of Judah.

22. And the key of the house of

astis; et domos diruistis ad muniendum murum.

11. Fossam quoque fecistis inter muros, aquis piscinæ veteris, et non respexistis ad fictorem ejus, et opificem ejus ab antiquo (*vel, eminus*) non vidistis.

12. Porro vocavit Dominus Iehova exercituum in die isto ad fletum et lamentum, ad calvitium et cincturam sacci.

13. Et ecce gaudium et lætitia, occidere bovem, mactare ovem, edere carnes, et bibere vinum, comedere, inquam, et bibere; quia cras moriemur.

14. Id revelatum est auribus Iehovæ exercituum, Si remittetur vobis hæc iniquitas, donec moriamini, dicit Dominus Iehova exercituum.

15. Sic dicit Dominus Iehova exercituum, Vade, ingredere ad fautorem istum, ad Sabna præfectum domus.

16. Quid tibi hic? et quis tibi hic? quod tibi hic excideris sepulchrum, sicut qui in excelso excidit sepulchrum suum, aut qui in rupe sculpit habitaculum sibi.

17. Ecce Iehova traducet te traductione insigni, et operiendo operiet te.

18. Convolvendo volvet te convolutione, quasi globum in terram longinquam manibus; ibi morieris; et ibi currus gloriæ tuæ ignominia domus domini tui.

19. Et propulsabo te de statione tua, et de sede tua te expellet.

20. Et erit in die illa: vocabo servum meum Eliakim, filium Helchiæ.

21. Et induam eum vestibus tuis, et balteo tuo roborabo eum; et potestatem tuam tradam in manum ejus, et erit pater incolæ Ierusalem et domi Iuda.

22. Et ponam clavem domus

David will I lay upon his shoulder: so he shall open, and none shall shut; and he shall shut, and none shall open.

23. And I will fasten him *as* a nail in a sure place; and he shall be for a glorious throne to his father's house.

24. And they shall hang upon him all the glory of his father's house, the offspring and the issue, all vessels of small quantity, from the vessels of cups, even to all the vessels of flagons.

25. In that day, saith the Lord of hosts, shall the nail *that is* fastened in the sure place be removed, and be cut down, and fall; and the burden that *was* upon it shall be cut off: for the Lord hath spoken *it*.

David super humerum ejus; aperiet, et nemo claudet; claudet, et nemo aperiet.

23. Et figam eum veluti clavum in loco fideli; eritque in solium gloriæ domui patris sui.

24. Et suspendent ab eo omnem gloriam domus patris sui, nepotes et pronepotes, omnia vasa minora, a vasis craterarum ad cuncta vasa melodiarum.

25. In die illa, dicit Iehova exercituum, recedet clavus fixus in loco fideli, frangetur et cadet, et dissipabitur onus quod fuit super ipsum; quia Iehova loquutus est.

1. *The burden of the valley of vision.* Isaiah again prophesies against Judea, which he calls *the valley of vision.* He gives this appellation to the whole of Judea rather than to Jerusalem, of which he afterwards speaks; but now in the preface he includes the whole of Judea. He appropriately calls it a "valley," for it was surrounded on all sides by mountains. It is a harsher view of the metaphor, which is adopted by some, that Jerusalem is called "a valley," because it was thrown down from its loftiness. The reason why he adds the words, *of vision,* is plain enough. The Lord enlightened the whole of Judea by his word; the prophets were continually employed in it, and that was the reason why they called them *seers.* (1 Sam. ix. 9.) There is also an implied contrast here, for valleys have less light than open plains, because the height of the mountains intercepts the light of the sun. Now, this valley, he tells us, is more highly enlightened than those countries which were exposed on all sides to the sun. It was by the extraordinary goodness of God that this happened; for he means, that it was enlightened, not by the rays of the sun, but by the word of God.

Besides, the Prophet unquestionably intended to beat down that foolish confidence with which the Jews were puffed up, because God had distinguished them above others by remarkable gifts. They abused his word and prophecies, as if by means of them they had been protected against all danger, though they were disobedient and rebellious against God. He therefore declares that visions will not prevent God from punishing their ingratitude; and he even aggravates their guilt by this mark of ingratitude, that amidst such splendour of heavenly doctrine they still continued to stumble like the blind.

What hast thou here? or, What hast thou now? He now addresses Jerusalem; not that this defeat affects Jerusalem alone, but because the whole country thought it safe to take refuge under the shadow of the sanctuary which then existed, and to lead the Jews to reflect, since this befell a fortified city, what would become of other cities which had no means of defence. He asks in astonishment, "What does it mean that every person leaves his house and flies to the house-top for the purpose of saving his life?" Among the Jews the form of house-tops was different from what is now customary with us, and hence arose that saying of Christ, "What you have heard in the ear proclaim on the house-tops." (Matt. x. 27.) When the inhabitants of Jerusalem fled to the house-tops, they left their houses open to be a prey to enemies, and this was a proof that they were exceedingly afraid. It is likewise possible that they went up to the house-tops for the purpose of throwing down javelins and other weapons against the enemies, whose arrival not only terrified them, but made them flee in consternation, and yet they did not escape danger.

2. *Thou that art full of noises.* He means that it was exceedingly populous; for where great multitudes of people are brought together, noise abounds; and therefore, amidst so crowded a population, there was less cause of fear. In order to make the representation still more striking, Isaiah has therefore added this circumstance, that instead of being, as they ought to have been, walls and bulwarks to defend the city, when there was no scarcity of men, they ignominiously turned their backs on the enemies, and fled to the tops of their houses. By these words he urges the Jews more strongly to consider the judgment of God; for when such overwhelming fear has seized the hearts of men, it is certain that God has struck them with trembling; as if he had said, " How comes

it that you have not greater firmness to resist? It is because God pursues and chases you."

These statements are taken from the writings of Moses, from which, as we have frequently remarked, the prophets borrow their instructions, but with this difference, that what Moses spoke in general terms they apply to the matter in hand. "The Lord shall cause thee to be smitten before thine enemies; thou shalt go out one way against them, and shalt flee seven ways before them. The Lord shall smite thee with madness, and blindness, and astonishment of heart." (Deut. xxviii. 25, 28.) He reproaches the Jews for their distressed condition, and with good reason; for it was proper to press the accusation more closely home, that they might learn to ascribe to their sins and transgressions all the afflictions and sufferings that they endured. The Lord had promised that he would continually assist them; and when they are now left destitute, let them acknowledge that they do not deserve such assistance, and that God has cast them off on account of their rebelliousness. The Lord does not deceive or make false promises, but by their own fault those wretched persons have shut themselves out from his aid and favour; and this is still more strongly expressed by the question, *What hast thou here?* It means that God gave practical evidence that Jerusalem had been deprived of her protector and guardian; for this mode of expression denotes something strange and extraordinary.

Thy slain men are not slain by the sword. To exhibit still more clearly the vengeance of God, he affirms that they who were slain there did not die bravely in battle. Thus he shews that all that they wanted was manly courage; for a timid and cowardly heart was a sure proof that they had all been forsaken by the Lord, by whose assistance they would have bravely and manfully resisted. He therefore does not mean that the defeat would be accompanied by shame and disgrace, but ascribes it to the wrath of God that they had not courage to resist; and unquestionably by this circumstance he beats down their foolish pride.

3. *All thy rulers are fled together.* This verse has been interpreted in various ways. The fact is abundantly plain,

but there is some difficulty about the words. As מ (*mem*) signifies *before* and *more than*, some explain מרחוק (*mĕrāchōk*)[1] to mean, "They fled before others, though they were situated in the most distant parts of the country, and were in greater danger." Others render it, "Although they were at a great distance from Jerusalem, still they did not cease to flee like men who are seized with terror, and never stop in their flight, because they continually think that the enemy is at their heels."

But a more natural interpretation appears to me to be, *They have fled from afar;* that is, "they who have resorted to Jerusalem as a safe retreat will be seized by enemies and vanquished;" for Jerusalem might be regarded as the general protection of the whole of Judea, and therefore, when a war broke out, the inhabitants rushed to it from every quarter. While they looked upon their habitation in Jerusalem as safe, they were taken prisoners. Others suppose it to refer to the siege of Sennacherib. (2 Kings xviii. 13; 2 Chron. xxxii. 1.) But I cannot be persuaded to expound the passage in this manner, for he speaks of the destruction of Jerusalem. When it was besieged by Sennacherib, the Lord immediately delivered it; none were taken or made prisoners, and there was no slaughter of men. These events therefore happened long after the death of the Prophet, and sacred history relates them, and informs us that in that destruction even the rulers betook themselves to flight; but they derived no advantage from their flight, nor did Jerusalem afford them any defence, for they fell into the hands of their enemies.

When he expressly mentions the *rulers*, this shews more strongly the shamefulness of the transaction, for they ought to have been the first to expose their persons for the safety of the people. They might be viewed as the shields which ought to have guarded and defended the common people. So long as Jerusalem kept its ground and was in a prosperous condition, these statements might be thought incredible, for it was a very strong and powerfully fortified city. But they chiefly boasted of the protection of God, for they thought that in some way God was bound to his "Temple;"

[1] Rendered in the English version, "from afar."

and their pride swelled them with the confident hope that, though all should be leagued against it, no power and no armies could bring it down. (Jer. vii. 4.) This prophecy might therefore be thought very strange, that they would have no courage, that they would betake themselves to flight, and that even in that manner they could not escape.

4. *Therefore I said.* Here the Prophet, in order to affect more deeply the hearts of the Jews, assumes the character of a mourner, and not only so, but bitterly bewails the distressed condition of the Church of God. This passage must not be explained in the same manner as some former passages, in which he described the grief and sorrow of foreign nations; but he speaks of the fallen condition of the Church of which he is a member, and therefore he sincerely bewails it, and invites others by his example to join in the lamentation. What has befallen the Church ought to affect us in the same manner as if it had befallen each of us individually; for otherwise what would become of that passage? "The zeal of thy house hath eaten me up." (Psalm lxix. 9.)

I will be bitter in my weeping.[1] He does not mourn in secret, or without witnesses; first, because he wishes, as I have already said, to excite others by his example to lamentation, and not to lamentation only, but much more to repentance, that they may ward off the dreadful judgment of God against them, which was close at hand, and henceforth may refrain from provoking his displeasure; and secondly, because it was proper that the herald of God's wrath should actually make evident that what he utters is not mockery.

Because of the spoiling of the daughter of my people. That he expresses the feelings of his own heart may be inferred from what he now declares, that he is bitterly grieved "on account of the daughter of his people." Being one of the family of Abraham, he thought that this distress affected his own condition, and intimates that he has good grounds for lamentation. By a customary mode of expression he calls the assembly of his people a *daughter.* Hence it ought to be observed, that whenever the Church is afflicted, the

[1] " I will weep bitterly. (Heb. I will be bitter in weeping.)"—Eng. Ver.

example of the Prophet ought to move us to be touched (συμπαθεία) with compassion, if we are not harder than iron; for we are altogether unworthy of being reckoned in the number of the children of God, and added to the holy Church, if we do not dedicate ourselves, and all that we have, to the Church, in such a manner that we are not separate from it in any respect. Thus, when in the present day the Church is afflicted by so many and so various calamities, and innumerable souls are perishing, which Christ redeemed with his own blood, we must be barbarous and savage if we are not touched with any grief. And especially the ministers of the word ought to be moved by this feeling of grief, because, being appointed to keep watch and to look at a distance, they ought also to groan when they perceive the tokens of approaching ruin.

The circumstance of his weeping publicly tended, as we have said, to soften the hearts of the people; for he had to deal with obstinate men, who could not easily be induced to lament. There is a passage that closely resembles it in Jeremiah, who bewails the miserable and wasted condition of the people, and says, that through grief "his heart fainteth,"[1] (Jer. iv. 31;) and in another passage, "O that my head were full of waters, and mine eyes a fountain of tears, that I might bewail the slain of my people!" (Jer. ix. 1.) When the prophets saw that they laboured in vain to subdue the obstinacy of the people, they could not avoid being altogether overwhelmed by grief and sorrow. They therefore endeavoured, by their moving addresses, to soften hard hearts, that they might bend them, if it were at all possible, and bring them back to the right path.

5. *It is a day of trouble.* He again declares that the Lord is the author of this calamity, and that the Jews may not gaze around in all directions, or wonder that their enemies prevail against them, he pronounces that they are fighting against God. Though this doctrine is frequently taught in Scripture, still it is not superfluous, and cannot be so earnestly inculcated as not to be forgotten when we come to

[1] "My soul is wearied because of murderers."—Eng. Ver. See our Author's view of that passage in his Commentary on Jeremiah, vol. i. p. 249.

practice. The consequence is, that we are not humbled in the presence of our Judge, and that we direct our eyes to outward remedies rather than to God, who alone could cure our distresses. He employs the word *day*, as is usual in Scripture, to signify an appointed time; for when God winks at the transgressions of men, he appears to make some abatement of the claims of his rank, which, however, he may be said to receive back again at the proper and appointed time.

In the valley of vision. It is not without good reason that he again calls it "the valley of vision," for the Jews believed that they would be protected against every calamitous event, because the Lord shone on them by the word. But having ungratefully rejected his instruction, they vainly trusted that it would be of avail to them; and indeed the Lord punishes the unbelief of men, not only out of the Church, but within the Church itself; and not only so, but he begins his chastisement at the Church, so that we must not abuse the gifts of God, or vainly glory in his name. (1 Peter iv. 17.)

And crying to the mountain.[1] This may refer either to God or to the Babylonians, or even to the exiles themselves. Conquerors raise a cry for the sake of increasing terror, and the vanquished either utter what is fitted to awaken compassion, or give vent to their grief by lamentation. The singular number may be taken for the plural, or rather it denotes that part of the city in which the temple was situated. Both meanings will agree well with the context, and it makes little difference whether we say that the enemies cried to Mount Zion, in order to encourage each other, or that, while they were destroying and plundering the city, a cry was heard in the neighbouring mountains, or that the citizens themselves caused their lamentations to resound to the mountains which surrounded the plain of Judea.[2]

6. *But Elam carrying the quiver.* Here commentators think that the discourse proceeds without any interruption, and that he makes known to the Jews the same judgment which he formerly proclaimed. But when I examine the

---

[1] "To the mountains."—Eng. Ver.
[2] "La plaine du Jordain;"—"The plain of the Jordan."

whole matter more closely, I am constrained to differ from them. I think that the Prophet reproaches the Jews for their obstinacy and rebellion, because, though the Lord had chastised them, they did not repent, and that he relates the history of a past transaction, in order to remind them how utterly they had failed to derive advantage from the Lord's chastisements. Such then is the manner in which these statements ought to be separated from what came before. First, he foretold those things which would come on the Jews, and now he shews how justly they are punished, and how richly they deserve those sharp chastisements which the Lord inflicts on them; for the Lord had formerly called them to repentance, not only by words, but by deeds, and yet no reformation of life followed, though their riches were exhausted, and the kingdom weakened, but they obstinately persisted in their wickedness. Nothing therefore remained but that the Lord should miserably destroy them, since they were obstinate and refractory.

The copulative ו (*vau*) I have translated *But*, which is the meaning that it frequently bears. Those who think that the Prophet threatens for a future period, preserve its ordinary meaning, as if the Prophet, after having mentioned God, named the executioners of his vengeance. But I have already given the exposition which I prefer, and the context will make it still more clear, that I had good reasons for being of that opinion.

When he speaks of the "Elamites" and the "Cyrenaeans," this applies better, I think, to the Assyrians than to the Babylonians; for although those nations had never made war against the Jews by troops under their own command, yet it is probable that they were in the pay of the Assyrian king, and that they formed part of his army while he was besieging Jerusalem. We have already remarked that, taking a part for the whole, by the "Elamites" are meant the eastern nations.

And Kir making bare the shield.[1] By *Kir* he undoubtedly means the inhabitants of Cyrenaica.[2] Because they

[1] "And Kir uncovered (Heb. made naked) the shield."—*Eng. Ver.*
[2] "Kir is now agreed to be identical with Κῦρος, the name of a river

were (πελτασταὶ) shieldsmen, he says that they "laid bare the shield;" for when they enter the field of battle, they draw the shields out of their sheaths.

7. *And the choice of the valleys*[1] *was full of chariots.* I do not find fault with the translation given by some interpreters, " in a chariot of horsemen," but I have chosen rather to translate literally the words of the Prophet; for I think that he means "a military chariot." At that time they made use of two kinds of chariots, one for carrying baggage, and another for the field of battle. Here he means those chariots in which the horsemen rode.

Had it been a threatening, it would have been proper to translate it in the future tense, " And it shall be ;" but as the words which immediately follow are in the past tense, and as there is reason to believe that the Prophet is relating events which have already taken place, I have not hesitated to make this beginning agree with what follows. " The choice of the valleys" means " the choicest valleys." He reminds the Jews of those straits to which they were reduced when the enemies were at their gates. They ought at that time to have sought help from God ; but those wretched people became more strongly alienated from God, and more shamefully manifested their rebellion, which shewed them to be men utterly abandoned, and therefore he reproaches them with this hardened obstinacy.

8. *And he took away the covering of Judah.* He shews in what distress of mind the Jews were when they were so closely besieged. Some refer this verb to God, and others to the enemy ; but I rather think it ought to be taken indefinitely, for by a mode of expression frequently used in the Hebrew language, "he took away," means that " the covering of Judah was taken away." By the word *covering* almost all think that either the Temple or God himself is meant, in whose name the Jews falsely boasted. But I

---

rising in the Caucasus, and emptying into the Caspian Sea, from which Georgia (Girgistan) is supposed to derive its name. Kir was subject to Assyria in the time of Isaiah, as appears from the fact that it was one of the regions to which the exiles of the ten tribes were transported. It may here be put for Media, as Elam is for Persia."—*Alexander.*

[1] " Thy choicest valleys, (Heb. the choice of thy valleys.)"—Eng. Ver.

interpret it more simply as denoting the armory, in which, as a secret place, they kept the instruments of war. He calls it a "covering," because they were not exposed to public view, but were concealed in a more sacred place. In short, he describes what commonly happens in a season of great alarm, because at such a time men run to arms, and the instruments of war, which had been formerly concealed, are brought forward.

And thou didst look in that day to the armory of the house of the forest. This latter clause agrees with what has been remarked, that they sought out, on such an occasion, every place which contained the means of arming themselves for a case of extreme urgency, the instruments of war having lain long concealed during peace. Sacred history informs us, that this "house of the forest" was built by Solomon, in order to contain the armory of the whole kingdom.[1] (1 Kings vii. 2.) The change of person, *thou didst look,* does not obscure the meaning, but rather confirms what I have already remarked, that the Prophet relates how eagerly the Jews at that time made every preparation for defending the city.

9. *And you have seen the breaches.* He proceeds with his narrative, for during prosperity and peace no one cares about bulwarks or instruments of war. It is necessity alone that arouses men and makes them active; peace and quietness make us indolent and cowardly. So long as they thought that they were far from danger, they disregarded the breaches of the wall; but when a report of war arose, they began to be anxious about them, and to make arrangements for preventing the entrance of the enemy.

Of the city of David. By "the city of David," he means the interior part of the city; for, like many other cities which we see, the city was divided into two parts. The whole of Jerusalem was surrounded by walls and ramparts;

[1] "The name of 'the house of the forest' was given to it, because it was constructed of 'cedars' taken from the forest of Lebanon, and because it rested on four rows of fifteen large pillars of cedar. When the inhabitants of Jerusalem heard of the invasion by the Assyrian army, they looked to this armory to draw from it arms for defending the city."—*Rosenmüller.* "It was built by Solomon within the city as a cool retreat; and here he laid up his choicest armory. 1 Kings vii. 2, and x. 17. See Neh. iii. 19."—*Stock.*

but the interior part was more strongly fortified, and was called "the city of David." The Temple was afterwards fortified, in consequence of which the city might be said to consist of three parts. Isaiah means that the Jews had nearly despaired as to the safety of the whole city, when they withdrew to the inmost and best fortified part of it; and indeed it is evident from sacred history, that everything was in a desperate condition. Hence also we may infer, that the prophecies were not collected in a regular order, and that those who drew them up in one volume paid no attention to the arrangement of dates.

The waters of the lower pool. He adds, that water was collected for necessary purposes, that the besieged might not be in want of it, and that the pool served for cisterns.

10. *And you numbered the houses of Jerusalem.* He means that the city was closely examined on all sides, that there might not be a house or building which was not defended. Others think that the houses were numbered, that they might have a supply of watchmen. But the former interpretation is preferable, and is confirmed by what the Prophet afterwards adds, that the houses were thrown down for the purpose of rebuilding the walls of the city. This is commonly neglected in the time of peace, and the houses of private individuals are often built on the very walls, and, on that account, must be thrown down in the time of war, to supply the means of fighting and of repelling the enemy, and also lest, by means of houses so near the wall, secret communications with the enemy should be maintained.

11. *You made also a ditch.* The first clause of this verse relates to the former subjects; for he means that they were reduced to the last necessity, and that the great approaching danger struck them with terror, so that they adopted every method in their power for defending themselves against the enemy.

And you have not looked to its maker. This second clause reproves them for carelessness, because they had given their whole attention to earthly assistance, and had neglected that which is of the greatest importance. Instead of resorting first of all to God, as they ought to have done, they forgot and despised him, and directed their attention to ramparts, and ditches, and walls, and other preparations of war; but their highest defence was in God. What I said at first is now more evident, that the Prophet does not foretell the destruction of the Jews, but declares what they have experienced, in order to shew how justly the Lord was angry with them, because they could not be amended or reformed by any chastisement. The alarming dangers to which they were exposed ought to have warned them against their impiety and contempt of God; but those dangers have made them still more obstinate. Though there is hardly any person so obstinate as not to be induced by adversity, and especially by imminent dangers, to bethink himself, and to consider if they have justly befallen him, if he has offended God and provoked his wrath against himself; yet the Prophet says, that there was not one of the Jews who remembered God in the midst of such distresses, and that therefore God justly ceased to take any concern about them.

Hence infer that it is a token of extreme and desperate wickedness, when men, after having received chastisements or afflictions, are not made better. We ought, first, to follow God and to render to him cheerful obedience; and secondly, when we have been practically warned and chastised, we ought to repent. And if stripes do us no good, what remains but that the Lord shall increase and double the strokes, and cause us to feel them heavier and heavier till we are hurled down to destruction? For it is vain to apply remedies to a desperate and incurable disease. This doctrine is highly applicable to our own times, in which so many strokes and afflictions urge us to repentance. Since there is no repentance, what remains but that the Lord shall try to the very utmost what can be done until he destroy us altogether?

To its maker. By these words he indirectly acknowledges that God does not blame our eagerness to repel the enemy and to guard against dangers; but that he blames the vain confidence which we place in outward defences. We ought to have begun with God; and when we disregard him, and resort to swords and spears, to bulwarks and fortifications, our excessive eagerness is justly condemned as treason. Let us therefore learn to flee to God in imminent dangers, and to betake ourselves, with our whole heart, to the sure refuge of his name. (Prov. xviii. 10.) When this has been done, it will be lawful for us to use the remedies which he puts into our hand; but all will end in our ruin if we do not first commit our safety to his protection.

He calls God the *maker* and *fashioner* of Jerusalem, because there he had his dwelling, and wished that men should call upon him. (1 Kings ix. 3.) As Jerusalem was a lively image of the Church, this title belongs also to us, for in a peculiar manner God is called the Builder of the Church. (Psalm cxxxii. 13, 14.) Though this may relate to the creation of the whole world, yet the second creation, by which he raises up from death, (Eph. ii. 1,) regenerates, and sanctifies us, (Psalm cx. 3,) is peculiar to the elect, the rest have no share in it. This title does not express a sudden but a continual act, for the Church was not at once created that it might afterwards be forsaken, but the Lord preserves and defends it to the last. "Thou wilt not despise the work of thy hands," says the Psalmist. (Psalm cxxxviii. 8.) And Paul says, "He who hath begun a good work in you will perform it till the day of Christ." (Phil. i. 6.)

This title contains astonishing consolation, for if God is the maker, we have no reason to fear if we depend on his power and goodness. But we cannot *look to* him unless we are endued with true humility and confidence, so that, being divested of all haughtiness and reduced to nothing, we ascribe the glory to him alone. This cannot be, unless we can also trust that our salvation is in his hand, and are fully convinced that we shall never perish, even though we be surrounded by a thousand deaths. It was an aggravation of their baseness, that the Lord's election of that city, which had been established by so many proofs, could not arouse the Jews to rely on the protection of God. As if he had said, What madness is it to think of defending the city when you despise him who made it!

From a distance, or *long ago.* The Hebrew word denotes either distance of place or length of time. If we refer it to place, the meaning will be, that the Jews are doubly ungrateful, because they have not beheld the Lord even at a distance. Here it ought to be observed, that we ought to look to God not only when he is near, but also when he appears to be at a very great distance from us. Now, we think that he is absent, when we do not perceive his present aid, and when he does not instantly supply our wants. In short, he shews what is the nature of true hope; for it is a carnal and gross looking at God, when we do not perceive his providence unless by visible favour, since we ought to ascend above the heavens themselves. Strictly and truly, no doubt, the Lord is always present, but he is said to be distant and absent with respect to us. This must be understood therefore to refer to our senses, and not to the fact itself; and therefore, although he appear to be at a distance during those calamities which the Church endures, still we ought to elevate our minds towards him, and arouse our hearts, and shake off our indolence, that we may call on him.

But the other meaning is equally admissible, that they did not look to God who created his Church, not yesterday or lately, but long ago, and who had proved himself to be her Maker during many ages. He is therefore called the ancient Maker of his Church, because if the Jews will apply their thoughts and careful search to the long succession of ages, they will perceive that he is the perpetual preserver of his workmanship; and this makes their ingratitude the less excusable.

12. *And the* LORD *of hosts called.* The wicked obstinacy of the people is exhibited by the Prophet with additional aggravations. What left them altogether without excuse was the fact, that while they were exposed to so great dangers, they despised the godly remonstrances of the prophets, and rejected the grace of God, when he wished to heal and restore them. It is a proof of consummate depravity, when men have so completely laid aside all feeling that they fearlessly despise both instruction and chastisements, and obstinately " kick against the pricks," (Acts ix. 5,) and this makes it evident that they have been " given over to a reprobate mind." (Rom. i. 28.)

When he says, that " the Lord called" them, this may be

explained in two ways; for although the Lord does not speak, still he calls loudly enough by stripes and chastisements. Let it be supposed that we are destitute of all Scripture, of prophets, teachers, and advisers, still he instructs us by distresses and afflictions, so that we may state, in a few words, that every chastisement is a *call* to repentance. But, unquestionably, the Prophet intended to express something more, namely, that in despising godly warnings, they did not scruple to treat with scorn God's fatherly invitation.

In that day. There is great weight also in mentioning *the day* of affliction, when danger threatened them, for they were admonished at the same time by the word and by strokes. The signs of God's anger were visible, the prophets uttered incessant cries, and still they became no better.

To baldness and girding with sackcloth. When he mentions *sackcloth* and *baldness*,[1] he employs the signs themselves to describe repentance; for repentance does not consist in sackcloth or haircloth,[2] or anything outward, but has its place in the heart. Those who sincerely repent are displeased with themselves, hate sin, and are affected with such a deep feeling of grief, that they abhor themselves and their past life; but as this cannot be done without, at the same time, making itself known by confession before men, on this account he describes the outward signs by which we give evidence of our conversion. Now, these things were at that time cast away among the Jews, when they made public declarations of repentance. The Prophet therefore means that they were called to repentance, to humble themselves before God, and to exhibit the evidences of repentance before men. Of themselves, indeed, the signs would not be sufficient, for repentance begins at the heart; and Joel gives warning to that effect, " Rend your hearts, and not your garments." (Joel ii. 13.) Not that he wished signs to be laid aside, but he shewed that they are not sufficient, and that of themselves they are not acceptable to God.

[1] " Le sac et l'arrachement des cheveux;"—" Sackcloth and pulling out the hair."
[2] " En sac ou cendre;"—" In sackcloth or ashes."

Hence infer what is our duty, when the tokens of God's anger are visible to us. We ought to declare publicly our repentance, not only before God, but also before men. The outward ceremonies, indeed, are of little consequence, and we are not commanded to wear sackcloth or to pull out our hair; but we must practise honestly and sincerely what is actually meant by these signs, disapprobation and confession of our guilt, humility of the heart, and reformation of the life. If we do not confess that we are guilty, and that we deserve punishment, we shall not return to a state of favour with God. In short, as culprits allow their beards to grow, and wear tattered clothes, in order to affect the hearts of the judges, so we ought to betake ourselves as suppliants to the mercy of God, and make a public declaration of our repentance.

But here we ought also to observe the usefulness of outward signs of repentance; for they serve as spurs to prompt us more to know and abhor sin. In this way, so far as they are spurs, they may be called causes of repentance; and so far as they are evidences, they may be called effects. They are causes, because the marks of our guilt, which we carry about us, excite us the more to acknowledge ourselves to be sinners and guilty; and they are effects, because, if they were not preceded by repentance, we would never be induced to perform them sincerely.

13. *And, behold, joy and gladness.* The Prophet does not here find fault with *joy* viewed in itself; for we see that Paul exhorts the godly to true joy, the "joy" which is "in the Lord," (Philip. iv. 4;) but now he censures the joy which is opposite to that sadness which commonly springs from repentance, of which Paul also speaks. (2 Cor. vii. 10.) No man can be under the influence of repentance and of a sincere feeling of the wrath of God, without being led, by the grief which accompanies it, willingly to afflict himself. The joy which is opposite to this grief is therefore sinful, because it proceeds from brutish indifference, and is justly blamed, since the Lord curses it. (Luke vi. 25.)

Slaying oxen and killing sheep. From what has been said, it is easy to see the reason why he censures them for "slaying oxen and killing sheep." These things are not in themselves sinful, and are not displeasing to God ; but as fasting is a part of a solemn declaration of repentance, which we make before men, so to slay cattle for feasting, when we ought to fast, is a proof of obstinacy and contempt of God ; for in this way men despise God's threatenings, and encourage themselves in their crimes.

Such is the statement which Isaiah intended to make in general terms. But it is absurd in the Papists to think of drawing from it an approbation of abstinence from eating flesh. Why do they not also include what the Apostle adds about wine ? They are so far from abstaining from the use of wine, that they freely indulge in drinking it, as a compensation for the want of flesh. But let us pass over these absurdities. Isaiah does not absolutely condemn the use of flesh or the drinking of wine, but he condemns the luxury and wantonness by which men are hardened in such a manner that they obstinately set aside God's threatenings, and treat as false all that the prophets tell them.

This ought to be carefully observed, for we do not always wear sackcloth and ashes ; but we cannot have true repentance without making it manifest by the fruits which it must unavoidably produce. In short, as he had described repentance by its signs, so he marks out obstinacy by its signs ; for as by fasting and other outward acts we testify our repentance, so by feastings and luxury we give proofs of an obstinate heart, and thus provoke more the wrath of God, in a similar manner to what we read about the days of Noah. (Gen. vi. 5 ; Matt. xxiv. 38, 39 ; Luke xvii. 27.) After having described intemperance and luxury in general terms, he particularly mentions eating and drinking, in which the Jews indulged to such an extent as if they had been able, in some measure, to combat the wrath of God, and to obliterate the remembrance of his threatenings.

For to-morrow we shall die. This clause shews plainly enough why the Prophet complained so loudly about eating flesh and drinking wine. It was because all the threatenings uttered by the prophets were turned by them into a subject of jesting and laughter. It is supposed that Paul quotes this passage, when, in writing to the Corinthians, he uses nearly the same words. (1 Cor. xv. 32.) But I am of a different opinion; for he quotes the opinion of the Epicureans, who lived for the passing day, and gave themselves no concern about eternal life, and therefore thought that they should follow their natural disposition, and enjoy pleasures as long as life lasted. Isaiah, on the other hand, relates here the speeches of wicked men, who obstinately ridiculed the threatenings of the prophets, and could not patiently endure to be told about chastisements, banishments, slaughter, and ruin. They employed the words of the prophets, and in the midst of their feasting and revelry, turned them into ridicule, saying, in a boasting strain, "*To-morrow we shall die.* If the prophets tell us that our destruction is at hand, let us pass the present day, at least, in cheerfulness and mirth."

Thus, obstinate minds cannot be struck with any terror, but, on the contrary, mock at God and the prophets, and give themselves up more freely to licentiousness. It certainly was frightful madness when, through indignation and wrath, they quoted with bitter irony the words which not only ought to have affected their minds, but ought to have shaken heaven and earth. Would that there were not instances of the same kind in the present day! For whenever God threatens, the greater part of men either vomit out their bitterness, or sneeringly ridicule everything that has proceeded from God's holy mouth.

14. *This is revealed.*[1] As if he had said, "Do you think that you can escape punishment for your wantonness, when God calls you to repentance?" It might be thought that here the Prophet says nothing that is new; for undoubtedly all things are known to God. But he adds this for the purpose of shaking off the indolence of men, who never would rise

---

[1] Rosenmüller, who is followed in this instance by Stock and Alexander, renders this clause, "Jehovah was revealed in my ears," remarking that נגלה (*niglah*) must here be taken for a reflective verb, and quoting as parallel passages, 1 Sam. ii. 27, and 1 Sam. iii. 21, in the former of which, instead of the literal rendering, "Revealing was I revealed?" our translators say, "Did I plainly appear?" while in the latter they make נגלה (*niglah*) a reflective verb, "The Lord revealed himself."—*Ed.*

so fiercely against God, if they did not think that they could deceive him; for whosoever knows that God is his witness, must also acknowledge that God is his judge. Hence it follows that wicked men, in their wantonness, rob God of his power; and therefore it is not without reason that they are summoned to his tribunal, that they may know that they must render an account to him.

If this iniquity shall be forgiven you till you die. He adds a dreadful threatening, that this wickedness shall never be forgiven. In the Hebrew language, the conditional particle, *if,* contains a denial, as if the Lord had said, "Do not think that I am true, or that I have any divine perfections, *if* I do not take vengeance on so great wickedness." The reason why the Jews, in their oaths, reserve something which is not expressed, is to accustom us to deeper reverence in this matter; for we entreat God to be our Judge and avenger if we speak falsely, and therefore we ought to restrain ourselves, so as not to make oaths at random. Here Isaiah states generally, that nothing is so displeasing to God as impenitence, by which, as Paul says, (Rom. ii. 5,) we "heap up for ourselves the treasures of God's wrath," and shut out all hope of pardon.

15. *Thus saith the Lord.* This is a special prediction against a single individual; for, having spoken of the whole nation, he turns to Shebna, whom he will afterwards mention. (Isaiah xxxvii. 2.) To this person the Prophet gives two titles, that of "scribe" or "chancellor," and that of "steward of the house," for while in this passage he calls him "steward," in the thirty-seventh chapter he calls him "scribe." This has led some to think that, at the time of this prediction, he had resigned his office as steward, and that Eliakim was put in his room. But this is uncertain, though the words of the Prophet, in reference to Shebna himself, lead us to conclude that he cherished wicked envy, which led him to attempt to degrade Eliakim from his rank. Nor is it improbable that this prediction was uttered, when Sennacherib's army was discomfited, and Jerusalem was saved in a miraculous manner. (2 Kings xix. 35; Isaiah xxxvii. 36.) During the interval, many things might have

happened which are now unknown to us; and it is not improbable that this treacherous scoundrel, having obtained the highest authority, made an unjust use of it to the injury of Eliakim. It is evident, from the history of the Book of Kings, that Shebna was a "scribe" or "secretary," and one of high rank, such as we now call chancellor.

There is greater difficulty about the word סֹכֵן, (*sōchēn.*) Some think that it means "treasurer," because סָכַן (*sāchăn*) signifies *to store up;* but, as he elsewhere calls him "chancellor," I think it is not probable that he was treasurer. Besides, the Prophet shews plainly enough that his office as governor was such as allowed others to have scarcely any share of authority along with him. Such a rank could not belong to a treasurer, and therefore I think that the Prophet means something else. As סָכַן (*sāchăn*) sometimes signifies "to abet," and "to foment," סֹכֵן (*sōchēn*) may here mean "an abettor," or, as we commonly say, "an accomplice." It is certain that this Shebna had communications with the enemy, and was a cunning and deceitful person; for he cherished a concealed friendship with the Egyptians and Assyrians, and held treacherous communications with them, so as to provide for his own safety in any event that might arise, and to maintain his authority.

Others think that סֹכֵן (*sōchēn*) is a word denoting the country to which he belonged, and that he was called a Sochnite from the city of which he was a native; for he is said to have been an Egyptian. I certainly do not reject that opinion, but I prefer the former; for he *abetted* both sides, and thought that, by his cunning, he would be preserved, even though everything should be turned upside down.

The particle הַזֶּה, (*hăzzēh,*) *this,* is evidently added in contempt. It is as if he had said, " *That* cunning man, ready for all shifts, (πανοῦργος,) who abets various parties, who curries favour on all sides." In this sense סֹכֵן (*sōchēn*) is used (1 Kings i. 2) when it relates to a maid who was about to be brought to the aged king in order to *cherish* him. Yet, if it be thought preferable to understand it as meaning a hurtful and injurious person, I do not object, for the word signifies also "to impoverish."

16. *What hast thou here?* Shebna had built a sepulchre at Jerusalem, as if he were to live there continually, and to die there. The Prophet therefore asks why he built a splendid and costly sepulchre in a lofty and conspicuous place, as is commonly done by those who wish to perpetuate the memory of their name in the world. He appears to glance at the ambition of a foreigner and a stranger in longing to be so magnificently buried out of his country, and yet eagerly joining with enemies for the destruction of Judea. What could have been more foolish than to erect a monument in that country for whose ruin he was plotting? And therefore he adds—

17. *Behold, the Lord will carry thee away.* As if he had said, "Thou shalt be cast out of that place into a distant country, where thou shalt die ignominiously." גבר (*gĕbĕr*) is commonly translated as in the genitive case; that is, "with the casting out of a man thou shalt be cast out." Again, גבר (*gĕbĕr*) denotes not an ordinary man, but a strong and brave man, and thus it comes to mean, "with a mighty and powerful casting out." Others render it in the vocative case, "O man!" as if he were addressing Shebna in mockery, "O illustrious man, who so proudly vauntest of thy greatness, who thinkest that thou art some hero!" But the former reading will be more appropriate. Yet here also commentators disagree; for, besides the exposition which I have mentioned, another is brought forward, that *men* will be carried to a greater distance than women. But I rather think that he alludes to the pride of Shebna, who had built so splendid a sepulchre, in order that his memory, like that of some distinguished man, might be handed down to posterity. "Thou wishest to be renowned after thy death: I will ennoble thee in a different manner. By a remarkable transportation will I remove thee to a foreign and distant country, where thou shalt be buried in an extraordinary manner."

First, on the word סכן (*sōchēn*) it is proper to remark how much God is displeased with a false and deceitful heart; for there is nothing which God more earnestly recommends to us than simplicity. He is called a ruler, because, being placed above others, he was likely to be dazzled by the lustre of his present greatness, as happens to those who, elated and puffed up by their success, dread no adversity, as if they had been placed beyond the reach of all danger. The Lord threatens that he will be the judge of such persons. Here it also deserves notice, that Isaiah could not, without making himself the object of strong dislike, utter this prediction, especially when addressed to a man of such an elevated station and so haughty; and yet he must not refuse this office, but must approach and threaten this man, as God had commanded him.

As to the *sepulchre*, we know that solicitude about burying the dead is not wholly condemned; for although " the want of burial," as one remarks, " is of little importance, yet the desire of being buried is natural to man, and ought not to be entirely disregarded." He does not blame him, therefore, for wishing to be buried, but for his ambition in building a tomb, by which he shewed his eagerness to obtain vain and empty renown. But there is another circumstance connected with Shebna that must be observed; for, having wished to deliver the city into the hands of the Assyrians by treachery, he thought that he would reign permanently. He hoped that the Assyrians, if they were successful, would bestow on him the government of the kingdom as the reward of his treachery, and that, if they were defeated, he would permanently retain his rank and authority.

But this will appear more clearly from the words themselves, *What hast thou here?* He was a foreigner, and as such he could honestly become united to the people of God; but, being a traitor and a foreigner, he had no right to that city or country which the Lord had specially assigned to his own people. Isaiah therefore asks, " Of what country art thou? Though thou hast no connection with the people of God by blood or relationship, dost thou wish not only to reign in this country during thy life, but to procure for thyself a settled abode in it after thou art dead? Wilt thou betray us to the Assyrians, and drive out the actual possessors, that thou, who art a foreigner, mayest enjoy that country, of which not even an inch belongs to thee?"

Hence infer that God is highly displeased with that ambition by which men endeavour to obtain undying renown in the world, instead of being satisfied with those honours which they enjoy during their life. They wish to be applauded after death, and in some measure to live in the mouth of men; and although death sets aside everything, they foolishly hope that their name will last through all ages. But God punishes their haughtiness and presumption, and causes those things which they wished to be the records of their glory to become their disgrace and shame. Either their memory is abhorred, so that men cannot see or hear anything connected with them without utter loathing, or he does not even permit them to be laid in their graves, but sends them to gibbets and to ravens, of which we read many instances in history, (Esther vii. 10,) and we have seen not a few in our own times.

Whenever I read this passage, I am forcibly reminded of a similar instance, resembling it indeed more closely than any other, that of Thomas More, who held the same office as Shebna; for it is well known that he was Lord Chancellor to the king of England. Having been a very bitter enemy of the gospel, and having persecuted good men by fire and sword, he wished that on this account his reputation should be extensive, and his wickedness and cruelty permanently recorded. He therefore ordered the praises of his virtue to be inscribed on a tomb which he had caused to be built with great cost and splendour, and sent his epitaph, which he had drawn up, to Basle, to Erasmus, along with a palfrey which he gave him as a present, to get it printed. He was so desirous of renown, that he wished to obtain during his life the reputation and praises which he hoped to enjoy after his death. Among other applauses the most conspicuous was, that he had been a very great persecutor of the Lutherans, that is, of the godly.[1] What happened? He was accused of treason, condemned, and beheaded; and thus he had a gibbet for his tomb. Do we ask more manifest judgments of God, by which he punishes the pride, the unbounded eagerness

[1] " C'est à dire, des enfans de Dieu;"—" That is, of the children of God."

for renown, and the blasphemous vaunting, of wicked men? In this inveterate enemy of the people of God, not less than in Shebna, we ought undoubtedly to acknowledge and adore God's overruling providence.

Another circumstance worthy of notice is, that this Shebna was a foreigner. Thus, all the tyrants and enemies of the people of God, though they be foreigners, would wish to cast out the actual lords of the soil, that they alone might possess the land; but at length the Lord drives them out, and strips them of all possession, so that they do not even continue to have a tomb.[1] There are innumerable instances in history. True, this does not always happen; but the instances which the Lord holds out to us, ought to lead our thoughts farther to consider his judgments against tyrants and wicked men, who wished to be applauded and celebrated, but are distinguished by some remarkable kind of death, so that their infamy becomes universally known. Thus, the renown of that sepulchre which Shebna had built is indirectly contrasted with the ignominy which quickly followed it.

18. *Turning he will turn thee.*[2] Isaiah continues the same discourse, in which he ridiculed the pride of Shebna, who had bestowed so much cost on building a sepulchre. This statement is connected with the first clause of the former verse; for, as he formerly said, "He will remove thee by an extraordinary removal," so he now says, "He will toss thee as a ball into an open plain." By this comparison he means that nothing will prevent the Lord from casting him out into a distant country, though he thinks that his power is firmly established; and since he had been so careful about his sepulchre, and had given orders about it, as if he had been certain as to his death, Isaiah declares that he will not die in Jerusalem, but in a foreign country, to which he shall be banished.

The chariot of thy glory. Under the word *chariot* he includes all the fame and rank of Shebna; as if he had said

---

[1] "Tellement qu'ils n'ont pas mesme un pied de terre pour estre interrez;"—"So that they have not even a foot of earth for a grave."
[2] "He will surely violently turn."—Eng. Ver.

that disgrace would be his reputation among foreigners. Thus, the Lord ridicules the mad ambition of those who look at nothing but the world, and who judge of their happiness by the glory of fading and transitory objects.

The shame of thy lord's house. He calls it " the shame of" the royal " house," either because he had polluted that holy place which might be regarded as the sanctuary of the Lord, or because Hezekiah had judged ill in elevating him to that station. That the mask of his high rank might not screen him from this prediction, the Prophet expressly states, that the office which he holds aggravates his guilt and renders him more detestable. Let princes, therefore, if they do not wish to expose themselves and their houses to reproaches, learn to act with judgment in appointing men to hold office.

19. *And I will cast thee out.* He says nothing new, but concludes the former prediction. Though in the next verse he will again mention Shebna, yet now he gives a brief summary of what has been already said. Shebna thought that he had a fixed abode in Jerusalem, so that, whatever might happen, he thought that he could not be driven or removed from it. But the Lord threatens that he will cast him out, and will banish him to a distant country. Thus, the Lord frequently overturns the thoughts of the wicked, (Psalm xxxiii. 10,) who, relying on their cunning and dexterity, toss about public affairs according to their own pleasure. The change of person shews that the Prophet speaks sometimes in his own name, and sometimes in the name of God.

20. *And it shall come to pass in that day.* It is uncertain at what time Eliakim was substituted in the room of Shebna; for we shall see, in the thirty-seventh chapter, that Eliakim was steward of the king's house when Shebna was chancellor. Whether or not any change took place during the interval cannot with certainty be affirmed; yet it is probable, as I lately hinted, that through the stratagems of this wicked man, Eliakim was afterwards driven from his office, and that Shebna, after having triumphed, was punished for his frauds which had been detected, and, having been driven or banished from Judea, fled to the Assyrians, and there received the

reward of his treachery. In like manner does it frequently happen to traitors, who, when they cannot fulfil their engagements, are hated and abhorred by those whom they have deceived; for, having been bold and rash in promising, they must be discovered to be false and treacherous.

The Jews allege that at last he was torn in pieces on account of his treachery, but no history supports that statement. Leaving that matter doubtful, it is certain that he was cast out or banished, and that he ended his days in a foreign country, and not at Jerusalem. It is probable that, after his banishment, Eliakim was again placed in his room.

I will call. It is certain that all princes and magistrates are called by the Lord, even though they be wicked and ungodly; for "all authority is from God," as Paul affirms. (Rom. xiii. 1.) But here the Prophet speaks of a peculiar *calling*, by which the Lord manifests his goodness towards his people, when he appoints such persons to be his servants, that it may be known that God governs by them; and they, on the other hand, are well aware of the purpose for which they have been appointed by God, and faithfully discharge the office assigned to them. Shebna had indeed been *called* for a time, but it was that he might be God's scourge; for nothing was farther from his thoughts than to obey God. Eliakim was a different kind of person; for he acknowledged himself to be a servant of God, and obeyed the holy calling.

I will call, means, therefore, " I will give a sign to my servant, that he may know that it is I who have raised him to that honourable rank." There is in this case a peculiar relation between the master and the servant, which does not apply to ungodly men when they obey their own inclination and wicked passions; but this man acknowledged the Lord and sincerely obeyed him. Lastly, this mark distinguishes the true servant of God from a wicked and hypocritical person, who had risen to honour by wicked practices.

21. *And I will clothe him.* He now explains more fully what he had briefly noticed in the former verse, that it was only by the purpose of God that Shebna was deposed, in order that Eliakim might succeed him. It is true, indeed,

that all the changes that happen in the world are directed by the providence of God; for he "girds kings with a girdle," as we are told in the book of Job, "and ungirds them, according to his pleasure." (Job xii. 18.) A witty saying was at one time current about the Roman emperors, "that they were theatrical kings;" because, as players, who perform their parts in the theatre, no sooner have laid aside the rank of a king, than they presently become poor mechanics; so the emperors, after having been thrown down from their lofty station, were speedily hurried to a disgraceful punishment. And yet it is certain that those insurrections did not take place by chance, or merely through the designs of men, or by military forces, but by the purpose of God, which directed the whole. But the Prophet declares, that there is this peculiarity in the case of Shebna, that his deposition will be a clear proof of the vengeance of God, and that the restoration of Eliakim will be regarded as a lawful form of government.

With thy robes and with thy girdle. By the *robes* and *girdle* are meant the badges of the magistrates' office. The *girdle* was an emblem of royalty, and the chief magistrates undoubtedly wore it as an honourable distinction. At Rome, also, the prætors wore this badge. Job says, that God ungirds kings when he deprives them of their royal rank. (Job xii. 18.) These things were foretold by the Prophet, that all might not only see clearly in this instance the providence of God, and acknowledge his purpose, but might perceive that this wicked man, who had raised himself improperly and by unlawful methods, was justly deposed.

He shall be a father. Wicked magistrates are indeed appointed by God, but it is in his anger, and because we do not deserve to be placed under his government. He gives a loose rein to tyrants and wicked men, in order to punish our ingratitude, as if he had forsaken or ceased to govern us. But when good magistrates rule, we see God, as it were, near us, and governing us by means of those whom he hath appointed. The Prophet means that Eliakim will perform the part of a father, because he has been endued with the Spirit of God. At the same time he reminds all godly persons that they will have good reasons for wishing the government of Eliakim, because it tends to the general advantage of the Church.

By the appellation *father*, he shews what is the duty of a good magistrate. The same thing has been taught by heathen writers, that "a good king holds the place of a father;" and when they wished to flatter those who crushed the commonwealth by the exercise of tyranny, nature suggested to them to call the tyrants by the honourable title of "fathers of their country." In like manner, philosophers, when they say that a family is the picture of a kingdom, shew that a king ought to hold the place of a father. This is also proved by the ancient titles given to kings, such as "Abimelech," (Gen. xx. 2, 8,) that is, "my father the king," and others of the same kind, which shew that royal authority cannot be separated from the feelings of a father. Those who wish to be regarded as lawful princes, and to prove that they are God's servants, must therefore shew that they are fathers to their people.

22. *And the key of the house of David.*[1] This expression is metaphorical, and we need not spend much time, as some do, in drawing from it an allegorical meaning; for it is taken from an ordinary custom of men. The keys of the house are delivered to those who are appointed to be stewards, that they may have the full power of opening and shutting according to their own pleasure. By "the house of David" is meant "the royal house." This mode of expression was customary among the people, because it had been promised to David that his kingdom would be for ever. (2 Samuel vii. 13; Psalm cxxxii. 11, 12.) That is the reason why the kingdom was commonly called "the house of David."

The key is put in the singular number for *keys*. Though "keys" are usually carried in the hands, yet he says that they are laid on the shoulders,[2] because he is describing an

[1] "As the robe and the baldric, mentioned in the preceding verse, were the ensigns of power and authority, so likewise was the key the mark of office, either sacred or civil."—*Lowth.*

[2] "To comprehend how the key could be borne on the shoulder, it will be necessary to say somewhat of the form of it; but, without entering into

important charge. Yet nothing more is meant than that the charge and the whole government of the house are committed to him, that he may regulate everything according to his pleasure; and we know that the delivering of keys is commonly regarded as a token of possession.

Some commentators have viewed this passage as referring to Christ, but improperly; for the Prophet draws a comparison between two men, Shebna and Eliakim. Shebna shall be deprived of his office, and Eliakim shall succeed him. What has this to do with Christ? For Eliakim was not a type of Christ, and the Prophet does not here describe any hidden mystery, but borrows a comparison from the ordinary practice of men, as if the keys were delivered to one who has been appointed to be steward, as has been already said. For the same reason Christ calls the office of teaching the word, (Matt. xvi. 19,) "the keys of the kingdom of heaven;" so that it is idle and foolish to spend much time in endeavouring to find a hidden reason, when the matter is plain, and needs no ingenuity. The reason is, that ministers, by the preaching of the word, open the entrance into heaven, and lead to Christ, who alone is "the way." (John xiv. 6.) By *the keys*, therefore, he means here the government of the king's house, because the principal charge of it would be delivered to Eliakim at the proper time.

23. *And I will fasten him* as *a nail in a sure place.* The particle of comparison must here be supplied, and therefore I have inserted in the text the word *as*. By נֶאֱמָן, (*nĕĕmān,*) *faithful,* he means what is "firm and sure." The

a long disquisition, and a great deal of obscure learning, concerning the locks and keys of the ancients, it will be sufficient to observe, that one sort of keys, and that probably the most ancient, was of considerable magnitude, and, as to the shape, very much bent and crooked. Homer, Odyss. xxi. 6, describes the key of Ulysses's store-house as εὐκαμπής, of a large curvature; which Eustathius explains by saying it was δρεπανοειδής, in shape like a reap-hook. The curve part was introduced into the key-hole, and, being properly directed by the handle, took hold of the bolts within, and moved them from their places. We may easily collect from this account, that such a key would lie very well upon the shoulder; that it must be of some considerable size and weight, and could hardly be commodiously carried otherwise. Ulysses's key was of brass, and the handle of ivory; but this was a royal key; the more common ones were probably of wood."—*Lowth.*

original idea of the word is "truth;" for where "truth" is, there firmness and certainty are found;[1] and therefore Hebrew writers employ the word "truth" to denote what is firm and certain. Isaiah employs an elegant metaphor, from which godly magistrates, who are few in number, ought to draw large consolation. They may conclude that not only has God raised them to that honourable rank, but they are confirmed and established, as if they had been *fixed* by his hand. And indeed, where the fear of the Lord dwells, there the stability, and power, and authority of kings, as Solomon says, are established by justice and judgment. (Prov. xvi. 12; xxv. 5; xxix. 14.)

This consolation ought to be of advantage to princes, not only that they may meet all danger courageously, but likewise that they may firmly and resolutely proceed in their office, and not turn aside on any account, or shrink from any danger. But there are very few who can actually relish this doctrine. Almost all are like Jeroboam, (1 Kings xii. 28,) and think that religion should yield to them, and, so far as they imagine, that it will be of service to them, follow it, or rather bend and change it for their own convenience. Their last thought is about God and religion; and we need not wonder if they are always in doubt about their own affairs, and are scarcely ever at rest; for they do not direct their thoughts to him from whom all authority proceeds. (Rom. xiii. 1.) Hence springs treachery, hence springs cruelty, covetousness, violence, and frauds and wrongs of every kind, in which the princes of the present day indulge with less restraint and with greater impudence than all others. Yet there are some in whom we see what is here said of Eliakim. The Lord guards and upholds them, and blesses that regard to equity and justice which he had bestowed upon them. If the Lord permits even tyrants for a time, because they have some appearance of regular government, what shall happen when a prince shall endeavour, to the utmost of his power, to defend justice and judgment, and the true worship

---

[1] "Ce mot est deduit de verité, laquelle est tousjours accompagnee de fermeté et asseurance;"—"This word is derived from truth, which is always accompanied by firmness and certainty."

of God? Will he not be still more confirmed and established by him who is the continual guardian of righteousness?

24. *And they shall hang upon him.* It is as if he had said that Eliakim would be fully qualified for discharging his duties, and would not be indolent in his office. Hence we infer that God does not exalt princes to honour, in order that they may live in indolence or gratify their own passions. The office of a prince is very laborious, if he discharges it properly, and if he do not copy the unmeaning countenances of those who imagine that they have been raised to that honour, that they may live in splendour and may freely indulge in every kind of luxury. If a prince wish to discharge his office in a proper manner, he must endure much toil. It must not be thought that the comparison of a *nail* is inapplicable to princely government, since it denotes an office full of activity and cares; and we know that metaphors do not apply at all points, but we ought to observe the purpose for which they are introduced.

All the glory of his father's house,[1] *the grandchildren and great-grandchildren.*[2] The expression, "his father's house," leaves no room to doubt that Eliakim was of royal blood;

---

[1] " In ancient times, and in the eastern countries, as the way of life, so the houses were much more simple than ours at present. They had not that quantity and variety of furniture, nor those accommodations of all sorts with which we abound. It was convenient and even necessary for them, and it made an essential part in the building of a house, to furnish the inside of the several apartments with sets of spikes, nails, or large pegs, upon which to dispose of, and hang up, the several moveables and utensils in common use, and proper to the apartment. These spikes they worked into the walls at the first erection of them—the walls being of such materials that they could not bear their being driven in afterwards; and they were contrived so as to strengthen the walls, by binding the parts together, as well as to serve for convenience. Sir John Chardin's account of this matter is this, ' They do not drive with a hammer the nails that are put into the eastern walls; the walls are too hard, being of brick; or if they are of clay, too mouldering; but they fix them in the brick-work as they are building. They are large nails with square heads like dice, well-made, the ends being so bent as to make them cramp-irons. They commonly place them at the windows and doors, in order to hang upon them, when they like, veils and curtains.'—(Harmer, Obser. i. p. 191.) And we may add, that they were put in other places too, in order to hang up other things of various kinds; as it appears from this place of Isaiah, and from Ezek. xv. 3, who speaks of a pin, or nail, to hang any vessel thereon."— *Lowth.*

[2] " The offspring and the issue."—Eng. Ver.

and therefore by his successors I understand not only those who were nearly related to him, but the whole family of David. He will have the charge of all that shall be in the king's house. By adding *grandchildren*, he likewise shews that this princely government will be of long duration, that it will not only last during the life of one individual, but will also extend to his successors.[1] For good princes are useful not only to their own age, but also to posterity, to whom they leave good laws, salutary regulations, and the traces of good government; so that their successors, even though they be wicked men, are ashamed to give themselves up all at once to abandoned wickedness, and, even against their will, are compelled through shame to retain something that is good. He shews that this will be the case with Eliakim, whose government will be so righteous that even posterity shall reap advantage from it.

The smaller vessels.[2] Metaphorically it denotes that there will be uniform justice, or equal laws, as the phrase is; and it is as if he had said, " He will not only support the nobles, but will likewise attend to the interests of the lowest rank." The more rarely this is found in a prince, so much higher praise does he deserve than if he favoured none but the rich and powerful; for these can guard and protect themselves, but the poor and feeble lie open as a prey to the attacks of others, and there is hardly any one that pleads their cause.

To all vessels of music.[3] By *vessels* the Hebrew writers denote instruments of all kinds, and the meaning is very extensive. When he speaks of *musical*[4] vessels, he follows out what he had said in a single word; for it serves to explain the word קטן, (*kātān,*) *little;* as if he had said that there

---

[1] " Mais s'estendra jusqu' a ceux qui viendront long temps apres;"—" But will extend to those who shall live long afterwards."

[2] " Here follow the names of utensils hung up in an eastern house, concerning which we must needs be uncertain. The meaning of the whole figure is, Eliakim shall be the support of all ranks in the state, of the meanest people as well as the highest."—*Stock.*

[3] " Even to all the vessels of flagons, (or, instruments of violins.)"—Eng. Ver.

[4] " The old interpretation of נבלים (*nĕbālīm*) as denoting musical instruments," says Professor Alexander, " though justified by usage, is forbidden by the context."

would be nothing so small, or minute, or insignificant, that he would not take charge of it.

25. *In that day.* It might be thought that this is inconsistent with what he had formerly said; but he no longer speaks of Eliakim, for he returns to Shebna, who was about to be cast down from his rank, as Isaiah had said. But for this, it might have been thought that there was no way by which Eliakim could arrive at that honour, but by the deposition of Shebna, who had arranged his matters so well, that no person thought it possible that he could be driven from his position. Yet though he has fortified himself by many defences, and thinks that he is at a great distance from all danger, still he shall be deprived of his office, and Eliakim shall be placed in his room.

In a sure place. When he calls it "a sure place," this must be understood with respect to men; for men judge that what is defended on all sides will be of long duration; but God casts it down with the smallest breath. It was only by way of concession that he called it "a sure place." Hence it ought to be inferred how foolishly men boast, and rely on their greatness, when they have been exalted to a high rank of honour; for in a very short time they may be cast down and deprived of all honour.

And the burden that was upon it shall be cut off. When wicked men are ruined, all who relied on their authority must also be ruined; and indeed it is in the highest degree reasonable that they who were united by the same bond of crimes, and who aided this wicked man as far as lay in their power, should share in the same punishment. It is difficult for those who place themselves under the protection of wicked men, and employ all their influence in behalf of them, not to be also partakers of their crimes; and if they were guiltless of crime, (which seldom, or rather, we may say, never happens,) still they are justly punished on this ground, that they have placed their trust on them as a very sure defence, and have depended wholly on their will and authority.

CHAPTER XXIII.

1. The burden of Tyre. Howl, ye ships of Tarshish; for it is laid waste, so that there is no house, no entering in: from the land of Chittim it is revealed to them.

2. Be still, ye inhabitants of the isle; thou whom the merchants of Zidon, that pass over the sea, have replenished.

3. And by great waters the seed of Sihor, the harvest of the river, *is* her revenue; and she is a mart of nations.

4. Be thou ashamed, O Zidon; for the sea hath spoken, *even* the strength of the sea, saying, I travail not, nor bring forth children, neither do I nourish up young men, *nor* bring up virgins.

5. As at the report concerning Egypt, *so* shall they be sorely pained at the report of Tyre.

6. Pass ye over to Tarshish; howl, ye inhabitants of the isle.

7. *Is* this your joyous *city*, whose antiquity *is* of ancient days? her own feet shall carry her afar off to sojourn.

8. Who hath taken this counsel against Tyre, the crowning *city*, whose merchants *are* princes, whose traffickers *are* the honourable of the earth?

9. The Lord of hosts hath purposed it, to stain the pride of all glory, *and* to bring into contempt all the honourable of the earth.

10. Pass through thy land as a river, O daughter of Tarshish: *there is* no more strength.

11. He stretched out his hand over the sea; he shook the kingdoms: the Lord hath given a commandment against the merchant-*city*, to destroy the strongholds thereof.

12. And he said, Thou shalt no more rejoice, O thou oppressed virgin, daughter of Zidon: arise, pass over to Chittim; there also shalt thou have no rest.

1. Onus Tyri. Ululate, naves Tharsis; quia devastatio facta est, ut non sit domus, non sit commeatus e terra Cittim. Revelatum est hoc eis.

2. Tacete incolæ insularum: negotiator Sidonis, trajicientes mare, qui te replebant.

3. In aquis multis semen Nili, messis fluminis fruges ejus; et fuit emporium gentium.

4. Erubesce, Sidon; quia dixit mare, fortitudo maris, dicens, Non parturivi, neque peperi, neque educavi adolescentes, neque extuli virgines.

5. Simul atque rumor pervenerit ad Ægyptios, dolebunt secundum rumorem Tyri.

6. Transite in Tharsis; ululate, habitatores insularum.

7. An hæc vobis exultans? à diebus antiquis vetustas ejus. Ducent eam pedes ejus, ut peregrinetur in terram longinquam.

8. Quis consultavit hoc super Tyrum coronantem? cujus negotiatores sunt Principes, cujus institores nobiles terræ?

9. Iehova exercituum ita decrevit ad profanandam superbiam omnium magnificorum, ut vilipendat omnes gloriosos terræ.

10. Transi instar fluminis è terra tua ad filiam Tharsis, quia non amplius cingulum.

11. Manum suam posuit super mare, concussit regna. Iehova mandavit super Canaan ut enervet robur ejus.

12. Et ait, Non adjicies ultra ut exultes, ubi oppressa fueris, virgo filia Sidon. Surge, ut transeas in Cittim. Atqui etiam illic non erit tibi requies.

13. Behold the land of the Chaldeans: this people was not, *till* the Assyrian founded it for them that dwell in the wilderness: they set up the towers thereof, they raised up the palaces thereof; *and* he brought it to ruin.

14. Howl, ye ships of Tarshish: for your strength is laid waste.

15. And it shall come to pass in that day, that Tyre shall be forgotten seventy years, according to the days of one king: after the end of seventy years shall Tyre sing as an harlot.

16. Take an harp, go about the city, thou harlot that hast been forgotten; make sweet melody, sing many songs, that thou mayest be remembered.

17. And it shall come to pass, after the end of seventy years, that the Lord will visit Tyre, and she shall turn to her hire, and shall commit fornication with all the kingdoms of the world upon the face of the earth.

18. And her merchandise and her hire shall be holiness to the Lord: it shall not be treasured nor laid up; for her merchandise shall be for them that dwell before the Lord, to eat sufficiently, and for durable clothing.

13. Ecce terra Chaldæorum, hic non fuit populus, Assur fundavit eam deserti incolis; erexerunt arces ejus; excitarunt palatia ejus; redegit eam in vastitatem.

14. Ululate, naves Tharsis; quia vastata est fortitudo vestra.

15. Accidet in die illa, ut sit in oblivione Tyrus septuaginta annis, secundum dies regis unius; a fine septuaginta annorum erit Tyro quasi canticum meretricis.

16. Sume citharam, circui urbem, meretrix oblivioni tradita, suavem fac melodiam, multiplica carmen, ut in memoriam revoceris.

17. Erit ergo a fine septuaginta annorum, ut visitet Iehova Tyrum; et tunc redibit ad mercedem suam, fornicabiturque cum omnibus regnis terræ quæ sunt super terram.

18. Sed (tandem) erit negotiatio ejus et merces ejus sancta Iehovæ; non reponetur neque recondetur; sed negotiatio ejus (addicta) erit iis qui habitabant coram Iehovæ, ut comedant ad satietatem, et habeant densum operimentum.

1. *The burden of Tyre.* Tyre was very wealthy, and highly celebrated, both on account of the variety and extent of its commercial intercourse with all nations, and on account of the flourishing colonies which sprang from it: Carthage, which was the rival of the Roman Empire, Utica, Leptis, Cadiz, and other towns, which also sent every year a present to Tyre, by which they acknowledged that they looked on Tyre as their mother. Isaiah threatens its destruction, because it had been hostile to the people of God, as we may infer from what is said by Ezekiel; for we ought carefully to attend to the cause of the destruction, because it was the design of the Prophet to shew that God testifies his fatherly regard to his people by opposing all her enemies. (Ezek. xxvi. 2.) Some think that this refers to the storming

of Tyre by Alexander, who took it with great difficulty. But the argument on which they rely, that Isaiah mentions *Chittim*,[1] has little force. By that name the Hebrew writers unquestionably denote the Macedonians, but under this word they likewise include other nations, such as the Greeks, and the countries that were beyond the sea. Nebuchadnezzar employed in that siege not only his own soldiers, but also foreigners, whom he brought from Greece and other places. It is for a reason altogether different, as we shall immediately see, that he mentions the Greeks, namely, that henceforth they will not take their ships to Tyre for the sake of carrying on merchandise.

But from the conclusion of this chapter I draw an argument for a contrary opinion, for Isaiah speaks of the restoration of Tyre, and it was never restored after having been stormed by Alexander. Besides, when I compare Ezekiel's words with those of Isaiah, I think that I see one and the same prediction. Now, he does not speak of Alexander, but of Nebuchadnezzar; and I cannot doubt that it must be explained in that manner. Not only so, but in the days of Ezekiel and Isaiah that city was under the dominion of a king, but historians relate that, when it was stormed by Alexander, it had been brought to the form of a republic. And if we consider the object of the prophecy, we shall be sufficiently confirmed in this opinion, for his aim is to comfort the Jews by threatening that the inhabitants of Tyre, by whom they had been oppressed, will not pass unpunished. For it would have been highly inconsistent that the Lord should punish other nations, and that this nation, which had been not less hostile, should escape punishment altogether, or be punished five hundred years afterwards. Every conjecture, therefore, leads us to this conclusion, that we should expound this passage as relating to Nebuchadnezzar.

Howl, ye ships of Tarshish. He employs various figures of speech, according to his custom, in illustrating the ruin of Tyre, in order to obtain greater credit to the prediction; for

---

[1] A slight change of spelling makes it necessary to remind the reader of the English Bible, that the " Chittim" were the descendants of Kittim, (Gen. x. 4.) a son of Javan, and grandson of Japheth.—*Ed.*

a plain narrative would have been ineffectual, or would not have exerted a powerful influence on minds naturally dull and sluggish, and therefore he sets before their eyes a lively portrait. This calamity, he declares, will be very grievous, because it will be felt even in distant countries. He bids the "ships howl," because, when Tyre has been destroyed, they will have nothing to do. The ships of the Cilicians are particularly mentioned by him, because, being neighbours, they traded often and extensively with the inhabitants of Tyre; and Cilicia is called by the Hebrews "Tarshish." It was impossible that there should not have arisen great inconvenience to that country at the destruction of Tyre; not only because commerce ceased for a time, but also because the articles of merchandise were carried off, and there was a disturbance of commercial relations,[1] as usually happens when the fortunes of rich men have been overthrown.

That there may be no entering in from the land of Chittim. What I have translated "that there may be no entering in," is explained by some to signify, that there may be no house "into which you can enter," but I think that I have faithfully conveyed the Prophet's meaning. And yet he does not mean that the Cilicians or the Greeks will be hindered from entering, but that they will not hold intercourse with Tyre as they were formerly accustomed to do, because it will not be, as formerly, a mart of nations.

Those who think that the Prophet speaks of the defeat accomplished by Alexander, separate this clause of the verse "from the land of Chittim" from what goes before, and connect it thus, "from the land of Chittim it was revealed to them." But, on the contrary, I join it differently in this way, "From not going from the land of Chittim;" that is, that the Greeks may no more enter as they were formerly accustomed to do. By the word "Chittim," he means both the Greeks and the western nations; as if he had said, "There will be an end put to commerce with the Greeks, so that they will no longer take their ships thither." Under

---

[1] "Et les papiers des marchans espars çà et là;"—"And the merchants' accounts scattered hither and thither."

this designation he includes also the inhabitants of Cyprus,[1] Sicily, and Italy, and other nations.

This was revealed to them. These words may be understood to refer both to the Greeks and to the inhabitants of Tyre. If they refer to the inhabitants of Tyre, the meaning will be, "When the report of the ruin of the city shall reach them, they will put an end to their wonted voyages, for they will avoid that harbour as they would avoid a rock;" and this is the meaning which I more readily adopt. Yet I do not reject the other interpretation, that the Prophet confirms his prediction, as we commonly speak of a thing that is certain, "Let this be regarded as addressed to you."

2. *Be silent, ye inhabitants of the islands.* This is intended to place in a more striking light the ruin of Tyre. There is a change of number in the word *island;* for although he uses the singular number, yet he means the islands of the Mediterranean sea, and the countries beyond the sea, especially the neighbours who frequently performed voyages to Tyre, and traded with it. He enjoins on them silence and stillness, because they will perform no more voyages to Tyre. He bids them "be silent" like persons who are stunned, on account of the grievous calamity which has befallen them, so that they do not even venture to open their mouth; for it was impossible that the nations who traded there should not feel it to be a heavy stroke, when a mercantile city like this was ruined, just as at the present day Venice or Antwerp could not be destroyed without inflicting great injury on many nations.

The merchant of Sidon. He mentions the inhabitants of *Sidon* in an especial manner, not only on account of their vicinity, but because they had a common origin. *Sidon* was highly celebrated, but greatly inferior to Tyre. Situated on the sea-shore, it was two hundred furlongs[2] distant from Tyre, and appeared both to be so near it, and to be so closely connected

---

[1] "Les Egyptiens;"—"The Egyptians."

[2] The Roman *stadium* or furlong = 125 paces = 625 feet. A Roman mile = 1000 paces = 5000 feet. An English mile = 1760 yards = 5280 feet. Therefore a Roman mile is to an English mile as 5000 to 5280, or as 125 to 132; and the number of English miles is to that of Roman miles in the inverse ratio of 132 to 125; so that 200 stadia = 25 Roman

with it by trade, that the poets frequently took Tyre for Sidon, and Sidon for Tyre. The Sidonians, therefore, were unquestionably greater gainers than others by imports and exports, and also by sales and merchandise, in consequence of being so near, and trading with it continually; for the wealth of Tyre overflowed on them, and, as the saying is, they flew under its wings. The result was, that they suffered more severely than others by the destruction of Tyre, and therefore the Prophet afterwards says, (verse 4,) *Be ashamed, O Sidon.*

Who replenished thee. He adds this general expression, either because it was filled with crowds and multitudes of men, when strangers flocked to it from various and distant countries, or because they who performed voyages to it for the sake of gain did, in their turn, enrich the city.

3. *And by great waters.* He intimates that the riches of Tyre will not prevent it from being destroyed; and therefore he extols its wealth, in order that the judgment of God may be more manifest, and that all may know that it was no ordinary calamity that befel it; and the more unexpected it was, the more evidently would it appear to be the work of God.

The seed of the Nile.[1] By an elegant expression he describes the wealth of Tyre; for since the Nile supplied it with wheat and other necessaries of life, and since a great quantity of corn was brought to it out of Egypt, he says that it had fields and *sowing* on the course of the Nile, just as the inhabitants of Venice say that their harvest is on the sea, because they have nothing that grows at home, but all that is necessary for food is brought to them by commerce. The Prophet speaks of the inhabitants of Tyre in the same manner; for it might be thought incredible that they whom the Nile so freely and abundantly supplied should be in want of food. He shews that this will be a vain boast, because they will be in want of all things; and these things,

---

miles = somewhat less than 24 English miles. It ought to be remembered, that the author does not profess to state the exact distance, but gives it in round numbers.—*Ed.*

[1] "The seed of Sihor."—Eng. Ver. "שחר, (*shĭchōr*.) and יאור, (*yĕōr*,) are the Hebrew and Egyptian names of the Nile. The first, according to its etymology, means *black*, and corresponds to Μέλας and *Melo*, Greek and Latin names of the same river, all derived from the colour of the water, or the mud which it deposits."—*Alexander.*

as we have already said, are described by Isaiah, that all may more fully acknowledge the avenging hand of God.

4. *Be thou ashamed, O Sidon; for the sea hath spoken.* This verse is added for the purpose of heightening the picture. We have explained the reason why he speaks particularly of Sidon. He calls Tyre, by way of eminence, (κατ' ἐξοχὴν,) *the sea,* as if she reigned alone in the midst of the sea.

I have not travailed. These words are immediately added, and belong (μιμητικῶς) to a fictitious address put into the mouth of Tyre, in which the Prophet wittily taunts the inhabitants of Tyre, who boasted of her colonies; for she " brought forth" other illustrious cities. " In ancient times," says Pliny, " she was famous for the cities which she built, Leptis, Utica, and that rival of the Roman empire, Carthage, which aspired to govern the whole world, besides Cadiz, which was built beyond the limits of the world. Her whole superiority now consists of scarlet and purple." (Plin. Hist. Nat., lib. v. c. 19.) Thus, Isaiah represents Tyre as bewailing her ancient glory, because she has ceased to be a mother, and because it is of no avail to her that she has brought forth so many children, and founded so many cities; for at an early period Carthage sent regularly every year a present to Tyre, for the purpose of doing homage to her as the mother. In this manner Tyre appeared to hold a higher rank than all other cities, since even Carthage, though a rival of the Roman empire, was in some respect subject to Tyre: but the Lord stripped her of all her ornaments in a moment, so that she bewailed her bereavement, as if she had never brought up any children.

5. *As soon as the report shall reach the Egyptians.*[1] In this verse he declares that this destruction will affect equally the inhabitants of Tyre and those of Egypt; and this confirms the exposition which we follow, that the present prophecy relates to a former devastation. The inhabitants of Tyre had been in alliance with the Egyptians, and both

[1] " As at the report concerning Egypt."—Eng. Ver. Luther's version runs thus:—" Gleichwie man erschrak, da man von Egypten hörete; also wird man auch erschrecken, wenn man von Tyrus hören wird;"—" Like as they were terrified when they heard of Egypt; so will they also be terrified when they shall hear of Tyre."—*Ed.*

countries had been under kingly government; not as in Alexander's time, when Tyre was a free state, and lived under its own laws. The alliance which existed between the inhabitants of Tyre and those of Egypt could not have been more appropriately described; and therefore he shews that this ruin extends also to the Egyptians, because they prompted the Jews to rebellion, and turned them aside from confidence in God. The former were open enemies; the latter, under the pretence of friendship, cherished dangerous hostility; and therefore both are justly punished.

6. *Pass ye over to Tarshish.* He addresses not only the inhabitants of Tyre, but foreigners who were connected with them by trading, and bids them go elsewhere and seek new harbours: and he mentions Cilicia, which was opposite to Tyre, as if he had said, "That shore, which was wont to be well supplied with harbours, will henceforth be forsaken, so that ships will sail in a very different direction;" for when a harbour or a mercantile city has been ruined, merchants commonly go in search of another.

Howl, ye inhabitants of the island.[1] "Island," as we have formerly explained, is here put for "islands;" for the change of number is very customary with Hebrew writers. He foretells that they will lament, because their support depended entirely on that traffic, and because their accounts and reckonings[2] were scattered about in all directions.

7. *Is this your exulting city?* The Prophet mocks at Tyre, and ridicules her pride, because she boasted of the antiquity of her name. He likewise confirms what all would suppose to be incredible; for this prediction was undoubtedly laughed at, seeing that the power of Tyre was unshaken, and her wealth was like a wall of brass. So much the more confidently does Isaiah speak, and threaten that her ruin is certain, and that, though she be more ancient than other cities, and though she be universally applauded on that ground, still this will not prevent her from being destroyed. The origin of Tyre is traced in profane history from time almost

[1] " Tyre at this time was seated on an island; after Alexander's conquest it was rebuilt on the continent."—*Stock.*

[2] " Leurs registres et papiers de comtes;"—" Their records and account-books."

out of mind, and is so obscure and intricate, that hardly anything can be ascertained; though they allege that it was founded by the Phenicians, as those who boast of the fame of antiquity call themselves natives of the soil. With this antiquity the Prophet contrasts banishment, intimating that, when God had determined to inflict punishment on that nation, her stability would be at an end.

Her feet shall carry her, to travel into a distant country. To follow wherever "the feet carry," is nothing else than to have long wanderings. Yet he also means that they will be deprived of their wealth, and will be in want of all things during their banishment, so that they will not have a conveyance of any kind, or a beast to carry them. Banishment is a very hard condition, when poverty is added to it; for it may be more easily endured where there are the means of supporting life; but when men must dwell in unknown countries in the deepest poverty, the misery is extreme. He adds the finishing stroke to their miseries by saying, that they must "travel into a distant country;" for the greater the distance, the harder is the banishment.

8. *Against crowning Tyre.* He adorns with this title the city which enriched many, as may be easily learned from the context; for when he calls her merchants "kings," he plainly states that by the word *crown* he intended to express metaphorically the magnificence of kings. This refutes the opinion of those who refer it to other cities. The general meaning is, that she enriches her citizens as if she made them kings and princes.

Some think that the Prophet added this verse, as if he were assuming the character of one who is astonished at the destruction of Tyre, in order to strike others with amazement; as if he had said, "Is it possible that Tyre should be so speedily overthrown, where riches, and troops, and defences, and fortifications, are so abundant, and where there is so much pomp and magnificence?" and as if he suddenly stopped, as we are wont to do, when anything unexpected has occurred. But it is better to connect it with the following verse, which removes every difficulty; for in that verse the Prophet himself immediately answers his own question, by which he intended to arouse the minds of his hearers to closer attention. He might have simply said, that these things were done by the purpose of the Lord; but we are sluggish, and stupid men would have treated them with contempt. By this question, therefore, he arouses their minds, that all may know that he is not speaking about an ordinary event, and that they may consider it more carefully; for the farther the judgments of God are removed from the ordinary opinions of men, so much the more ought they to excite our astonishment.

He formerly spoke in the same manner about Egypt, when he intended to shew that the destruction of it could not be reckoned one of the ordinary changes. (Isaiah xix.) Since therefore it was incredible that Tyre could be overthrown by man, the Prophet justly infers that God is the author of its ruin. On this account he calls her the mother or nurse of kings, that he may place in a more striking light the glory of the divine judgment; for if it had been any ordinary state, its fall would have been viewed with contempt; but when it was adorned with the highest rank, who would think that this happened in any other way than by the purpose of God?

Whose merchants are princes.[1] In like manner the merchants of Venice in the present day think that they are on a level with princes, and that they are above all other men except kings; and even the factors look on men of rank as

[1] "The trade carried on by the Phenicians of Sidon and Tyre," says an able historian, "was extensive and adventurous; and both in their manners and policy, they resemble the great commercial states of modern times, more than any people in the ancient world." After mentioning the navigation to Tyre as the earliest route of communication with India, he goes on to say, "To this circumstance, which, for a considerable time, secured to them a monopoly of that trade, was owing, not only the extraordinary wealth of individuals, which rendered the 'merchants of Tyre, princes, and her traffickers the honourable of the earth,' (Isaiah xxiii. 8,) but the extensive power of the state itself, which first taught men to conceive what vast resources a commercial people possess, and what great exertions they are capable of making." He adds in a note, "The power and opulence of Tyre, in the prosperous age of its commerce, must have attracted general attention. In the prophecies of Ezekiel, who flourished two hundred and sixty years before the fall of Tyre, there is the most particular account of the nature and variety of its commercial transactions that is to be found in any ancient writer, and which conveys, at the same time, a magnificent idea of the extensive power of that state."—*Robertson's Historical Disquisition concerning the Knowledge which the Ancients had of India.*

beneath them. I have been told, too, that at Antwerp there are factors who do not hesitate to lay out expenses which the wealthiest of the nobility could not support. We are wont to put questions, when no reply can be given but what we wish ; and this is an indication of boldness.

9. *To profane the pride,* or, *to profane the loftiness;* for it may be read either way, because loftiness leads to pride, and where loftiness or a high spirit is found, there seldom is humility. But it will be better to read it *Pride,* which alone provokes the vengeance of God, when men, under pretence of their excellence, vaunt themselves above measure. To "profane" and to "despise" mean the same thing ; for those who are high in rank imagine that they are separated from others, and consider themselves to have something indescribably lofty belonging to them, as if they ought not to mingle with the crowd of human beings. But God strips them of their rank, degrades them, and treats them as vile and worthless.

From this passage let us learn, that we ought to contemplate the providence of God in such a manner as to ascribe to his almighty power the praise which it deserves for righteous government. Although the rectitude by which God regulates his judgments is not always apparent or made visible to us, still it is never lawful to separate his wisdom and justice from his power. But as the Scriptures very frequently state and clearly explain the reason why God does this or that, we ought carefully to examine the cause of his works.

That invention which the Schoolmen have introduced, about the absolute power of God, is shocking blasphemy. It is all one as if they said that God is a tyrant who resolves to do what he pleases, not by justice, but through caprice. Their schools are full of such blasphemies, and are not unlike the heathens, who said that God sports with human affairs. But in the school of Christ we are taught that the justice of God shines brightly in his works, of whatever kind they are, " that every mouth may be stopped," (Rom. iii. 19,) and that glory may be ascribed to him alone.

The Prophet therefore assigns the causes of so great an overthrow, that we may not think that God acts without a reason ; for the inhabitants of Tyre were proud, ambitious, lewd, and licentious. These vices follow in the train of wealth and abundance, and commonly abound in mercantile cities. For this reason he shews that God is provoked on account of these vices, that all who are left may be taught by this example to pay greater attention to their own interests, and not to abuse the gifts of God for parade and luxury. Such is the benefit which we ought to draw from it, for we must not imagine that it is a bare history which is related to us.

But a question arises, Does God hate the exalted rank of princes and lords? For he raises on high princes, senators, nobles, and all classes of magistrates and rulers; and how then can he hate them? I reply, the high station occupied by princes is not in itself hateful to God, but only on account of the vice which is accidental to it, that when they have been highly exalted, they despise others, and do not think that they are men. Thus, pride is almost always an attendant of high station, and therefore God hates it; and, in a word, he must rebuke that haughtiness of which he declares that he is an enemy.

10. *For there is not any longer a girdle.*[1] מָזוּחַ (*mēzăch*) is translated by some *a girdle,* and by others *strength.* Those who translate it *girdle,* suppose the meaning to be that Tyre will be so completely plundered, that she will not even have a *girdle* left; and that the allusion is to the vast wealth laid out in merchandise, for the poorest of the merchants sell girdles. But I think that Isaiah alludes to the situation of the city, which was protected on all sides by ditches, mounds, ramparts, and the sea.

11. *He stretched out his hand over the sea.* It is thought that the prediction which the Prophet uttered, about the destruction of Tyre, is here confirmed by examples; namely, that the Lord has given so many examples of his power in overturning the greatest kingdoms, that we ought not to think it strange if he now overturn Tyre, however flourishing and wealthy it may be. And indeed this manner of speaking is frequently employed in Scripture, if it be not

---

[1] " There is no more strength."—Eng. Ver. " There is no mound now left."—*Stock.*

made plain by manifest examples and by actual demonstration. It is therefore believed that the Prophet here calls to remembrance the deliverance from Egypt, when the Lord divided the sea, (Exod. xiv. 21, 22,) and again, when he drove out seven kings, and brought his people into the land of Canaan. (Josh. vi. viii. and x.) But when I take a closer view of the words of the Prophet, I am more disposed to explain them as referring to the present state of matters; for he speaks here of Tyre, whose riches covered the whole sea.

He shook the kingdoms. What he says about the *kingdoms* is, because she could not perish alone, but must at the same time involve many kingdoms in her ruin. Thus the whole world must have undergone some change, as appears from history; and finally, the Prophet himself draws the conclusion, that the Lord commanded that this mart of nations should be overthrown.

Jehovah hath given commandment concerning Canaan.[1] The word כנען (*chĕnăăn*) has led commentators to think that the Prophet here speaks of the Canaanites, and refers to the proof which God gave of his vengeance against them. But there is little force in that argument; for כנען (*chĕnăăn*) is often taken for a common noun, just as, a little before, (verse 8,) he used the word כנעניה (*chinyăneihā*) to mean *her factors.* The riches of Tyre having consisted of merchandise and trading, Isaiah described it by naming the principal part. By the expression, *hath given commandment,* he extols the providence of God, that the Jews may know that all that appears to be permanent in the world stands and falls according to the will of God, and that there is no need of the instruments of war for overturning the best fortified place, but the mere expression of the will of God is enough.

12. *And he said, Thou shalt not add any more to rejoice.*[2] All this belongs to one and the same object; for, since a plain description would not have had sufficient weight, the Prophet confirms his prediction by many words. It was

---

[1] "The Lord hath given a commandment against the merchant-city."— Eng. Ver. "Jehovah hath given a charge concerning Canaan."—*Stock.*
[2] "And he said, Thou shalt no more rejoice."—Eng. Ver.

incredible that a city so celebrated and powerful, so well defended and fortified, and associated with many allies and confederates, should be destroyed and overturned. When he says, *Thou shalt not add,* he does not intend to shut out the hope of restoration which he will give soon afterwards; for this threatening ought to be limited to the time of the ruin of Tyre, " Thou shalt not live wantonly, as formerly thou wert wont to do."

O virgin. Metaphorically he calls her *a virgin,* because, previous to that time, the riches of Tyre were untouched, and had suffered no injury. This is not praise of chastity, but a witty manner of saying that the treasures which had been laid up in faithful custody will be violated. " Formerly thou didst skip lightly, like heifers in the bloom of youth; but when thou hast suffered violence, there will be an end of thy mirth;" just as if one should say, that the city of Venice has not lost her virginity because it has not been taken by force since it was built.

Daughter of Sidon. He continues to speak of Tyre, but gives it this name, because it was built by the Sidonians, though the daughter excelled the mother, as frequently happens in human affairs. The convenience and situation of the place gave a superiority to the inhabitants of Tyre, and Sidon became but an appendage. From the book of Kings it is evident enough (1 Kings v. 1) that the monarchy of Tyre had a high reputation, but here the Prophet looked at its origin.

Pass over to Chittim. When he bids them *pass over to Chittim,* he banishes them not only into Cilicia, but into countries still more distant; for under this name he includes Greece, Italy, and other countries; as if he had said, " When thou shalt change thy residence on account of banishment, thou shalt have no settled habitation in neighbouring countries; but thou must wander through the whole world, shalt be dragged into unknown countries, and even there thou shalt find no rest." Lastly, he means that the ruin will be so lamentable, that they will not have among neighbours, and, after crossing the sea, they will not have among foreigners, a place of rest.

13. *Behold, the land of the Chaldeans.* He now confirms by an example what he predicted about the taking of Tyre; for those things could scarcely obtain credit, especially among the inhabitants of Tyre, who thought that they were very far from such ruin. I am aware that this passage is explained in various ways, but I shall not spend time in refuting the opinions of others. It will be enough if I shall state, as far as I am able to form a judgment of it, the Prophet's real meaning.

The people of the Chaldeans was not; that is, they had no name; for, if we inquire into their origin, they were descended from the Assyrians, as is evident from Gen. x. 11. He therefore says truly, that they were not at first a nation, but were concealed under the name of another, so that they did not form a separate body.

Ashur founded it for the inhabitants of the wilderness. The words which we have rendered "inhabitants of the wilderness" others translate *ships,* but we do not approve of that exposition. What we at first stated is preferable, namely, that the Assyrians gave a settled condition to the Chaldeans, who formerly led a wandering life in the deserts under skins,[1] but were collected into cities, and trained to higher civilisation, by the Assyrians. This is also the meaning of the word עוררו, (*gnōrĕrū,*) namely, that they erected and built cities; for we cannot agree with those who render it "to destroy."[2] What happened?

He brought it to ruin. That is, to use a common expression, "The daughter has devoured the mother;" for the Assyrian monarchy was overturned by the Chaldeans, though it was more powerful and flourishing than all the others. It will be said, what has this to do with Tyre? We answer, it is because Tyre will be overthrown by the Assyrians and Chaldeans. Since therefore the Chaldeans, who formerly

---

[1] "Sous des tentes de peaux;"—"Under tents of skins."
[2] "They raised up the palaces thereof."—*Eng. Ver.* "Erected her palaces."—*Stock.* Professor Alexander renders it, "They have roused up her palaces;" but says, "According to the usual interpretation, the *towers* mentioned are those used in ancient sieges; the masculine suffix refers to עַם, (*gnām;*) the feminine suffix to Tyre; and עורר (*gnōrēr*) may be taken either in the sense of *raising,* (from ערר, *gnārăr,*) or in that of *rousing,* (from עור, *gnūr,*) that is, filling with confusion and alarm."

were no people, could conquer the Assyrians and subject them to their power, why should we wonder if both united should conquer Tyre? Since the Lord gave such a display of his power in the case of the Assyrians, why should Tyre rely on her riches? She will undoubtedly be made to feel the hand of God, and her power will be of no avail to her.

14. *Howl, ye ships of Tarshish.* He repeats what he formerly said; for the Cilicians, on account of their vicinity, constantly traded with the inhabitants of Tyre. He bids their ships *howl,* because, when that harbour is shut up, the merchants will be struck with amazement at not having their ordinary intercourse. He calls that harbour which they visited, *their strength,* not only because it was a place of resort that might be relied on, but because there was no other way in which their voyages could yield profit.

15. *And it shall come to pass in that day.* After having spoken of the taking of Tyre, he next declares how long her calamity shall endure. It happens that cities which have been ruined are suddenly restored, and regain their former position; but the Prophet testifies that this city will be desolate and ruinous for *seventy years.* By *being forgotten* he means that there will be no merchandise, because she will not have the ordinary course of trade.

According to the days of one king.[1] Some think that *the days of one king* relate to David, but that is exceedingly frivolous, for "the days of a king" are put for the age of a man, in the same manner as the age of a man is shewn by the Psalmist to be generally limited to seventy years. (Psalm xc. 10.) But why did he mention "a king" rather than any other man? It was because Tyre had a king, and reckoned time by the life of a king. This contributed greatly to establish the certainty of the prediction, for the Prophet could not have ascertained it by human conjectures.

Tyre shall have a song like that of a harlot. By " the

[1] "That is, of one kingdom. See Dan. vii. 17, and viii. 20. Nebuchadnezzar began his conquests in the first year of his reign; from thence to the taking of Babylon by Cyrus are seventy years; at which time the nations conquered by Nebuchadnezzar were to be restored to liberty." —*Lowth.*

song of a harlot" he employs a beautiful comparison to denote merchandise; not that in itself it ought to be condemned, for it is useful and necessary to a commonwealth, but he alludes to the fraud and dishonesty with which it frequently abounds, so that it may justly be compared to the occupation of a harlot.

16. *Take a harp.* He compares Tyre to a harlot, who, after having spent the whole period of her youth in debauchery, has at length grown old, and on that account is forsaken and despised by all, and yet cannot forget her former gain and lewdness, but desires to grow young again and renew her loves, and, in order to attract men, goes about the city, delighting their ears by songs and musical instruments. Such prostitutes are seized with some kind of madness, when they perceive that they are disregarded on account of their old age; and we see that Horace mocks at Lydia on this account.[1] Thus Tyre, after having been ruined, and as it were buried in oblivion, will again put forth her efforts, and schemes, and contrivances, for recovering her former condition.

Make sweet melody. By the "harp" and "sweet melody," he means the tricks, and frauds, and blandishments, and flatteries of merchants, by which they impose on men, and as it were drive them into their nets. In a word, he shews by what methods mercantile cities become rich, that is, by deceitful and unlawful methods; and therefore he says, that Tyre will regale their ears by pleasant melody.

Sing many songs. That is, Tyre will add fraud to fraud, and allurements to allurements, that at length she may attract all to her, may be again remembered by men, and recover her former celebrity. In short, as an old harlot contrives methods for regaining the favour of men, and allures them by painting, and ornaments, and dress, and songs, and musical instruments, so will Tyre recover her wealth and power by the same arts with which she formerly succeeded. And yet he does not on that account exhort

---

[1] " Que le poete Horace s'est moqué d'une putain nommee *Lydia* pour la mesme occasion;"—" That the Poet Horace mocked at a prostitute named *Lydia* for the same reason."

Tyre to restore herself in this way, but proceeds with his prophecy.

17. *Jehovah will visit Tyre.*[1] Although the Lord will afflict Tyre in such a manner that she will appear to be ruined, yet he declares that she will obtain mercy, because, rising at length out of her ruins, she will be restored to her former vigour. Such a restoration is justly ascribed to the favour of God; for otherwise the same thing must have happened to them as Malachi foretells would happen to the Edomites, that the Lord would overturn and destroy all that men would build. (Mal. i. 4.) Consequently they would never have returned to their former condition if the Lord had not aided them.

From these words we ought to draw a profitable doctrine, that though the Lord is a severe judge towards the wicked, yet he leaves room for the exercise of his compassion, and is never so harsh as not to mitigate his chastisements, and at length to put an end to them. And if he is such towards the wicked, what will he be towards those whom he has adopted, and on whom he determines to pour out his goodness? When kingdoms therefore are re-established, when cities are rebuilt, and nations regain their freedom, this is brought about solely by the providence of God, who, whenever he pleases, lays low what is high, (1 Sam. ii. 7; Luke i. 52,) and quickly raises up and restores what was fallen.

And then she will return to her hire. This ought to be viewed as a contrast to the former statement, for the meaning is, that Tyre will be no better, and will not be reformed

---

[1] " Tyre, after its destruction by Nebuchadnezzar, recovered, as is here foretold, its ancient trade, wealth, and grandeur; as it did likewise after a second destruction by Alexander. It became Christian early with the rest of the neighbouring countries. St. Paul himself found many Christians there. (Acts xxi. 4.) It suffered much in the Diocletian persecution. It was an archbishopric under the patriarchate of Jerusalem, with fourteen bishoprics under its jurisdiction. It continued Christian till it was taken by the Saracens in 639; was recovered by the Christians in 1124; but in 1280 was conquered by the Mamalukes, and afterwards taken from them by the Turks in 1516. Since that time it has sunk into utter decay, is now a bare rock, ' a place to spread nets upon,' as the Prophet Ezekiel foretold it should be. (Ezek. xxvi. 14.) See Sandy's Travels; Vitringa on the place; Bishop Newton on the Prophecies, Dissert. xi." —*Lowth.*

by so severe a chastisement, because she will quickly return to her natural disposition; for he accuses her of ingratitude. We see instances of the same kind every day. There is scarcely a corner of the world in which the Lord has not exhibited proofs of his judgment. To those whom he has chastised he allows time to breathe, but they become no better. Isaiah says that this will happen to Tyre.

She will commit fornication. "She will not repent, but, on the contrary, will return to her former courses. *She will commit fornication,* as she was formerly accustomed to do." He unquestionably speaks of buying and selling, but continues to employ the comparison which he had adopted; not that he wishes to condemn the occupation of a merchant, as we have already said, but that it is so largely mingled with the corruptions of men as to resemble closely the life of a harlot; for it is so full of tricks, and hidden stratagems, and deep-laid traps, (as we often see,) that it appears to have been contrived for the purpose of ensnaring and deceiving men. How many new and unheard of contrivances for making gain and exacting usury are every day invented, which no one who has not been long trained in the school of merchandise can understand? We need not wonder, therefore, that the Prophet made use of this comparison, for it means that Tyre will have no more honesty than before in mercantile transactions.

18. *But her merchandise and her hire shall be holiness to the Lord.* This was another instance of the divine compassion towards Tyre. Though she had been restored, yet she was not converted to God, but continued to follow dishonest practices, so that she justly deserved to be ruined. And indeed she was again punished severely, when Alexander took the city by storm; but still the kingdom of Christ, as Luke informs us, was erected there. (Acts xxi. 4.) This verse ought therefore to be viewed as contrasted with the former, as if he had said, "*And yet* the merchandise of Tyre shall be consecrated to God." Here we have an astonishing proof of the goodness of God, which penetrated not only into this abominable brothel, but almost into hell itself. The restoration of Tyre ought thus to be regarded as a

proof of the goodness of God; but the former favour was small in comparison with the second, when God consecrated her to himself.

But a question arises, "Could that which the inhabitants of Tyre obtained by cheating and unlawful methods be offered to God in sacrifice?" For God abhors such sacrifices, and demands an honest and pure conscience. (Prov. xxi. 27; Isaiah i. 13.) Many commentators, in expounding this passage, give themselves much uneasiness about this question, but without any good reason; for the Prophet does not mean that the merchandise of Tyre will be consecrated to God while she continues to commit fornication, but describes a time subsequent to her change and conversion. At that time she will not lay up riches for herself, will not amass them by unlawful methods, but will employ them in the service of God, and will spend the produce of her merchandise in relieving the wants of the godly. When he used a word expressive of what was disgraceful, he had his eye on the past, but intimated that she would unlearn those wicked practices, and change her disposition.

It shall not be treasured nor laid up. He describes, in a few words, the repentance of Tyre, who, having formerly been addicted to avarice, has been converted to Christ, and will no longer labour to amass riches, but will employ them in kind and generous actions; and this is the true fruit of repentance, as Paul admonishes, that "he who stole should steal no more, but, on the contrary, should labour that he might relieve the poor and needy." (Eph. iv. 28.) Isaiah foretells that the inhabitants of Tyre, who formerly, through insatiable avarice, devoured the riches of all, will henceforth take pleasure in generous actions, because they will no longer have an insatiable desire of gain. It is an evidence of brotherly love when we relieve our neighbours, as it is an evidence of cruelty if we suffer them to be hungry, especially when we ourselves have abundance.

Her merchandise shall be for them that dwell before the Lord. He next mentions a proper method of exercising generosity, which is, to employ their wealth in aiding the servants of God. Though he includes all godly persons, yet he alludes to the Levites and priests, some of whom sacrificed, while others made ready the sacrifices, and others kept watch, and, in short, all were ready to perform their duty; and therefore they were said to "dwell before the Lord." (Numb. iii. and iv.) The same thing may justly be said of all the ministers of the Church. But as all believers, of whatever rank they are, belong to the sanctuary of God, and have been made by Christ "a royal priesthood," (1 Peter ii. 9; Rev. i. 6,) that they may stand in the presence of God so I willingly regard this passage as relating to all "the household of faith," (Gal vi. 10,) to whom attention is especially due; for Paul holds them out as having the highest claims, and enjoins that they shall be first relieved. If the tie which binds us universally to mankind ought to prevent us from "despising our own flesh," (Isaiah lviii. 7,) how much more the tie that binds the members of Christ, which is closer and more sacred than any natural bonds?

We ought also to attend to this mode of expression, by which we are said to "dwell before God;"[1] for though there is not now any "Ark of the Covenant," (Heb. ix. 4,) yet, through the kindness of Christ, we approach more nearly to God than the Levites formerly did. We are therefore enjoined to "walk before him," as if we were under his eye, that we may follow holiness and justice with a pure conscience. We are enjoined to walk before him, and always to consider him as present, that we may be just and upright.

That they may eat till they are satisfied.[2] The Prophet means that we ought to supply the wants of brethren with greater abundance and generosity than what is customary among men; for when neighbours ought to be relieved, men are very niggardly. Few men perform cheerfully any gratuitous duty, or labour, or kindness; for they reckon that they give up and take from their own property all that they bestow on others. For the purpose of correcting this error,

---

[1] "The revenues of Tyre shall be employed in supporting the worshippers of the true God. The prophecy intimates that Tyre should be converted to the religion of Christ as it was in the earliest times of the gospel. Of the same event David also had prophesied in Psalm xlv. 12; lxxii. 10; lxxxvii. 4."—*Stock.*

[2] "Afin qu'ils mangent leur saoul;"—"That they may eat their fill."

God highly commends cheerfulness; for the command which Paul gives to deacons, " to distribute joyfully," (Rom. xii. 8,) ought to be applied to all; and all ought to remember that passage which declares that " God loveth a cheerful giver." (2 Cor. ix. 7.)

It deserves our attention, also, that the Prophet says that what is bestowed on the poor is consecrated to God; as the Spirit elsewhere teaches, that " with such sacrifices God is well pleased." (Heb. xiii. 16; 2 Cor. ix. 12.) Never was it on his own account that he commanded sacrifices to be made, nor did he ever stand in need of them. But under the law he ordained such exercises of piety; and he now commands us to bestow and spend on our neighbours something that is our own, and declares that all that we lay out on their account[1] is " a sacrifice of sweet savour," (Philip. iv. 18,) and is approved and accepted by him. This ought powerfully to inflame us to the exercise of kindness and generosity, when we learn that our alms are so highly applauded, and that our hands, as well as our gift, are consecrated to God.

CHAPTER XXIV.

1. Behold, the Lord maketh the earth empty, and maketh it waste, and turneth it upside down, and scattereth abroad the inhabitants thereof.

2. And it shall be, as with the people, so with the priest; as with the servant, so with his master; as with the maid, so with her mistress; as with the buyer, so with the seller; as with the lender, so with the borrower; as with the taker of usury, so with the giver of usury to him.

3. The land shall be utterly emptied, and utterly spoiled: for the Lord hath spoken this word.

4. The earth mourneth *and* fadeth away; the world languisheth *and* fadeth away; the haughty people of the earth do languish.

1. Ecce Iehova evacuat terram, denudat eam, evertit faciem ejus, et incolas ejus dissipat.

2. Et erit ut populus, ita sacerdos; ut servus, ita dominus ejus; ut ancilla, ita domina ejus; ut emptor, ita venditor; ut mutuo dans, ita qui mutuo accipit; ut fœnerator, ita qui accipit fœnori, (*vel, ut creditor, ita debitor.*)

3. Evacuando evacuabitur terra, et direptione diripietur; quoniam Iehova pronunciavit hoc verbum.

4. Luxit, cecidit terra; elanguit, cecidit orbis; elanguerunt qui erant sublimis populus terræ.

[1] " Tout ce que nous employons pour la necessité de nos freres;"—
" All that we spend for relieving the want of our brethren."

5. The earth also is defiled under the inhabitants thereof; because they have transgressed the laws, changed the ordinance, broken the everlasting covenant.
6. Therefore hath the curse devoured the earth, and they that dwell therein are desolate: therefore the inhabitants of the earth are burned, and few men left.
7. The new wine mourneth, the vine languisheth, all the merry-hearted do sigh.
8. The mirth of tabrets ceaseth, the noise of them that rejoice endeth, the joy of the harp ceaseth.
9. They shall not drink wine with a song; strong drink shall be bitter to them that drink it.
10. The city of confusion is broken down; every house is shut up, that no man may come in.
11. *There is* a crying for wine in the streets; all joy is darkened, the mirth of the land is gone.
12. In the city is left desolation, and the gate is smitten with destruction.
13. When thus it shall be in the midst of the land among the people, *there shall be* as the shaking of an olive-tree, *and* as the gleaning-grapes when the vintage is done.
14. They shall lift up their voice, they shall sing for the majesty of the Lord, they shall cry aloud from the sea.
15. Wherefore glorify ye the Lord in the fires, *even* the name of the Lord God of Israel in the isles of the sea.
16. From the uttermost part of the earth have we heard songs, *even* glory to the righteous. But I said, My leanness, my leanness, woe unto me! the treacherous dealers have dealt treacherously; yea, the treacherous dealers have dealt very treacherously.
17. Fear, and the pit, and the snare, *are* upon thee, O inhabitant of the earth.
18. And it shall come to pass, *that* he who fleeth from the noise of the fear shall fall into the pit; and

5. Et terra fallax fuit sub incolis suis; quoniam transgressi sunt leges, mutarunt statutum, dissolverunt fœdus seculi.
6. Itaque maledictio consumpsit terram, et desolati sunt incolæ ejus; ideo combusti sunt, inquam, incolæ terræ; et pauci residui sunt facti homines.
7. Periit vinum, elanguit vitis, gemuerunt omnes qui læto erant corde.
8. Cessavit gaudium tympanorum, desiit strepitus exultantium, quievit lætitia citharæ.
9. Cum cantico non bibent vinum; amara erit sicera bibentibus eam.
10. Contrita est civitas vanitatis; clausa est omnis domus, ne quis ingrediatur.
11. Clamor est super vino in plateis; obscuratum est omne gaudium; migravit lætitia terræ.
12. Residua est in urbe vastitas, et vastatione percussa est porta.
13. Quia sic erit in medio terræ, in medio populorum, quasi decussio olivæ, et quasi racemi, cum peracta est vindemia.
14. Hi levabunt vocem suam; jubilabunt in altitudine Iehovæ, vociferabuntur a mari.
15. Propterea in vallibus glorificate Iehovam, in insulis maris nomen Iehovæ Dei Israel.
16. Ab extremo terræ laudes audivimus, gloriam (*vel, gratulationem*) justo, et dixi, Macies mihi, macies mihi, væ mihi. Prævaricatores prævaricati sunt; prævaricatione, inquam, prævaricatores prævaricati sunt.
17. Pavor, et fovea, et laqueus super te, O incola terræ.
18. Et accidet ut qui effugerit a voce pavoris, incidat in foveam; et qui ascenderit e medio foveæ capi-

he that cometh up out of the midst of the pit shall be taken in the snare: for the windows from on high are open, and the foundations of the earth do shake.

19. The earth is utterly broken down, the earth is clean dissolved, the earth is moved exceedingly.

20. The earth shall reel to and fro like a drunkard, and shall be removed like a cottage; and the transgression thereof shall be heavy upon it; and it shall fall, and not rise again.

21. And it shall come to pass in that day, *that* the Lord shall punish the host of the high ones *that are* on high, and the kings of the earth upon the earth.

22. And they shall be gathered together, *as* prisoners are gathered in the pit, and shall be shut up in the prison, and after many days shall they be visited.

23. Then the moon shall be confounded, and the sun ashamed, when the Lord of hosts shall reign in mount Zion, and in Jerusalem, and before his ancients gloriously.

atur laqueo. Quoniam fenestrae de excelso apertae sunt; et commota sunt fundamenta terrae.

19. Contritione contrita est terra; dissolutione dissoluta est terra; commotione commota est terra.

20. Agitatione agitata est terra, sicut ebrius; et transferetur sicut tabernaculum; et gravis erit super eam iniquitas ejus; et corruet, neque adjiciet ut resurgat.

21. Et erit in die illa, visitabit Iehova super exercitum excelsum in excelso, et super reges terrae super terram.

22. Et congregabuntur congregatione instar vinctorum in carcere, et claudentur in ergastulo; deinde post multos dies visitabuntur.

23. Erubescet luna, et pudefiet sol; cum regnaverit Iehova exercituum in monte Sion, et in Ierusalem; et coram senibus suis gloria.

1. *Behold, Jehovah maketh the earth empty.* This prophecy, so far as I can judge, is the conclusion of all the descriptions that have been given from the thirteenth chapter downwards, in which Isaiah foretold destruction not only to the Jews and to Israel, but to the Moabites, Assyrians, Egyptians, and other nations. In short, having, as it were, surveyed all the countries which were near the Jews and known to them, he gives a brief summary of the whole. Some view this as referring to Israel, and others to the Jews, and think that their destruction is foretold; but as he mentions *the world*, I can view it in no other light than as a comprehensive statement of all that he formerly said about each of them, and at different times. Nor is this view contradicted by the fact that he immediately mentions *the priest*, which might lead us to believe that these things relate to none but the people of God; for although he speaks of all the nations, yet because the Jews always hold the highest rank, Isaiah must have had them especially in his

eye, for he was appointed to them. It may be said to have been accidental that he mentions other nations; and therefore we ought not to wonder if, after having made reference to them, he speaks particularly about his own people in a single word.

Others suppose that he means "the whole world," but think that he refers to the last day, which I consider to be an excessively forced interpretation; for, after having threatened the Jews and other nations, the Prophet afterwards adds a consolation, that the Lord will one day raise up his Church and make her more flourishing; which certainly cannot apply to the last judgment. But by the term *the earth*, I do not think that the Prophet means the whole world, but the countries well known to the Jews; just as in the present day, when we speak of what happens in the world, we almost never go beyond Europe, or think of what is passing in India; for this may be said to be our world. Thus, Isaiah speaks of "the earth" known to himself and to all whom he addressed, and of the people who inhabited the neighbouring countries. In short, we may limit the term "World" to the Egyptians, Assyrians, Moabites, Tyrians, and such like; as if he had said, " Hitherto I have spoken of various calamities, which threatened many nations,' and still in part threaten some of them; but I may sum up all by saying, 'The Lord will overturn and strip the face of the earth of all its ornaments.'"

And maketh it bare.[1] Some translate בלקה, (*bōlĕkāch,*) *he uncovereth the earth,* that the enemies may have free entrance into it. But I choose rather to translate it, "he maketh bare the earth," because the earth is said to be " covered," when it is inhabited by a great multitude of men, and when it abounds in fruits and flocks; and it is said to be "uncovered" or "laid bare," when it is deprived of its inhabitants, and when its covering is taken away from it, as if one were stripped of his raiment and ornaments. Now, this must have happened not only to the Jews, but to the Assyrians, Egyptians, and other nations, which he had mentioned; and therefore to all of them together he threatens their ruin.

[1] " And maketh it waste."—Eng. Ver.

2. *And it shall be.* By these words he means the utmost desolation, in which there will be no longer any distinction of ranks or any appearance of a commonwealth; for so long as there is a tolerably regular form of government, some distinction continues to be maintained between " the people" and " the priests." By a figure of speech, in which a part is taken for the whole, (συνεκδοχικῶς,) he mentions one department instead of the whole class, as is frequently done in the Scriptures; though we might take כֹּהֲנִים, (*kōchănīm,*) to mean those who hold any high rank; for Hebrew writers frequently give this name to princes, and especially to those who are of royal blood; but I have no reluctance to view it as an instance of the figure of speech which I have mentioned.

Since Isaiah reckons this confusion among the curses of God, and declares that, when the distinction of ranks is laid aside, it is a terrible display of the vengeance of God, we ought to conclude, on the other hand, how much God is pleased with regular government and the good order of society, and also how great a privilege it is to have it preserved among us; for when it is taken away, the life of man differs little from the sustenance of cattle and of beasts of prey. We ought therefore not only to acknowledge the dreadful vengeance of God, but also to lay it to the blame of our own sins, whenever he breaks down order and takes away instruction and courts of law; for when these fall, civilisation itself falls along with them. It ought also to be considered that, when the Lord executes his judgments, he spares no rank, not even the most sacred. What was this order of priests, which the Lord had so splendidly adorned, and had determined to consecrate to himself, and of which the people also boasted as if it had been unchangeable and eternal? Yet even the rank of priesthood is involved in the judgment of God, because there is no respect of persons, but, on the contrary, the more highly any have been favoured, and the higher the rank to which they have been exalted, the more severely will he punish them, if they shall shew themselves to be ungrateful and abuse his benefits.

As the servant, so his master; as the buyer, so the seller.

This statement is to the same effect with what goes before; for these ranks are manifestly lawful, and are not usually set aside, unless when the Lord determines to chastise his people with dreadful vengeance, as we have already said; for in a well-ordered society the distinction between master and servant must be observed. In like manner, no public government can be lasting without the transactions of commerce; and therefore, when the distinction between rich and poor has been taken away, every scheme for gaining a livelihood among men is destroyed. The meaning of the Prophet is, that all civil government will be broken up, because in such calamities, they who were the wealthiest are reduced to the lowest poverty. In short, he describes the most appalling desolation, which will be followed by unwonted change.

3. *By emptying shall the earth be emptied.* He confirms what he had already said, and declares that those changes will not be accidental, but that they are the work of God. In the first verse, he had expressly stated that God is making preparations for emptying the earth: he now asserts that it will happen, and adds the reason, that God hath purposed and determined to do it.

4. *The earth hath lamented.* Isaiah proceeds with his subject; for all this tends to explain the desolation of the whole world, that is, of the world which was known to the Jews. According to his custom, he illustrates the judgment of God more clearly by figures, which are fitted to produce an effect on sluggish minds.

The lofty people of the earth.[1] By the "lofty ones" we must understand those eminent persons who held a higher rank than others; for this is more wonderful than if the common people had fallen. Yet if it be thought preferable to explain it as relating peculiarly to the Jews, I have no objection; for although the Assyrians and Egyptians excelled them in wealth and power, still the Jews held the highest rank in this respect, that they had been adopted by God. But I prefer the other exposition, which makes the meaning to be, that the Lord would inflict punishment, not

[1] "The haughty people of the earth. (Heb. the height of the people.)" —Eng. Ver.

only on common people, but also on those who surpassed others in rank and splendour.

5. *And the earth was deceitful.*[1] Others render it "defiled" or "polluted," because כנף (*chănăph*) means "to be wicked." Both renderings may be appropriate; but the next verse appears to demand that we explain it to mean *false;* for he appears to illustrate and exhibit it more fully immediately afterwards, when he says that "the earth has been consumed by a curse."

Under its inhabitants. Whether תחת (*tăhăth*) be translated " *Under* its inhabitants," or, " *On account of* its inhabitants," is of little importance. There is a kind of mutual bargain between the land and the husbandmen, that it gives back with usury what it has received: if it does not, it deceives those who cultivate it. But he assigns a reason, imputing blame to them, that they render it barren by their wickedness. It is owing to our fault that it does not nourish us or bring forth fruit, as God appointed to be done by the regular order of nature; for he wished that it should hold the place of a mother to us, to supply us with food; and if it change its nature and order, or lose its fertility, we ought to attribute it to our sins, since we ourselves have reversed the order which God had appointed; otherwise the earth would never deceive us, but would perform her duty.

Because they have transgressed the laws. He immediately assigns the reason why the earth is unfaithful, and deceives her inhabitants. It is because those who refuse to honour God their Father and supporter, will justly be deprived of food and nourishment. Here he peculiarly holds up to shame the revolt of his nation, because it was baser and less excusable than all the transgressions of those who had never been taught in the school of God. The word תורה (*tōrāh*) is applied to "the Law," because it denotes instruction; but here, in the plural number, תורת (*tōrōth*,) it denotes all the instruction that is contained in the "Law." But as the "Law" contains both commandments and promises, he adds two parts for the purpose of explanation.

[1] "The earth also is defiled."—*Eng. Ver.* "The earth is even polluted."—*Stock.* "And the land has been profaned."—*Alexander.*

They have changed the ordinance. The Hebrew word חֹק (*chōk*) means "an ordinance," and on that account some think that it denotes ceremonies, and others that it denotes morals. We may render it "commandments;" and I understand it to mean not only ceremonies, but everything that belongs to the rule of a holy life.

They have broken the everlasting covenant. The third term employed by him is בְּרִית, (*berīth*,) by which he means a covenant and contract. This word is limited to those "contracts" by which the Lord, who adopted his people, promised that he would be their God. (Ex. xix. 6; xxix. 45; Lev. xxvi. 12.) He therefore charges them with ingratitude, because, when the Lord revealed himself by all these methods, and gave proofs of his love, they were disobedient and rebellious, "transgressed the laws," and "broke the holy covenant."

But why does he address himself to the Jews? Because he knew that he had been appointed to be their Prophet, that he might especially give instructions to them. Hence we may infer what is the rule of a holy life. It is contained in that law which we ought to follow if we wish that God should approve of our life; if we turn aside from it, we must be wicked and abandoned. We ought also to remark, that it is the will of God that in his word we should consider not only his commandments and laws, but also his covenant; for the chief part of the word consists of promises, by which he adopts and receives us as his own people. Besides, the Prophet unquestionably intended to use a variety of terms in order to express his meaning more strongly; as if he had said, "There is nothing about us that is sound and pure; everything is polluted and corrupted."

He calls it "the covenant of eternity," or "the everlasting covenant," because it ought to be perpetual and inviolable, and to be in force in every age. It was to be transmitted, in uninterrupted succession, from father to son, that it might never be effaced from the memory of man, but might be kept pure and entire. He therefore represents in strong terms their treachery and wickedness, because they dared to violate that covenant which God had made with them, and to overthrow what the Lord intended to be firm and permanent. This was monstrous; and therefore we ought not to wonder that the earth takes vengeance for this wickedness, and refuses to give food to men.

6. *Therefore hath the curse devoured the earth.* Some render it *perjury*,[1] but as אלה (*ālāh*) signifies also a "curse," I have no doubt that here he employs it to denote a "curse," and alludes to those curses which Moses in the law threatens against wicked men and transgressors of the law. (Lev. xxvi. 16; Deut. xxviii. 15.) We know that the earth was cursed on account of the transgression of our first parent, so that it brought forth thorns and thistles instead of fruits. (Gen. iii. 17, 18.) The Lord mitigated this curse, so that, although men were ungrateful and unworthy, still it yielded them food. But when we do not cease to sin, and when we add sin to sin, is it not in the highest degree just that the earth should become barren and unfruitful, in order that we may more clearly perceive this curse, and that it may make a deeper impression on our senses?

And its inhabitants are made desolate. I think that אשם (*āshăm*) here means "to make desolate," rather than "to forsake;" and this is apparent from the context, on which account I have translated it "are made desolate." But perhaps it will be thought preferable to take the copulative ו (*vau*) as signifying *because*, and then the meaning will be, "The earth accursed by God is burnt up, *because* its inhabitants have acted wickedly."[2]

Therefore the inhabitants of the earth are burned, and few men left. The word חרו (*chārū*) may be taken metaphorically, and I prefer this view of it, which makes the meaning to be, that those whom the wrath of God has consumed are burned up; because the destruction is compared

---

[1] "On account of the sin of perjury is the earth consumed."—*Jarchi.* "אלה (*ālāh*) does not here mean false swearing, as explained in the Targum, and by Jarchi and Kimchi, but the curse of God attending the violation of his law."—*Alexander.*

[2] "אשם (*āshăm*) is taken by some of the early writers in the sense of being *desolate*. Its true sense is that of being recognised as guilty, and treated accordingly. It therefore suggests the ideas both of guilt and punishment."—*Alexander.*

to a conflagration. When he adds, "that few will be left," we learn from it that this prediction cannot be explained as relating to the last day of judgment, and that, on the contrary, the Prophet foretells and confirms those desolations which threatened various nations, and that he does so in order that the godly may fear, and may be led to repentance, and may be prepared for enduring all things.

7. *The wine hath failed.* The same subject is continued, and the Prophet threatens chiefly against the Jews the desolation of the land. He gives a long description in order to affect them more deeply, and impress them with a conviction of the judgment of God. Their luxury, intemperance, and feasting, are rapidly surveyed, because amidst so great abundance they proudly disobeyed God. Such ingratitude was not peculiar to the Jews or to that age, but it is universally found that they who enjoy abundance rebel against God, and indulge themselves too freely. On this account the Prophet censures them; as if he had said, "Hitherto you have been plunged in luxuries and pleasures, but the Lord will cause you to lead a very different kind of life." Isaiah speaks of the future as if it had been present, in order to place it more clearly before their eyes.

9. *They shall not drink wine with a song.* To drink wine is not in itself evil, because God has appointed it for the use of man; but here the Prophet describes the banquets of drunkards, which were full of licentiousness, songs, and insolence. Again, because they abused their enjoyment of plenty, he threatens them with want, which men almost bring upon themselves, when by their luxury they turn to a bad use the goodness of God.

Strong drink shall be bitter. He adds, that if they drink wine, it will be "bitter" to them; because sorrow commonly deprives men of a relish both for what they eat and for what they drink. The meaning may be thus summed up, "Though they have abundance of wine, yet they will be deprived of the use of it, because they will feel such sorrow as shall take away all relish for it." "Strong drink shall be *bitter;*" that is, you shall no longer enjoy those pleasures and delights in which you have hitherto indulged.

10. *The city of vanity*[1] *is broken down.* I do not object to viewing this as relating especially to the desolation of Jerusalem. Yet it may be gathered from the context that it applies also to other cities; for shortly afterwards he uses the plural number in summoning the nations to appear before the same tribunal. But as the Prophet had his own countrymen chiefly in view, we may properly consider it to denote Jerusalem, which he calls "the city of vanity," either because there was no solid virtue in it, or because it was destroyed.

The word תֹהוּ (*tōhū*) may refer either to the destruction itself, or to their crimes, by which they provoked the wrath of God against them. If it be thought better to refer it to their crimes, it will denote "the city of confusion," in which nothing is regular or properly arranged; and I approve of this interpretation. Yet it may refer to the punishment; for it declares, in my opinion, the cause of the destruction, and gives up the city to ruin, because justice and good government are banished from it.

Every house is shut up. This is a proof of solitude, and the only reason why it is added is, to express the desolation of that city.

11. *There is a cry about wine.* He means, that there will be a scarcity of wine; for where want or hunger is found, it is accompanied by unceasing complaints, not only in private, but "in the streets" and public places. He therefore points out those doleful sounds and complaints, but, at the same time, reproves their luxury and intemperance, because they were not satisfied with what was necessary, but greedily swallowed wine, and abandoned themselves to every kind of enjoyment. We must supply the contrast. "Hitherto you have had abundance of wine and of food, and you have taken occasion from it to grow insolent against God; and therefore you will justly be deprived of them, and, instead of your wanton indulgence, wailings and lamentations will be heard in the streets."

All joy is darkened. The metaphor in this second clause deserves attention; for, as we say that joy brightens when

---

[1] "The city of confusion."—Eng. Ver.

it obtains its object, so the Prophet here says, that "joy is darkened," because sorrow may be said to be a cloud drawn over it. To *rejoice* is not in itself evil, any more than to drink; and the Prophet does not censure joy simply considered, but excessive and immoderate mirth. When men are merry, they lay no restraint on themselves on account of that dissoluteness or love of disorder (ἀταξίαν) which is natural to them. The Jews, having behaved insolently and lived luxuriously, are deservedly threatened with the vengeance of God, because most justly is joy taken from us when we know not how to make a right use of the Lord's benefits, or to rejoice in him. It thus becomes necessary that he should take away our pleasures and delights, and compel us to sigh and groan.

12. *In the city is left desolation.* By an elegant mode of expression he describes the desolation of Jerusalem or of many other cities. The ornament and perfection of cities consists of men; and therefore, when their inhabitants have been removed, cities are said to be deserted. The Prophet says ironically, that "ruin" will be left; but the word שׁמה (*shămmāh*) is rendered by others *desolation,* which amounts to the same thing.

And the gate is smitten with desolation. He mentions the *gates,* because in them the crowded population of the city was seen, for there the people assembled, and there the courts of justice were held. At first, therefore, he mentions the whole city, and next he names one part of it, but for the purpose of setting the matter in a stronger light; for although cities be deprived of their inhabitants, yet some are to be seen in the gates; but if the gates be altogether empty, there must be grievous solitude in the whole city.

13. *For it shall be in the midst of the land.* As this statement is inserted between the threatenings and the consolation, the Prophet appears to address the chosen people, and not all the nations indiscriminately; if we do not rather say that he describes the dispersion, by which the Jews were divided, as it were, into many nations. But this being a harsh and forced interpretation, I interpret it as simply meaning that some hope is left to the ruined nations,

and certainly this prediction applies strictly to the kingdom of Christ; and therefore we need not wonder that some part of the salvation is also promised to the Gentiles.

As the shaking of an olive-tree. The Prophet has elsewhere used the same metaphor, but it was when he spoke of the Church alone. (Isaiah xvii. 5, 6.) On that occasion he said that some seed of God would be left, that believers might not think that the Church was utterly ruined; for when "the olives are shaken," still a few olives are left, and some grapes after the vintage; and in like manner, after the terrible destruction which shall fall upon the Church, a small number of the godly will be left. But now he extends the same promise to other parts of the world, as they were to become partakers of the same grace through Christ. Yet there is still a mixture of threatening; as if he had said, that the earth will be deprived of its inhabitants in exactly the same manner as the trees and vines are stripped of their fruits.

14. *They shall lift up their voice.* He follows out and increases the consolations which he had briefly sketched; for, having formerly (Isaiah x. 19-22) said that, out of that vast multitude, a few drops would be left, which would nevertheless overflow the whole world, in like manner he now says, that the small number of the godly, which shall be left out of an abundant vintage, will nevertheless rejoice and utter a voice so loud that it will be heard in the most distant countries. This was done by the preaching of the gospel; for, as to the condition of Judea, it appeared to be entirely ruined by it: the national government was taken away, and they were broken down by foreign and civil wars in such a manner that they never could rise above them. The rest of the world was dumb in singing the praises of God, and deaf to hear his voice; but as the Jews were the first fruits, I shall willingly admit that they are here placed in the highest rank.

Hence we obtain a remarkable consolation, that the Lord can in a moment restore his Church, and make it most flourishing; or rather, he can, as it were, create it out of nothing; for even out of death, as we have seen, he brings life. Now, this is contrary to nature and to ordinary custom, that so small a number of persons should lift up their voice, and be heard in distant places; for where there are few persons, there is silence, and where there is a crowd, there is commonly a noise. It is therefore a work of God, which goes beyond the course of nature and the ability of men; for otherwise it would appear as if the Prophet uttered what was contradictory, that when the whole of Judea had been laid waste and the world had been emptied, there would be few or almost none left, and yet that their shouting would be heard everywhere. This is in itself incredible, or rather absurd; but, as we have already said, it is an astonishing work of God.

They shall cry aloud from the sea. By those heralds he means not only those who were the descendants of the Jews according to the flesh, but those who were descended from them by faith. The *crying aloud* denotes not only cheerful voices, expressive of gladness and joy, but likewise confidence; for they will freely and boldly utter with a loud voice the praises of God. He states, at the same time, that it is right that believers should be employed in extolling God's perfections and not their own claims to approbation. By *the sea*, he obviously means distant countries, and those which lay beyond the sea and were unknown to the Jews.

15. *Wherefore glorify Jehovah in the valleys.*[1] God's benefits ought to excite us to gratitude, and we testify it by singing his praises. "What return shall we make," as David says, "for all the benefits which he has bestowed on us, but to take the cup of thanksgiving for salvation, and call on the name of the Lord?" The Prophet therefore observes this order; having spoken of the restoration of the Church, he exhorts us to offer the sacrifice of praise.

By *the valleys*, he means countries that are hidden and, as it were, separated from others; for those which are surrounded by mountains are separated and disjoined by nature. The consequence is, that the inhabitants of valleys are less civilized, because they have fewer opportunities of conversing with each other. The meaning is the same as if the Pro-

[1] "In the fires, (or, valleys.)"—*Eng. Ver.*

phet had said, that there will not be a corner so obscure or retired that the praises of God shall not be heard in it.

The name of Jehovah the God of Israel. He uses the expression, "the name of the God of Israel," in order to intimate that all nations will call upon the true God; for, as all nations have a knowledge of God that is natural to them, so all easily turn aside to superstition and false worship. (Rom. i. 19.) But here he speaks of spreading the true religion through the whole world; and this makes it still more evident that the prophecy relates to the kingdom of Christ, under which true religion has at length penetrated into foreign and heathen nations.

16. *From the uttermost part[1] of the earth.* This verse contains two statements which have some appearance of being at variance with each other. It begins with a joyful description of the praises of God, and next passes on to complaints and lamentations, in which he bewails the treachery of transgressors, who overturn religion and godliness. So far as relates to praises, we have said that we can neither praise God nor call upon him, till he reveal himself to us, and give a taste of his goodness, that we may entertain hope and confident expectation of life. Hence those sayings of David, "In the grave who shall praise thee, O Lord? In death who shall confess to thee?" (Psalm vi. 5.) When we feel nothing but the wrath of God, we are dumb to his praises; and therefore when he says that the praises of God will be heard, he means that the gospel will be spread through the whole world; that men may acknowledge God to be their Father, and may thus break forth into his praise. "From the uttermost part" is a phrase that deserves attention; for at that time the praises of God were confined to Judea, and were not heard at a distance; but afterwards they began to resound everywhere. (Psalm lxxvi. 1, 2.)

Glory to the righteous. Some consider this to be spoken by all believers, as if the song were, "God is glorified on account of his righteousness." Others read the two clauses as

---

[1] "The uttermost part. (Heb. wing.)"—Eng. Ver. The Septuagint translates it literally, ἀπὸ τῶν πτερύγων τῆς γῆς, "from the wings of the earth."—*Ed.*

one, "We have heard that glory is given to the righteous God." Those who think that the heralds of God's praises are called "righteous," bring out a very good sense, but do not attend to the word "Glory," or at least are constrained to render the word צבי (*tzēbī*) *joy*.[1] He makes use of the preterite, "We have heard," instead of the future tense; and his reason for doing so is, that he intended to cheer the hearts of the godly by some consolation; "We shall again hear the praises of God;" for this is more than if he had said, "They will be heard." He speaks also in the first person, in order to include the whole body of the Church, and thus to awaken the attention of the godly.

God is called *righteous;* and we know that this expression frequently occurs in Scripture, but it belongs to him in a different manner from that in which it belongs to men; for men are called "righteous," on account of the "righteousness" which has been communicated to them; but God, who is the fountain of righteousness, is called "righteous," on account of what he performs. (Deut. xxxii. 4; Psalm vii. 9; xi. 7.) And that is a proof of this congratulation and thanksgiving, because from the communication of this righteousness we obtain salvation and life; and therefore, wherever the righteousness of God is, it must be followed by praises and thanksgivings.

When the Prophet predicted these things, how incredible might they appear to be! for among the Jews alone was the Lord known and praised. (Psalm lxxvi. 2.) To them destruction is foretold, and next the publication of the word, and the

[1] There is a considerable diversity of opinion about the application of the term *righteous* in this passage. Many commentators agree with CALVIN in thinking that God is here called *righteous*. Bishop Stock has slightly modified this view by applying the designation to the Messiah. "By the righteous," says he, "is probably meant one person, the Messiah, (see Acts vii. 52; xxii. 14,) whose kingdom the Prophet beholds in vision, and joins in the chorus of joy at its approach; a joy, however, which is presently interrupted by a reflection on the wickedness of the greater part of his countrymen at that time, who should reject the Lord that bought them. Therefore he saith, Wo is me! destruction shall overtake the inhabitants of the land." Instead of "Glory to the righteous," the Septuagint renders it, ἐλπὶς τῷ εὐσεβεῖ, "hope to the godly man." Professor Alexander's rendering is, "Praise to the righteous;" and he remarks, "צדיק (*tzăddīk*) is not an epithet of God (Henderson) or Cyrus (Hendewerk), but of righteous men in general."—*Ed.*

celebration of the praises of God; but how could these things be done, when the people of God had been destroyed? Hence we may infer that there were few who believed these predictions. But now that those events have taken place, it is our duty to behold with admiration so great a miracle of God, because, when the Jews had been not only broken down, but almost annihilated, still there flashed from them a spark by which the whole world was enlightened, and all who were kindled by it burst forth into a confession of the truth.

My leanness.[1] This passage is explained in various ways; for some translate רזי (*rāzī*) *secret*, and others *leanness*. Those who translate it *secret* understand the Prophet to mean that a double secret has been revealed to him, because the Lord has determined to reward the good and to punish the wicked; for when men look only at the outward appearance of things, and see that the wicked succeed to their wish, and that the godly are overwhelmed by afflictions, they are distressed, and doubt whether the affairs of men are governed by the hand of God, or all things happen by chance; and Solomon shews that thoughts of this kind are the seed of ungodliness. (Eccl. viii. 11.) On this account the Psalmist also says, that he "entered into the sanctuary of God," that he might examine the subject in another manner than by human reason. (Psalm lxxiii. 17.) If we adopt that interpretation, the meaning will be, "Though it appear as if there were no reward to the righteous, yet I hold this as a secret imparted to me, that it will be well with them; and although the wicked think that they will escape, yet I know that they will not pass unpunished." But as this ingenuity appears to be too far-fetched, I prefer a more simple interpretation; and, besides, there immediately follows an interjection expressive of lamentation, אוי, (*ōi*,) *Wo!* so that I do not think that Isaiah speaks here about the righteous or about their reward.

Others more correctly explain it *leanness;* as if he had said, that through grief he shrinks and grows lean; for as the prosperous and flourishing condition of that people might

---

[1] "My leanness. (Heb. leanness to me, or, my secret to me.)"—Eng. Ver.

be called "fatness," so its wretched and distressed condition might be called "leanness." Here the Prophet stands forth as the representative of the whole race; and when the Lord cuts it down, he justly complains of his "leanness." This interpretation, I have said, is probable; for when the Prophet saw the people diminishing in numbers, he had good reason for bewailing that diminution. We know that, when the grace of God was very abundantly poured out, the ancient people was greatly diminished, and the posterity of Abraham was almost annihilated.

But we must see if the Prophet does not look farther than to the rejection of his nation, so as to bewail the condition of his bowels, when he foresees that the Church will be heavily distressed; for רז, (*rāz*,) which some translate *secret*, may properly be understood to denote the internal part of the body In this way the exclamation would be, "My bowels, or my entrails, are pained;" for in a pathetic discourse there is no absurdity in supposing that a word is supplied. When the Lord has extended his Church, it appears to be in a flourishing state, and free from all danger; but when its very inwards or bowels, that is, its own members, give it uneasiness, it is grievously tormented. Hypocrites arise, by whom it is more annoyed than by enemies who "are without." (Rev. xxii. 15.)

Such is also the import of those groanings, אוי, (*ōi*,) *wo to me;* and Isaiah, I have no doubt, intended to intimate that the godly should not think that they will be happy in this world, but should believe that they must maintain a continual strife, even when they might imagine that there is nothing to hinder them from enjoying uninterrupted tranquillity and peace. He wishes to express the feeling of poignant grief which torments the Church inwardly, even in her very bowels; and this affliction is the more deeply to be lamented, because it cannot be avoided; for, as some one says, the Church can neither flee from internal and domestic enemies, nor put them to flight. Isaiah can scarcely find terms adequate to express this misery.

The treacherous dealers have dealt treacherously. These words abundantly confirm the expositions which have been already given. How heavy this affliction is, and how deeply it ought to be deplored, we ourselves have abundantly experienced, and still experience every day. Whence arose Popery, and all its corruption, but from this internal evil? for it was an imposthume ($ἀπόστημα$) bred in the very bowels of the Church, which sent forth offensive and diseased matter. How comes it also that, when the Church begins to revive, we see doctrine corrupted and discipline overturned not only by the common people, but by those who ought to have given a good example to others? Is it not because the Church is always subject to this evil?

17. *Fear, and the pit, and the snare.* The Prophet here discourses against the sins of the people. Formerly he declared that not only one nation, but very many and very distant nations, would have abundant grounds of thanksgiving. He now passes to another doctrine; for I think that these words ought to be separated from what goes before, because Isaiah again threatens the wicked, that they may know that amidst the highest prosperity of the Church they will be miserable. For the sake of cherishing their indifference, wicked men are accustomed rashly to apply the promises of God to themselves, though they do not at all belong to them; and therefore the prophets usually mingle threatenings with them. It is also possible that Isaiah delivered this discourse separately from the rest, and on a different occasion; for neither the prophets themselves nor other learned men divided the chapters. We have often seen different subjects joined together, and others divided which ought to have been joined, which was undoubtedly done through ignorance. However that may be, the Prophet returns to the wicked, and threatens against them severe and dreadful judgment.

This description of "fear, the pit, and the snare," is intended to touch the feelings; for if he had said, in a single word, that destruction awaits the wicked, they would not have been greatly moved. But there is room for doubting if he addresses the Jews alone. For my own part, I should not be much inclined to dispute about this matter; but I think it is more probable that these threatenings related also to other nations, and even to the whole world, of which he had formerly prophesied.

O inhabitant of the earth. By "the world" we understand those countries which were known to the Jews, as we have already explained. The meaning is, "Thou art pressed by afflictions so diversified, that thou hast no means of escape." Amos gives a similar description: "He who shall flee through dread of a lion shall meet a bear; and if he go into the house, when he leaneth on a wall, a serpent shall bite him." (Amos v. 19.) Isaiah formerly said that lions would be sent against the Moabites who had escaped from the battle. (Isaiah xv. 9.) God has an endless variety of scourges for punishing the wicked. It is as if he had said, "Know that you cannot escape the hand of God; for he has various methods by which he takes vengeance on their crimes, and thus overtakes those who had hoped to escape by a variety of contrivances. He who escapes from the battle shall be tormented with hunger; and when he is freed from hunger, he will meet some other calamity, as if nets had been laid on all sides to ensnare you."

For the windows from on high are open, and the foundations of the earth are shaken. This argument confirms what had been already said, that it is impossible for them to escape the vengeance of God, who has prepared for it a free course in heaven and in earth, from the utmost height of heaven down to the depths of the earth. Some think that he alludes (Gen. vii. 11) to the deluge; but, in my opinion, the meaning is simpler, that the wrath of God will be revealed above and below; as if he had said, "The Lord will arm heaven and earth to execute his vengeance against men, that wherever they turn their eyes, they may behold nothing but destruction."

19. *By breaking down is the earth broken down.* He heightens his description of punishments by using various modes of expression. A little afterwards he will point out the cause of this "shaking," which is, that men by their sins had drawn down on themselves such destruction. He now declares that this evil is incurable. We have formerly said that the Prophet explains the same thing in various ways, and

for the purpose of striking and arousing those minds which are naturally very sluggish; for there is in the flesh a carelessness which produces contempt of God, and we have too much experience of it both in ourselves and in others. In order, therefore, that the prophets might arouse those who were careless and asleep in their vices, they adorn their style; not because they cared about being thought eloquent, but that they might make their hearers more attentive, and sting them to the quick. Hence the allusions of which these verses are full; hence the brilliant metaphors in the style; hence the threatenings and terrors announced in various ways; the object of all is, that careless men may be aroused.

Now, this doctrine ought to be limited to the wicked; not because the godly are exempted from those evils, for they are afflicted as well as other men; but because, when the godly betake themselves to God, and rely wholly upon him, they are not shaken in this manner, and remain firm and steadfast against every assault; while wicked men, who despised the judgments of God, and took unbounded liberties in transgression, are terrified and alarmed, and never find rest.

20. *And shall be removed like a tent.* This does not mean that any change will take place in the position of the earth; but these words, as we have already said, must be referred to men; as if he had said, that there would be no kingly power and no regular government. In short, he intended to describe those changes which he had spoken of in the tenth chapter.

And the transgressions thereof shall be heavy upon it. When he says that "the earth is laden with its iniquity," he has very appropriately assigned this reason, that we may understand that God is never angry with men without a cause; for we ourselves are the authors of all the evils which we suffer. God is by nature disposed to kindness, and regards us with a father's love; and therefore it is our own fault that we are treated with sharpness and severity, and we have no reason to blame him.[1]

[1] "Nous n'avons raison aucune d'accuser celuy qui nous frappe;"—"We have no reason to blame him who strikes us."

And it shall fall, and not rise again. He at length repeats what he briefly stated a little before, that there will be no remedy for those evils. Some think that this relates to the Jews, whose form of government was entirely taken away, so that they were broken down and scattered, and were scarcely reckoned in the rank of men. But I give a more extensive interpretation, that the distresses of the world will be so severe, that it cannot be restored to its original condition. Men always contend against adverse events, and their minds are full of confidence. Having endured calamities, they think that there will be some room for breathing, and their minds are swelled with false hopes, which the Prophet therefore takes away, that they may not in future deceive themselves by unfounded expectation. Yet it ought to be observed, that this general statement does not set aside the exception which Isaiah formerly made.

21. *And it shall come to pass.* This passage has tortured the minds of many commentators, and various interpretations have been offered by various writers. Some think that this relates to the sun and the stars, and others, that it relates to the devils, who will be punished along with the wicked. Others refer it to the Jews, on whom God had bestowed a remarkable privilege. But I cannot adopt any of those interpretations.[1] The simple and genuine meaning, therefore, appears to me to be, that no power will be so high as to be exempted from those scourges of God; and though they raise themselves above the clouds, yet the hand of God will reach them; as it is said in the Psalm, " Whither shall I go from thy Spirit? and whither shall I flee from thy face? If I ascend into heaven, thou art there; if I take the wings of the morning, and dwell in the uttermost parts of the sea, there also shall thy hand pursue me." Psalm cxxxix. 7-10.

[1] " Interpreters have commonly assumed that 'the host of the high place' is the same with the 'host of heaven,' and must therefore mean either stars (Jerome), or angels (Aben Ezra), or both (Gesenius). Grotius understands by it the images of the heavenly bodies worshipped in Assyria. Gesenius finds here an allusion to the punishment of fallen angels, and then makes this a proof of recent origin, because the Jewish demonology was later than the time of Isaiah. It may be doubted whether there is any reference to the hosts of heaven at all."—*Alexander.*

Jehovah will visit upon the army on high.[1] This is a metaphor by which he denotes kings and princes, who shine and sparkle in the world like stars; and he afterwards explains this metaphor in direct language, by adding, *upon the kings of the earth;* for I do not think that they ought to be separated, as if he were speaking of different subjects, but that there is a repetition of the same statement, so that the latter clause explains the former. But perhaps it will be thought preferable to explain it thus: "he will visit on the kingdoms of the earth," even on those things which appear to surpass the rank of men; for some things rise so much above others, that they appear as if they did not belong to the ordinary rank. The word *visit* must relate to punishment, as even the context shews plainly enough.

22. *And they shall be gathered together, and shall be shut up in prison.* He continues his subject in the beginning of the verse. The mode of expression is metaphorical; for they were not all captives, but God reduced them to servitude, as if a man held in his hand the enemies whom he subdued. He therefore brings forward God as a conqueror, who shuts up enemies in prison, as captives are commonly shut up. We know that men, as it were, flee from God, and despise him, so long as he spares them, and exercises any forbearance towards them; and on this account also he threatens that they shall be thrown into prison in large masses, that they may not solace themselves with their multitude.

Afterwards they shall be visited. When he adds that after a time "they shall be visited," it is not simply a promise, but includes also a threatening to this effect, "As formerly by their obstinacy they mocked God, and excessively prolonged the time of sinning, so God will punish without making haste, till at length, though late, they acknowledge the cause of their distresses." Thus earthly judges frequently do not deign to admit into their presence the malefactors who have offended them, but plunge them into darkness and filth, and gradually wear them out, in order to subdue their obstinacy. Again, as there are two ways in which God visits the world,

[1] "The Lord shall punish (Heb. visit upon) the host of the high ones." — Eng. Ver.

either when he punishes the wicked, or when he shews to the elect the tokens of a Father's kindness, the word *visit* here signifies " to look upon ;" and thus the Prophet softens the harshness of the threatening. It was necessary that the hearts of the godly should be supported amidst these distresses, that they might not faint; and on their account, therefore, after various threatenings, the prophets are wont to add consolations. As these statements tended to support believers, they were undoubtedly addressed to the Jews, among whom chiefly faith was found, or rather, there was none to be seen anywhere else.

After many days. This also deserves attention. It was intended to try the faith of the godly ;[1] for we are hasty in our desires, and would wish that God should immediately perform his promises : we complain that he is slow, and we cannot brook any delay. It is therefore our duty to wait patiently for that mercy ; and no delay, however long, should make us lose heart. Yet it ought also to be observed, that this does not refer to all ; for, as we saw a little before, God had determined to save but a small remnant ; and this ought to quicken us the more, that, being humbled by slow and long-continued punishments, we may meet God who visits us.

23. *The moon shall be confounded.* Many commentators think that the Prophet waxes still more wroth against the Jews, so far as to say, that the sun and moon and stars are ashamed of their unbelief, and that not only men, but creatures devoid of speech, will abhor them ; but this appears to be far removed from the meaning and design of the Prophet. I have no doubt that he continues to give the consolation which he had glanced at in the former verse ; " When the Lord shall visit his people, and cleanse the Church from its defilement, he will establish a kingdom so illustrious that it will darken the sun and stars by its brightness." This mode of expression is frequently employed by the prophets, and we have formerly seen it. Since, therefore, God will establish your kingdom on Mount Zion, so great will be its splendour in the restoration of the people, that those things

[1] " Des enfans de Dieu ;"—" Of the children of God."

which dazzle the eyes of men, will be dark in comparison of it; and, for the purpose of expressing this, he has mentioned those objects which surpass all others in brightness.

When the Lord of hosts shall reign in Mount Zion. Some think that the word *reign* denotes God's vengeance; but this is inaccurate, for although the Lord is said to reign when he discharges the office of a Judge, yet the complex phrase, "the reign of God in Mount Zion," always denotes mercy and salvation. He speaks of the restoration of the Church, and hence it follows, that it is only in Christ that those things are fulfilled.

And before his elders glory. By expressly mentioning the "elders," he employs a figure of speech frequently used in Scripture, by which the chief part of the Church is taken for the whole body of it. And yet it is not without a special design that he denotes, by the term "elders," not only the priests, but other governors who preside over discipline and morals, and by whose moderation and prudence others ought to be guided. Under their name he includes the whole nation, not only because they represent the whole body, and because the common people are in some measure concealed under their shadow, but likewise that believers may entertain hope of future restoration; for otherwise it would have been of little or no avail that a scattered multitude should be left like a mutilated body or a confused mass. Not without good reason did he use the phrase, "and before his elders," that the Jews might know that the power of God would be visibly and strikingly displayed; not that it can be perceived by the bodily senses, but by faith. He reigns in such a manner, that we feel that he is present with us; and if we did not comprehend this, it would yield us no consolation.

Glory.[1] Instead of "glory" some read "gloriously," and others, "glorious." I prefer to take it simply as a substantive, though there is little difference in the meaning. He shews how great will be the splendour and glory of God, when the kingdom of Christ shall be established, because all

---

[1] "And before his ancients gloriously; (or, there shall be glory before his ancients.)"—Eng. Ver. "Before his ancients shall he be glorified."—*Lowth.* "And before his elders shall there be glory."—*Alexander.*

that is brilliant must be obscured, and the glory of Christ alone must hold a high and prominent place. Hence it follows, that then only does God receive his just rights, and the honour due to him, when all creatures are placed in subjection, and he alone shines before our eyes.

CHAPTER XXV.

1. O Lord, thou *art* my God: I will exalt thee, I will praise thy name: for thou hast done wonderful *things; thy* counsels of old *are* faithfulness *and* truth.
2. For thou hast made of a city an heap; *of* a defenced city a ruin: a palace of strangers to be no city; it shall never be built.
3. Therefore shall the strong people glorify thee, the city of the terrible nations shall fear thee.
4. For thou hast been a strength to the poor, a strength to the needy in his distress, a refuge from the storm, a shadow from the heat, when the blast of the terrible ones *is* as a storm *against* the wall.
5. Thou shalt bring down the noise of strangers, as the heat in a dry place; *even* the heat with the shadow of a cloud: the branch of the terrible ones shall be brought low.
6. And in this mountain shall the Lord of hosts make unto all people a feast of fat things, a feast of wines on the lees; of fat things full of marrow, of wines on the lees well refined.
7. And he will destroy in this mountain the face of the covering cast over all people, and the veil that is spread over all nations.
8. He will swallow up death in victory; and the Lord God will wipe away tears from off all faces: and the rebuke of his people shall he take away from off all the earth: for the Lord hath spoken *it*.
9. And it shall be said in that day, Lo, this *is* our God; we have waited for him, and he will save us: this *is*

1. Iehova Deus meus es tu: exaltabo te; celebrabo nomen tuum; quia fecisti rem mirificam; consilia iam olim decreta, veritatem firmam.
2. Quia posuisti ex urbe acervum, urbem munitam in ruinam; palatium extraneorum, ut non sit civitas, nec unquam ædificetur.
3. Propterea glorificabit te populus fortis; civitas gentium robustarum timebit te.
4. Nam fuisti fortitudo pauperi; fortitudo, inquam, egeno in afflictione ejus; refugium ab inundatione, umbra ab æstu, quia spiritus fortium (*aut, violentorum*) quasi turbo (*vel, inundatio*) contra murum.
5. Sicut æstum in arido, strepitum alienorum humiliabis, æstum in umbra nubis; clamorem (*vel, cantum, vel, excisionem*) fortium humiliabit.
6. Et faciet Iehova exercituum cunctis populis in monte isto convivium pinguium, convivium defecatorum; pinguium, inquam, medullatorum; defecatorum liquidorum.
7. Et destruet in monte isto faciem involucri quo involuti sunt populi omnes, et operimentum quod expansum est super omnes gentes.
8. Destruxit mortem in æternum. Et absterget Dominus Iehova lachrymam a cunctis faciebus, et opprobrium populi sui auferet ab universa terra; quia Iehova locutus est.
9. Et dicetur in die illa: Ecce Deus noster iste; expectavimus eum, et salvabit nos. Iste Iehova; expec-

the Lord; we have waited for him, we will be glad and rejoice in his salvation.

10. For in this mountain shall the hand of the Lord rest, and Moab shall be trodden down under him, even as straw is trodden down for the dunghill.

11. And he shall spread forth his hands in the midst of them, as he that swimmeth spreadeth forth *his hands* to swim; and he shall bring down their pride together with the spoils of their hands.

12. And the fortress of the high fort of thy walls shall he bring down, lay low, *and* bring to the ground, *even* to the dust.

tavimus eum, exultabimus, et lætabimur in salute ejus.

10. Nam quiescet manus Iehovæ in monte isto; et triturabitur Moab subter eum, sicut trituratur palea in sterquilinio.

11. Et extendet manum suam sub medio ejus, sicut extendit natator ad natandum; et humiliabit superbiam ejus, cum brachiis manuum suarum.

12. Et munitionem sublimitatis murorum tuorum sternet, humiliabit, dejiciet in terram, ad pulverem.

1. *O* LORD, *thou art my God.* Hitherto Isaiah has prophesied about the judgments of God, which threatened not only a single nation, but almost the whole world. Now, it was impossible that the contemplation of calamities so dismal as those which he foresaw should not give him great uneasiness; for godly persons would desire that all mankind should be saved, and, while they honour God, they desire also to love all that belongs to him; and, in short, so far as any man sincerely fears God, he has a powerful and lively feeling of the divine judgments. While wicked men stand amazed at the judgments of God, and are not moved by any terror, godly men tremble at the slightest token of his anger. And if this be the case with us, what do we suppose was experienced by the Prophet, who had almost before his eyes those calamities which he foretold? For, in order that the ministers of the word might be convinced of the certainty of what they taught, it was necessary that they should be more powerfully impressed by it than the generality of men.

Since therefore the Lord held out to Isaiah, as in a picture, those dreadful calamities, he found it necessary, under the overpowering influence of grief and anxiety, to betake himself to the Lord; otherwise the confused emotions of his mind would have agitated him beyond measure. He therefore takes courage from the belief that, in the midst of these tempests, the Lord still determines to promote the advantage of his Church, and to bring into subjection to himself those who were formerly estranged. Isaiah therefore remains firm and steadfast in his calling, and does not allow himself to be drawn aside from his purpose, but continually relies on the expectation of mercy, and therefore perseveres in celebrating the praises of God. Thus we learn that this thanksgiving is connected with the former prophecies, and that Isaiah considers not only what he foretold, but why the Lord did it; that is, why the Lord afflicted so many nations with various calamities. It was, that he might subdue those who were formerly incorrigible, and who rushed forward with brutal eagerness, who had no fear of God, and no feeling of religion or godliness.

Thou art my God. Being as it were perplexed and confused, he suddenly raises his thoughts to God, as we have already said. Hence we ought to draw a very useful doctrine, namely, that when our minds are perplexed by a variety of uneasy thoughts on account of numerous distresses and afflictions which happen daily, we ought immediately to resort to God, and rely on his providence; for even the smallest calamities will overwhelm us, if we do not betake ourselves to him, and support our hearts by this doctrine. In order to bring out more fully the meaning of the Prophet, the word *but* or *nevertheless* may be appropriately inserted in this manner: "Whatever temptations from that quarter may disturb me, nevertheless I will acknowledge thee to be my God." Thus he promises that he will give to God the praise which is due to him; and this cannot be, unless a firm belief of his grace dwell in our hearts, and hold a superiority, from which grace springs a joy, which yields to us the most abundant ground for praises, when we are certain of our salvation, and are fully convinced that the Lord is our God. Accordingly, those who are influenced by no desire to praise God, have not believed and have not tasted the goodness of God; for if we actually trust in God, we must be led to take great delight in praising his name.

For thou hast done a wonderful thing. He uses the word פלא, (*pĕlĕ,*) *wonderful,* in the singular number instead of the plural. The Prophet does not confine his view to the present appearance of things, but looks to the end; for even men who in other respects are heathens, behold in the government of the world astonishing events, the sight of which overwhelms them with amazement; which undoubtedly happened to the inhabitants of Tyre and Sidon, and to the Babylonians and Moabites. But those only who have tasted his goodness and wisdom can profit by the works of God; for otherwise they undervalue and despise his works, and do not comprehend their excellence, because they do not perceive their end, which is, that God, wonderfully bringing light out of darkness, (2 Cor. iv. 6,) raises his Church from death to life, and regulates in the best manner, and directs to the most valuable purpose, those things which to the eye of man appear to be confused.

Counsels which have been already decreed of old.[1] Now, in order to bestow still higher commendation on the providence of God, he adds, that the "counsels have been already decreed of old;" as if he had said, that to God nothing is sudden or unforeseen. And indeed, though he sometimes appears to us to act suddenly, yet all things were undoubtedly ordained by him before the creation of the world. (Acts xv. 18.) By this word, therefore, the Apostle means that all the miracles which happen contrary to the expectation of men, are the result of that regular order which God maintains in governing the world, arranging all things from the beginning to the end. Now, since we do not understand those secret decrees, and our powers of understanding cannot rise so high, our attention must therefore be directed to the manifestation of them; for they are concealed from us, and exceed our comprehension, till the Lord reveal them by his word, in which he accommodates himself to our weakness; for his decree is ($ἀνεξεύρητον$) unsearchable.

Firm truth.[2] From the eternal decrees of God the Prophet thus proceeds to doctrines and promises, which he undoubtedly denotes by the word *truth;* for the repetition would be frivolous, if this word did not signify a relation;

---

[1] "Faithfulness and truth."—*Eng. Ver.* "Perfectly true."—*Stock.* "Truth, certainty."—*Alexander.*

[2] "Counsels of old."—*Eng. Ver.* "Counsels of old time."—*Stock.*

because, when God has revealed to us his purpose, if we believe his sayings, he then appears to be actually true. He commends the firmness and certainty of the word, when he says that it is "steadfast truth;" that is, that everything that comes from God, everything that is declared by him, is firm and unchangeable.

2. *For thou hast made of a city a heap.* Some refer this to Jerusalem; but I think that there is a change of the number, as is very customary with the prophets; for the Prophet does not speak merely of a single city, but of many cities, which he says will be reduced to heaps. As to the view held by some, that the Romans made Jerusalem a palace, it has nothing to do with the Prophet's meaning, which will be easily enough understood, if we keep in remembrance what has been already stated, that the Prophet does not confine his thoughts to those calamities by which the Lord afflicts many nations, but extends his view to the end of the chastisements. In this manner the Lord determined to tame and subdue the obstinacy of men, whom he would never have brought into subjection to him without having been broken down by various afflictions.

A palace of foreigners,[1] *that it may not be a city.* The Prophet does not merely mean that, when the natives have been driven out, "foreigners" will inhabit the cities which have been taken; for that would not agree with what he immediately adds, "that it may be no longer a city;" but that wandering bands of men who shall be in want of a habitation will there find abundance of room, because there will be no inhabitants left. Since ארמון (*armōn*) denotes a magnificent palace, the Prophet thus says ironically, that highwaymen will dwell as in palaces, on account of the vast extent of the place which shall be deserted.

3. *Therefore shall the strong people glorify thee.* This is the end which I mentioned;[2] for if the Lord should destroy the world, no good result would follow, and indeed destruction could produce no feeling but horror, and we would never

---

[1] "*Of foreigners*, a term with the Jews synonymous to barbarians or enemies; as the Romans confounded *hospites* with *hostes*, being to them nearly the same thing."—*Stock.*

[2] See page 191.

be led by it to sing his praise; but, on the contrary, we must be deprived of all feeling, when we perceive nothing but wrath. But praises flow from a sense of grace and goodness. It is therefore as if he had said, "Thou wilt not only strike and afflict, O Lord, but wilt cause the chastisements to be not without effect; for by them thou wilt subdue the fierceness of men, so that those who were formerly estranged from thee shall bend their neck to thee." This passage should lead us to observe how much we need chastisements, which train us to obedience to God; for we are carried away by prosperity to such an extent, that we think that we have a right to do anything, and we even grow wanton and insolent when God treats us with gentleness.

The city of the terrible nations shall fear thee. When the Prophet next mentions *fear*, he shews that this praise does not consist in words or outward gestures, but in the sincere feeling of the heart. Hence we infer that he now speaks of the entire worship of God; but, as many persons think that they have fully discharged their duty, as soon as they have made a confession with the mouth, he adds, for the sake of explanation, "The nations shall fear thee." When he calls them strong and powerful, by these epithets he denotes their pride and arrogance; for they were elated by their prosperity. They rebel against God, and cannot be made humble or submissive, unless they have been deprived of all things. To such views, therefore, ought our thoughts to be directed amidst those calamities which we perceive. The fierceness of men must be restrained and subdued, that they may be prepared for receiving doctrine and for rendering true obedience. So long as they shall be blinded by their wealth and vain confidence, they will fearlessly mock at the judgments of God, and will never yield subjection to him.

4. *For thou hast been a strength to the poor.* Hence we see the fruit of conversion, namely, that the Lord raises us from the dead, and brings us, as it were, out of the grave, stretching out his hand to us from heaven, to rescue us even from hell. This is our first access to him, for it is only in our poverty that he finds the means of exercising his kindness. To us in our turn, therefore, it is necessary that we

be poor and needy, that we may obtain assistance from him; and we must lay aside all reliance and confidence in ourselves, before he display his power in our behalf. This is the reason why he visits us with chastisements and with the cross, by which he trains us, so that we may be able to receive his assistance and grace.

A refuge from the storm, a shadow from the heat. It is not without good reason that Isaiah adorns this description by these comparisons; for numerous and diversified temptations arise, and, in order to bear them courageously, it is necessary that the weak minds of men should be strengthened and fortified. On this account he says that God will be "a strength to the poor, a refuge from the storms, and a shadow from the heat;" because, whatever may be the nature of the dangers and assaults which threaten them, the Lord will protect his people against them, and will supply them with every kind of armour.

The breath of the strong or *of the violent ones.* In this passage, as in many others, (Gen. viii. 1; Ex. xv. 10; 1 Kings xix. 11,) רוח (*rūăch*) signifies "the blowing of the wind," and denotes the tremendous violence with which wicked men are hurried along against the children of God; for not only do they "breathe out threatenings and terrors," (Acts ix. 1,) but they appear to vomit out fire itself.

A storm or *flood against the wall.* This is to the same purport as the former; for by this figure he means, that wicked men, when they obtain liberty to do mischief, rush on with such violence that they throw down everything that comes in their way, for to overthrow and destroy walls is more than if the water were merely flowing over the fields.

5. *As the heat in a dry place.* If the Lord did not aid when violent men rush upon us, our life would be in imminent danger; for we see how great is the rage of wicked men, and if the Lord overturn walls, what can a feeble man do against him? These things therefore are added in order to magnify the grace of God, that we may consider what would become of us if the Lord did not render assistance.

Yet there are two ways in which commentators explain this passage. Some understand it to mean, that wicked men will be consumed by God's indignation, in the same manner as the violence of the heat burns up the fields which are in themselves barren. Others render it in the ablative case, *As if by heat,* and make the meaning to be, " Though wicked men, relying on their power, are so violent, yet the Lord will prostrate them in a moment, as if they were overpowered ' by heat in a dry place.' " But I consider the meaning to be different, for, after having shewn how great is the rage of wicked men against believers, he adds :

Thou wilt bring them down, O Lord. Alluding to the metaphor of the deluge, which he had formerly used, he says, " Thou wilt quench their heat, which would otherwise consume us, even as rain, or a shower, falling from heaven, quenches the heat that scorched the thirsty fields." And thus the passage flows naturally; for the other interpretation is forced, and does violence, as the saying is, to the letter.

The noise of the strong ones will he lay low.[1] This clause is tortured in various ways. Some think that זמיר (*zĕmīr*) means *seed;* others that it means *a root;* as if he had said, that God will not only destroy wicked men, but will utterly root them out. This meaning would be probable, were it not opposed by the metaphor of the heat. In my opinion, therefore, it is more correctly interpreted by others to mean " singing and shouting," or " cutting off," although even those interpreters do not fully succeed in getting at the meaning of the Prophet. He therefore confirms the preceding statement, that the violence of wicked men, or the shouting which they haughtily and daringly set up, will presently be laid low, as the heat of the sun is overpowered by the falling rain, which is meant by *the shadow of a cloud.*

6. *And the* LORD *of hosts shall make.* This passage has received various interpretations. Some think that the Prophet threatens the Jews, and threatens them in such a manner as to invite various nations to a banquet. This mode of expression is also found in other passages, for the Lord is said to fatten the wicked for the day of slaughter. Those

[1] " The branch of the terrible ones."—Eng. Ver. " So shall the song of the tyrants be brought low."—*Alexander*.

commentators think that, as if the Jews were exposed as a prey to the Gentiles on account of their impiety, the Gentiles are invited to a banquet; as if the Lord had said, " I have prepared a splendid entertainment for the Gentiles; the Romans shall plunder and prey on the Jews." But, in my opinion, that view of the passage cannot be admitted, nor will it be necessary for me to give a long refutation of it, after having brought forward the true interpretation. Others explain it as if Isaiah were speaking of the wrath of God in this manner, " The Lord will prepare a banquet for all nations; he will give to them to drink the cup of his anger, that they may be drunken."

But the Prophet had quite a different meaning, for he proceeds in making known the grace of God, which was to be revealed by the coming of Christ. He employs the same metaphor which is also used by David, when he describes the kingdom of Christ, and says, that " the poor and the rich will sit down at this feast, and will eat and be satisfied." (Psalm xxii. 26, 29.) By this metaphorical language he means, that no class of men will be excluded from partaking of this generous provision. Formerly it seemed as if the Lord nourished the Jews only, because they alone were adopted, and, as it were, invited to the feast provided for his family; but now he admits the Gentiles also, and extends his beneficence to all nations.

Will make for all nations a feast of fat things. This is an implied contrast when he says, *to all nations*, for formerly he was known to one nation only. (Psalm lxxvi. 1.) By " a feast of fat things" is meant a banquet consisting of animals that have been well fattened.

Of liquids purified.[1] Some render the Hebrew word שְׁמָרִים, (*shĕmārīm,*) *dregs*, but inaccurately, for it means " old wines," such as the French call, *vins de garde*, " wines that have been long kept," and that are preferable to ordinary wines, especially in an eastern country, where they carry their age better. He calls them liquids which contain no dregs or sediment.

In short, it is sufficiently evident that he does not here

---

[1] " Of wines on the lees well refined."—Eng. Ver.

threaten destruction against Gentiles or Jews, but that both are invited together to a very splendid banquet. This is still more evident from Christ's own words, when he compares the kingdom of heaven to a marriage-feast which the King prepared for his Son, to which he invites all without exception, because those who were at first invited refused to come. (Matt. xxii. 2, 3.) Nor have I any doubt that he speaks of the preaching of the gospel; and as it proceeded from Mount Zion, (Isaiah ii. 3,) he says that the Gentiles will come to it to feast; for when God presents to the whole world spiritual food for feeding souls, the meaning was the same as if he had prepared a table for all. The Lord invites us at the present day, that he may fill and satisfy us with good things; he raises up faithful ministers to prepare for us that feast, and gives power and efficacy to his word, that we may be satisfied with it.[1]

In this mountain. As to the word *mountain*, though the servants of God do not now come out of the mountain to feed us, yet by this name we must understand the Church; for nowhere else can any one partake of this food. That feast is not set down in streets and highways, the table is not spread everywhere, and this banquet is not prepared in all places. In order that we may feast, we must come to the Church. That place was mentioned, because there alone God was worshipped, and revelations proceeded from it; as also the gospel came forth from it. When he says that this banquet will be rich and sumptuous, the design of this is to commend the doctrine of the gospel; for it is the spiritual food with which our souls are fed, and is so exquisitely delightful that we have no need of any other.

7. *And he will destroy the face of the covering.*[2] Here also commentators differ, for by the word *covering* is meant the disgrace with which believers are covered in this world, so that the glory of God is not seen in them; as if he had said, " Though many reproaches oppress the godly, yet God will take away those reproaches, and will make their condition

---

[1] " Que nous en soyons remplis et rassassiez;"—" That we may be filled and satisfied with it."
[2] " Le voile qui cache la face de tous les peuples;"—" The veil which covers the face of all people."

glorious. I pass by other interpretations; but, in my opinion, the true meaning is, that the Lord promises that he will take away the veil by which they were kept in blindness and ignorance; and therefore it was by the light of the gospel that this darkness was dispelled.

In that mountain. He says that this will be in mount Zion, from which also the light of the word shone on the whole world, as we have already seen. (Isaiah ii. 3.) This passage, therefore, must unavoidably be referred to the kingdom of Christ; for the light did not shine on all men till Christ, the Sun of Righteousness, arose, (Mal. iv. 2,) who took away all the veils, wrappings, and coverings. And here we have another commendation of the gospel, that it dispels the darkness, and takes away from our eyes the covering of errors. Hence it follows, that we are wrapped up and blinded by the darkness of ignorance, before we are enlightened by the doctrine of the gospel, by which alone we can obtain light and life, and be fully restored. Here, too, we have a confirmation of the calling of the Gentiles, that is, of our calling; for not only the Jews, but all nations, which formerly were buried in every kind of errors and superstition, are invited to this banquet.

8. *He hath destroyed death eternally.*[1] The Prophet continues his subject; for in general he promises that there will be perfect happiness under the reign of Christ, and, in order to express this the more fully, he employs various metaphors admirably adapted to the subject. That happiness is real, and not temporary or fading, which not even death can take away; for amidst the highest prosperity our joy is not a little diminished by the consideration that it will not always last. He therefore connects two things, which render happiness full and complete. The first is, that the life is perpetual; for to those who in other respects are happy for a time, it is a wretched thing to die. The second is, that this life is accompanied by joy; for otherwise it may be thought that death would be preferable to a sorrowful and afflicted life. He next adds that, when all disgrace has been removed, this life will be glorious; for otherwise less

[1] " He will swallow up death in victory."—Eng. Ver.

confidence would have been placed in the prophecy, in consequence of the wretched oppression of the people.

But it is asked, To what period must we refer these promises? for in this world we must contend with various afflictions, and must fight continually; and not only are we "appointed to death," (Psalm xliv. 22,) but we "die daily." (1 Cor. xv. 31.) Paul complains of himself and the chief pillars of the Church, that they are "a spectacle to all men," and endure insults of every kind, and are even looked upon as (καθάρματα) "cleansings" and (περιψήματα) "sweepings," or "offscourings."[1] (1 Cor. iv. 9, 13.) Where or when, therefore, are these things fulfilled? They must undoubtedly be referred to the universal kingdom of Christ;—universal, I say, because we must look not only at the beginning, but also at the accomplishment and the end: and thus it must be extended even to the second coming of Christ, which on that account is called "the day of redemption" and "the day of restoration;" because all things which now appear to be confused shall be fully restored, and assume a new form. (Luke xxi. 28; Acts iii. 21; Rom. viii. 23; Eph. iv. 30.) This prediction relates, no doubt, to the deliverance from Babylon; but as that deliverance might be regarded as the earnest and foretaste of another, this promise must undoubtedly be extended to the last day.

Let us therefore direct all our hope and expectation to this point, and let us not doubt that the Lord will fulfil all these things in us when we have finished our course. If we now "sow in tears," then undoubtedly we shall "reap with joy" and ecstasy. (Psalm cxxvi. 5.) Let us not dread the insults or reproaches of men, which will one day procure for us the highest glory. Having obtained here the beginnings of this happiness and glory, by being adopted by God, and

---

[1] "When we consider the expression which follows, (evidently meant, by a parallelism, to be exegetical,) πάντων περίψημα, there is little doubt that the sense of περικαθάρματα is 'the cleansings up,' as περίψημα is 'the sweepings up or around;' metaphorically denoting 'the vilest things' or 'persons,' the very 'outcasts' of society."—*Bloomfield* on 1 Cor. iv. 13. "Περίψημα denotes filings or scrapings of any kind, and also the sweepings that are cleared away with a brush."—CALVIN on Corinthians, vol. i. p. 166.

beginning to bear the image of Christ, let us firmly and resolutely await the completion of it at the last day.

For Jehovah hath spoken it. After so many dreadful calamities, it might be thought that such an event was incredible; and therefore the Prophet shews that it proceeds not from man, but from God. When Jerusalem had been overthrown, the worship of God taken away, the temple destroyed, and the remnant of the people oppressed by cruel tyranny, no man would have believed it to be possible that everything would be raised to its original condition. It was necessary to combat with this distrust, to which men are strongly inclined; and therefore the Prophet confirms and seals these promises. "Know that God communicated to me these declarations; fix your minds therefore on him, and not on me; let your faith rely on him 'who cannot lie' or deceive." (Titus i. 2.)

9. *And it shall be said.* The verb אָמַר (*āmăr*) is indefinite, "He shall say;" but as the discourse does not relate to one or another individual, but to all in general, I chose to render it in a passive form.[1] This is an excellent conclusion; for it shews that God's benefits are not in any respect doubtful or uncertain, but are actually received and enjoyed by men. The Prophet declares that the banquet, of which he formerly spoke, (verse 6,) will not in vain be prepared by God; for men shall feast on it, and possess everlasting joy.

Lo, this is our God. That joyful shout, which he declares will be public, is the actual test and proof, so to speak, of the experience of the grace of God. This passage ought to be carefully observed; for the Prophet shews that there will be such a revelation as shall fix the minds of men on the word of God, so that they will rely on it without any kind of hesitation; and if these things belong, as they undoubtedly do belong, to the kingdom of Christ, we derive from them this valuable fruit, that Christians, unless they are wanting to themselves, and reject the grace of God, have undoubted truth on which they may safely rely. God has

---

[1] "J'ay mieux aimé le tourner, On dira;"—"I chose rather to render it, It shall be said."

removed all ground of doubt, and has revealed himself to them in such a manner, that they may venture freely to declare that they know with certainty what is his will, and may say with truth what Christ said to the Samaritan woman, "We worship what we know." (John iv. 22.) Having been informed by the gospel as to the grace offered through Christ, we do not now wander in uncertain opinions, as others do, but embrace God and his pure worship. Let us boldly say, "Away with all the inventions of men!"

It is proper to observe the contrast between that dark and feeble kind of knowledge which the fathers enjoyed under the law, and the fulness which shines forth to us in the gospel. Though God deigned to bestow on his ancient people the light of heavenly doctrine, yet he made himself more familiarly known through Christ, as we are told; "No man hath seen God at any time; the only-begotten Son, who is in the bosom of the Father, hath declared him." (John i. 18.) The Prophet now extols that certainty which the Son of God brought to us by his coming, when he "sheweth to us the Father." (John xiv. 9.) Yet, while we excel the ancient people in this respect, that the reconciliation obtained through Christ makes God, as it were, more gracious to us, there is no other way in which God can be known but through Christ, who is "the pattern and image of his substance." (Heb. i. 3.) "He who knoweth not the Son, knoweth not the Father." (John xiv. 7.) Though Jews, Mahometans, and other infidels, boast that they worship God, the creator of heaven and earth, yet they worship an imaginary God. However obstinate they may be, they follow doubtful and uncertain opinions instead of the truth; they grope in the dark, and worship their own imagination instead of God. In short, apart from Christ, all religion is deceitful and transitory, and every kind of worship ought to be abhorred and boldly condemned.

Nor is it without good reason that the Prophet employs not only the adverb *Lo*, but the demonstrative pronoun *This*,[1] in order to attest more fully the presence of God, as, a little afterwards, by repeating the declaration of certainty

[1] "Ces deux mots, *Voici, Cestui-ci;*"—"These two words, *Lo, This.*"

and confidence, he expresses the steadfastness that will be found in those who shall worship God through Christ. It is certain that we cannot comprehend God in his majesty, for he "dwelleth in unapproachable light," (1 Tim. vi. 16,) which will immediately overpower us, if we attempt to rise to it; and therefore he accommodates himself to our weakness, gives himself to us through Christ, by whom he makes us partakers of wisdom, righteousness, truth, and other blessings. (1 Cor. i. 30.)

This is Jehovah. It is worthy of observation that, when he calls Christ the God of believers, he gives to him the name "Jehovah;" from which we infer that the actual eternity of God belongs to the person of Christ. Besides, since Christ has thus made himself known to us by the gospel, this proves the base ingratitude of those who, not satisfied with so full a manifestation, have dared to add to it their own idle speculation, as has been done by Popery.

We have waited for him. He expresses the firmness and perseverance of those who have once embraced God in Christ; for it ought not to be a temporary knowledge, but we must persevere in it steadfastly to the end. Now, Isaiah speaks in the name of the ancient Church, which at that time had its seat, strictly speaking, among the Jews alone; and therefore, despising as it were all the gods that were worshipped in other countries, he boldly declares that he alone, who revealed himself to Abraham, (Gen. xv. 1,) and proclaimed his law by the hand of Moses, (Exodus xx. 1, 2,) is the true God. Other nations, which were involved in the darkness of ignorance, did not "wait for" the Lord; for this "waiting" springs from faith, which is accompanied by patience, and there is no faith without the word.

Thus he warns believers that their salvation rests on hope and expectation; for the promises of God were as it were suspended till the coming of Christ. Besides, we ought to observe what was the condition of those times; for it appeared as if either the promise of God had come to nought, or he had rejected the posterity of Abraham. Certainly, though they looked very far, God did not at that time appear to them; and therefore they must have been endued with astonishing patience to endure such heavy and sharp temptations. Accordingly, he bids them wait quietly for the coming of Christ; for then they will clearly perceive how near God is to them that worship him.

The same doctrine ought to soothe us in the present day, so that, though our salvation be concealed, still we may "wait for the Lord" with firm and unshaken hope, and, when he is at a distance, may always say, *Lo, here he is.* In times of the greatest confusion, let us learn to distinguish him by this mark, *This is he.*[1] As to the words, though he says, in the past tense,[2] "We rejoiced and were glad in his salvation;" yet the words denote a continued act; and, a little before, he had said in the future tense, "He will save us." The meaning may be thus summed up, "Christ will never disappoint the hopes of his people, if they call on him with patience."

10. *For the hand of Jehovah shall rest.* The design of the Prophet in the beginning of this verse, I have no doubt, was to comfort the godly, who but for this would have thought that God had forsaken and abandoned them; for the opinion of those who view it as describing the judgment which the Lord was about to execute on the Jews, has no foundation whatever; but the meaning is the same as if he had said, that the Lord will always assist his Church. I am aware that "the hand of God" rests also on the reprobate, when he does not cease to pursue them with his vengeance, till he completely overwhelm them; but here the word "hand" denotes assistance, and not chastisements, and therefore by the word "rest," is meant the uninterrupted continuance of defence or protection.

We draw from this a profitable doctrine, that although God scatters innumerable blessings over the whole world, in such a manner that wicked men also obtain a share of them,

---

[1] " C'est-ci l'Eternel ;"—" This is the Eternal."

[2] " This is a strange oversight. נגילה (*nagîlah*) and נשמחה (*nismĕchāh*) are in the future tense, and are so rendered by our Author in his version, " Exultabimus et lætabimur,"—" We will rejoice and be glad." "The augmented futures at the close," says Professor Alexander, alluding to the He paragogic, "may either denote fixed determination ('we will rejoice, we will be glad') or a proposition, ('Let us then rejoice,') for which the language has no other distinct form."—*Ed.*

yet his "hand" does not "rest," or is not continually present, but in the holy *mountain;* that is, in the Church, where he is worshipped. It ought also to be observed, that Jerusalem had been chastised, before she received these blessings; for he had formerly threatened chastisements and punishments, to which he added this consolation.

And Moab shall be trodden down under him. In this clause he gives an additional view of the grace of God; for, by inflicting punishment on the enemies of the Church, he will shew how dearly he values its salvation. The Jews had no enemies more deadly than the Moabites, though their ancestors[1] were near relatives. By a figure of speech (συνεκδοχικῶς) in which a part is taken for the whole, he includes under this name all the enemies of the Church, and especially those who are somewhat related to them, and who are more destructive than all others. He shews that, though for a time they are victorious and oppress the Church, yet eventually they shall be punished. His object is, that under their afflictions believers may not lose heart, as if their condition were unhappy, while wicked men are cheerful and prosperous; for the "treading down," which is here mentioned, will quickly follow. Consequently, if at the present day we see the Church disturbed and oppressed by those who are somewhat related to us, and who even assume the name and title of the Church, let us comfort our hearts by this promise.

As straw is trodden down in the dunghills.[2] The word מדמנה, (*Mădmēnāh*,) which we translate "dunghill,"[3] is supposed by some to be the name of a city, which is also mentioned by Jeremiah, (xlviii. 2.) But what if we should say that the Prophet alludes to the city, which was probably situated in a fertile soil, and thus conveys a stronger censure, and presses harder on the Moabites? As if he had said,

---

[1] That is, Abraham and Lot. (Gen. xi. 31; xix. 37.)

[2] "As straw is trodden down for the dunghill, (or, thrashed in Madmenah.)"—(Eng. Ver.)

[3] Professor Alexander renders it, "in the water of the dunghill," and remarks, "The Keri, or Masoretic reading in the margin, has במו, a poetical equivalent of ב, the preposition. The Kethib, or textual reading, which is probably more ancient, is במי, *in the water.* This, with the next word, may denote a pool in which the straw was left to putrefy."

"As straw is trodden down in their fields, so will the Lord tread down the Moabites." I do not dislike other interpretations, but consider it to be not improbable that he alludes to the fertility of the soil in which that city was situated. Yet in my version I have not hesitated to follow the common opinion.

11. *And he shall spread out.* The Prophet now explains and confirms the former statement; but he employs a different metaphor, by which he means, that the Lord will spread out his hand to the innermost part of the country of Moab, and not merely to its extremities. Some explain the metaphor thus: "As the arms are stretched out in swimming, so the Lord will chastise the Moabites on all sides." Others think that it expresses the doubling of punishments, as if he had said, "The Lord will not only punish the Moabites, but will again and again take vengeance for the cruelty which they exercised against the children of God."

But we might take another way of explaining that metaphor. Those who swim do not rush forward with the utmost violence, but gently spread out and quickly draw back their arms, and yet they cut and subdue the waters. In like manner, the Lord does not always put forth great strength to cut down the wicked, but without any effort, without the use of armies, without any noise or uproar, he destroys and puts them to flight, however valiant or well prepared for battle they may appear to be. And I approve of this explanation, because it takes nothing from the meaning formerly given, and explains more clearly, that the wicked are often brought to nothing by the hand of God, though he do not openly thunder from heaven. When he says, "*In the midst of it,*" he shews that no part will be hidden in such a manner as not to be overtaken by this vengeance.

12. *And the fortress.* The Prophet now directs his discourse to the country of Moab. It was highly fortified, and was proud of its walls and fortifications; and he affirms that the lofty towers, and other defences, however strong and seemingly impregnable, will be of no avail. The ancients, it is well known, had quite a different method of fortifying from what is practised among us.

He will bring down, lay low, and cast to the ground. The three words here employed, for conveying the meaning more strongly, are not superfluous; for it was necessary to beat down that pride which swelled the hearts of the Moabites, and which, as we formerly saw,[1] made them intolerable. The Prophet therefore mocks at them, "As if the Lord could not cast down that loftiness of which you boast!"

To the dust. The meaning of this clause is as if he had said, "He will not only level it with the ground, but will reduce it *to dust,* so that there will not even be a trace of the ancient ruin." This passage contains an excellent and highly seasonable consolation; for the enemies of the Church in the present day are so haughty, that they mock not only at men, but at God himself, and are so much swelled and puffed up by their power, that they imagine themselves to be invincible; but, in opposition to their bulwarks and defences, we ought to bring forward this declaration of the Prophet, "The Lord will quickly bring down and lay them low." Yet we must patiently endure to see them strong and powerful, till the full time for their destruction arrive.

CHAPTER XXVI.

1. In that day shall this song be sung in the land of Judah; We have a strong city: salvation will *God* appoint *for* walls and bulwarks.
2. Open ye the gates, that the righteous nation which keepeth the truth may enter in.
3. Thou wilt keep *him* in perfect peace, *whose* mind *is* stayed *on thee;* because he trusteth in thee.
4. Trust ye in the Lord for ever: for in the Lord Jehovah *is* everlasting strength.
5. For he bringeth down them that dwell on high; the lofty city, he layeth it low: he layeth it low, *even* to the ground; he bringeth it *even* to the dust.

1. In die illa cantabitur canticum in terra Iuda: Urbs fortitudinis nobis; salutem posuit muros et vallum.
2. Aperite portas, et ingredietur gens justa, custodiens veritates.
3. Cogitatio fixa: custodies pacem, pacem; quoniam in te confisum est.
4. Sperate in Iehova in perpetuum; quia in Iah Iehova fortitudo seculorum.
5. Nam incurvabit incolas sublimitatis, civitatem exaltatam humiliabit; humiliabit, inquam, eam ad terram, deducet ad pulverem.

---
[1] See *Commentary on Isaiah,* vol. i. p. 488.

6. The foot shall tread it down, *even* the feet of the poor, *and* the steps of the needy.

7. The way of the just *is* uprightness: thou, most upright, dost weigh the path of the just.

8. Yea, in the way of thy judgments, O Lord, have we waited for thee; the desire of *our* soul *is* to thy name, and to the remembrance of thee.

9. With my soul have I desired thee in the night; yea, with my spirit within me will I seek thee early: for when thy judgments *are* in the earth, the inhabitants of the world will learn righteousness.

10. Let favour be shewed to the wicked, *yet* will he not learn righteousness: in the land of uprightness will he deal unjustly, and will not behold the majesty of the Lord.

11. Lord, *when* thy hand is lifted up, they will not see: *but* they shall see, and be ashamed for *their* envy at the people; yea, the fire of thine enemies shall devour them.

12. Lord, thou wilt ordain peace for us: for thou also hast wrought all our works in us.

13. O Lord our God, *other* lords besides thee have had dominion over us; *but* by thee only will we make mention of thy name.

14. *They are* dead, they shall not live; *they are* deceased, they shall not rise: therefore hast thou visited and destroyed them, and made all their memory to perish.

15. Thou hast increased the nation, O Lord, thou hast increased the nation: thou art glorified: thou hadst removed *it* far *unto* all the ends of the earth.

16. Lord, in trouble have they visited thee; they poured out a prayer *when* thy chastening *was* upon them.

17. Like as a woman with child, *that* draweth near the time of her delivery, is in pain, *and* crieth out in her pangs; so have we been in thy sight, O Lord.

18. We have been with child, we have been in pain, we have as it

6. Calcabit eam pes; pedes pauperis, gressus inopum.

7. Semita justi rectitudines; rectam viam justi æquabis, (*vel, tu, qui rectus es, viam justi æquabis.*)

8. Etiam in via judiciorum tuorum, Iehova, speravimus in te, ad nomen tuum, et memoriam tui desiderium animæ.

9. Anima mea desideravit te per noctem; quin et spiritu meo intra me te mane (*vel, sedulo*) quæram; nam ex quo fuerint judicia tua in terra, justitiam discent incolæ terræ.

10. Impius gratiam obtinebit, nec discet justitiam; in terra rectorum operum perversè aget, nec videbit magnificentiam Iehovæ.

11. Iehova, utcunque exaltata fuerit manus tua, non videbunt; videbunt et pudefient æmulatione populi; quin et ignis hostium tuorum vorabit eos.

12. Iehova, ordinabis nobis pacem; nam et omnia opera nostra operatus es nobis.

13. Iehova Deus noster, subjugaverunt nos domini præter te; tantum in te recordabimur nominis tui.

14. Mortui non vivent; occisi non resurgent; propterea visitasti, et exterminasti eos; et perdidisti omnem memoriam eorum.

15. Addidisti genti, Iehova; addidisti genti; glorificatus es; dilatasti omnes fines terræ.

16. Iehova, in tribulatione visitaverunt te, effuderunt precationem, dum castigatio tua super eos.

17. Sicut prægnans, quæ ad partum propinquat, dolet, clamat in doloribus suis; sic nos fuimus à facie tua, Iehova.

18. Parturivimus, doluimus, ac si peperissemus ventum, salus non

were brought forth wind; we have not wrought any deliverance in the earth, neither have the inhabitants of the world fallen.

19. Thy dead *men* shall live, *together with* my dead body shall they arise. Awake and sing, ye that dwell in dust: for thy dew *is as* the dew of herbs, and the earth shall cast out the dead.

20. Come, my people, enter thou into thy chambers, and shut thy doors about thee: hide thyself as it were for a little moment, until the indignation be overpast.

21. For, behold, the Lord cometh out of his place to punish the inhabitants of the earth for their iniquity: the earth also shall disclose her blood, and shall no more cover her slain.

est facta terræ, et non ceciderunt incolæ orbis.

19. Vivent mortui tui, cadaver meum resurgent. Evigilate, et cantate, incolæ pulveris. Quoniam ros herbarum ros tuus; et terra mortuos ejiciet, (*vel, terram Gigantum prosternes; vel, terra Gigantes cadere faciet.*)

20. Veni, popule mi, intra in cubicula tua; claude ostia post te: lateas paululum ad momentum, donec transeat indignatio.

21. Nam ecce Iehova egreditur e loco suo, ut visitet iniquitatem habitatoris terræ contra eum. Et discooperiet terra sanguines suos, et non teget amplius super occisis suis.

1. *In that day shall a song be sung.* Here the Prophet begins again to shew that, after the return of the people from captivity, they will be defended by God's power and guardianship, and that under his protection Jerusalem will be as safe as if she had been surrounded by bulwarks, ramparts, a ditch, and a double wall, so that no enemy could find entrance.

It is proper to observe the time when "this song was sung." The Prophet had foretold the calamity that would befall the Church, which was not yet so near at hand, but happened a short time after his death. When the people were led into captivity, they would undoubtedly have despaired, if they had not been encouraged by such promises. That the Jews might cherish a hope that they would be delivered, and might behold life in the midst of death, the Prophet composed for them this song, even before the calamity occurred, that they might be better prepared for enduring it, and might hope for better things. I do not think that it was composed solely that, when they had been delivered, they might give thanks to God, but that even during their captivity, though they were like dead men, (Ezek. xxxvii. 1,) they might strengthen their hearts with this confidence, and might also train up their children in this expectation, and hand down these promises, as it were, to posterity.

We have formerly[1] seen the reason why these and other promises were put by Isaiah into the form of verse. It was, that, having been frequently sung, they might make a deeper impression on their memory. Though they mourned in Babylon, and were almost overwhelmed with sorrow, (hence these sounds, (Psalm cxxxvii. 4,) " How can we sing the Lord's song in a foreign land ?") yet they must have hoped that at a future period, when they should have returned to Judea, they would give thanks to the Lord and sing his praises ; and therefore the Prophet shews to them at a distance the day of deliverance, that they may take courage from the expectation of it.

We have a city of strength. By these words a full restoration of Jerusalem and of the people is promised, because God will not only deliver the captives and gather those that are scattered, but will also preserve them safe, after having brought them back to their country. But not long afterwards believers saw that Jerusalem was destroyed, (2 Kings xxv. 9,) and the Temple thrown down, (2 Chr. xxxvi. 19,) and after their return nothing could meet their eye but hideous ruins ; and all this Isaiah had previously foretold. It was therefore necessary that they should behold from the lofty watch-tower of faith this restoration of Jerusalem.

He hath made salvation to be walls and a bulwark. He now defines what will be "the strength of the city ;" for the " salvation" of God will supply the place of a " wall," towers, ditches, and mounds. As if he had said, " Let other cities rely on their fortifications, God alone will be to us instead of all bulwarks." Some allege that the words may be read, " He hath set a wall and bulwark for salvation ;" and I do not set aside that rendering. But as a more valuable doctrine is contained in the Prophet's words, when nothing is supplied, it serves no good purpose to go far for a forced interpretation ; especially since the true and natural interpretation readily presents itself to the mind, which is, that God's protection is more valuable than all ditches and walls. In

---
[1] See vol. i. p. 162.

like manner, it is also said in the psalm, "Thy mercy is better than life," (Psalm lxiii. 3;) for as David there boasts of enjoying, under God's shadow, greater safety and freedom from care than if he had been fortified by every kind of earthly defence, so Isaiah here says, that there will be good reason for laying aside fear, when God shall have undertaken to guard his people. Now, since this promise extends to the whole course of redemption, we ought to believe that at the present day God is still the guardian of his Church, and therefore, that his power is of more avail than if it had been defended by every kind of military force. Accordingly, if we wish to dwell in safety, we must remain in the Church. Though we have no outward defences, yet let us learn to be satisfied with the Lord's protection, and with his sure salvation, which is better than all bulwarks.

2. *Open ye the gates.* This "song" was undoubtedly despised by many, when it was published by Isaiah; for during his life, the inhabitants of Jerusalem were wicked and ungodly, and the number of good men was exceedingly small. But after his death, when they had been punished for their wickedness, it was in some measure perceived that this prediction had not been uttered in vain. So long as wicked men enjoy prosperity, they have no fear, and do not imagine that they can be brought low. Thus the Jews thought that they would never be driven out of Judea, and carried into captivity, and hoped that they would continue to dwell there. It was therefore necessary to take away from them every pretence for being haughty and insolent; and such is the import of the Prophet's words:

And a righteous nation, which keepeth the truth, shall enter in. "The inhabitants of the restored city shall be unlike the former; for they will maintain righteousness and truth. But at that time this promise also might appear to have failed of its accomplishment; for when they had been driven out of the country and led into captivity, no consolation remained. Accordingly, when the Temple had been destroyed, the city sacked, and all order and government overthrown and destroyed, they might have objected, "Where are those 'gates' which he bids us 'open?' Where are the people who shall 'enter?'" Yet we see that these things were fulfilled, and that nothing was ever foretold which the Lord did not accomplish. We ought, therefore, to keep before our minds those ancient histories, that we may be fortified by their example, and, amidst the deepest adversity to which the Church is reduced, may hope that the Lord will yet raise her up again.

When the Prophet calls the nation "righteous and truthful," he not only, as I mentioned a little before, describes the persons to whom this promise relates, but shews the fruit of the chastisement; for when its pollution shall have been washed away, the holiness and righteousness of the Church shall shine more brightly. At that time wicked men were the majority, good men were very few, and were overpowered by the multitude of those who were of an opposite character. It was therefore necessary that that multitude, which had no fear of God, and no religion, should be taken away, that God might gather his remnant. Thus, it was a compensation for the destruction, that Jerusalem, which had been polluted by the wickedness of her citizens, again was actually devoted to God; for it would not have been enough to regain prosperity, if newness of life had not shone forth in holiness and righteousness.

Now, as the Prophet foretells the grace of God, so he also exhorts the redeemed people to maintain uprightness of life. In short, he threatens that these promises will be of no avail to hypocrites, and that the gates of the city will not be opened for them, but only for the righteous and holy. It is certain that the Church was always like a barn, (Matt. iii. 12,) in which the chaff is mingled with the wheat, or rather, the wheat is overpowered by the chaff; but when the Jews had been brought back into their country, the Church was unquestionably purer than before. Those who returned must have been animated by a good disposition, to undertake a journey so long, and beset by so many annoyances, embarrassments, and dangers; and many others chose rather to remain in captivity than to return, thinking that to dwell in Babylon was a safer and more peaceful condition than to return to Judea. Such persons must have had a seed of piety, which led them to take possession of those promises which were granted to the fathers. Now, though the Church even at that time was stained by many imperfections, still this description was comparatively true; for a large portion of the filth had been swept away, and those who remained had profited in some degree under God's chastisements.

A righteous nation, which keepeth the truth. Some distinguish these terms in this manner, " A nation *righteous* before God, and *upright* before men." But I take the meaning to be more simple; that, after having called the nation "righteous," he shews in what righteousness consists; that is, where there is uprightness of heart, which has nothing feigned or hypocritical, for nothing is more opposite to righteousness than hypocrisy. And though no man ever existed who advanced so far that he could receive the commendation of being perfectly righteous, yet the children of God, who with their whole heart aim at this "truth," may be said to be keepers of it. But perhaps it will rather be thought that, by a figure of speech, one part is taken for the whole, to describe what is true righteousness; that is, when all deceit and all wicked practices have been laid aside, and men act towards each other with sincerity and truth.

If any man wish to make use of this passage for upholding the merits of men, the answer is easy ; for the Prophet does not here describe the cause of salvation, or what men are by nature, but what God makes them by his grace, and what kind of persons he wishes to be members of his Church. Out of wolves he makes sheep, as we have formerly seen.[1] So long as we live here, we are always at a great distance from perfection, and are in continual progress towards it; but the Lord judges of us according to that which he has begun in us, and, having once led us into the way of righteousness, reckons us to be righteous. As soon as he begins to check and reform our hypocrisy, he at once calls us true and upright.

[1] See CALVIN on Isaiah, vol. i. p. 384.

3. *The thought is fixed; thou wilt keep peace, peace.*[1] As the Hebrew word יֵצֶר (*Yĕtzĕr*) signifies both "imagination" or "creature," and "thought," some render it, "By a settled foundation thou wilt keep peace;" as if the Prophet meant, that when men, amidst the convulsions of the world, continue to rest firmly on God, they will always be safe. Others render it, "For the fixed thought thou wilt keep peace;" which amounts to nearly the same thing, that they who have fixed their minds on God alone will at length be happy; for in no other way does God promise that he will be the guardian of his people than when they rely on his grace with settled thoughts, and without change or wavering. Since, however, the sign of the dative case is not added, but the Prophet in a concise manner of expression says, "Fixed or steadfast thought," let my readers judge if it be not more appropriate to view it as referring to God, so as to make the meaning to be, that the peace of the Church is founded on his eternal and unchangeable purpose; for, in order to prevent godly minds from continual wavering, it is of the highest importance to look to the heavenly decree.

It is undoubtedly true that we ought constantly to hope in God, that we may perceive his continual faithfulness in defending us; and believers are always enjoined not to be driven about by any doubt, or uncertainty, or wavering, but firmly to rely on God alone. Yet the meaning which is more easily obtained from this passage, and comes more naturally from the words of the Prophet, is, that it is a fixed and unchangeable decree of God, that all who hope in him shall enjoy eternal peace; for if *fixed thought* means the certainty and steadfastness of the godly, it would be superfluous to assign the reason, which is—

Because he hath trusted in thee. In short, both modes of expression would have been harsh, that "continual peace is prepared for imagination," or "for thought." But it is perfectly appropriate to say that, when we trust in God, he never disappoints our hope, because he has determined to guard us for ever. Hence it follows, that, since the safety

[1] "Thou wilt keep him in perfect peace (Heb. peace, peace) whose mind (or, thought, or, imagination) is stayed on thee."—Eng. Ver.

of the Church does not depend on the state of the world, it is not moved or shaken by the various changes which happen daily; but that, having been founded on the purpose of God, it stands with steady and unshaken firmness, so that it can never fall.

There is also, I think, an implied contrast between God's fixed thought and our wandering imaginations; for at almost every moment there springs up something new which drives our thoughts hither and thither, and there is no change, however slight, that does not produce some doubt. We ought therefore to hold this principle, that we do wrong if we judge of God's unshaken purpose by our fickle imaginations; as we shall elsewhere see, " As far as the heavens are from the earth, so far are my thoughts from your thoughts, O house of Israel." (Isaiah lv. 9.) We ought therefore above all to hold it certain, that our salvation is not liable to change; because the purpose of God is unchangeable.

Thou wilt keep peace, peace. What has now been stated explains the reason of the repetition of the word *peace;* for it denotes uninterrupted continuance for ever. By the word *peace* I understand not only serenity of mind, but every kind of happiness; as if he had said, that the grace of God alone can enable us to live prosperously and happily.

4. *Trust ye in Jehovah for ever.* As to the words, some read in the second clause, " Trust in God, the strong Jehovah of ages;" but as צוּר (*tzūr*) is not always an adjective, but signifies *strength,* I reject that meaning as forced, besides that it has little relation to the subject, as will immediately appear. There is also little ground for the ingenuity of those who infer from this passage the divinity of Christ, as if the Prophet said, that " Jehovah is in Jah;" for the twofold name of God is given for the express purpose of magnifying his power.

He now exhorts the people to rest safely on God, and therefore, after the preceding doctrine, there is now room for exhortation. Besides, it would have been vain to say that our peace is in the hand of God, and that he is our faithful guardian, if we had not been taught and instructed on this subject, and at the same time urged by exhortations. Yet he exhorts us not only to earnest hope, but to perseverance; and this discourse applies properly to believers, who have already learned what it is to trust in the Lord, and who need to be strengthened, because they are still weak, and may often fall, in consequence of the various motives to distrust with which they are called to struggle. He therefore does not enjoin them merely to trust in the Lord, but to remain steadfastly in trust and confidence to the end.

For in Jah Jehovah is the strength of ages.[1] We ought to attend to the reason which is here assigned, namely, that as the power of God, which is the object of faith, is perpetual, so faith ought to be extended so as to be equally perpetual. When the Prophet speaks of the strength and power of God, he does not mean power which is unemployed, but power active and energetic, which is actually exerted on us, and which conducts to the end what he had begun. And this doctrine has a wider application, for it bids us truly believe that we ought to contemplate the nature of God; for, as soon as we turn aside from beholding it, nothing is seen but what is fleeting, and then we immediately faint. Thus ought faith to rise above the world by continual advances; for neither the truth, nor the justice, nor the goodness of God, is temporary and fading, but God continues always to be like himself.

5. *For he will bring down the inhabitants of loftiness.*[2] He now explains more fully what is that power of God of which he spoke. It is that which we ourselves feel, and which is exerted for our benefit. The two clauses are therefore closely connected, that " the proud are laid low by the power of God," and that " the lowly and despised are placed in their room ;" for it would not have yielded full consolation to tell us, in the first place, that " the proud will be laid low," if he had not likewise added, that " the lowly will be exalted," so as to hold dominion over the proud. We therefore acknowledge, that in our own experience God

[1] " For in the Lord Jehovah is (Heb. the Rock of ages) everlasting strength."—Eng. Ver.
[2] " For he bringeth down them that dwell on high."—Eng. Ver.

works powerfully for our salvation, and this yields to us a ground of hope.

Under the word *loftiness* he includes not only bulwarks and fortifications of every kind, (for the ancients were wont to build their cities in lofty places,) but also wealth and magnificence. He therefore means, that no defence can prevent God from casting down the wicked, and laying them low. Towers and bulwarks, indeed, are not displeasing to God; but as it rarely happens that they who are strong and powerful are not proud, so *loftiness* frequently denotes *pride.* Unquestionably he speaks of the wicked, who have abundance of arms, forces, and money, and imagine that they are protected against God himself. He likewise comforts the Jews, as we have formerly said,[1] because the invincible power of Babylon might have terrified them and thrown them into despair, if the Lord had not supported them by this promise: "You have no reason for being terrified at the greatness or strength of Babylon; for she will quickly fall, and will not stand before the power of the Lord."

7. *Straightnesses are the way of the righteous man.* He does not praise the righteousness of the godly, as some have falsely supposed, but shews that, through the blessing of God, they are prosperous and successful during the whole course of their life. Having only stated briefly in the beginning of the verse, that "their ways are plain and smooth," he explains more fully in the second clause, ascribing it to the grace of God that in an open plain, as it were, the righteous proceed in their course, till they reach the goal.

Thou wilt weigh the straight path of the righteous. The word *weigh* contains a metaphor, that God, by applying a balance, as it were, brings to an equal measure those things which in themselves were unequal. The Hebrew word ישר (*yāshār*) is ambiguous, for it may refer either to God or to the path. Accordingly some render it, *Thou, who art upright, will direct the path of the righteous;*[2] and in other

[1] See *Commentary on Isaiah,* vol. i. p. 407.
[2] It will be observed, that this accords very nearly with our English version.—*Ed.*

passages God is called *upright*. (Deut. xxxii. 4; Psalm xxv. 8.) There would also be propriety in the allusion, that the *straightnesses* of which he spoke proceed from God, for he alone is *straight* or *upright*. But the other version appears to be more natural.[1]

He promises in general, that God will take care of the righteous, so as to lead them, as it were, by his hand. When the wicked prosper and the righteous are oppressed, everything in this world appears to be moved by chance; and although Scripture frequently declares and affirms that God takes care of them, (Psalm xxxvii. 5; 1 Peter v. 7,) yet we can scarcely remain steadfast, but waver, when everything that happens to them is unfavourable. Yet it is true that the ways of the righteous are made plain by God's balance, however rough and uneven they may appear to be; and not only so, but he has committed them to the guardianship of his angels, " lest they should be injured, or dash their foot against a stone." (Psalm xci. 11.) But for this, they would easily fall or give way through exhaustion, and would hardly ever make way amidst so many thorns and briers, steep roads, intricate windings, and rough places, did not the Lord lead out and deliver them.

Let us therefore learn to commit ourselves to God, and to follow him as our leader, and we shall be guided in safety. Though snares and artifices, the stratagems of the devil and wicked men, and innumerable dangers, may surround us, we shall always be enabled to escape. We shall feel what the Prophet says here, that our ways, even amidst deep chasms, are made plain, so that there is no obstacle to hinder our progress. And, indeed, experience shews, that if we are not led by God's guidance, we shall not be able to push our way through rugged roads; for so great is our weakness that we shall scarcely advance a single step without stumbling at

---

[1] Bishop Stock's rendering is, " The road of the just is the direct road; rightly the path of the just dost thou make even;" and he makes the following annotations:—" *The direct road* to happiness, the object of all human pursuit. 'Rightly,' or with reason, ' the path of the just dost thou make even,' smooth before him, till he reaches his journey's end. ' The straight road is the short one,' says the divine as well as the geometrician."—*Ed.*

the smallest stone that comes in our way. Satan and wicked men not only entangle and delay us by many perplexities, and not only present to us slight difficulties, but cause us to encounter sometimes high mounds and sometimes deep pits, which even the whole world would be unable to avoid.

It is therefore proper for us to acknowledge how much we need heavenly direction, and to confess with Jeremiah, " I know, O Lord, that the way of man is not in himself; and it is not in man that walketh to direct his steps." (Jer. x. 23.) Let us not be puffed up with vain confidence, as if the result were placed in our own power. Let us not boast, as James warns us, that " we shall do this or that." (James iv. 15.) Such is the manner of rash men, who act as if they could do everything at their own pleasure; while it is not in our power, as Solomon tells us, to direct our tongue so as to give a proper answer. (Prov. xvi. 1.) In vain, therefore, do men form plans, and deliberate, and decide about their ways, if God do not stretch out his hand. But he holds it out to the righteous, and takes peculiar care of them; for, while the providence of God extends to all, and while he supplies the wants of young ravens (Psalm cxlvii. 9) and sparrows, (Matt. x. 29,) and of the smallest animals, yet he has a fatherly kindness towards the godly, and delivers them out of dangers and difficulties.

8. *Yea, in the way of thy judgments.* This verse contains a very beautiful doctrine, without which it might have been thought that the former statements were without foundation. Since he said that God will be our guide during the whole of life, so that we shall neither wander nor stumble, and while, on the other hand, we are pressed by so many straits, we might conclude that those promises have not been actually fulfilled. Accordingly, when he tries our patience, we ought to strive, and yet to trust in him. Here the Prophet gives us this instruction, that, though our eyes are not gratified by an easy and delightful path, and though the road is not made smooth under our feet, but we must toil through many hard passages, still there is room for hope and patience.

By *the way of judgments* he means adversity, and the

word *judgment* often has this meaning in Scripture. But here is a mark which distinguishes the godly from hypocrites; for in prosperity hypocrites bless God, and speak highly of him; but in adversity they murmur, and curse God himself, and plainly shew that they had no confidence in him, and thus judge of God according as their prosperity lasts. The godly, on the other hand, when they are tried by afflictions and calamities, are more and more excited to place confidence.[1]

The particle אף, (*ăph*,) *Even*, is inserted for the sake of emphasis, as if the Prophet had said, that believers are earnest in the worship of God, not only so long as he treats them with gentleness, but that, if he deal harshly with them, still they do not faint, because they are supported by hope. It is therefore the true test of sincere godliness, when not only while God bestows his kindness upon us, but while he withdraws his face, and afflicts us, and gives every sign of severity and displeasure, we place our hope and confidence in him. Let us learn to apply this doctrine to our own use, whenever we are hard pressed by the calamities of the present life; and let us not cease to trust in him, even when our affairs are in the most desperate condition.[2] "Though he slay me," says Job, "I will trust in him;" and David says that, "though he walk amidst the shadow of death, he will trust and not be afraid, because he knows that God is with him." (Job xiii. 15; Psalm xxiii. 4.)

To thy name. The Prophet aims at shewing what is the source of that unwearied earnestness which prevents the godly from sinking under the greatest calamities. It is because they are free from wicked desires and from excessive solicitude, and in their aspirations boldly rise to God. For, in consequence of our disorderly passions and cares holding us bound, as it were, to the earth, our hearts either wander astray, or sink into indolence, so that they do not freely rise to God; and as the essence of God is hidden from us, this makes us more sluggish in seeking him. From his

---

[1] " A se fier en Dieu ;"—" To trust in God."

[2] " Encor que les choses soyent du tout hors d'espoir ;"—" Even when matters are altogether beyond hope."

hidden and incomprehensible essence, therefore, the Prophet draws our attention to the name of God, as if he enjoined us to rest satisfied with that manifestation of it which is found in the word; because there God declares to us, as far as is necessary, his justice, wisdom, and goodness, that is, himself.

And to the remembrance of thee. It is not without good reason also that he has added the word *remembrance;* for it means that the first perception or thought is not enough, but that continual meditation is enjoined; because without its aid all the light of doctrine would immediately vanish away. And indeed the true and sincere knowledge of God inflames us to desire him, and not only so, but also prompts us to desire to make progress, whenever the "remembrance" of it occurs to our minds. The knowledge of God, therefore, comes first; and next, we must be employed in frequent "remembrance;" for it is not enough that we have once obtained knowledge, if love and desire do not grow through constant meditation. Hence, also, we perceive that the knowledge of God is not a dead imagination.

9. *My soul hath desired thee.* This is a stronger expression of the former statement; for, having previously spoken in the person of believers, he had said that the desire of their soul was towards God. He now adds, with regard to himself, *My soul hath desired;* as if he had said, "I have all the faculties of my soul directed towards seeking thy name." The word נפש (*nĕphĕsh*) frequently denotes the vital *Soul;* but as the Prophet here employs two words, I distinguish them so as to make נפש (*nephesh*) mean the desire or will, and רוח (*rūăch*) the intellectual parts; for we know that these are the chief parts of the human soul, namely, the Understanding and the Will, both of which God justly claims for himself. Such is also the import of that passage, "Thou shalt love the Lord thy God with all thy heart, with all thy mind, and with all thy strength." (Deut. vi. 5; Matt. xxii. 37.) The Prophet therefore shews, that all the faculties of his soul are directed to this point, to seek God and embrace him.

Others take רוח, (*rūăch,*) *the Spirit,* to mean the regenerated part; and so by נפש (*něphěsh*) they understand the natural soul, and by רוח, (*rūăch*,) *the Spirit*, they understand the grace of God, which is supernatural. But this cannot be admitted; for the sensual man (ψυχικός) never seeks God; and we perceive how strongly we are opposed by our feelings when we rise to God, and with what difficulty we conquer that aversion. It is unnecessary, therefore, to refute this interpretation, for it is directly contrary to Scripture; and from many similar passages it is sufficiently plain that the Spirit and Soul mean the understanding and the heart.

In the night. By *the night* Scripture often means adversity, which is compared to darkness and gloominess. But I interpret it somewhat differently, as if the Prophet had said, "There is no time so improper or unreasonable that I may not call upon thee or pray to thee." That interpretation differs little from the former, but is rather more general; for night is supposed to be set apart for rest, and at that time all the desires and labours of men[1] cease; and, in short, there is little difference between a sleeping and a dead man. He says, therefore, that at the time which is devoted to rest and repose he rises to seek God, so that no occasion turns him aside;—not that those who are asleep have any active thought, but that sleep itself, if we turn to God, is a part of our course; and although we slumber and are silent, still we praise him by hope and confidence.

In the morning[2] *will I seek thee.* By *the night* the Prophet does not literally mean *sleep;* and this is perfectly evident from the present clause, in which *night* is contrasted with *morning,* which denotes continuance.

The inhabitants of the earth will learn righteousness. We must observe the reason assigned, when he says that "the inhabitants of the earth learn righteousness from the judgments of God," meaning that by chastisements men are taught to fear God.[3] In prosperity they forget him, and

[1] "Tous les desirs et travaux des hommes."
[2] "Early."—(Eng. Ver.) In the marginal reading of the Author's version, he renders it "earnestly."—*Ed.*
[3] "Que les hommes sont enseignez à craindre Dieu par les verges dont il les frappe;"—"That men are taught to fear God by the scourges with which he strikes them."

their eyes are as it were blinded by fatness; they grow wanton and petulant, and do not submit to be under authority; and therefore the Lord restrains their insolence, and teaches them to obey. In short, the Prophet confesses that he and others were trained, by God's chastisements, to yield submission to his authority, and to intrust themselves to his guardianship; because if God do not, with uplifted arm, claim his right to rule, no man of his own accord yields obedience.

10. *The wicked man will obtain favour.*[1] Isaiah contrasts this statement with the former. He had said that the godly, even when they are afflicted, or see others afflicted, still rely on the love of God, and trust in him. But now he declares, on the other hand, that the wicked cannot be brought in any way to love God, though he endeavour, by every sort of kindness, to draw and gain them over; and that, whatever aspect the Lord assume towards them, they do not become better.

This verse appears, at first view, to contradict the former, in which the Prophet said, that the justice of God is acknowledged in the earth, when he executes his judgments, and shews that he is the Judge, and punishes the transgressions of men; while he says here that the wicked cannot in any way be led or persuaded to worship God, and that they are so far from being made better by the chastisements, that even acts of kindness make them worse. The good effect of chastisements certainly does not appear in all; for wicked men do not at all profit by them, as we see in Pharaoh, whom chastisements and scourges rendered more obstinate. (Exod. vii. 13.) But although he spoke indiscriminately about "the inhabitants of the earth," yet he strictly included none but God's elect, with whom indeed even some hypocrites share the profit that is gained; for sometimes, though reluctantly, they are moved by reverence for God, and are restrained by the dread of punishments.[2] But as the Prophet here describes sincere repentance, by " the inhabitants of the earth" he means only the children of God.

[1] "Let favour be shewed to the wicked."—Eng. Ver.
[2] "Et se retiennent en bride de crainte qu'ils ont d'estre fouettez;"—"And are kept in check through fear of being chastised."

Some view it as a question, " Shall favour be shewn to the wicked?" or, " Why should the wicked man obtain favour?" as if the Prophet insinuated that they do not deserve that God should deal gently with them. But I choose rather to explain it thus, " Whatever may be the acts of kindness by which God draws the wicked, they will never learn to act uprightly." The Prophet therefore has limited the statement made in the former verse.

In the land of upright actions he will deal unjustly. This is added in order to shew more strongly the baseness of this ingratitude. It was a sufficiently heinous offence that they abused the acts of God's kindness, and by means of them became more rebellious; but it is their crowning wickedness, that " they deal wickedly in the land" which the Lord had consecrated to himself. What he now says relates to Judea, but may be extended also to other countries in which God is now worshipped; but at that time there was no other country on which Isaiah could bestow that title, for in no other was there any knowledge of God. (Psalm lxxvi. 2.)

Thus he calls Judea "the land of upright actions." I give this interpretation, because, since the Prophet employs נכֹחוֹת (*nekōchōth*) in the feminine gender, the word *upright* cannot apply to men.[1] He therefore bestows this title, because the law was there in full force, (Psalm lxxvi. 1, 2,) and that nation had been peculiarly chosen by God; and it was added, as I have already said, in order to exhibit more strongly the ingratitude of the nation. Some extend it indiscriminately to the whole world, because, wherever we live, God supports us on the condition of our maintaining uprightness. This is too far-fetched; but, since God has now spread abroad his kingdom in every direction, wheresoever men call on his name, that is " the land of upright actions;"[2] so that we are worthy of double condemnation, if, after having been stimulated by benefits so numerous and so great, we do not testify our gratitude by the practice of godliness and by good works.

[1] Accordingly, our English version, instead of "upright actions," uses the term "uprightness," which corresponds to the Author's French version, "la terre de droiture," " the land of uprightness."—*Ed.*

[2] " La terre de droiture;"—." The land of uprightness."

When he adds, that the reprobate *will not behold the majesty of the Lord,* this does not in any degree palliate, but rather doubles their criminality; because it is base and shameful indolence not to observe the glory of God which is openly manifested before our eyes. The wicked are thus rendered the more inexcusable, because, how numerous soever may be the methods by which the Lord makes known his name, still they are blind amidst the clearest light. There is never any lack of testimonies by which the Lord openly manifests his majesty and glory, but, as we have formerly seen,[1] few consider them. God manifests his glory not only by the ordinary works of nature, but likewise by some astonishing miracles and demonstrations, by means of which he gives us abundant instruction about his goodness, wisdom, and justice. Wicked men shut their eyes, and do not observe them, though in trifling matters they are very clear-sighted; and the Prophet now censures them severely for this wickedness.

Others think that it is a threatening against the reprobate, *they shall not behold the majesty of the Lord,* as if they did not deserve to obtain this view of the works of God. Though this is true, yet, as this clause is closely connected with the former, the Prophet continues to censure the indolence of those who do not direct their minds to the works of God, but, on the contrary, become stupid. On this account, we ought to think it the less wonderful that so few repent, though very many demonstrations of the righteousness of God are openly made; for infidelity is always blind to behold the works of God.

11. *O Jehovah, though thy hand is lifted up.* This is an explanation of the former statement; for he brings forward nothing that is new, but shews more clearly what he had formerly stated in a few words. He had already said that the wicked " will not behold the majesty of the Lord;" and now he explains that "majesty" to be that which is visible in the works of God. He does not send us to that hidden majesty which is concealed from us, but leads us to the

---

[1] The Author refers to his exposition of Isaiah v. 12. See *Commentary on Isaiah,* vol. i. p. 176.

works, which he denotes figuratively (μετωνυμικῶς)[1] by the *hand*. Here he again censures the wicked, and shews that they cannot be excused on the plea of ignorance; for, though they perceive nothing, still the hand of God is openly visible; and it is nothing but their blind ingratitude, or rather their voluntary indolence, that hinders them from perceiving it. Some might plead ignorance, and allege that they did not see these works; but the Prophet says that God's hand is "lifted up," and not merely exerted, so that it is not only visible to a few persons, but shines conspicuously.

They shall see and be ashamed. He shews plainly that this " beholding" is different from that of which he formerly spoke, when he said that the wicked " do not see the glory of the Lord;" for they do see, but do not observe or take any notice of it; but at length "they shall see," but too late, and to their great hurt. After having long abused the patience of God, and proved that they were obstinate and rebellious, they will at length be constrained to acknowledge the judgments of God. Thus Cain, (Gen. iv. 13, 14,) Esau, (Gen. xxvii. 38,) and others like them, who too late repented of their crimes, (Heb. xii. 17,) though they fled from the face of God, yet were constrained to see that he was their Judge. Thus, in those who despise him, God frequently produces a feeling of remorse, that he may display his power; but such knowledge is of no avail to them.

In this manner, therefore, the Prophet threatens wicked men, after having accused them of blindness, in order to shew that they have no plea of ignorance; and he forewarns them that the time will come when they shall know with whom they have to do, and that they will then feel that they ought not to despise that heavenly name which they now treat as fabulous, and scorn. They shut their eyes, and act without restraint, and make us a laughing-stock, and do not think that God will be their Judge, but rather turn into ridicule our distresses and afflictions. Thus they look down

---

[1] Μετωνυμία, or *metonymy*, denotes that figure of rhetoric by which one word is exchanged for another on account of a connection of idea, such as, " Moses and the prophets," for their works, or, as in this passage, the " hand" for the works performed by it.—*Ed.*

on us as from a lofty place, and grow more and more hardened; but at length they will understand that the true worshippers of God have not lost their labour.

And shall be ashamed. In order to shew that this beholding of the glory of God is not only of no advantage, but hurtful to them, he says that they shall behold with *shame* the blessing of God towards believers, in which they will have no share.

Through their envy of the people. This tends to shew more strongly the severity of the punishment, that not only will they burn with "envy," when they shall see that the children of God have been delivered from those distresses, and have been exalted to glory, but there will likewise be added another evil, that they will be consumed by the fire of the enemy. By "the envy of the people," therefore, is here meant the indignation which wicked men feel when they compare the lot of godly men with their own.

Yea, the fire of thine enemies shall devour them. By *the fire of the enemies,* he means that "fire" with which God consumes his "enemies." He employs the word "fire" to denote God's vengeance; for here it must not be taken for visible "fire" with which we are burned, nor even for the thunderbolt alone, but is a metaphorical expression for dreadful anguish, as we find that in many other passages Scripture denotes by this term, God's severest vengeance. (Deut. xxxii. 22; Job xx. 26, and xxii. 20.) No language indeed can sufficiently express this anguish. Yet I do not object to the suggestion, that the Prophet alludes to the destruction of Sodom and Gomorrah. (Gen. xix. 24.)

12. *O Jehovah, thou wilt ordain peace for us.* This statement tends to the consolation of the godly, as if he had said, "We shall see what will be the end of the wicked; for thou wilt prevent them from sharing with thy children, and wilt take them away as enemies by fire, but we shall be happy." The Hebrew verb שפת, (*shāphăth,*) which signifies "to ordain," has the same import as the word "establish;" as if he had said, "Thou wilt prepare peace for us in uninterrupted succession:" for the wicked also enjoy peace, but not of long duration; but our peace is fixed on the Lord, and

has a firm foundation, and never comes to an end. By the word *peace* he means perfect happiness. Hence infer, that the children of God alone, who rest on him, are happy; for the life of the wicked, to whatever extent it may abound in pleasures and luxuries, when everything proceeds to their wish, is most miserable. There is therefore no solid foundation for peace but in God's fatherly love.

All our works. By *works* he means all the blessings which the Lord bestows on those who believe in him; as if he had said, "Transactions, business, actions," and everything included in the French phrase *nos affaires,* or in the corresponding English phrase *our affairs.* Accordingly, those who have quoted this passage for the purpose of overturning free-will have not understood the Prophet's meaning. It is undoubtedly true that God alone does what is good in us, and that all the good actions which men perform are from his Spirit. But here the Prophet merely shews that we have obtained from the hand of God all the good things which we enjoy; and hence he infers that his kindness will not cease till we shall have obtained perfect happiness. Now, since God is the author of all good things, we ought chiefly to consider those which hold the first and highest place; for if we ought to acknowledge that we have received from God those things by which we support this life, much more those which belong to the salvation of the soul. If, therefore, we ought to acknowledge his kindness in small matters, how much more ought we to acknowledge it in matters of the greatest importance and value? But there is no reason why we should bring forward this passage against the Papists; for they might easily evade it, and we have a great number of other passages exceedingly conclusive.

In this passage, therefore, the Prophet appears to exhort the godly to testify their gratitude; for he bids them declare the acts of God's kindness, so as to acknowledge that they are indebted to him for everything which they possess; and this contains a profitable doctrine, namely, that from past events and benefits received, the godly reason even as to God's future kindness, and infer that he will also take care of them for the future. Having therefore experienced God's kindness, let us also learn to hope for the future; and since he hath shewn himself to be so kind and bountiful, let us steadfastly fix our hearts in the hope of future assistance.

This example has been followed by all the saints, and in this way they have strengthened their faith. Thus David says, "Thou wilt not despise the work of thy hands." (Psalm cxxxviii. 8.) Paul says, "He who hath begun in us a good work will perform it." (Philip. i. 6.) Jacob also says, "I am less than the compassions and the truth which thou hast shewn to thy servant; but thou saidst, I will surely do thee good." (Gen. xxxii. 10, 12.) God is not like men, to be capable of being wearied by doing good, or exhausted by giving largely; and therefore the more numerous the benefits with which he has loaded us, so much the more ought our faith to be strengthened and increased.

13. *O Lord our God.* This verse contains a complaint of the saints, that they were oppressed by the tyranny of the wicked. This song was composed in order to refresh the hearts of believers, who were to be cruelly banished from that land which was a figure of eternal happiness, that, having been deprived of sacrifices and holy assemblies, and almost of every consolation, crushed by the heavy yoke of the Babylonians, banished from their country, loaded with reproach and sore afflictions, they might direct their groanings to God, in order to seek relief. He speaks, therefore, in the name of believers, who to outward appearance had been rejected by God, and yet did not cease to testify that they were the people of God, and to put their trust in him.

Other lords besides thee have had dominion over us. Not without cause do they complain that they are placed under a different dominion from that of God, for he had received them under his sole guardianship. Hence it follows that, if they had not been estranged from him, they would not have endured so hard a lot as to be exposed to the tyranny and caprice of enemies. It may be thought that the government of all princes is "besides God," or different from that of God, even though they govern in his name. But the Prophet does not speak of those who govern for our benefit, but of those who are opposed to true worship and to holy doctrine. David was indeed a ruler who exercised dominion separate from that of God, but at the same time he was a genuine servant of God for the general advantage of the whole people; and therefore he maintained the true religion, which those rulers wished altogether to overthrow. Most justly did it befall the Jews, that, in consequence of having refused to obey God, who treated them with the greatest kindness, they were subjected to the tyranny of wicked men.

There is an implied contrast between God and the pious kings who governed the people in his name and by his authority, and the tyrants who oppressed them by governing with most unjust laws. This will be made more evident by a similar passage in Ezekiel, "I gave them," says God, "good laws, by which they might live; but because they did not execute my judgments, and despised my statutes, and profaned my Sabbaths, and cast their eyes upon the idols of their fathers, for this reason I gave them statutes that were not good, and judgments by which they could not live." (Ezek. xx. 11, 24, 25.) Since they might formerly, through the blessing of God, have been prosperous and happy, if they had obeyed his word, the prophet Ezekiel threatens that they will be subjected to tyrants who will compel them to obey their cruel enactments, and that without profit or reward. Isaiah now deplores a similar calamity. "When the Lord ruled over us, we could not be satisfied with our lot, and now we are compelled to endure severe tyranny, and suffer the just punishment of our wickedness." The same complaint may be made by believers who live under the Papacy, or who in any way are compelled, by unjust laws, to observe superstition; for they are subject to a government which is "besides God," or different from that of God, and endure bondage worse than barbarous, which not only fetters their bodies, but conducts their souls to torture and slaughter.

In thee only. This clause appears to be contrasted with the former to this effect, "Although irreligious men wish to withdraw from thy dominion, yet we will continue under it; for we are fully convinced that we are thine." But we may draw from it more abundant instruction, that, although the feeling of the flesh pronounces that those who are cruelly oppressed by enemies have been forsaken by God, and laid open to be a prey, yet the Jews do not cease to boast in God when they do not perceive that he is near them; for the mere remembrance of his name supports them, and gently cherishes their hope. There is thus a very emphatic contrast between "the remembrance of the name of God" and the immediate experience of his grace; for steadfastly to embrace God, even though he is absent, is a proof of uncommon excellence.

Others render it, *In thee and in thy name;* but the word *and* is not in the passage. There is here exhibited to us consolation, which is great and highly necessary in these times, when the base ingratitude of men, by shaking off the yoke of God, has brought down upon itself a most cruel tyranny; and we need not wonder if we already see it abound in many places in which men call on the name of God. Yet the godly ought not to faint on this account, provided that they support themselves by this consolation, that God never entirely forsakes those who find abundant consolation in the remembrance of his name. But at the same time it is necessary to testify this faith, so as to choose to die a thousand times rather than depart from God by profaning his name; for when any one goes astray through the fear of men, it is certain that he never has truly tasted the sweetness of the name of God. So long, therefore, as we freely enjoy the word, let us be diligently employed in it, so that, when necessity shall demand it, we may be armed, and that it may not appear that we have indulged at our ease in idle speculation.

14. *The dead shall not live.*[1] The Prophet again speaks of the unhappy end of the wicked, whose prosperity often agitates and vexes us, as we read in the Psalms of David. (Psalm xxxvii. 1, and lxxiii. 3, 17.) That our eyes may not be dazzled by the present appearances of things, he foretells that their end will be very miserable. Others interpret this passage as relating to believers, who appear to die without any hope of a resurrection; but unquestionably he speaks of

---

[1] "(They are) dead, they shall not live."—Eng. Ver.

the reprobate, and this will be still more evident from an opposite statement which he makes at the nineteenth verse. There is a contrast between the resurrection of good men and wicked men,[1] between whom there would be little difference, were it not evident that the latter are sentenced to eternal death, and that the former will receive a blessed and everlasting life: and not only does eternal death await the wicked, but all the sufferings which they endure in this world are the commencement of everlasting destruction; for they cannot be soothed by any consolation, and they feel that God is their enemy.

The slain shall not rise again.[2] The word which we render *slain* is rendered by others *giants;*[3] but as in many passages of Scripture רפאים[4] (*rĕphāīm*) denotes *slain*, so also in this passage it will be more appropriate, for otherwise there would be no contrast. (Psalm lxxxviii. 11; Prov. ii. 18; ix. 18; xxi. 16.)

Therefore hast thou visited and destroyed them. This is added for the sake of explanation; for it assigns the reason why the reprobate perish without hope, namely, because it is the purpose of God to destroy them. In the wrath of God they have nothing to look for but death and ruin.

15. *Thou hast added to the nation.* This verse is explained in various ways. Some think that the Prophet here declares that the godly are not merely oppressed by one kind of affliction, but are plunged, as it were, into the lowest misery, and that they see no end of their distresses. Others explain it simply to mean, "O Lord, thou hast bestowed on thy nation various blessings," and think that the Prophet mentions the blessings which God bestowed on his people in

---

[1] "Des fideles et des infideles;"—"Of believers and unbelievers."

[2] "(They are) deceased, they shall not rise."—Eng. Ver.

[3] Professor Alexander renders רפאים (*rĕphāīm*) *ghosts;* and remarks, "It is here a poetical equivalent to מתים, (*mĕthīm*,) and may be variously rendered shades, shadows, spirits, or the like. The common version (*deceased*) leaves too entirely out of view the figurative character of the expression. *Giants*, on the contrary, is too strong, and could only be employed in this connection in the sense of gigantic shades, or shadows."

[4] As if the reading had been not *rĕphāīm*, but *rōphĕīm*, the Seventy render it ἰατροὶ οὐ μὴ ἀναστήσουσι, "*physicians* shall not rise again."—*Ed.*

various ways, as if he had said, "The people have experienced, not only in one instance, but in innumerable ways, the Lord's kindness and bounty."

But when I attend to what follows, *Thou hast enlarged*, that is, "Thou hast extended thy kingdom, which formerly was confined within narrow limits," I choose rather to view the two statements as closely connected; for the latter clause is an interpretation of the former. Besides, it agrees well with what follows, that *God is glorified;* for we know that in nothing does the glory of God shine more conspicuously than in the increase of the Church. It is as if he had said, "Thou hadst formerly a small people, but thou hast multiplied and increased it;" for the Gentiles were admitted and joined to the Jews on condition that they should be united into one people. Thus the Lord added a vast multitude, for the children of Abraham were called out of all nations.

We must therefore supply, not "Thou hast added blessings," but "Thou hast added a greater number;" and the meaning is, "O Lord, thou wast not satisfied with that small number, and hast gathered for thyself out of all nations an innumerable people." This relates to the kingdom of Christ, which has been spread through the whole world by the preaching of the gospel; and in this passage the Prophet speaks highly of this wide extension, and expresses it by the phrase, *Thou hast enlarged.* This mode of expression is not at variance with the ordinary way of speaking, when an enlargement of a kingdom or of territories is expressed. And yet the Prophet does not mean that the land was enlarged, but that, by spreading the worship of God on all sides, mutual intercourse produced larger space and greater freedom of habitation; for contentions had the effect of narrowing it.[1] We have here a promise of the calling of the Gentiles, which must have greatly comforted godly men during that banishment and miserable dispersion of the Church, so that, although they saw it to be amazingly weakened and diminished, still they were convinced that it would be increased in such a manner that not only would they be

---

[1] "Faisoyent que la demeurance estoit plus estroite et moins libre;"—"Made habitation to be narrower and less free."

innumerable, but foreign and distant nations would be added to them.

16. *O Jehovah, in tribulation they have visited thee.* This might be explained as relating to hypocrites, who never flee to God but when they have been constrained by distresses and afflictions. But since the Lord instructs believers also by chastisements, as the Prophet formerly shewed, (verses 8 and 9,) I choose rather to refer it simply to them, that not only they may know that God has justly punished them, but that the bitterness of the afflictions may likewise be sweetened by the good result of the chastisement, and that they may be better instructed in the fear of the Lord, and may profit more and more every day. Isaiah therefore speaks in the person of the Church, that whenever godly men read this statement, they might acknowledge that amidst their distresses and afflictions they were nearer to God than when they enjoyed prosperity, by means of which almost always (such is the depravity of our nature) we become excessively proud and insolent. On this account we must be curbed and tamed by chastisements; and this thought will soften the harshness of punishments, and make us less ready to shrink from them if we think that they are profitable to us.

They poured out a prayer. The Hebrew word לחש (*lăchăsh*)[1] signifies a *muttering.* This word therefore must not be taken for a prayer pronounced in words,[2] but for that which indicates that the heart is wrung with sore pains, as those who are tortured by extreme anguish can hardly speak or express the feelings of their hearts. It therefore denotes, that calling upon God which is sincere and free from all hypocrisy; such as men will aim at when in sore affliction they utter groans as expressive of intense pain. In prosperity men speak with open mouths; but when they are cast down by adversity, they hardly venture to mutter, and express their feelings with the heart rather than with the tongue. Hence arise those unutterable groans of which

[1] "Que nous avons traduit Prière;"—"Which we have translated Prayer."
[2] "Pour une prière articulee;"—"For an articulated prayer."

Paul speaks. (Rom. viii. 26.) It is in reference to the godly, therefore, that Paul makes this declaration, and to them must this doctrine be limited; for wicked men, although some lamentations are extorted from them by pain, become more hardened and more and more obstinate and rebellious.

17. *As a woman with child.* Here two things ought chiefly to be remarked. First, he compares believers to women in labour, who, we know, endure exquisite pain; and, accordingly, he says that their anguish breaks out into loud and violent cries. Hence we infer that the Prophet does not only speak of that sorrow which arises from outward distresses and annoyances, but rather describes that dreadful anguish by which the hearts of the godly are sorely and dreadfully tormented, when they perceive that God is angry with them, and when their consciences reprove them. There is no bodily pain so acute that it can be compared to that anguish, and this is plainly expressed by the phrase *in thy sight.*

18. *We have as it were brought forth wind.* The second thing to be remarked is, that he goes beyond the limit of the metaphor; for when there is no end to their distresses, the condition of the godly is worse than that of women in labour, who, as soon as they are free from their pains, break out into joy at the sight of what they have brought forth, (John xvi. 21,) and forget all their sorrows. The godly, on the other hand, he tells us, are continually bringing forth; for new troubles and anxieties constantly await them, and when they think that the birth is at hand, they bring forth nothing but anguish. That is what he means by *wind*,[1] namely, that there is no removal or abatement of pain; and immediately afterwards he thus explains it, *Salvations have not been wrought for the land*,[2] that is, we have not beheld any deliverance.

And the inhabitants of the world have not fallen. וּבַל
יִפֹּלוּ (ūbăl yĭppĕlū,) that is, *have not fallen;* for נָפַל (nāphăl)

---

[1] "An obvious phrase for inanity. See below, chap. xxxiii. 11. They who think of a female disorder, termed *empneumatosis*, should remember that it is an uncommon disorder, and that metaphors are not drawn from objects or events of rare occurrence."—*Stock.*

[2] "We have not wrought any deliverance in the earth."—Eng. Ver.

signifies " to fall." Others explain it " to dwell." If we take it in that sense, the meaning will be, " The Jews shall not dwell," that is, they shall not return to their own land ; the inhabitants who possess it shall not perish. But if we follow the ordinary interpretation, we must view it as referring to the wicked. " The inhabitants of the world annoy us, and do not fall ; everything goes on prosperously with them."

So long as the wicked flourish, the children of God must be unhappy, and become like women in labour ; and this condition must be quietly endured by us, if we wish to have a place in the Church of God. It is, indeed, the common lot of all to endure numerous and endless afflictions ; and hence comes the old proverb, " It is happy not to be born, or, when born, immediately to depart out of life." But we see that the godly are visited with sore anguish and very heavy afflictions beyond others ; for in this manner God wishes to try their faith, that, after having laid aside their desires and forsaken the world, they may serve him. Since, therefore, the Lord has a peculiar care of them, he must chastise them, while he permits wicked men to indulge in unbounded licentiousness.

Here we are also reminded that we must endure not merely one or another calamity, and must not imagine that, when we have endured some afflictions, there are none in reserve for us ; for we ought always to be prepared to endure new ones. When God begins to chastise his people, he does not immediately cease. We shall " bring forth wind" when we think that the birth is at hand ; other calamities will break out, and we shall be continually attacked by additional sorrows. We must therefore maintain this warfare so long as it shall please God to employ us in it. Accordingly, we shall follow the ordinary interpretation, *have not fallen ;* for, as the Lord cheers his people, when he manifests to them his salvation and punishes the wicked, so he gives them occasion to groan, so long as they behold their enemies placed in a lofty position and exercising high authority. And if the Lord in this manner tried his Church in former times, we need not wonder that we experience the same thing in the present day.

By *the inhabitants of the world* he means heathens and irreligious men; for he contrasts the rest of the world with Judea, which he formerly called, by way of eminence, (κατ' ἐξοχὴν,) *the land,* and mentions its inhabitants apart.

19. *Thy dead men shall live.* Isaiah continues the same consolation, and addresses his discourse to God, thus shewing that there is nothing better for us than to bring our thoughts to meet in God, whenever we must struggle with temptations; for there is nothing more dangerous than to wander in our thoughts, and to give way to them, since they can do nothing else than toss us up and down and drive us into error. Nothing therefore is safer for us than to betake ourselves to God, on whom alone our hearts can rest; for otherwise we shall meet with many things that tend to shake our faith. The general meaning is, that as God guards believers, though they are like "dead men," yet they "shall live" amidst death itself, or shall rise again after their decease.

But it may be asked, of what time does Isaiah speak? For many interpret this passage as relating to the last resurrection. The Jews refer it to Messiah's kingdom, but they are mistaken in thinking that it is immediately fulfilled by the Messiah's first coming. Christians are also mistaken in limiting it to the last judgment; for the Prophet includes the whole reign of Christ from the beginning to the end, since the hope of living, as we shall immediately see, goes beyond this world. Now, in order to understand more fully the whole of the Prophet's meaning, we ought first to consider that life is promised, not indiscriminately, but only to "God's dead men;" and he speaks of believers who die in the Lord, and whom he protects by his power. We know that "God is the God of the living, and not of the dead." (Matt. xxii. 32.) Accordingly, if we are God's people, we shall undoubtedly live; but in the meantime we must differ in no respect from dead men, for "our life is hidden," (Col. iii. 3,) and we do not yet see those things for which we hope. (Rom. viii. 23, 24.)

So then he speaks simply of the dead, that is, of the condition of believers, who lie in the shadow of death on account of various afflictions which they must continually endure. Hence it is evident, that this must not be limited to the last resurrection; for, on the contrary, we say that the reprobate, even while they live, are dead, because they do not taste God's fatherly kindness, in which life consists, and therefore perish in their brutal stupidity. But believers, by fleeing to God, obtain life in the midst of afflictions, and even in death itself; but because they have in prospect that day of the resurrection, they are not said literally to live till that day when they shall be free from all pain and corruption, and shall obtain perfect life; and, indeed, Paul justly argues, that it would be a subversion of order, were they to enjoy life till the appearance of Christ, who is the source of their life. (Col. iii. 3, 4.)

Thus we have said that Isaiah includes the whole reign of Christ; for, although we begin to receive the fruit of this consolation when we are admitted into the Church, yet we shall not enjoy it fully till that last day of the resurrection is come, when all things shall be most completely restored; and on this account also it is called "the day of restitution." (Acts iii. 21.) The only remedy for soothing the griefs of the godly is, to cast their eyes on the result, by which God distinguishes them from the reprobate. As death naturally destroys all the children of Adam, so all the miseries to which they are liable are forerunners of death, and therefore their life is nothing else than mortality. But because the curse of God, through the kindness of Christ, is abolished, both in the beginning and in the end of death, all who are ingrafted into Christ are justly said to live in dying; for to them all that is evil is the instrument of good. (Rom. viii. 28.) Hence it follows, that out of the depths of death they always come forth conquerors till they are perfectly united to their Head; and therefore, in order that we may be reckoned among "God's dead men," whose life he faithfully guards, we must rise above nature. This is more fully expressed by the word נבלה, (*nĕbēlāh,*) or *dead body.*

My dead body, they shall arise. As if he had said, "The long-continued putrefaction, by which they appear to be consumed, will not hinder the power of God from causing them to rise again entire." So far as relates to the phrase, some render it, "With my dead body." Others explain it, "Who are my dead body." Others supply the particle of comparison, "Like as my dead body ;" but as the meaning is most fully brought out if, without adding or changing anything, we take up simply what the words mean, I choose to view them as standing in immediate connection. At least, this word is inserted for the express purpose that the Prophet may join himself to the whole Church, and thus may reckon himself in the number of "God's dead men" in the hope of the resurrection.[1]

As to his mentioning himself in particular, he does so for the sake of more fully confirming this doctrine; for thus he testifies his sincerity, and shews that this confession is the result of faith, according to that saying, "I believed, therefore I spake." (Psalm cxvi. 10 ; 2 Cor. iv. 13.) But for this, irreligious men might discourse concerning the mercy of God and eternal life, though they had no sincere belief of them ; for even Balaam knew that he spoke what was true, and yet he derived no benefit from his predictions. (Num. xxiii. 19 ; xxiv. 13.) Very differently does the Prophet speak in this passage ; for he professes to belong to the number of those who shall obtain life, and then declares that he willingly endures all the troubles and calamities by which the Lord humbles and slays him, and that he chooses rather to endure them than to flourish along with the wicked. In this manner he testifies, that he does not speak of things unknown, or in which he has no concern, but of those things which he has learned by actual experience ; and shews that his confidence is so great that he willingly ranks himself in the number of those "dead bodies" which, he firmly believes, will be restored to life, and therefore chooses to be a dead body, and to be so reckoned, provided that he be accounted a member of the Church, rather than to enjoy life in a state of separation from the Church.

This gives greater force to his doctrine, and he contrasts it with the statement which he formerly made (verse 14)

---

[1] "Esperant avoir part de leur resurrection ;"—"Hoping to share in their resurrection."

about wicked men, *they shall not live;* for the hope of rising again is taken from them. If it be objected, that resurrection will be common not only to believers but also to the reprobate, the answer is easy; for Isaiah does not speak merely of the resurrection, but of the happiness which believers will enjoy. Wicked men will indeed rise again, but it will be to eternal destruction; and therefore the resurrection will bring ruin to them, while it will bring salvation and glory to believers.

Awake and sing, ye inhabitants of the dust. He gives the name, *inhabitants of the dust,* to believers, who are humbled under the cross and afflictions, and who even during their life keep death constantly before their eyes. It is true that they enjoy God's blessings in this life;[1] but by this metaphor Isaiah declares that their condition is miserable, because they bear the image of death; for "the outward man" must be subdued and weakened, till it utterly decay, "that the inward man may be renewed." (2 Cor. iv. 16.) We must therefore be willing to be humbled, and to lie down in the dust, if we wish to share in this consolation.

Accordingly, he bids the dead men "awake and sing," which appears to be very inconsistent with their condition; for among them there is nothing but mournful silence. (Psalm vi. 5; lxxxviii. 11.) He thus draws a clear distinction between God's elect, whom the corruption of the grave and the "habitation in the dust" will not deprive of that heavenly vigour by which they shall rise again, and the reprobate, who, separated from God the source of life, and from Christ, fade away even while they live, till they are wholly swallowed up by death.

For thy dew is the dew of herbs.[2] He now promises "the

---

[1] "En ceste vie."
[2] Bishop Lowth's rendering is, "For thy dew is as the dew of the dawn." Bishop Stock follows him very closely: "For as the dew of day-light is thy dew," and remarks:—"*A dew of rays,* that is, as I conceive, a dew able to abide the solar rays, or a *steady* dew, in opposition 'to the early dew that passeth away' of Hosea vi. 4, and xiii. 3; which the Prophet there parallels with 'the morning cloud.' The comparison of Isaiah intimates that the refreshing of Israel should not be transient, but lasting." Professor Alexander, with his usual learning and judgment, produces a formidable array of conflicting authorities, but vindicates the usual ren-

dew of herbs," and thus illustrates this doctrine by an elegant and appropriate comparison. We know that *herbs*, and especially those of the meadows, are dried up in winter, so that they appear to be wholly dead, and, to outward appearance, no other judgment could be formed respecting them; yet the roots are concealed beneath, which, when they have imbibed the *dew* at the return of spring, put forth their vigour, so that *herbs* which formerly were dry and withered, grow green again. In this manner will the nation regain its former vigour after having been plentifully watered with the *dew* of the grace of God, though formerly it appeared to be altogether withered and decayed.

Such comparisons, drawn from well-known objects, have great influence in producing conviction. If "herbs" watered by "dew" revive, why shall not we also revive when watered by the grace of God? Why shall not our bodies, though dead and rotten, revive? Does not God take more care of us than of herbs? And is not the power of the Spirit greater than that of "dew?" Paul employs a similar argument in writing to the Corinthians, when he treats of the resurrection; but as he applies his comparison to a different purpose, I think it better to leave it for the present, lest we should confound the two passages. It is enough if we understand the plain meaning of the Prophet.

And the earth shall cast out the dead. Others render the clause in the second person, "Thou wilt lay low the land of giants,"[1] or "Thou wilt lay low the giants on the earth." I do not disapprove of this interpretation, for the words admit of that meaning; but the former appears to agree better

dering. "There are," he says, "two interpretations of ארות, (ōrōth,) both ancient, and supported by high modern authorities. The first gives the word the usual sense of אור, (ōr,) *light;* the other, that of *plants,* which it has in 2 Kings iv. 39. To the former it may be objected, that it leaves the plural form unexplained, that it arbitrarily makes *light* mean *life*, and that it departs from the acknowledged meaning of ארות (ōrōth) in the only other place where it occurs. The second interpretation, on the other hand, assumes but one sense of the word, allows the plural form its proper force, and supposes an obvious and natural allusion to the influence of dew upon the growth of plants. In either case, the reference to the dew is intended to illustrate the vivifying power of God."—*Ed.*

[1] As to the interpretation of רפאים (rĕphāīm) by *giants*, see page 231, note 3.

with the scope of the passage, though it makes little difference as to the substance of the doctrine. These words must relate to that consolation of which we have formerly spoken.

20. *Come, my people.* In this verse he exhorts the children of God to exercise patience, to shut themselves up, and to bear with moderation their troubles and afflictions, and to stand unmoved in opposition to the fierce tempests which seemed likely to overwhelm them. This exhortation was highly necessary; for the lamentable state to which the nation was afterwards reduced was, to outward appearance, very inconsistent with that promise. The Prophet, therefore, when the people are distressed and know not where to go, takes them, as it were, by the hand, and conducts them to some retired spot, where they may hide themselves in safety till the storms and tempests are abated. When he calls them "his own people," he speaks in the name of God, and not in his own.

Enter into thy chamber. By *chamber* he means calmness and composure of mind, by which we encourage and strengthen our hearts with firm belief, and calmly wait for the Lord, as Habakkuk, after having foretold the calamities which were about to fall on the Jews, says that he will go up "to his watch-tower," that is, to a place of safety, in which he may patiently and silently await the result. (Hab. ii. 1.) Isaiah gives a similar injunction in this passage, that the godly, when they see that they are attacked by various storms which they are unable to resist, should shut themselves up in a "chamber," or some place of retirement.

Shut thy doors behind thee. As it would not be enough that we should once be fortified against the fierce attacks of tempests, he bids us also "shut the doors." This relates to steadfastness; as if he enjoined us to take good heed not to leave any chink open for the devil; for he will easily break through and penetrate into our hearts, if the smallest entrance be allowed him.

Hide thyself for a little moment. When he bids them "hide" or "conceal" themselves, he means that it will be a very safe refuge for believers, if they are courageous and patiently wait for the Lord; for though we must boldly and valiantly maintain the contest, yet since the power of God is displayed in our weakness, (2 Cor. xii. 9,) there is nothing better for us than to take refuge, with all humility, under God's wings, that they who tremble may be placed by him in perfect safety.

Again, because we are naturally rash, and hurried away by impatience, when we do not see that the Lord's assistance is immediate, on this account he says that these storms are " momentary."[1] True, we must continually struggle with afflictions, and, so long as we live, must not hope to see an end of them; and, consequently, the afflictions are, in our opinion, of very long duration. But if we compare them with that eternity, in which we shall possess immortal joys, it will be but " a very little moment." In like manner, Paul also shews that the light and momentary afflictions which we endure in this life, ought not to be compared to that weight of eternal glory which we expect to receive. (2 Cor. iv. 17; Rom. viii. 18.)

Till the indignation pass over. By adding this he intends to remove all doubt from believers, as if he promised that they would quickly be delivered. I interpret " indignation" as meaning simply the affliction which proceeds from the Lord's anger. Others refer it to enemies; and I do not object to that interpretation, but prefer the former; for we see that the prophets earnestly teach that no evil happens to us that does not come from the hand of God, who does not inflict them on us without good reason, but when he has been provoked by our iniquities and transgressions. (Amos iii. 6.) We are thus reminded that God's wrath against the Church will not last always, but that, like storms and tempests, it will come to an end, and on this account believers endure it more patiently. Hence it is said elsewhere, (Micah vii. 9,) " I will bear the Lord's wrath;" for they know that he chastises them for their salvation. He introduces the Lord speaking, as I mentioned a little before, that his exhortation may have greater authority.

21. *For, behold, Jehovah cometh out of his place.* It is a

[1] " Que ces tourbillons et orages passent, et sont de petite duree;"— " That these whirlwinds and storms pass away, and are of short duration."

very grievous temptation to the godly, when they see that the wicked exercise their rage without being punished, and that God does not restrain them; for they look upon themselves as forsaken by him. Isaiah therefore meets this temptation, and shews that the Lord, though he keep himself out of view for a time, will in due season gird himself for yielding assistance, and for revenging the injuries which his people have received.

By the word *cometh out*, he describes God stretching out his hand to his people in such a manner as if it had formerly been concealed, because the saints did not perceive his aid. For this reason he says, that the Lord " cometh out," and that he appears in public to yield assistance and exercise judgment, as if he had formerly dwelt like a private person at home. But perhaps there is an allusion to the sanctuary; and this mode of expression occurs frequently in the prophets. (Mic. i. 3; Hab. iii. 13; Zech. xiv. 3.) Though heathen nations despised the ark of the covenant which was laid up in a place little renowned, yet believers knew, by communications of power and grace which they quickly obtained, that it was not in vain or to no purpose that they called on God in that holy place. Yet this principle always holds good, that, though unbelievers ridicule the temple as some mean hut, still God will " come forth" from it at his own time, that the whole world may know that he is the protector of his people.

This meaning is more appropriate than if we were to interpret God's *place* to mean heaven, from which he " cometh forth;" for Isaiah intended to express something more. When the prophets mention heaven, they exhibit to us the majesty and glory of God; but here he refers to our senses, that is, when we see that God, who formerly appeared to remain concealed and to be at rest, gives us assistance. He employs the demonstrative particle הנה, (*hinnēh*,) *behold*, and the participle of the present tense יצא, (*yōtzē*,) *coming forth*, in order to express certainty, and that believers may not be displeased at bridling their feelings till his coming.

To visit the iniquity. This is to the same purport with what goes before; for it would have been inconsistent with the nature of God, who is the judge of the world, to allow the wicked freely to indulge in sin without being punished. The word *visit* contains a well-known metaphor; because, so long as God delays or suspends his judgments, we think that he sees nothing, or that he has turned away his eyes. There is emphasis, also, in the phrase עליו, (*gnālāiv*,) *upon him;* as it is frequently said that the wicked are taken in "the snares which they have laid," (Psalm ix. 16,) or "in the pit which they have digged." (Psalm lvii. 6.) The meaning therefore is, that all the injuries inflicted will fall on the heads of those who were the authors of them.

The earth also shall disclose her blood.[1] This also is highly emphatic. When innocent blood is shed and trodden under foot by wicked men, the earth drinks it up, and as it were receives it into her bosom; and, in the meantime, the death of the godly appears to be forgotten, and to be blotted out for ever from remembrance, so that it shall never come to be beheld even by God himself. Men indeed think so, but God makes a widely different declaration; for he declares, that those murderers will one day be "disclosed" and brought into judgment.

On this account he calls it "the blood, or bloods, of the earth," which the earth has drunk up; and in like manner it is said, that "the earth opened her mouth" when the blood of Abel was shed. (Gen. iv. 11.) In that passage the Lord represents in strong terms the aggravation of that guilt, by saying, that the earth was polluted with that blood, and therefore he shews how "precious in his sight is the death of the saints," (Psalm cxvi. 15,) how great is the care which he takes of them, and that at length he will not permit their death to pass unpunished. The earth itself will take up arms to avenge the murders and cruelties which the godly have endured from tyrants and enemies of the truth; and not a drop of blood has been shed of which they will not have to render an account. We ought therefore to call to remembrance this consolation, and to keep it constantly before our eyes, when the wicked slay, mock, and ridicule us, and inflict upon us every kind of outrage and cruelty.

[1] "Her blood (Heb. bloods)."—Eng. Ver.

God will at length make known that the cry of innocent blood has not been uttered in vain; for he never can forget his own people. (Luke xviii. 7.)

CHAPTER XXVII.

1. In that day the Lord, with his sore, and great, and strong sword, shall punish leviathan the piercing serpent, even leviathan that crooked serpent; and he shall slay the dragon that *is* in the sea.

2. In that day sing ye unto her, A vineyard of red wine.

3. I the Lord do keep it; I will water it every moment: lest *any* hurt it, I will keep it night and day.

4. Fury *is* not in me: who would set the briers *and* thorns against me in battle? I would go through them, I would burn them together.

5. Or let him take hold of my strength, *that* he may make peace with me; *and* he shall make peace with me.

6. He shall cause them that come of Jacob to take root: Israel shall blossom and bud, and fill the face of the world with fruit.

7. Hath he smitten him, as he smote those that smote him? *or* is he slain according to the slaughter of them that are slain by him?

8. In measure, when it shooteth forth, thou wilt debate with it: he stayeth his rough wind in the day of the east wind.

9. By this therefore shall the iniquity of Jacob be purged; and this *is* all the fruit to take away his sin; when he maketh all the stones of the altar as chalk-stones that are beaten in sunder, the groves and images shall not stand up.

10. Yet the defenced city *shall be* desolate, *and* the habitation forsaken, and left like a wilderness: there shall the calf feed, and there shall he lie down, and consume the branches thereof.

1. In die illa visitabit Iehova gladio suo duro, et magno et forti, super Leviathan serpentem penetrantem, et super Leviathan serpentem flexuosum, et occidet draconem qui est in mari.

2. In die illa vineae ruboris canite.

3. Ego Iehova custodio eam, singulis momentis irrigabo eam; ne visitet eam (*hostis,*) noctu et interdiu custodiam ipsam.

4. Furor non est mihi. Quis me committat cum vepre et spina (*aut, veprem spinae*)? Gradiar hostiliter per eam, incendam penitus.

5. An apprehendet robur meum, ut faciat mecum pacem, mecum, inquam, pacem faciat?

6. In posterum radices mittet Iacob; pullulabit et florebit Israel, et implebuntur facies orbis fructu.

7. An juxta plagam percutientis eum percussit eum? An juxta caedem caedentium eum caesus est?

8. In mensura in emissione ejus disceptabis cum ea, etiam cum flaverit vento suo violento in die Euri.

9. Itaque hoc modo expiabitur iniquitas Iacob; et hic omnis fructus, ablatio peccati ejus; cum posuerit cunctos lapides altaris sicut lapides calcis confractos, ut non resurgant luci et imagines.

10. Civitas tamen munita erit solitaria; locus habitatus erit desertus, ac derelictus quasi solitudo. Ibi pascetur vitulus, et ibi accubabit et absumet summitates ejus.

11. When the boughs thereof are withered, they shall be broken off: the women come, *and* set them on fire; for it *is* a people of no understanding: therefore he that made them will not have mercy on them, and he that formed them will shew them no favour.

12. And it shall come to pass in that day, *that* the Lord shall beat off from the channel of the river unto the stream of Egypt, and ye shall be gathered one by one, O ye children of Israel.

13. And it shall come to pass in that day, *that* the great trumpet shall be blown, and they shall come which were ready to perish in the land of Assyria, and the outcasts in the land of Egypt, and shall worship the Lord in the holy mount at Jerusalem.

11. Dum arescet messis ejus, frangent (*vel, secabunt*) eam, mulieres venientes accendent eam; quia non est populus intelligens; propterea non miserebitur ejus factor ejus, et fictor ejus non erit illi propitius.

12. Accidet tamen in die illa, ut excutiat Iehova ab alveo fluminis ad fluvium Ægypti; et vos congregabimini unus ad unum, filii Israel.

13. Accidet etiam die illa, ut clangatur tuba magna; et venient qui perierant in terra Assur, et qui dissipati erant in terra Ægypti; et adorabunt Iehovam in monte sancto, in Ierusalem.

1. *In that day.* Here the Prophet speaks in general of the judgment of God, and thus includes the whole of Satan's kingdom. Having formerly spoken of the vengeance of God to be displayed against tyrants and wicked men who have shed innocent blood, he now proceeds farther, and publishes the proclamation of this vengeance.

On leviathan. The word "leviathan" is variously interpreted; but in general it simply denotes either a large serpent, or whales and sea-fishes, which approach to the character of monsters on account of their huge size.[1] Although this description applies to the king of Egypt, yet under one class he intended also to include the other enemies of the Church. For my own part, I have no doubt that he speaks allegorically of Satan and of his whole kingdom, describing him under the figure of some monstrous animal, and at the same time glancing at the crafty wiles by which he glosses over his mischievous designs. In this manner he

---

[1] "The word *leviathan*, which, from its etymology, appears to mean *contorted, coiled*, is sometimes used to denote particular species, (*e.g.*, the crocodile,) and sometimes as a generic term for huge aquatic animals, or the larger kind of serpents, in which sense the corresponding term תנין (*tănnīn*) is also used. They both appear to be employed in this case to express the indefinite idea of a formidable monster, which is in fact the sense now commonly attached to the word *dragon*."—*Alexander.*

intended to meet many doubts by which we are continually assailed, when God declares that he will assist us, and when we experience, on the other hand, the strength, craft, and deceitfulness of Satan. Wonderful are the stratagems with which he comes prepared for doing mischief, and dreadful the cruelty which he exercises against the children of God. But the Prophet shews that all this will not prevent the Lord from destroying and overthrowing this kingdom. It is indeed certain that this passage does not relate to Satan himself, but to his agents or instruments,[1] by which he governs his kingdom and annoys the Church of God. Now, though this kingdom is defended by innumerable cunning devices, and is astonishingly powerful, yet the Lord will destroy it.

To convince us of this, the Prophet contrasts with it *the Lord's sword, hard, and great, and strong,* by which he will easily slay an enemy that is both strong and crafty. It ought therefore to be observed, that we have continually to do with Satan as with some wild beast, and that the world is the sea in which we sail. We are beset by various wild beasts, which endeavour to upset our ship and sink us to the bottom; and we have no means of defending ourselves and resisting them, if the Lord do not aid us. Accordingly, by this description the Prophet intended to describe the greatness of the danger which threatens us from enemies so powerful and so full of rage and of cunning devices. We should quickly be reduced to the lowest extremity, and should be utterly ruined, did not God oppose and meet them with his invincible power; for by his sword alone can this pernicious kingdom of Satan be destroyed.

But we must observe what he says in the beginning of the verse, *In that day.* It means that Satan is permitted, for some time, to strengthen and defend his kingdom, but that it will at length be destroyed; as Paul also declares, "God will quickly bruise Satan under your feet." (Rom. xvi. 20.) By this promise he shews that the time for war is not yet ended, and that we must fight bravely till that enemy be subdued, who, though he has been a hundred times van-

[1] Ses organes et instrumens.

quished, ceases not to renew the warfare. We must therefore fight with him continually, and must resist the violent attacks which he makes upon us; but, in order that we may not be discouraged, we must keep our eye on that day when his strong arm shall be broken.

On leviathan the piercing serpent, and on leviathan the crooked serpent. The epithets applied to "leviathan" describe, on the one hand, his tricks and wiles, and, on the other hand, his open violence; but at the same time intimate that he is endued with invincible power. Since בריח (*bārīăch*) signifies a crowbar, that word denotes metaphorically the power of piercing, either on account of venomous bites, or on account of open violence. The second name, עקלתון, (*gnăkāllāthōn,*) is derived from the verb עקל, (*gnākăl,*) to bend; and hence it comes to be applied to crooked and tortuous foldings.

2. *Sing to the vineyard of redness.*[1] He now shews that all this will promote the salvation of the Church; for the Lord attends to the interests of his people, whom he has taken under his guardianship and protection. In order, therefore, that the Church may be restored, Satan and all his kingdom shall be utterly destroyed. The object of all the vengeance which God takes on his enemies is to shew that he takes care of the Church; and although in this passage the Prophet does not name the Church, he shews plainly enough that he addresses her in this congratulation.

This figure conveys the meaning even more strongly than if he had spoken expressly of the people of Israel; for since the whole excellence of a vineyard depends partly on the soil in which it is planted, and partly on diligent cultivation, if the Church of God is a vineyard, we infer that its excellence is owing to nothing else than the undeserved favour of God and the uninterrupted continuance of his kindness. The same metaphor expresses also God's astonishing love towards the Church, of which we spoke largely under the fifth chapter.[2]

He calls it *a vineyard of redness,* that is, very excellent;

---

[1] "Chantez à la vigne rouge;"—"Sing to the red vineyard."
[2] See *Commentary on Isaiah,* vol. i. p. 162.

for in Scripture, if we compare various passages, " red wine" denotes excellence. He says that this song may at that time be sung in the Church, and foretells that, though it would in the mean time be reduced to fearful ruin, and would lie desolate and waste, yet that afterwards it will be restored in such a manner as to yield fruit plentifully, and that this will furnish abundant materials for singing.

3. *I Jehovah keep it.* Here the Lord asserts his care and diligence in dressing and guarding the vine, as if he had said, that he left nothing undone that belonged to the duty of a provident and industrious householder. Not only does he testify what he will do, when the time for gladness and congratulation shall arrive, but he relates the blessings which the Jews had already received, that their hope for the future may be increased. Yet we must supply an implied contrast with the intermediate period, during which God appeared to have laid aside all care of it, so that at that time it differed little from a wilderness. This then is the reason why the Lord's vineyard was plundered and laid waste; it was because the Lord forsook it, and gave it up as a prey to the enemy. Hence we infer that our condition will be ruined as soon as the Lord has departed from us; and if he assist, everything will go well.

I will water it every moment. He next mentions two instances of his diligence, that he " will water it every moment," and will defend it against the attacks of robbers and cattle and other annoyances. These are the two things chiefly required in preserving a vineyard, cultivation and protection. Under the word *water* he includes all that is necessary for cultivation, and promises that he will neglect nothing that can carry it forward. But protection must likewise be added; for it will be to no purpose to have cultivated a vineyard with vast toil, if robbers and cattle break in and destroy it. The Lord, therefore, promises that he will grant protection, and will not permit it to suffer damage, that the fruits may ripen well, and may be gathered in due season. Though the vine may suffer many attacks, and though enemies and wild beasts may assail it with great violence, God declares that he will interpose to preserve it unhurt and free from all danger. Moreover, since he names a fixed day for singing this song, let us remember that, if at any time he cease to assist us, we ought not entirely to cast away hope; and therefore, if he permit us to be harassed and plundered for a time, still he will at length shew that he has not cast away all care of us.

4. *Fury is not in me.* This verse contains excellent consolation; for it expresses the incredible warmth of love which the Lord bears towards his people, though they are of a wicked and rebellious disposition. God assumes, as we shall see, the character of a father who is grievously offended, and who, while he is offended at his son, still more pities him, and is naturally inclined to exercise compassion, because the warmth of his love rises above his anger. In short, he shews that he cannot hate his elect so as not to bear fatherly kindness towards them, even while he visits them with very severe punishments.

Scripture represents God to us in various ways. Sometimes it exhibits him as burning with indignation, and having a terrific aspect, and sometimes as shewing nothing but gentleness and mercy; and the reason of this diversity is, that we are not all capable of enjoying his goodness. Thus he is constrained to be perverse towards the perverse, and holy towards the holy, as David describes him. (Psalm xviii. 25.) He shews himself to us what we suffer him to be, for by our rebelliousness we drive him to severity.

Yet here the Prophet does not speak of all indiscriminately, but only of the Church, whose transgressions he chastises, and whose iniquities he punishes, in such a manner as not to lay aside a father's affection. This statement must therefore be limited to the Church, so as to denote the relation between God and his chosen people, to whom he cannot manifest himself otherwise than as a Father, while he burns with rage against the reprobate. Thus we see how great is the consolation that is here given; for if we know that God has called us, we may justly conclude that he is not angry with us, and that, having embraced us with a firm and enduring regard, it is impossible that he shall ever deprive us of it. It is indeed certain that at that time God hated many persons who belonged to that nation; but, with respect to their adoption, he declares that he loved them. Now, the more kindly and tenderly that God loved them, so much the more they who provoked his anger by their wickedness were without excuse. This circumstance is undoubtedly intended to aggravate their guilt, that their wickedness constrains him, in some measure, to change his disposition towards them; for, having formerly spoken of his gentleness, he suddenly exclaims,—

"*Who shall engage me in battle with the brier and thorn?*" or, as some render it, "Who shall set me as a brier and thorn?" Yet it might not be amiss also to read, "Who shall bring against me a brier, that I may meet it as a thorn?" for there is no copulative conjunction between those two words. Yet I willingly adhere to the former opinion, that God wishes to have to deal with thistles or thorns, which he will quickly consume by the fire of his wrath. If any one choose rather to view it as a reproof of those doubts which often arise in us in consequence of unbelief, when we think that God is inflamed with wrath against us, as if he had said, "You are mistaken in comparing me to the brier and thorn," that is, "You ascribe to me a harsh and cruel disposition," let him enjoy his opinion, though I think that it is different from what the Prophet means.[1]

Others think that God assumes the character of a man who is provoking himself to rage; as if he had said, "I do not choose to be any longer so indulgent, or to exercise such forbearance as I have formerly manifested;" but this is so forced, that it does not need a lengthened refutation. It is true, indeed, that since God is gentle and merciful in his nature, and there is nothing that is more foreign to him than harshness or cruelty, he may be said to borrow a nature that does not belong to him.[2] But the interpretation which I have given will of itself be sufficient to refute others, namely, that God complains bitterly that he will as soon

[1] "Si quelqu'un est de cet advis, je n'empesche point qu'il ne le suive;"—"If any one is of that opinion, I do not hinder him from following it."

[2] "Tellement qu'il est contraint comme l'emprunter d'ailleurs quand il se courrouce;"—"So that he is compelled, as it were, to borrow it from another quarter when he is enraged."

fight with thorns as with his vineyard, for when he considers that it is his inheritance, he is compelled to spare it.

I will pass through them in a hostile manner, and utterly consume them. These words confirm my former exposition; for the burning relates to "briers and thorns," and he declares that, if he had to deal with them, he would burn them all up, but that he acts more gently, because it is his vineyard. Hence we infer that, if God is not enraged against us, this must be attributed, not to any merits of men, but to his election, which is of free grace. By these words, מי יתנני, (*mi yittĕnēnī*,) "Who shall give me?" he plainly shews that he has just cause for contending with us, and even for destroying us in a hostile manner, were he not restrained by compassion towards his Church; for we would be as thorns and briers, and would be like wicked men, if the Lord did not separate us from them, that we might not perish along with them. If the phrase במלחמה, (*bămmilhāmāh*,) *in battle*, which we have translated "in a hostile manner," be connected with the question, "Who shall set me?" it will not ill agree with the meaning.[1]

5. *Will she take hold of my strength?* או (*ō*) is frequently a disjunctive conjunction,[2] and therefore this passage is explained as if the particle had been twice used, "*Either* let her take hold of my strength, *or* let her make peace with me;" that is, "If she do not enter into favour with me, she will feel my strength to her great loss." Others explain it somewhat differently, "Who shall take hold of my strength?" that is, "Who shall restrain me?" But I pass by this interpretation, because I consider it to be too far-fetched. I return to that which is more generally received.

It is supposed that God threatens the Jews in order to try all the ways and methods by which they may be brought

[1] That is, instead of making it the beginning of the following sentence, "In battle (or, in a hostile manner) I will pass through them," it might be read as the conclusion of the question, "Who shall engage me with briers and thorns in battle?" And this concluding suggestion accords with our English version.—*Ed*.

[2] "Of the various senses ascribed to או, (*ō*,) such as *unless, oh that if*, &c., the only one justified by usage is the disjunctive sense of *or*."—*Alexander*.

back to the right path; for God is laid under a necessity to urge us in various ways, because we are accustomed to abuse his forbearance and goodness. On this account he frequently threatens to punish us for our ingratitude, as Isaiah appears to do in this passage, "If they do not choose to avail themselves of my kindness, and repent, that they may return to favour with me, they shall feel my strength,[1] which I have hitherto restrained." Yet another meaning equally appropriate might perhaps be drawn from it, as if God exhorted his people to acknowledge his power, which leads them to seek reconciliation; for whence comes that brutish indifference which makes us view without alarm the wrath of God, but because we do not think of his power with due reverence?

But I prefer to view it as a question, as in other passages also it frequently has this meaning.[2] "Will he take hold of my strength, so as to enter into peace with me?" As if a father, anxious and perplexed about his son, were to groan and complain, "Will not this scoundrel[3] allow himself to receive benefit? for I know not how I ought to treat him; he cannot endure severity, and he abuses my goodness. What shall I do? I will banish him till he repent, and then he will feel how great is that fatherly power by which I have hitherto preserved him. Since he does not permit me to exercise forbearance, he must be treated with the utmost rigour of the law. Will he not then perceive how great my power is, that he may come into a state of favour with me?" We shall understand this better, if we consider that the source of all our distresses is, that we are not affected with a sense of the divine goodness; for if we should take into consideration the greatness of the blessings which we have received from God, we should quickly be drawn aside from our iniquities and transgressions, and should desire to return into a state of favour with him.

Here we see what care about our salvation is manifested

[1] "Ils sentiront la pesanteur de ma main;"—"They shall feel the weight of my hand."
[2] That is, our Author is of opinion that אִן (ō) frequently has the same force as the Latin interrogative particle *An.*— *Ed.*
[3] "Ce vaut-neant-ci;"—"This good-for-nothing."

by our Heavenly Father, who wishes us to take hold of his power and goodness, that we may know how great it is, and may partake of it more and more abundantly; for he would wish to deal with us on the same familiar terms as with his children, if we did not prevent him by our wickedness. Since, therefore, we are incapable of enjoying his fatherly tenderness, he must display his strength and majesty, that, being awed by it, and affected by the anticipation of the judgment, we may humbly entreat him, and sincerely implore peace and pardon. Now, this is done when we are truly[1] converted to him; for, so long as we please ourselves, and flatter our vices, we cannot but displease him; and, on the other hand, if we enter into peace with him, we must make war against Satan and sin.

How earnestly God desires to be reconciled to us appears still more clearly from the repetition of the words. He might have said, in a single word, that he is merciful and ready to bestow pardon; and therefore, when he twice repeats the words, *that he may make peace with me*, he declares that willingly and most earnestly he hastens to blot out all our offences.

6. *Afterwards*[2] *shall Jacob put forth roots.* He now gives actual proof of that love of which he formerly spoke. In order to understand it better, we must consider the condition of that ancient people; for it was the heritage of God, not through its own merits, but by the blessing of adoption. The Lord might justly have been offended at that nation to such an extent as to destroy it utterly, and blot out its name; but he refrained from exercising such severity, because he had to deal with his vineyard and heritage. He

---

[1] " Sans feintise ;"—" Without hypocrisy."

[2] Such is CALVIN's translation of באים, (*baīm*,) *coming*, which, occupying a somewhat anomalous position at the beginning of the verse, has perplexed the critics. The usual and best defended supplement is ימי, (*yāmīm*,) *days*, and thus the construction is supposed to be, " In coming days." The French version takes *ci-apres*, " hereafter ;" the Italian has *Ne' giorni a venire*, " In the days to come ;" Luther's version has Es wird dennoch dazu kommen, " Yet it will *come* to this." Our English version connects the word with " Jacob," and makes it to signify " Them that come of Jacob," which is countenanced by the Septuagint, οἱ ἐρχόμενοι τέκνα Ἰακώβ, " They that come, the children of Jacob," but does not appear to have the support of any modern critic or version.—*Ed.*

aimed at nothing more than that the people should acknowledge their guilt and return to his favour; and therefore he followed up the former statement with this promise, lest the people, struck with excessive terror at that power which exhibits the judgments of God and his chastisements and stripes, should grow disheartened; for the contemplation of the judgment of God might throw us into despair, if we did not entertain some hope of being restored. Accordingly, he says—

Jacob shall again put forth roots. " Though I shall lessen my Church, and reduce it to a very small number, yet it shall be restored to its ancient and flourishing condition, so as to fill the whole world; for, after having once been reconciled, it will be more and more increased." This metaphor borrowed from *roots* is highly elegant; for by the wrath of the Lord we are as it were cut off, so that we appear to be completely slain and dead; but to whatever extent the Lord afflicts his Church, he never allows the roots to die, but they are concealed for a time, and at length bring forth their fruit.

And the face of the world shall be filled with fruit. What he now says, that "the world shall be filled with the fruit" of those roots, was accomplished at the coming of Christ, who collected and multiplied the people of God by the gospel; and Israel was united with the Gentiles in one body, so that the distinction which formerly existed between them was removed. (Eph. ii. 14.) Now, we know that the gospel, and all the fruit that sprung from it, proceeded from the Jews. (Isaiah ii. 3; John iv. 22.)

7. *Hath he smitten him?*[1] He confirms the former statement, and shews that, even in chastisements, there are certain and manifest proofs of the goodness and mercy of God; for while the Lord chastises his people, he moderates the severity in such a manner as always to leave some room for compassion. There are various ways of explaining this verse. Some interpret it thus: " Did I smite Israel as his enemies smote him? The Assyrians did not at all spare

---

[1] " Hath he smitten him as he smote (Heb., according to the stroke of) those that smote him?"—Eng. Ver.

him: they acted towards him with the utmost cruelty. But I laid a restraint on my wrath, and did not smite as if I wished to destroy him; and thus I gave abundant evidence that I am not his enemy." But I prefer another and commonly received interpretation, which leads us to understand that a difference between believers and the reprobate is here declared; for God punishes both indiscriminately, but not in the same manner. When he takes vengeance on the reprobate, he gives loose reins to his anger; because he has no other object in view than to destroy them; for they are "vessels of wrath, appointed to destruction," (Rom. ix. 22,) and have no experience of the goodness of God. But when he chastises the godly, he restrains his wrath, and has another and totally different object in view; for he wishes to bring them back to the right path, and to draw them to himself, that provision may be made for their future happiness.

But it may be asked, Why does the Prophet employ a circuitous mode of expression, and say, "according to the stroke of him that smote him?" I answer, he did so, because the Lord often employs the agency of wicked men in chastising us, in order to depress and humble us the more. It is often a very sore temptation to us, when the Lord permits us to be oppressed by the tyranny of wicked men; for we have doubts whether it is because he favours them, or because he deprives us of his assistance, as if he hated us. To meet this doubt, he says that he does indeed permit wicked men to afflict his people, and to exercise their cruelty upon them for a time, but that he will at length punish them for their wickedness more sharply than they punished the godly persons. Yet, if any one choose to adopt the former interpretation, namely, that the Lord will not deal with us as with enemies, I have no objection. Hence arises also that saying, that "it is better to fall into the hands of God than into the hands of men;" for the Lord can never forget his covenant, that he will deal in a gentle and fatherly manner with his Church. (2 Samuel xxiv. 14; 1 Chron. xxi. 13.)

8. *In measure.* This is the second proof of the divine com-

passion towards all the elect, whom he chastises for this purpose, that they may not perish; and, by mitigating the punishments which he inflicts upon them, he pays such regard to their weakness that he never permits them to be oppressed beyond measure. As to the word בסאסאה, (*bĕsăssĕāh,*) *in measure,* all interpreters agree that it denotes moderation; for otherwise we could not bear the hand of the Lord, and would be overwhelmed by it; but he keeps it back, and " is faithful," as Paul says, " not to suffer us to be tempted beyond what we are able to bear." (1 Cor. x. 13.) Thus also Jeremiah prays to the Lord to " chastise him in judgment," that is, with moderation, accommodating the stripes to his weakness. (Jer. x. 24.)

In her shooting forth, בשלחה, (*bĕshăllĕchāch.*) Interpreters are not agreed as to the meaning of this word. Some think that it means, " by engaging them in internal wars with each other," and others, " that God will punish their sins by that sword which they have drawn and put into his hand." But as I cannot approve of either of those interpretations, I pass them by. I approve more highly of those who interpret it, " in her shootings forth," that is, in plants; so as to mean, that in inflicting punishment, the Lord attacks not only their outward circumstances, but also their persons. We know that the Lord's chastisements are various. The more light and moderate are those by which he takes from us only external blessings, which are called " the good things of fortune." So then God punishes believers in such a manner as not only to afflict their persons, but to take from them what is necessary for the support of life, such as corn, wine, oil, and other things of that kind which the earth produces; for שלח (*shălăch*) signifies to " shoot forth," and to " produce."

But I have another exposition which comes nearer to the Prophet's meaning, that *in shooting forth* God contends with the Church, because, though he cuts down the branches and even the trunk, yet his wrath does not extend to the roots, so as to prevent the tree from again shooting forth; for there is always some remaining vigour in the roots, which he never permits to die. And this agrees with what goes before, when he promised (verse 6) that Israel would bring forth " fruit." This explains what he formerly said, *in measure;* namely, that he will not pull up the root; for the Lord cuts down what appears outwardly, such as branches and leaves, but defends the root and preserves it safe. But, on the other hand, he tears up the reprobate by the roots, and cuts them down in such a manner that they can never rise again.

Though he blow with his violent wind. Some translate it, " he blew with his wind," but I think that the meaning is made more clear by saying, " though he blow." He continues the metaphor, by which he had alluded to herbs and plants, which a violent wind causes to wither, but only in appearance ; for the root is always safe. Thus though the Lord attacks believers with great violence, and takes away all their beauty and comeliness, so that they appear to be entirely slain, yet he usually preserves in them some internal vigour.

In the day of the east wind. When the Prophet spoke of " the day of the east wind," he had his eye on the situation of Judea, to which, as we learn from other passages, that easterly wind was injurious. We know that each country has its own particular wind that is injurious to it ; for in some countries the north wind, in others the south wind, and in others the east or equinoctial wind, occasions great damage, throwing down the corn, scorching or spoiling all the fruits, blasting the trees, and scarcely leaving anything in the fields uninjured. By " the east wind" in this passage, is supposed to be meant " the equinoctial wind," which in many countries is very destructive.

9. *Therefore in this manner shall the iniquity of Jacob be expiated.* After having spoken of the chastisement of the people, he begins to state more clearly that the Lord promotes the interests of his people by these chastisements, so that they derive benefit from them. He had mentioned this formerly, but now he explains it more fully, that all the chastisements which God inflicts will tend to wash away the sins of his people, that thus they may be reconciled to God.

A question arises, Are our sins expiated by the stripes

with which God chastises us? For if it be so, it follows that we must satisfy God for our sins, as the Papists teach. These two things are closely connected. If God punish us for our sins in order to expiate them, when punishments are not inflicted, satisfactions must come in their room. But this difficulty will be easily removed, if we consider that here the Prophet does not handle the question, whether we deserve the forgiveness of sins on account of our works, or whether the punishments which God inflicts on us may be regarded as making amends for them. He simply shews that chastisements are the remedies by which God cures our diseases, because we are wont to abuse his goodness and patience. God must therefore bring us to acknowledgment of our sins, and to patience; and thus the punishments which he inflicts as chastisements for our sins are remedies, because our desires may be said to be consumed by them as by fire,[1] to which also Scripture frequently compares them. (Psalm lxvi. 10; lxxxix. 46.) In no respect can they yield satisfaction, but men are prepared by them for repentance. Hence he shews, therefore, that the godly have no reason for exclaiming against God's chastisements, and that they ought to acknowledge, on the contrary, that their salvation is thus promoted, because otherwise they would not acknowledge the grace of God. If any person wish to have a short reply, we may state it in a single word, that chastisements expiate our offences indirectly, but not directly, because they lead us to repentance, which again, in its turn, brings us to obtain the forgiveness of sins.

And this is all the fruit, the taking away of his sin. Some render it in the genitive case, "the fruit *of* the taking away of his sin;" but I prefer to read it in the nominative case. כֹּל, (*chōl,*) *all*, frequently means, "great and abundant;" and therefore it denotes the plentiful fruit by which the chastisements will be followed. In a word, he intends to commend to us God's chastisements on the ground of their usefulness, that the godly may bear them with calmness and moderation, when they know that by means of them they

---

[1] "Ne plus ne moins que si le feu y avoit passé;"—"In exactly the same manner as if fire had passed on them."

are purged and prepared for salvation.[1] And immediately afterwards the Prophet explains his meaning more clearly by speaking of abolishing superstitions. So long as the people of Israel enjoyed prosperity, they did not think of repentance; for it is natural to men that prosperity should make them insolent and harden them more and more. He therefore shews how, in chastising his people, God also takes away their sin, because, having formerly indulged in wickedness and proceeded to greater lengths in sinning in consequence of his goodness and forbearance, they shall now know that they were justly punished, and shall change their life and conduct.

When he shall have made all the stones of the altar. Here Isaiah, by a figure of speech, exhibits a single class, so as to explain the whole by means of a part, and describes in general terms the removal of idolatry and superstitions; for he does not speak of the *altar* which was consecrated to God, but of that which they had erected to their idols. Thus, when the stones of it shall have been broken, and the idols thrown down and destroyed, so that no trace of superstition shall be seen, the iniquity of the people shall at the same time be removed.

Hence it ought to be remarked, first, that we ought not to expect pardon from the Lord, unless we likewise repent of our sins; for whosoever flatters himself must be the object of the anger of God,[2] whom he does not cease to provoke, and our iniquity is taken away only when we are moved by a true feeling of repentance. Secondly, it ought to be observed, that though repentance is an inward feeling of the heart, yet it brings forth its fruits before men. In vain do we profess that we fear God, if we do not give evidence of it by outward works; for the root cannot be separated from its fruits. Thirdly, it ought to be inferred, that idolatry is chiefly mentioned here, because it is the source of all evils. So long as the pure worship of God and the true religion are maintained, there is also room for the

[1] " Et mis en chemin de salut ;"—" And led into the way of salvation."
[2] " Quiconque se flatte en son ordure, il attirera sur sa teste infailliblement l'ire de Dieu;"—" Whosoever flatters himself in his pollution will infallibly draw down on his head the wrath of God."

duties of brotherly kindness, which necessarily flow from it; but when we forsake God, he permits us also to fall into every kind of vices. And this is the reason why, under the name of idolatry, he includes likewise other acts of wickedness. Besides, we see that he condemns not only statues and images, but everything that had been invented by the Jews contrary to the injunction of the law; and hence it follows that he sets aside every kind of false worship.

That groves and images may never rise again. By adding this, he shews how strongly God abhors idolatry, the remembrance of which he wishes to be completely blotted out, so that not even a trace of it shall henceforth be seen. Yet the Prophet intended to express something more, namely, that our repentance ought to be of such a kind that we shall steadfastly persevere in it; for we will not say that it is true repentance, if any one, through a sudden impulse of feeling, shall put down superstitions, and afterwards shall gradually allow them to spring up and bud forth; as we see to be the case with many who at first burn with some appearance of zeal, and afterwards grow cold. But here the Prophet describes such steadfastness that they who have once laid aside their filth and pollution maintain their purity to the end.

10. *Yet the defenced city shall be desolate.* Here the copulative ו (*vau*) is generally supposed to mean *for*, and some take it for *otherwise*. There will thus be a twofold interpretation; for if we translate it *because*, the Prophet will assign a reason for the former statement, but that exposition is rejected by the context, and is altogether absurd. With greater plausibility it is taken for *otherwise;* for this threatening might be appropriately introduced, " If you do not repent, you see what awaits you, the defenced city shall be like a wilderness." But I consider that exposition to be a departure from the natural meaning, and therefore I choose rather to take it as signifying *nevertheless* or *yet*.

The Prophet means that Jerusalem and the other cities of Judea must " nevertheless" be destroyed, and that, although the Lord wishes to spare his people, it is impossible for them to be preserved. Godly men would have grown disheartened, when they saw that holy city overthrown and the temple demolished; but from these predictions they learned that God would have abundance of methods for preserving the Church, and were supported by that consolation. So then the Prophet intended to meet this very sore temptation; and hence also we learn that we ought never to lose courage, though we suffer every hardship, and though the Lord treat us with the utmost severity. Although this threatening extends to the whole of Judea, yet I think it probable that it relates chiefly to Jerusalem, which was the metropolis of the nation.

There shall the calf feed. This metaphor is frequently employed by the prophets when they speak of the desolation of any city; for they immediately add, that it will be a place for pasture. Here we ought to take into account the judgment of God, which places *calves* and brute beasts in the room of the Jews who had profaned the land by their crimes. Having been adopted by God to be his children, with good reason ought they to have obeyed so kind a Father; but since they had shaken off the yoke and given themselves up to wickedness, it was the just reward of their ingratitude, that the land should be possessed by better inhabitants, taken not from the human race but from brute beasts.

And shall browse on its tops.[1] What he says about the "tops" tends to shew more strongly the desolation; as if he had said that there will be such abundance of grass that the calves will crop none but the tender parts. סעיף (*sāīph*) signifies also *branch;* but as branches naturally rise high, I take it here for *summit* or *top.* It might also be thought that there is an allusion to the beauty of the city, and that as its houses formerly were lofty and magnificent, when these have been thrown down, nothing will be seen in it but herbs and leaves, the "tops" of which the calves which enjoy abundant pasture will eat in disdain.

11. *When its harvest shall wither.*[2] Some think that the Prophet has in his eye the metaphor of a vineyard, which he employed at the beginning of the chapter, and therefore

---

[1] "And consume the branches thereof."—Eng. Ver.
[2] "When the boughs thereof are withered."—Eng. Ver.

they translate קָצִיר, (kātzīr,) *branches.* The word is certainly ambiguous; but as קָצִיר (kātzīr) means also a *harvest,* and as the metaphor of a *harvest* is more appropriate, I prefer to take it in that sense. Nor do I translate it, "When the harvest shall be withered," but "When the harvest shall wither." In this passage *wither* means nothing else than to approach to maturity. Before the harvest of the land is ripe, it shall be cut down; as if he had said, "The Lord will take away from thee the produce which thou thoughtest to be already prepared for thee and to be in thy hand."

The women coming shall burn it. When he says that "women shall come," he means that God will have no need of robust soldiers to execute his judgment, and that he will only make use of the agency of women. This exhibits in a still stronger light the disgracefulness of the punishment, for he threatens that the calamity shall also be accompanied by disgrace; because it is more shameful and humiliating to be plundered by "women," who are unused to war, than by men.

For it is a people of no understanding. At length he assigns the reason of so heavy a calamity. At first sight it might appear to be excessively harsh that the Lord should permit the people whom he had chosen to be wretchedly tormented and scattered, and not to render them any assistance; for it is inconsistent with his kindness and fatherly love which he bears towards them. But the Prophet shews that God had good reason for punishing the Jews with such severity; for they were destitute of knowledge and sound "understanding."

Nor is it without reason that he pronounces ignorance to have been the source of all evils; for since "the fear of God is the beginning of wisdom," (Prov. i. 7; Psalm cxi. 10,) they who despise God and obey the wicked passions of their flesh are justly condemned by the Spirit of God as blind and mad. And yet such ignorance does not at all excuse us or lessen the guilt of our wickedness; for they who sin are conscious of their sinfulness, though they are blinded by their lust. Wickedness and ignorance are therefore closely connected, but the connection is of such a nature that ignorance proceeds from the sinful disposition of the mind.

Hence it comes that " ignorance," or " ignorances," is the general name given by the Hebrew writers to every kind of sin, and hence also that saying of Moses, " O that they were wise and understood!" (Deut. xxxii. 29.) Any man will easily perceive this, if he consider how great is the power of evil passions to trouble us ; for when we have been deprived of the light of doctrine, and are void of understanding, the devil drives us as it were to madness, so that we do not dread the arm of God, and have no respect for his holy word.

Therefore their Maker will not have compassion on them. For the purpose of still heightening their terror, he at length takes away all hope of pardon ; for even if a remnant was preserved, the wrath of God did not on that account cease to rage against the multitude at large. The Prophet here calls God the *Maker* and *Creator* of Israel, not in the same manner that he is called the Creator of heaven and earth, (Gen. i. 1,) but inasmuch as he has formed his Church by the Spirit of regeneration. In like manner Paul also declares, that in that sense we are αὐτοῦ ποίημα, *his workmanship*, (Eph. ii. 10,) as we have already stated in the exposition of another passage.[1] (Isaiah xix. 25.) Isaiah made this statement, in order to exhibit more strongly the ingratitude of the people, and to shew how justly they deserve to be punished, since, after having been formed and preserved by God, they treated him with dishonour and contempt.

12. *And yet it shall come to pass on that day.* He softens the harshness of the former statement ; for it was a dreadful judgment of God, that the people were deprived of all hope of mercy and favour. The particle ו (*vau*) must therefore be explained as in the tenth verse, " *Nevertheless,* or, *and yet it shall come to pass on that day.*"

That Jehovah shall thrash. The Prophet speaks metaphorically ; for he compares the gathering of the Church to the " thrashing" of wheat, by which the grain is separated from the chaff. The meaning of the metaphor is, that the people were so completely overwhelmed by that captivity that they appeared to be nothing else than grain concealed

[1] See p. 83.

or scattered here and there under the chaff. It was necessary that the Lord should "thrash," as with a fan, what was concealed amidst the confused mass ; so that this gathering was justly compared to "thrashing."

From the channel of the river to the river of Egypt. By this he means Euphrates and the Nile ; for the people were banished, partly into Chaldea or Assyria, and partly into Egypt. Many fled into Egypt, while others were carried captive into Babylon. He therefore foretells that the Lord will gather his people, not only from Chaldea, and from the whole of Mesopotamia, but also from Egypt.

And you shall be gathered one by one. לאחד אחד, (*lĕăhăd ĕhād,*) which we have translated "one by one," is translated by others "each out of each place ;" but this is an excessively forced exposition, and the exposition which I have stated appears to me more simple. Yet there are two senses which the words will bear ; either, "I will gather you into one body," or "I will gather you, not in companies nor in great numbers, but one after another," as usually happens when men who had wandered and been scattered are gathered ; for they do not all assemble suddenly, but approach to each other by degrees. The Jews were scattered and dispersed in such a manner that they could not easily be gathered together and formed into one body ; and therefore he shews that this dispersion will not prevent them from being restored to a flourishing condition. This was afterwards fulfilled ; for the Jews were gathered and brought back, not by a multitude of horsemen or chariots, not by human forces, or swords, or arms, as Hosea states, but solely by the power of God. (Hosea i. 7.)

13. *It shall also come to pass in that day.* This is the explanation of the former verse. He speaks metaphorically, and shews that so great will be the power of God, that he will easily bring back his people. As kings assemble large armies by the sound of a trumpet, so he shews that it will be easy for the Lord to gather his people, on whom prophecy had not less efficacy than the trumpet by which soldiers are mustered.

And they shall come who were perishing. He calls them

perishing, because they were miserably scattered, and appeared to be very near destruction, without any hope of being restored. The enemies, while their monarchy lasted, would never have permitted their captives to return, nor had they led them into banishment in a distant country with any other design than that of gradually casting into oblivion the name of Israel.

And who had been scattered in the land of Egypt. What he adds about Egypt contains a more remarkable testimony of pardon, namely, that those who fled into Egypt, though they did not deserve this favour, shall be gathered. They had offended God in two respects, as Jeremiah plainly shews; first, because they were obstinate and rebellious; and, secondly, because they had refused to obey the revelation, (Jer. xxviii. 10, 11;) for they ought to have submitted to the yoke of the Babylonians rather than flee into Egypt in opposition to the command of God.

And shall worship Jehovah in the holy mountain. At length, he describes the result of their deliverance, that the Jews, having returned from captivity into their country, may again worship God their deliverer in a pure and lawful manner. By the *mountain* he means the temple and sacrifices. This was indeed accomplished under Darius, but the Prophet undoubtedly intended to extend this prophecy farther; for that restoration was a kind of dark foreshadowing of the deliverance which they obtained through Christ, at whose coming the sound of the spiritual trumpet, that is, of the gospel, was heard, not only in Assyria or Egypt, but in the most distant parts of the world. Then were the people of God gathered, to flow together to Mount Zion, that is, to the Church. We know that this mode of expression is frequently employed by the prophets when they intend to denote the true worship of God, and harmony in religion and godliness; for they accommodated themselves to the usages of the people that they might be better understood. We know also that the gospel proceeded out of Zion; but on this subject we have spoken fully at the second chapter.[1]

---

[1] See *Commentary on Isaiah,* vol. i. p. 96.

CHAPTER XXVIII.

1. Woe to the crown of pride, to the drunkards of Ephraim, whose glorious beauty *is* a fading flower, which *are* on the head of the fat valleys of them that are overcome with wine!

2. Behold, the Lord hath a mighty and strong one, *which,* as a tempest of hail, *and* a destroying storm, as a flood of mighty waters overflowing, shall cast down to the earth with the hand.

3. The crown of pride, the drunkards of Ephraim, shall be trodden under feet:

4. And the glorious beauty, which *is* on the head of the fat valley, shall be a fading flower, *and* as the hasty fruit before the summer; which *when* he that looketh upon it seeth, while it is yet in his hand he eateth it up.

5. In that day shall the Lord of hosts be for a crown of glory, and for a diadem of beauty, unto the residue of his people,

6. And for a spirit of judgment to him that sitteth in judgment, and for strength to them that turn the battle to the gate.

7. But they also have erred through wine, and through strong drink are out of the way: the priest and the prophet have erred through strong drink, they are swallowed up of wine, they are out of the way through strong drink; they err in vision, they stumble *in* judgment.

8. For all tables are full of vomit *and* filthiness, so *that there is* no place *clean.*

9. Whom shall he teach knowledge? and whom shall he make to understand doctrine? *them that are* weaned from the milk, *and* drawn from the breasts.

10. For precept *must be* upon precept, precept upon precept; line upon line, line upon line; here a little, *and* there a little:

1. Væ coronæ superbiæ temulentorum Ephraim; quia decor gloriæ ejus erit flos deciduus, quæ est super caput vallis pinguium, oppressorum a vino.

2. Ecce durus et fortis Domino, sicut inundatio grandinis, turbo subvertens; sicut impetus aquarum vehementium inundantium, dejiciens in manu ad terram.

3. Pedibus conculcabitur corona superbiæ temulentorum Ephraim.

4. Et erit flos deciduus decor gloriæ ejus, quæ est super caput vallis pinguium, quasi fructus præcox ante æstivos, quem qui viderit, aspiciens eum dum adhuc in manu est, devorat.

5. In illa die erit Iehova exercituum in corona gloriæ, et diadema decoris reliquiis populi sui,

6. Et in spiritum judicii sedenti super tribunal, et in fortitudinem propulsantibus prœlium ad portam.

7. At isti quoque præ vino errarunt, præ sicera hallucinati sunt. Sacerdos et propheta errarunt præ sicera, absorpti sunt a vino; hallucinati sunt præ sicera, errarunt in visione, impegerunt in judicio.

8. Quoniam omnes mensæ plenæ sunt vomitu stercoreo, ut locus non vacet.

9. Quem docebit scientiam, et quem intelligere faciet doctrinam? Abductos a lacte, abstractos ab uberibus?

10. Quoniam præceptum ad præceptum, præceptum ad præceptum; instructio ad instructionem, instructio ad instructionem; paululum ibi, paululum ibi.

11. For with stammering lips, and another tongue, will he speak to this people.

12. To whom he said, This *is* the rest *wherewith* ye may cause the weary to rest; and this *is* the refreshing: yet they would not hear.

13. But the word of the Lord was unto them precept upon precept, precept upon precept; line upon line, line upon line; here a little, *and* there a little; that they might go, and fall backward, and be broken, and snared, and taken.

14. Wherefore hear the word of the Lord, ye scornful men, that rule this people which *is* in Jerusalem:

15. Because ye have said, We have made a covenant with death, and with hell are we at agreement; when the overflowing scourge shall pass through, it shall not come unto us: for we have made lies our refuge, and under falsehood have we hid ourselves.

16. Therefore thus saith the Lord God, Behold, I lay in Zion for a foundation a stone, a tried stone, a precious corner-*stone*, a sure foundation: he that believeth shall not make haste.

17. Judgment also will I lay to the line, and righteousness to the plummet; and the hail shall sweep away the refuge of lies, and the waters shall overflow the hiding-place.

18. And your covenant with death shall be disannulled, and your agreement with hell shall not stand; when the overflowing scourge shall pass through, then ye shall be trodden down by it.

19. From the time that it goeth forth it shall take you: for morning by morning shall it pass over, by day and by night; and it shall be a vexation only *to* understand the report.

20. For the bed is shorter than that *a man* can stretch himself *on it;* and the covering narrower than that he can wrap himself *in it.*

21. For the Lord shall rise up as *in* mount Perazim, he shall be wroth

11. Quoniam balbis labiis et lingua exotica loquetur ad populum istum.

12. Quoniam illis dixit, Hæc est requies; requiescere facite lassum, et hoc refrigerium; et noluerunt audire.

13. Erit igitur illis verbum Iehovæ regula ad regulam, regula ad regulam; instructio ad instructionem, instructio ad instructionem; paululum ibi, paululum ibi; propterea ibunt, et corruent retrorsum, conterentur, irretientur et capientur.

14. Propterea audite verbum Iehovæ, viri illusores, qui dominamini populo huic, qui est in Ierusalem.

15. Quia dixistis, Percussimus fœdus cum morte, et cum inferno fecimus pactum; flagellum inundans cum transierit, non veniet ad nos; quia posuimus mendacium refugium nostrum, et sub vanitate sumus absconditi.

16. Quare sic dicit Dominus Iehova: Ecce ego ponam in Sion lapidem, lapidem probationis, angulum pretiosum, fundamentum solidum. Qui credit non festinabit.

17. Et ponam judicium ad regulam, et justitiam ad mensuram (*vel, trutinam.*) Everret grando fiduciam mendacii, et latibulum aquæ inundabunt.

18. Et abolebitur pactum cum morte; visio vestra cum inferno non stabit, flagellum inundans cum transierit, tunc eritis ei in conculcationem.

19. Ex quo transierit, rapiet vos utique mane quotidie, transibit interdiu et noctu. Et erit ut terror (*vel, commotio*) duntaxat intelligere faciat auditum.

20. Quoniam contractus est lectus, ut non sufficiat; angusta erit stragula colligendo.

21. Quoniam sicut in monte Perazim stabit Iehova, et sicut in valle

as *in* the valley of Gibeon, that he may do his work, his strange work; and bring to pass his act, his strange act.	Gibeon, irascetur (*vel, tumultuabitur*) ad faciendum opus suum, alienum opus suum; ad designandum facinus suum, alienum facinus suum.
22. Now therefore be ye not mockers, lest your bands be made strong; for I have heard from the Lord God of hosts a consumption, even determined upon the whole earth.	22. Nunc itaque ne sitis illusores; ne forte constringantur vincula vestra. Quoniam consumptionem et finitionem audivi a Domino Iehova exercituum super universam terram.
23. Give ye ear, and hear my voice; hearken, and hear my speech.	23. Auscultate, et audite vocem meam; advertite et audite sermonem meum.
24. Doth the plowman plow all day to sow? doth he open and break the clods of his ground?	24. An quotidie arat arator, ut seminet? aperit et confringit glebas agri sui?
25. When he hath made plain the face thereof, doth he not cast abroad the fitches, and scatter the cummin, and cast in the principal wheat, and the appointed barley, and the rye, in their place?	25. Annon cum æquaverit faciem ejus, tunc sparget viciam, seret cyminum, et ponet triticum in mensura, hordeum demensum, et speltam suo modo?
26. For his God doth instruct him to discretion, *and* doth teach him.	26. Docet eum rectitudinem Deus suus, et instituit eum.
27. For the fitches are not thrashed with a thrashing-instrument, neither is a cart-wheel turned about upon the cummin; but the fitches are beaten out with a staff, and the cummin with a rod.	27. Certe non triturabitur vicia tabula dentata, nec rota plaustri super cyminum circumferetur; quia baculo excutitur vicia, et cyminum virga.
28. Bread-*corn* is bruised; because he will not ever be thrashing it, nor break *it with* the wheel of his cart, nor bruise it *with* his horsemen.	28. Triticum licet trituretur, non in perpetuum triturat ipsum, nec rotam plaustri sui perpetuo strepere facit, ne dentibus suis conterat ipsum.
29. This also cometh forth from the Lord of hosts, *which* is wonderful in counsel, *and* excellent in working.	29. Etiam hoc ab Iehova exercituum egressum est, qui mirificus est, consilio et magnificus opere.

1. *Wo to the crown of pride.* Isaiah now enters on another and different subject from that which goes before it; for this discourse must be separated from the former one. He shews that the anger of the Lord will quickly overtake, first, Israel, and afterwards the Jews; for it is probable that the kingdom of Israel was still entire when the Prophet uttered these predictions, though nothing more can be affirmed with certainty than that there is good reason to believe that the ten tribes had not at that time been led into captivity.

Accordingly, the Prophet follows this order. First, he shews that the vengeance of God is not far from Israel, because various sins and corruptions of every kind prevailed in it; for they were swelled with pride and insolence, had plunged into their luxuries and given way to every kind of licentiousness, and, consequently, had broken out into open contempt of God, as is usually the case when men take excessive liberties; for they quickly forget God. Secondly, he shews that God in some measure restrains his anger by sparing the tribe of Judah; for when the ten tribes, with the half tribe of Benjamin, had been carried into captivity, the Jews still remained entire and uninjured. Isaiah extols this compassion which God manifested, in not permitting his Church to perish, but preserving some remnant. At the same time he shews that the Jews are so depraved and corrupted that they do not permit God to exercise this compassion, and that, in consequence of the wickedness which prevailed among them, not less than in Israel, they too must feel the avenging hand of God. This order ought to be carefully observed; for many persons blunder in the exposition of this passage, because the Prophet has not expressly mentioned the name of Israel, though it is sufficiently known that *Ephraim* includes the ten tribes.

As to the words, since the particle הוֹי (*hōi*) very frequently denotes "wishing evil on a person," I was unwilling to depart from the ordinary opinion of commentators, more especially because the Prophet openly threatens in this passage; yet if the translation, *Alas the crown!* be preferred, I have no objection.

For the excellence of its glory shall be a fading flower.[1] The copulative ו (*vau*) signifies *for* or *because.* He compares the "glory" and "excellence" of Israel to "a fading flower," as will afterwards be stated. In general, he pronounces a curse on the wealth of the Israelites; for by the word "Crown" he means nothing else than the wicked confidence with which they were puffed up, and which proceeded from the excess of their riches. These vices are almost always joined together, because abundance and fulness produce

---

[1] "Whose glorious beauty is a fading flower."—Eng. Ver.

cruelty and pride; for we are elated by prosperity, and do not know how to use it with moderation. They inhabited a rich and fertile country, and on this account Amos (iv. 1) calls them "fat cows," which feed on the mountain of Samaria. Thus, being puffed up by their wealth, they despised both God and men. The Prophet calls them "drunkards," because, being intoxicated by prosperity, they dreaded no adversity, and thought that they were beyond the reach of all danger, and that they were not even subject to God himself.

A fading flower. He alludes, I doubt not, to the crowns or chaplets[1] which were used at banquets, and which are still used in many places in the present day. The Israelites indulged in gluttony and drunkenness, and the fertility of the soil undoubtedly gave occasion to their intemperance. By calling it "a fading flower" he follows out his comparison, elegantly alluding to flowers which suddenly wither.

Which is on the head of the valley of fatness.[2] He says that that glory is "on the head of the valley of fatness," because they saw under their feet their pastures, the fertility of which still more inflamed their pride. שְׁמָנִים (*shĕmānīm*) is translated by some "of ointments;" but this is inapplicable, for it denotes abundance and fulness, which led them to neglect godliness and to despise God. By the word "head" or "top," he alludes to the position of the country, because the Israelites chiefly inhabited rich valleys. He places on it a crown, which surrounds the whole kingdom; because it was flourishing and abounded in every kind of wealth. This denotes riches, from which arose sluggishness, presumption, rashness, intemperance, and cruelty. This doctrine relates to us also; for the example of these men reminds us that we ought to use prosperity with moderation,

---

[1] "Wo to Samaria, the proud chaplet of the drunkards of Ephraim, which stands at the head of a rich valley belonging to a race of sots! 'Sebaste, the ancient Samaria, is situated on a long mount of an oval figure, having first a fruitful valley, and then a ring of hills running round about it.'—*Maundrell*, p. 58. Hence it is likened to a chaplet, or wreath of flowers, worn upon the head by Jews, as well as Greeks and Romans, at their banquets, as may be seen, Wisd. ii. 7, 8."—*Stock*.

[2] "De la vallee grasse;"—"Of the fat valley."

otherwise we shall be very unhappy, for the Lord will curse all our riches and abundance.

2. *Behold, the Lord hath a mighty and strong one.* This may refer to the Assyrians, as if he had said, that they will be ready at God's command to fight under his authority, as soon as they shall be called. Yet I prefer to take it without a substantive, to mean either "a staff," or some other instrument, by which the Lord will cast them down from this lofty pride.

As a deluge of hail. He compares it to "a deluge" or to "hail," by which both herbs and flowers are thrown down, and all the beauty of the earth is marred. Thus he continues the metaphor of the "fading flower," which he had introduced at the beginning of the chapter; for nothing can be more destructive to flowers than a heavy shower or "hail." He makes use of the demonstrative particle הִנֵּה, (*hinnēh*,) *behold;* because wicked men are not moved by any threatenings, and therefore he shews that he does not speak of what is doubtful, or conjecture at random, but foretells those things which will immediately take place.

Casting them down with the hand to the earth. בְּיָד, (*bĕyād*,) which I have translated "with the hand," is translated by Jerome, "a spacious country," which does not agree with the words. Others take it for "strength," so as to mean a violent casting down. But the plain meaning appears to me to be, that the glory and splendour of the Israelites will be laid low, as if one threw down a drunk man "with the hand." The same statement is confirmed by him in the third verse.

4. *And the excellence of its glory.* He repeats nearly the same words; for we know how difficult it is to terrify and humble those who have been blinded by prosperity, and whose eyes success covers in the same manner that fatness would. As Dionysius the Second,[1] in consequence of gorging himself at unseasonable banquets, was seized with such blindness that he constantly stumbled, so pleasures and luxuries blind the minds of men in such a manner that they no longer know either God or themselves. The Prophet therefore inculcates the same truth frequently on the minds

[1] "Tyran de Sicile;"—"Tyrant of Sicily."

of men who were stupid and amazed, that they might understand what would otherwise have appeared to them to be incredible.[1]

As the hasty fruit before the summer. He now illustrates the subject by another metaphor exceedingly beautiful and appropriate; for the first-ripe fruits are indeed highly commended, because they go before others, and hold out the expectation of the rest of the produce; but they last but a short time, and cannot be preserved, for they are quickly eaten up either by pregnant women, or by children, or by men who do not make a proper selection of their food. He says that the happiness of the Israelites will be of that sort, because their flourishing prosperity will not be of long duration, but will be swallowed up in a moment. What Isaiah declared about the kingdom of Israel, applies also to the whole world. By their ingratitude men prevent all the goodness which the Lord has bestowed on them from reaching maturity; for we abuse his blessings and corrupt them by our wickedness. The consequence is, that hasty and short-lived fruits are produced, which could not yield to us continual nourishment.

5. *In that day shall the Lord of hosts.* After having spoken of the kingdom of Israel, he passes to the tribe of Judah, and shews that, amidst this severe vengeance of God, there will still be room for compassion, and that, although ten tribes perished, yet the Lord will preserve some *remnant*, which he will consecrate to himself; so that there will be in it *a crown of glory and diadem of excellence*, that is, that the Church is never disfigured in such a manner that the Lord does not adorn it with beauty and splendour.

Yet I do not extend this prophecy indiscriminately to all the Jews, but to the elect who were wonderfully rescued from death; for although he calls the tribe and half-tribe *a remnant*,

---

[1] Justin, in a rapid sketch of that tyrant, informs us that, " after having defeated his rivals, he abandoned himself to indolence and gluttony, which brought on such weakness of sight that he could not bear day-light; that the consciousness of being despised on account of his blindness made him more cruel than before, and led him to fill the city with murders as much as his father had filled the jails with prisoners, so that he became universally hated and despised."—*Justin, Hist.* l. xxi. c. 11. The appalling facts are confirmed by other historians.—*Ed.*

as compared with the other ten tribes, yet, as we advance, we shall see that he makes a distinction between the tribe of Judah itself and the others. Nor ought we to wonder that the Prophet speaks differently about the same people, directing his discourse, sometimes to a body corrupted by crimes, and sometimes to the elect. Certainly, as compared with the ten tribes, which had revolted from the worship of God and from the unity of faith, he justly calls the Jews a *remnant* of the people; but when he leaves out of view this comparison, and considers what they are in themselves, he remonstrates with equal justice against their corruptions.

I am aware that some expound it differently, on account of what is said immediately afterwards about *wine and strong drink*, (verse 7,) and think that this statement ought to be viewed in connection with the beginning of the chapter. Yet perhaps the Lord spares the Jews. But how would he spare them? They are in no respect better than the others; for they are equally in fault,[1] and must also be exposed to the same punishments. But those commentators do not consider that the Prophet holds out an instance of the extraordinary kindness of God, in not exercising his vengeance at the same time against the whole family of Abraham, but, after having overthrown the kingdom of Israel, granting a truce to the Jews, to see if they would in any degree repent. Neither do they consider that, by the same means, he employs the circumstance which he had stated for placing in a stronger light the ingratitude of the people, that is, that they ought to have been instructed by the example of their brethren;[2] for the calamity of Israel ought to have aroused and excited them to repentance, but it produced no impression on them, and did not make them better. Although therefore they were unworthy of so great benefits, yet the Lord was pleased to preserve his Church in the midst of them; for this is the reason why he rescued the tribe of Judah, and the half-tribe of Benjamin, from that calamity.

[1] "Puis donc qu'ils sont coulpables d'une mesme ingratitude;"—"Since they are guilty of the same ingratitude."
[2] "Aux despens de leurs freres;"—"At the expense of their brethren."

Now, since the tribe of Judah was a small portion of the nation, and therefore was despised by the haughty Israelites, the Prophet declares that in God alone there is enough of riches and of glory to supply all earthly defects. And hence he shews what is the true method of our salvation, namely, if we place our happiness in God; for as soon as we come down to the world, we gather fading flowers, which immediately wither and decay. This madness reigns everywhere, and more than it ought to be among ourselves, that we wish to be happy without God, that is, without happiness itself. Besides, Isaiah shews that no calamities, however grievous, can prevent God from adorning his Church; for when it shall appear that everything is on the eve of destruction, God will still be a crown of glory to his people. It is also worthy of observation, that Isaiah promises new splendour to the Church only when the multitude shall be diminished, that believers may not lose courage on account of that dreadful calamity which was at hand.

6. *And for a spirit of judgment.* He explains the manner in which the Lord will adorn that "remnant" with additional splendour; for he holds out instances of the true art of civil government, which mainly contributes to the upholding of nations. It consists chiefly of two things, *counsel* and *strength.* The internal administration must be conducted by counsel and wisdom, and "strength" and force are needed against enemies who are without. Since therefore it is by these two defences that kingdoms and commonwealths defend and uphold their rank, he promises to his people the spirit of "wisdom" and "strength." At the same time he shews that it is God who gives both, and that they ought not to be expected from any other; for magistrates will not be able to rule and to administer justice in a city, and military generals will not be able to repel enemies, unless the Lord shall direct them.

7. *But they also have erred through wine.* He returns to the irreligious despisers of God, who were Jews in name only, and proves their ingratitude to be highly aggravated, because, though they had before their eyes a striking proof of the anger of God, when they saw their brethren severely

chastised, and notwithstanding experienced God's forbearance towards themselves, yet neither that example of severity, nor the conviction of the divine goodness, could bring them back into the right path, or make them in any respect better, although the Lord spared them. Here he speaks of "wine and strong drink" metaphorically; for I do not understand it to relate to ordinary drunkenness, against which he remonstrated at the beginning of the chapter, but, on the contrary, he says that they were like drunk men, because they wanted knowledge and sound understanding. If the word *as* be supplied before the words "through wine and through strong drink," the meaning will be more easily understood. I do acknowledge that by continued drunkenness men become, as it were, brutalized, and I have no doubt that drunkenness and excessive eating and drinking contributed also to stupify the minds of the Jews; but if we examine the whole of the context, it will be easy to see that the madness which he condemns is metaphorical.

The priest and the prophet have erred. He proceeds still farther to exhibit their aggravated guilt, and says that not only the common people were drunk, but the priests themselves, who ought to have held out the light and pointed out the path to others; for, as Christ declares, they may be regarded as "the salt of the earth." (Matt. v. 13.) If they are mad, what shall the common people be? "If the eye is blind," what shall become of the other parts of the body? (Matt. vi. 23.)

They have erred in vision. The most grievous thing of all is, when he says that they err not only in the more flagrant transgressions of life, but in *vision* and *judgment.* Hence we ought to infer how desperate was the condition of the Jewish Church, and here, as in a mirror, we may behold our transgressions. It is indeed something monstrous that, after so many chastisements which God has employed for cleansing it, the Church is so deeply corrupted; but such is our wickedness that we fight against his strokes,[1] and though he continually restrains us, and uses unceasing

[1] "Que nous regimbons contre l'esperon;"—"That we kick against the spur."

efforts to purify us from our sins, we not only render all his remedies useless, but bring upon ourselves new diseases. We ought not therefore to wonder that in the present day, after the numerous scourges and afflictions with which the Church has been chastised, men appear to be obstinate, and even become worse, when Isaiah testifies that the same thing took place in the ancient Church. True, indeed, the goodness of the Lord rose above the base and shameful wickedness of that nation, and still preserved the Church; but this was accomplished by his secret power, contrary to the expectation of all; for it would be of no advantage to us, if he employed ordinary remedies.

Hence also it is evident how silly and childish is the boasting of the Papists, who always have in their mouth " The Church," and use as a pretext the names of priests, bishops, and pontiffs, and wish to fortify themselves by their authority against the word of God, as if that order could never err or mistake. They think that they have the Holy Spirit confined within their brains, and that they represent the Church, which God never forsakes. But we see what the Prophet declares concerning the priests, whose order was more splendid and illustrious. If ever there was a Church, there certainly was one at that time among the Jews; and that order derived from the word of God support to which they have no claim. And yet he shews that not only were they corrupt in morals, but erred " in vision and judgment," and that the prophets, whom we know that God added to the priests, out of the ordinary course, on account of the carelessness of the priests, were nevertheless blind in that sacred office of teaching and in revelations. Nothing therefore is more idle than, under the pretext of an office which bears a splendid title, to hold out as exempt from the danger of erring those who, having forsaken God, and not only cast away all regard to religion, but even trodden shame under their feet, defend their tyranny by every means in their power.

8. *For all tables are full of vomiting.* He pursues the same metaphor, and draws, as it were, a picture of what usually happens to men who are given up to drunkenness;

for they forget shame, and not only debase themselves like beasts, but shrink from nothing that is disgraceful. It is certainly an ugly and revolting sight to see "tables covered with vomiting;" and, accordingly, under this figure Isaiah describes the whole life of the people as shameful beyond endurance. There can be no doubt that the Prophet intended to express by a single word, that no sincerity or uprightness was left among the Jews. If we approach their tables, we can find nothing but foul drunkenness; if we look at their life, no part of it is pure or free from crimes and enormities. Doctrine itself is so corrupt that it stinks as if it were polluted by vomiting and filth. In expounding allegories, I have no intention to enter, as some do, into ingenious disquisitions.

9. *Whom shall he teach knowledge?* Here the Prophet shews by an expression of amazement, that the disease of the people is incurable, and that God has no other remedies adapted to cure them, for he has tried every method without effect. When he calls wanderers to return to the right path, and unceasingly warns those who are thoughtlessly going astray, this undoubtedly is an extraordinary remedy; and if it do no good, the salvation of those who refuse to accept of any aid from a physician is utterly hopeless.

Those who are weaned from the milk. The Prophet complains that the stupidity of the people may be said to hinder God from attempting to cure them of their vices; and therefore he compares the Jews to very young infants,[1] or who are but beginning to prattle, and whom it would be a waste of time to attempt to teach. Justly indeed does Peter exhort believers to draw near, "like infants newly born, to suck the milk of pure doctrine;" for no man will ever shew himself to be willing to be taught until he has laid aside that obstinacy which is the natural disposition of all.[2] (1 Pet. ii. 2.) But now the Prophet condemns another kind of infancy, in which men who are stupified by their vices

---

[1] "A des petits enfans n'agueres sevrez;"—"To young infants hardly weaned."

[2] "Que tous apportent du ventre de la mere;"—"Which all bring from their mother's womb."

pay no more regard to heavenly doctrine than if they had no understanding whatsoever. It is therefore a mistake to connect this statement of the Prophet with that passage in the Apostle Peter, as if Isaiah represented God as desirous to obtain disciples who had divested themselves of all pride, and were like infants lately weaned; for the Prophet, on the contrary, loudly complains, that to "teach doctrine" is useless, and merely provokes ridicule among stupid and senseless persons, who are "children, not in malice, but in understanding," as Paul speaks. (1 Cor. xiv. 20.) From what follows it will more clearly appear that, since they were unfit for receiving doctrine, God cannot be accused of undue severity if he reject them, and if he resolve not to bestow useless labour by thundering in their ears any longer.

10. *For precept must be on precept.* This shews plainly that the Lord complains of spending his labour to no purpose in instructing this unteachable people, just as if one were to teach children, who must have elementary instructions repeated to them over and over again, and quickly forget them, and when the master has spent a whole day in teaching them a single letter, yet on the following day and afterwards, the same labour must be renewed, and though he leave nothing untried that care or diligence can do, still they will make no progress under him. Those who change the words of this verse, in order to avoid offending the ears of the readers,[1] obscure the Prophet's meaning through a foolish affectation of copiousness of language, and even destroy the elegance of the style; for, by using the same words, he intended to express a repetition which is constant and unceasing, and full of annoyance. The metaphor, as I have already said, is taken from children, to whom teachers do not venture to give long lessons, because they are incapable of them, but give them, as it were, in little drops. Thus, they convey the same instructions a second and third time, and oftener; and, in short, they continue to receive elementary instructions till they acquire reason and judgment. By a witty imitation he repeats the words, "here a little, there a little."

[1] "Afin de ne fascher les oreilles des lecteurs."

Instruction upon instruction.[1] The word קַו (*kăv*) is improperly, in my opinion, translated by some interpreters *line,* as if the Prophet alluded to the slow progress of a building, which rises gradually by " lines." That would be a harsh and far-fetched metaphor, for this passage relates to elementary instruction conveyed to children. I acknowledge that the same Hebrew word is used in the eighteenth chapter, where we have translated it " Line by line,"[2] and in many other passages; but here the connection demands a different meaning, as is also the case in Psalm xix. 4, where, however, the word *line*[3] or *dimension* could be admitted with greater propriety than in this verse. Yet I admit that it is taken metaphorically for an instruction or rule; for as in buildings קַו (*kăv*) denotes the " rule" or " plumb-line," as we shall see that it means in a later portion of this chapter, we need not wonder that it is applied to other rules.

11. *For with stammering lips.*[4] Some supply, that " it is as if one should say;" but that is superfluous. I therefore view these words as relating to God, who became, as the Prophet tells us, a barbarian[5] to a people without understanding. This reproof must have wounded them to the quick, because by their own fault they made God, who formed our tongues, to appear to be " a stammerer." He does not as yet threaten them, but lays the blame on their indolence, that they rendered the proclamation of heavenly doctrine a confused noise, because of their own accord they shut their eyes, and thus derived no advantage from it. Their infatuation, in not hearing God speaking to them, is compared by the Prophet to a prodigy.

12. *For he said to them.* Some explain it by circumlocu-

[1] " Line upon line."—Eng. Ver.
[2] " De toutes parts, ou, ligne apres ligne;"—" On all sides, or, line after line."
[3] The reader may consult the Author's exposition, and the Translator's notes. *Commentary on the Book of Psalms,* vol. i. pp. 312, 313.—*Ed.*
[4] " For with stammering lips. (Heb. Stammerings of lips.)"—Eng. Ver.
[5] " But since this patience has been lost upon them, a stronger way shall be taken to force their attention. God will thunder in their ears, what to them will appear jargon, the language of a foreign nation, by whom they shall be carried into captivity."—*Stock.*

tion in this manner: "If one should say to them, This is the rest, they refuse to hear." But this is a feeble exposition, and does not connect the various parts of the passage in a proper manner. On the contrary, the Prophet assigns the reason why God appears to the Jews to be a barbarian: it is, because they had not ears. Words were spoken to the deaf. It was to no purpose that the Lord offered to them rest. This deafness arose from obstinacy, for they wickedly and rebelliously rejected doctrine. Their wickedness was doubly inexcusable in refusing rest which was offered to them, and which all men naturally desire. It was in itself intolerable baseness to be deaf to the voice of God speaking, but it was still more foul ingratitude deliberately to reject a blessing which was in the highest degree desirable. Accordingly, he points out the benefit which they might have derived from the obedience of faith, and of which they deprived themselves by their own wickedness. He therefore reproaches them with this ignorance and blindness; for it springs from their own stubbornness in maliciously turning away their eyes from the light which was offered to them, and choosing rather to remain in darkness than to be enlightened.

Hence it follows that unbelievers, as soon as God has exhibited to them his word, voluntarily draw down on themselves wretched uneasiness; for he invites all men to a blessed rest, and clearly points out the object by which, if we shape the course of our life, true happiness awaits us; for no man who has heard heavenly doctrine can go astray except knowingly and willingly. We learn from it how lovely in our eyes heavenly doctrine ought to be, for it brings to us the invaluable blessing of enjoying peace of conscience and true happiness. All confess loudly that there is nothing better than to find a place of security; and yet, when rest is offered, many despise it, and the greater part of men even refuse it, as if all men expressly desired to have wretched perplexity and continual trembling: and yet no man has a right to complain that he errs through ignorance; for nothing is clearer or plainer than the doctrine of God, so that it is vain for men to plead any excuse. In short, nothing can be more unreasonable than to throw the blame on God, as if he spoke obscurely, or taught in a confused manner. Now, as God testifies in this passage that he points out to us in his word assured rest, so, on the other hand, he warns all unbelievers that they suffer the just reward of their wickedness when they are harassed by continual uneasiness.

Cause the weary to rest. Some explain it thus, that God demands the duties of brotherly kindness, in order that he may be reconciled to us, and that those duties are here included, a part being taken for the whole. But I think that the Prophet's meaning is different, namely, that God points out to us that rest by which our weariness may be relieved, and that consequently we are convicted of deeper ingratitude, if even necessity, which is a very sharp spur, does not quicken us to seek a remedy. This saying of the Prophet corresponds nearly to the words of Christ, "Come to me, all ye that labour and are heavy laden, and I will give you rest." (Matt. xi. 28.) In a word, Isaiah informs the Jews that they have this choice, "Do they prefer to be refreshed and relieved, or to sink under the burden and be overwhelmed?" This confirms a passing remark which I made a little before, that God does not in vain exhort those who seek repose to come to him, as we shall elsewhere see, "I have not in vain said to the house of Jacob, Seek me." (Isaiah xlv. 19.) Since, therefore, if we do not stand in the way, we shall be taught by his word, we may safely rely on the doctrine which is contained in it; for he does not intend to weary us out by vain curiosity, as men often draw down upon themselves much distress and anguish by idle pursuits.

Besides, when he shews that this rest is prepared for the weary who groan under the burden, let us at least be taught by the distresses which harass us to betake ourselves to the word of God, that we may obtain peace. We shall thus find that the word of God is undoubtedly fitted to soothe our uneasy feelings, and to give peace to our perplexed and trembling consciences. All who seek "rest" in any other way, and run beyond the limits of the word, must always be subjected to torture or wretched uncertainty, because they attempt to be wise and happy without God. We see that this is the condition of the Papists, who, having despised this peace of God, are wretchedly tormented during their whole life; for Satan tosses and drives them about in such a manner that they are tormented with dreadful uneasiness, and never find a place of rest.

13. *The word of the Lord shall therefore be to them.* Although the Prophet repeats the same words, yet the meaning is somewhat different; for, having formerly spoken of voluntary stupidity, he now threatens the punishment of it, namely, that God will strike them with such bewilderment, that they shall be totally deprived of the benefit of saving doctrine, and shall perceive in it nothing but an empty sound. In short, he concludes, from what goes before, that since they had not profited by the word of God, the Jews shall be justly punished for their ingratitude; not that the word shall be taken from them, but that they shall be deprived of sound judgment and understanding, and shall be blind amidst the clearest light. Thus God blinds and hardens the reprobate more and more on account of their disobedience.

Paul quotes this passage (1 Cor. xiv. 21) when he reproves the Corinthians for foolish affectation, in consequence of their being so much under the influence of ambition, that they regarded with the highest admiration those who spoke in a foreign tongue, as the common people are accustomed to stare at everything that is unknown and uncommon. This passage in the writings of Paul has been misunderstood, because these words of the Prophet have not been duly weighed. Now, Paul applies these words most appropriately to his object; for he shews that the Corinthians are under the influence of a foolish and absurd admiration, and that they improperly aspire to those things from which they can derive no advantage; in short, that they are "like children, not in malice, but in knowledge and understanding;" that thus they voluntarily draw down on themselves the curse which the Prophet here threatens; and that the word of God becomes to them precept on precept, and they receive no more instruction from it than if a person were to bawl out to them in an unknown tongue. It is the height of madness to bring upon themselves, by idle affectation, that blindness and stupidity which the Lord threatens against obstinate and rebellious men. Paul therefore explains and renders more intelligible this statement made by the Prophet, for he shews that they who abuse the doctrine of salvation do not deserve to make progress in it in any way whatever.

We have seen a passage closely resembling it in which the Prophet compared his doctrine to " sealed letters." (Isaiah viii. 16.) Afterwards we shall find that the Prophet compares it to a book that is "shut." (Isaiah xxix. 11.) This takes place when, on account of the ingratitude of men, God takes from them judgment and sound understanding; so that, " seeing they do not see, and hearing they do not hear," and thus are most justly punished. (Isaiah vi. 9; Mark iv. 12.) This ought to be carefully observed; for frequently we think that all is well with us, and are highly delighted with ourselves, because we continue to enjoy the word.[1] But of what avail will it be to us, if it do not enlighten our understandings and regulate our hearts? We thus draw down upon ourselves a heavier judgment, and therefore we need a twofold grace; first, that God would shine on us by his word; and secondly, that he would open our understandings and dispose our hearts to obedience, otherwise we shall derive no more aid from the brilliancy of the gospel than blind men derive from the brightness of the sun. By this punishment, therefore, we are reminded that we must not abuse the word of God, but must look directly to the object which the Lord holds out to us in the word.

They shall fall backward, and be broken and snared. At length he describes the destruction of those who are blind to this brightness of the word; for nothing remains for them but to be thrown down headlong, because they have departed from the right path, and therefore they must stumble and fall. He means that the fall will not be slight, for they shall be *bruised* by it. By the word *snared* he employs an-

[1] " De ce que la parole est au milieu de nous;"—" Because the word is in the midst of us."

other metaphor, namely, that for all unbelievers "snares" are prepared, by which they shall be entangled and drawn to destruction. We had a similar sentiment on a former occasion, (Isaiah viii. 15,) and expressed in nearly the same words;[1] for there the Prophet speaks on the same subject, the blinding of the people, who by their obstinacy had provoked the wrath of God. He shews that they who go astray, in opposition to the word of God, are always very near destruction. Either they shall meet with stumblingblocks on which they shall "stumble," or with snares by which they shall be "ensnared." In short, it will be impossible that evil shall not befall those who do not keep the path which God has pointed out; for either they shall openly "fall and be bruised," or through concealed traps they shall fall into a "snare."

14. *Wherefore hear ye the word of the Lord.* He goes on to address to them still stronger reproof, and at the same time mingles with it a consolation in order to encourage the hearts of the godly. While he threatens utter destruction against the wicked, he leaves for believers ground of consolation, by declaring that their salvation is dear and precious in the sight of God.

Ye scornful men. By this term he means men who are addicted to sophistry and deceit, who think that by jeers and cunning they can escape the judgment of God; for ליץ (*lūtz*)[2] signifies to *jeer* or *scorn*. Now, he addresses not ordinary men, but rulers and governors, who, in governing the people, thought that they surpassed other men in sharpness and dexterity, but turned their acuteness to cunning, by which they acted hypocritically towards God himself, and therefore, in keen irony, he calls them "scorners;" as if he had said, "You think that you have enough of craftiness to mock God, but you will not succeed in mocking him." (Gal. vi. 7.) The Prophet's chief and severest contest was

---

[1] See *Commentary on Isaiah*, vol. i. p. 282.

[2] From which the noun לצון (*lātzōn*) is derived. The phrase אנשי לצון (*ănshē lātzon*) literally signifies "men of scorn," and is so rendered by Stock and others; but the force of the Hebrew idiom is fully brought out by the word "scoffers," as in Lowth, or by "scornful men," as in the English Version.—*Ed.*

with the nobles; for although all ranks were exceedingly corrupted, yet the nobles, being puffed up with a false belief of their own wisdom, were more obstinate than the rest. It has commonly been found, in almost every age, that the common people, though they are distinguished by unrestrained fierceness and violence, do not proceed to such a pitch of wickedness as nobles or courtiers, or other crafty men, who think that they excel others in ability and wisdom. The ministers of the word ought chiefly, therefore, to arm themselves against ingenious adversaries. None can be more destructive; for they not only of themselves do injury, but excite others to the same kind of scorn and wickedness, and frequently, through the estimation in which they are held, and the splendour of their reputation, they dazzle the common people who are less clear-sighted. It is a dreadful and monstrous thing when the governors of the Church not only are themselves blinded, but even blind others, and excite them to despise God, and ridicule godly doctrine, and taunt it by their jeers, and, in short, employ their utmost ingenuity for overturning religion; but in opposition to such persons we ought to encourage our hearts by the example of the Prophet, that we may not sink or lose heart in this contest. He shews us also the way in which we ought to treat such persons.[1] We ought not to spend much time in teaching them, (for instruction would be of little use,) but must threaten them severely, and terrify them by the judgment of God.

This people which is in Jerusalem. Their guilt is highly aggravated by the consideration that they inhabit the very sanctuary of God, and infect with their pollution God's chosen people.

15. *Because ye have said.* The Prophet next assigns the reason why he called them "scorners;" it was because they had thrown off all fear of God. He likewise describes the manner in which they acted, by saying that they promised to themselves that they would escape punishment amidst all their crimes and enormities, and became the more daring, and, as if they had obtained greater liberty to pursue wicked

[1] " Ces moqueurs;"—" Those mockers."

courses, rushed forward without dread wherever their unruly passions carried them.

We have struck a league with death, and with hell have we made a compact. This is what he means by the league into which they had entered with death and the grave; for by despising and boldly ridiculing all God's threatenings and chastisements, they thought that they were out of all danger. חֹזֶה (chōzĕh) means what he had formerly expressed by בְּרִית, (berīth,) for it is a repetition of the same statement. Literally it signifies *seeing*,[1] and denotes what is conveyed by the French phrase, *avoir intelligence,* or by the English phrase, "to have a mutual understanding." There appears to be also an implied contrast between prophetic visions and that deceitful craftiness on which veterans in wicked arts value themselves.

We have made lies our refuge. It is certain that those cunning men never broke out into such boasting as to utter those offensive words, for that would have been childish and absurd.[2] Besides, though they despised God and set at nought all his admonitions, they undoubtedly wished to be held in some estimation by the people, and would never have confessed that they "made lies their refuge;" but the Prophet looked at their feelings and aims, and not at their pretexts, and took into account their actions and dispo-

---

[1] " חֹזֶה (*chōzĕh*) is properly a participle (*seeing*) often used as a noun to denote a *seer* or prophet. Here the connection seems distinctly to require the sense of league or covenant. That there is no error in the text may be inferred from the substitution of the cognate form חָזוּת (*chăzūth*) in verse 18. Hitzig accounts for the transfer of meanings by the supposition that in making treaties it was usual to consult the *seer* or prophet. Ewald supposes an allusion to the practice of necromantic art or divination as a safeguard against death, and translates the word ײַאל, (*oracle.*) The more common explanation of the usage traces it to the idea of an *interview* or *meeting,* and the act of looking one another in the face, from which the transition is by no means difficult to that of mutual understanding or agreement."—*Alexander.* Buxtorf renders it "a seer, or prophet," and, by a transferred meaning, "provision," or "foresight," "We have made provision, we have looked forward, we have acted with foresight;" and adds, that the Chaldee version renders it שְׁלָמָא, (*shĕlama,*) *peace.*—*Ed.*

[2] " Car c'eust esté une chose trop ridicule et dont les petits enfans se fussent moquez ;"—" For it would have been too absurd, and even young children would have laughed at it."

sitions, and not their words. Whoever, then, flatters himself and his vices, and fearlessly despises God's threatenings, declares that he has "entered into a league with death," which he does not at all dread, notwithstanding the Lord's threatenings.

The Prophet, therefore, reproves in general that carnal presumption by which men are led to forgetfulness of the judgment of God, and willingly deceive themselves, as if they could escape the arm of God: but chiefly he attacks Lucianists[1] and censorious men, who place their wisdom in nothing else than in irreligious contempt of God; and the more eager they are to conceal their dishonour, the more earnestly does the Prophet expose them, as if he had dragged forth to the light, from a deep concealment, their cunning wiles, and as if he had said, "This is the dexterity, skill, and cunning of the wise men of this world, who are exposed on every hand to troubles and afflictions, and yet imagine that they are concealed and safe. They unquestionably deserve to seek salvation from falsehood, for they disregard God's salvation, and despise and ridicule him." Their tricks, and cunning, and imposture, are indeed concealed by them under plausible names, and they do not think that they are falsehoods; but the Prophet calls them by their proper names.

When the overflowing scourge shall pass through. As to "the overflowing scourge," the Prophet here includes two metaphors; for he compares the calamities and afflictions by which God chastises the transgressions of the world to a "scourge," and then says, that they are so rapid and violent that they resemble a "flood." Against those calamities, however severe and distressing, wicked men of this description think that they are fortified by lying and deceit, and hope that they shall be able to escape them, though they overflow far and wide over the whole world. They perceive the judgments of God, and the calamities to which men are exposed; but, because they do not observe the hand and

[1] Lucian is often alluded to by our Author as the type of daring and scornful infidels. See *Commentary on a Harmony of the Evangelists,* vol. ii. p. 283, n. 1.—*Ed.*

providence of God, and ascribe everything that happens to fortune, they therefore seek to obtain such defences and safeguards as may drive such "scourges" away from them.

16. *Therefore thus saith the Lord God.* Isaiah now comforts the godly, and threatens against the wicked such punishment as they deserved. In the first instance, he brings forward consolation, because the godly were a laughingstock to those crafty men, as we see at the present day that irreligious men laugh at our simplicity, and reckon us to be fools, because amidst such deep adversity and sore afflictions we still hope that it will turn out to our advantage. In opposition to this insolence of the reprobate, the Prophet encourages and supports the hearts of the godly to pass by with indifference, and reckon of no account their jeers and reproaches, and to believe firmly that their hope will not be confounded or vain.

Behold, I lay in Zion a stone, a stone of trial. The demonstrative particle *behold* expresses certainty; as if he had said, "Though wicked men despise my words, and refuse to believe them, yet I will perform what I have promised." The pronoun *I* is emphatic, that the prophecy may be more firmly believed. As to the words, the genitive בחן, (*bōchăn,*) *of trial,* which is used instead of an adjective along with *stone,* may be taken both in an active and in a passive sense, either for a stone by which the whole building is "tried," or examined as by a standard, or for a "tried stone." The former meaning appears to me to be more appropriate, and undoubtedly the usage of the Hebrew language requires us to interpret it rather in an active sense. He calls it therefore a trying stone, or a trier, on account of the effect produced; because by this stone the whole building must be squared and adjusted, otherwise it must unavoidably totter and fall.

A precious corner-stone, a sure foundation. He calls it a corner-stone, because it supports the whole weight of the building, and by this name, which is also given to it in Psalm cxviii. 22, he commends its force and strength. Lastly, he calls it a "foundation," and, so to speak, a "fundamental foundation," proceeding gradually in the commendation of it; for he shews that it is not an ordinary stone, or one of many which contribute to the building, but that it is a highly valuable stone, on which the whole weight of the building exclusively rests. It is a stone, but a stone which fills the whole corner; it is a corner-stone, but the whole house is founded on it. As "another foundation cannot be laid," so on it alone must the whole Church, and every part of it, rest and be built. (1 Cor. iii. 11.)

He that believeth shall not make haste. This clause is interpreted by some as an exhortation, " He that believeth, let him not make haste." But I prefer to take it in the future tense, both because that meaning agrees best with the context, and because it is supported by the authority of the Apostle Paul. I do acknowledge that the Apostles followed the Greek translation,[1] and used such liberty, that while they were satisfied with giving the meaning, they did not quote the exact words. Yet they never changed the meaning, but, taking care to have it properly applied, they gave the true and genuine interpretation. Whenever, therefore, they quote any passage from the Old Testament, they adhere closely to its object and design.

Now, Paul, when he quotes this prophecy, adopts the Greek version, " He that believeth shall not be ashamed." (Rom. ix. 33; x. 11.) And certainly the design of the Prophet is to shew, that they who believe will have peace and serenity of mind, so that they shall not desire anything more, and shall not wander in uncertainty, or hasten to seek other remedies, but shall be fully satisfied with this alone. That is not a departure from the meaning, for the word signifying *to make haste* conveys the idea of eagerness or trembling. In short, the design of the Prophet is, to extol faith on account of this invaluable result, that by means of it we enjoy settled peace and composure. Hence it follows that, till we possess faith, we must have continual perplexity and distress; for there is but one harbour on which we can safely rely, namely, the truth of the Lord, which alone will give us peace and serenity of mind.

This fruit of faith is elsewhere described by the same

[1] Commonly called the Septuagint.—*Ed.*

Apostle Paul, when he says that, "being justified by faith, we obtain peace with God." (Rom. v. 1.) The Apostles and evangelists shew that this "stone" is Christ, because the Church was actually settled and founded at the time when he was presented to the view of the world. (Matt. xxi. 42; Acts iv. 11; Rom. ix. 33; 1 Pet. ii. 6.) First, in him the promises have their firmness; secondly, the salvation of men rests on him alone, and therefore if Christ be taken away, the Church will fall down and be ruined. The state of the fact therefore shews, that these statements must undoubtedly be referred to Christ, without whom there is no certainty of salvation; and therefore at every moment ruin is at hand. Next, we have the authority of evangelists and Apostles; and indeed the Holy Spirit conveys that instruction by their mouth.

But it will be proper to examine it more closely, that we may see in what manner these things are applied to Christ. First, it is not without good reason that Isaiah represents God as speaking, whose peculiar work it is to found the Church, as we have already seen elsewhere, and as the Prophet will afterwards declare; and this statement occurs very frequently in the Psalms. For if all men devote their labour to it, they will not be able to lay the least stone. It is God alone, therefore, who founds and builds his Church, though he employs for this purpose the labours and services of men. Now, by whom was Christ given, but by the Father? So then it was the heavenly Father who did and accomplished these things, and who appointed Christ to be the only foundation on which our salvation rests.

But was not this stone laid before? Did not the Church always rest on this foundation? I acknowledge that it did, but only in hope; for Christ had not yet been revealed, and had not fulfilled the office of a Redeemer. On this account the Prophet speaks of it as a future event, that believers may be fully persuaded that the Church, which they saw not only tottering and falling, but grievously shaken and almost laid in ruins, will yet be made firm by a new support, when it shall rest on a stone laid by the hand of God.

I lay in Zion. He says that it is "in Zion;" because Christ must come out of it, which contributes greatly to confirm our faith, when we see that he came out of that place which was appointed for this purpose so long before. Now, at the present day, "Mount Zion" is everywhere; for the Church has spread to the ends of the world.

Christ is truly "the stone of trial," for by him must the whole building be regulated, and we cannot be the building of God, if we are not adapted to him. Hence also Paul exhorts us to "grow in him who is the head, from whom the whole body must be joined and united." (Eph. iv. 15.) Our faith must be wholly applied to Christ, that he may be our rule. He is also the "corner-stone," on which rests not only one part of the building, but its whole weight, and the foundation itself. "No man," as Paul says, "can lay any other foundation than Jesus Christ." (1 Cor. iii. 11.) This is the reason why, when the Lord promises by the mouth of Isaiah the restoration of his Church, he reminds us of the foundation; for it was wasted in such a manner that it resembled a ruin, and there was no way in which it could be restored but by Christ. As to Christ being called also the "stone of stumbling," this is accidental; for the fault lies on ungrateful men, who, having rejected him, find him to be altogether different from what he would have been to them. But on this subject we have spoken at chap. viii. 14.[1]

17. *And I will lay judgment to the line.* The ruinous condition of the Church being such that believers hardly ventured to hope that it would be improved, he shews that God has in his hand the ready means of forming the Church entirely anew. As he lately mentioned a building, so now, by a different metaphor, he shews that there is no reason to fear that God will not at length finish the work of building which has been begun. Yet indirectly he reproves the pride and insolence of those who wished to be accounted pillars of the Church, while they were endeavouring, as far as lay in their power, to raze it to the foundation. Although, in consequence of an almost total extinction of the light of faith, and a frightful corruption of the worship of God, the

---

[1] See *Commentary on Isaiah,* vol. i. p. 280.

state of the people was hideous, yet they boasted of their royal priesthood, in the same manner as we see the Papists at the present day shamelessly utter similar boasting, though lamentable confusion cries aloud that the form of the Church has utterly perished among them. For this reason the Prophet describes what will be the reformation of the Church.

Judgment to the line, and righteousness to the measure or plummet. It is probable that קָו, (*kāv,*) *a line,* and מִשְׁקֹלֶת, (*mishkōlĕth,*) *a plummet,* mean the same thing, as may be inferred with greater certainty from another passage : " I will stretch over Jerusalem the rope or line of Samaria, and the plummet of the house of Ahab." (2 Kings xxi. 13.) Yet I do not deny that he alludes to the examination of weights ; but both metaphors are taken from buildings, in which the master-builders and masons try everything by a rule, in order to preserve a due proportion in every part. Thus it is said that the Lord administers equal judgment, when he restores the Church, in which otherwise everything is disordered and confused, as in a hideous ruin, when the ungodly are exalted and enjoy prosperity, while the godly are despised and sorrowful.

He makes the same statement concerning "righteousness," that he will measure or try it by his weights, and will regulate everything by a rule ; for by *righteousness* and *judgment* he means a proper and lawful administration of the Church, as contrasting with the masks and disguises boasted of by those who fear the title of Bishops. The meaning is, that this foundation is laid, not only that the Church may be commenced, but that it may be perfectly restored, to use a common phrase, " from top to bottom" (De fonds en comble.)

The hail shall sweep away the reliance of falsehood. This second part of the metaphor denotes also a very exact equality. Nothing then will be wanting to the building, if Christ be laid for the foundation ; and, on the other hand, if he be not there, all will be vanity and confusion. Now since there was no room for "judgment and righteousness," but by sweeping away the false confidences, he declares that they shall be all swept away, because the violence of God's anger shall cast down all loftiness, and the flood shall penetrate all the hiding-places of thoughtless indifference. He therefore threatens that hypocrites, with all their boasting, shall nevertheless perish, even though the Lord preserve the Church; for he does not speak of chastisements, as if the wicked would be corrected by them, because, on the contrary, they become hardened and more obstinate. The cleansing, therefore, he shews, will be such as to drag them forth from their hiding-places and strip them of false and empty confidence; for wicked men think that they are so thoroughly concealed by their falsehood and deceit, that they shall never feel strokes, and therefore they please and flatter themselves amidst their iniquities and crimes; but the *waters* will easily reach them; that is, the wrath of God, which shall rush down upon them like a deluge, will easily break through their lurking-places.

18. *And your covenant with death shall be disannulled.* Formerly he directed his reproof against hypocrites, who obstinately mocked at God and all his threatenings; and he checked their thoughts in imagining that "they had made a covenant with death," (verse 15,) that is, in promising to themselves that all their transgressions would pass unpunished; as if by jeers and laughter they could escape the arm of God. He now threatens that, when they shall be fully aware that they must render an account to God, they shall be struck with fear and dread, whether they will or not;[1] for that state of ease and indifference into which they are sunk, arises from a kind of lethargy or drunkenness, which hinders them from perceiving the alarming nature of their disease; but the Lord will arouse them from their sleep, however profound, and will annul their imaginary compacts.

In short, he means that that peace which the wicked enjoy, while they slumber in their sins, will not be perpetual; for they shall be compelled, even against their will, to acknowledge that God is their judge, and, when they shall wish to enjoy repose, and while they are careless and unprepared, they shall be suddenly seized and agitated by strange terrors and anguish of mind. Their case is similar to that of malefactors, who, if they have broken out of prison and

[1] "Voire en despit de leurs dents;"—"Even in spite of their teeth."

escaped, mock their judges, and utter reproachful and forward and insolent language against them, but, when they see the officers of justice close at their heels, suddenly tremble, and find that all their joy is turned into mourning, and that their condition is far worse than if they had not broken out of prison. Thus the wicked enjoy some momentary gladness, which they obtain by forgetfulness of their guilt ; but the Lord immediately lays his hand on them, and terrifies their consciences in such a manner that they can find no rest.

19. *From the time that it shall pass.* He expresses more in this verse than in the preceding one ; for he declares that the destruction of the reprobate is close at hand, though they promise to themselves everlasting happiness. Wicked men indeed perceive that they are liable to many calamities, but yet they flatter and stupify themselves, and imagine that in this way they can ward off their calamities. They have in their mouth proverbs of this sort, " Let us not distress ourselves before the time : Let us enjoy the season while it lasts : Let us be cheerful, and not give ourselves uneasiness when we can avoid it." But he threatens that there hangs over their heads a hidden destruction,[1] and adds :

It shall seize you every morning, and shall pass every day by day and night. By " every morning" is meant " quickly and continually ;" for it is only when they feel distress that wicked men are touched with the fear of God. Frequently indeed they are afraid when there is no danger ; but it is a blind terror, for they do not understand whence their alarm proceeds. While God threatens, they are unconcerned, because they do not acknowledge him to be their judge, and thus they have no serious thoughts about God till they feel his hand. When he again repeats " in the morning," and afterwards adds, " by day and by night," he means, as I have said, that the scourge will be constant and daily ; that they may not persuade themselves that it will be a light calamity, or deceive themselves by the hope of any mitigation ; for,

---

[1] " Qu'il leur pend une horrible calamité sur leurs testes, laquelle ils ne voyent point ;"—" That there hangs over their heads a dreadful calamity which they do not see."

while the wrath of God against believers is momentary, against unbelievers it is eternal, for it never ceases to pursue them to the end.

Terror alone shall cause them to understand the report.[1] Here commentators differ. Jerome's translation is, "Terror shall give understanding to the report." But they come nearer to the meaning of the Prophet who give this interpretation, "The report alone shall make you understand," that is, "The men to whom the messenger shall come will be rendered obedient to God by the report alone." For my own part, I adopt a simpler view, though I do not choose to refute the expositions given by others. "It will come to pass that terror alone shall enable you to understand doctrine." As if he had said, "Hitherto I have not succeeded in my exhortations to you, but the Lord will find out a new method of instructing you, that is, chastisements and calamities, by which he will terrify you in such a manner that you shall know with whom you have to do." It is as if a grieved and sorrowful father were thus to remonstrate with a disobedient and incorrigible son, "Since you despise my advices, you must one day be taught by the executioner."[2]

Thus Isaiah threatens wicked men, who mocked at all his threatenings, and tells them that they do not care for the assistance of prophets, but that one day they will actually

---

[1] "And it shall be a vexation only to understand the report. Or, when he shall make you to understand doctrine."—(Eng. Ver.) "And even the report alone shall cause terror."—*Lowth*. "And it shall be terror merely to hear the report of it."—*Stock*. "And only vexation (or distress) shall be the understanding of the thing heard."—*Alexander*. "E'l sentirne il grido non produrrà altro che commovimento;"—"And to hear the cry of it will produce nothing but distress."—(Ital. Ver.)

[2] "There are three interpretations of the last clause, one of which supposes it to mean, that the mere report of the approaching scourge should fill them with distress; another, that the effect of the report should be universal distress; a third, that nothing but a painful experience would enable them to understand the lesson which the Prophet was commissioned to teach them. שְׁמוּעָה (*shĕmūgnāh*) meaning simply what is heard, may of course denote either rumour or revelation. The latter seems to be the meaning in verse 9, where the noun stands connected with the same verb as here. Whether this verb ever means simply to perceive or hear, may be considered doubtful; if not, the preference is due to the third interpretation above given, viz., that nothing but distress or suffering could make them understand or even attend to the message from Jehovah."—*Alexander*.

know with what sincerity and truth they addressed them, and yet that it will be of no advantage to them, because knowledge so late will leave no room for repentance. We must "seek the Lord while there is time." (Isaiah lv. 6.) Pharaoh was made no better by the chastisements which he received, (Exod. viii. 15,) and Esau gained nothing by his tears, when he saw that he had been stripped of his birthright, (Gen. xxvii. 38 ; Heb. xii. 17 ;) for they were not followed by any repentance or any amendment of life. By the word "terror" he shews how "dreadful it is to fall into the hands of the living God," (Heb. x. 31,) and that they who despise his word are never allowed to pass unpunished. He employs the word שְׁמוּעָה (shĕmūgnāh) to denote what is heard, that is, doctrine.

20. *For the bed shall be short.* By this metaphor he adorns the former statement ; for he compares the reprobate, who are pressed down by the hand of God, to those who have concealed themselves in a "short and narrow bed," in which they can scarcely stretch their limbs or lift their head, and where, in short, instead of rest, they feel sharp pains. He means that the Jews will be shut up in such a manner that they shall be overwhelmed with the severity of their distresses, and that the "bed," which is given to man for rest, will be an instrument of torture.

If they seek a "covering," he says that "it will be too short to wrap themselves in it," and that it is an addition to their former distress, that amidst those heavy calamities they will want all necessary comforts. He chose to express this by the metaphor of a "narrow covering," that they may know that their condition will be in the highest degree wretched ; because the vengeance of God will pursue them on all sides, both above and below, so that they shall have no abatement or mitigation, and shall find no relief. The Lord employs these metaphors, in order to accommodate himself to our weakness ; because otherwise we cannot understand how dreadful is the judgment of God. Hence therefore we learn how dreadful are the terrors which shake and confine wicked men, when the Lord pursues them ; they search eagerly for places of concealment, and would willingly hide themselves in the centre of the earth; but the Lord drags them forth to light, and confines and hems them in, so that they cannot move.

21. *For as in Mount Perazim.* Since he speaks here of the reprobate, the Prophet holds out nothing but terrors and cruel punishment; for while the Lord deals kindly and gently with his children, he shews that he will be an object of terror to the reprobate. For this purpose he produces examples, in which the Lord displayed his arm in defence of his people, as when he routed the Philistines in the valley of Perazim, when David pursued them, (2 Sam. v. 20; 1 Chron. xiv. 11,) and at another time, when the Amorites and other enemies were slain by the Israelites in the valley of Gibeon, with Joshua as their leader, to whom the Lord granted that the "sun and moon should stand still," that they might more easily pursue their enemies. (Joshua x. 10-14.)

Shall Jehovah rise up. By the word "rise up" he points out the power of God, because we think that he is lazy and indolent, when he does not punish the reprobate. It is therefore said that he "rises up" or stands erect, when he openly exhibits to us proofs of his power, and such as especially manifest the great care which he takes of his Church. Although the manner was different, (for in ancient times he "rose up" in defence of his chosen people against foreigners, but now he threatens war against the Jews,) yet Isaiah skilfully applies these examples; for by driving out internal enemies God will promote the advantage of his Church not less than if he directed his strength and arms against foreigners. He would thus reckon them in the number of enemies, though they falsely boasted that they were his people.

His strange work. [1] Some think that this "work" is called "strange," because nothing corresponds better to the nature of God than to be merciful and to pardon our sins; and that when he is angry, he acts against his will, and assumes a character that is foreign to him and that is contrary to his

---

[1] "La sua opera strana, la sua operazione straordinaria;"—"His strange work, his extraordinary act."—Ital. Ver.

nature. By nature he is gentle, compassionate, patient, kind, slow to anger, as Scripture declares by many words and by a variety of expressions his infinite compassion. (Exod. xxxiv. 6; Psalm ciii. 8.) Others explain it to mean that the "work" is "strange," because formerly he was wont to defend his people, and that it is monstrous that he now proceeds to attack and exterminate them, as if they were enemies.

For my own part, I consider "strange" to mean simply what is uncommon or wonderful; for this appellation is given to what is rare and unusual among men, and we know that they almost always view with astonishment whatever is new. It is as if he had said, "The Lord will punish you, and that not in a common or ordinary way, but in a way so amazing that at the sight or hearing of it, all shall be struck with horror." It is certain that all the works of God are so many proofs of his power, so that they ought justly to excite our admiration; but because, through constant habit and looking at them, they are despised by us, we think that he does nothing unless he adopt some extraordinary methods. On this account Isaiah quotes ancient examples, in order that we may know that, though to men this vengeance be new and amazing, yet to God it is far from being new, since for a long period he has given proofs of his power and ability not less remarkable than these. Yet I willingly admit that the Prophet contrasts the wicked Israelites with the Philistines and Canaanites, as if he had said, "The Lord formerly performed miracles when he wished to save his people; he will now perform them in order to destroy that people; for since the Israelites have degenerated, they shall feel the hand of God for their destruction which their fathers felt for their salvation."

22. *Now therefore.* He again reminds those wicked men, whom he had formerly called "scorners," (verse 14,) that their cunning, and contempt, and jeers, and mockery, will avail them nothing, because all their ingenuity will be thwarted; and he exhorts them to repentance, if there still be any of them that are capable of being cured. For this reason he repeats the same threatenings, in order to arouse them.

Lest your chains be more firmly fastened. He says that all that they will gain by resistance will be to draw themselves more firmly into their nets. Instead of "chains," there are some who render מוֹסְרִים (*mōsĕrīm*) "chastisements;" but this does not agree with the context. The metaphor of "chains" is highly appropriate in this passage; for, as the fox which has fallen into a snare, fastens the knot more firmly by his attempts to extricate himself and escape, so wicked men by their disobedience entangle and fasten themselves more and more. They desire to escape the hand of God, and kick against the spur, like an unruly horse which bends all its strength to shake off its rider; but all that they accomplish by their obstinacy and stubbornness is to receive heavier and severer blows.

Be ye not mockers. This shews us how we ought to deal with wicked men, when we see that they are altogether destitute of the fear of God. All that remains for us to do is, to warn them that their jeers and scorn will be attended by no success in resisting the vengeance of God which hangs over them. We are also reminded that we ought not to sport with God, since we see, as in a mirror, what has been the end of those who despised the warnings and threatenings of the prophets since the beginning of the world.

For I have heard a consumption. That his prediction may be firmly believed, he declares that he brings nothing forward which God did not reveal. כלה (*chălāh*) sometimes signifies "perfection," and sometimes "consumption," as we formerly stated.[1] (Isaiah x. 23.) Here it must denote "consumption," for the Prophet means nothing else than that God has determined speedily to destroy the whole earth by a general slaughter. This includes two things; first, that dreadful and grievous destruction is about to overtake the world, (unless it be thought better to limit the word "earth" to Judea, to which I do not object,) and, secondly, that the day is fixed and is not distant. The word *hearing* is here used to denote Revelation. He says that it has been made known to him; for, as the Lord determined to make use of the ministry of the prophets, so he revealed to them

---

[1] See *Commentary on Isaiah*, vol. i. p. 360.

his secrets, that they might be, as it were, interpreters of them.

Upon the whole earth. As if he had said, " The whole world abounds with shocking impiety, reprobate men have grown wanton in their wickedness, as if there would be no judgment of God ; but throughout the whole world, or in every part of Judea, God will shew that he is judge and avenger, and not a corner of the earth will be exempted from troubles and calamities, because they have despised the word." Now, although these things were revealed in the age of Isaiah, yet they belong not less to other times, in which God shews that he is always like himself, and is wont to execute his judgments by the same method and rule.[1]

23. *Give ear and hear my voice.* Isaiah makes use of a preface, as if he were about to speak of something important and very weighty ; for we are not wont to demand attention from our hearers, unless when we are about to say what is very important. And yet he seems here to speak of common and ordinary subjects, as for example, about agriculture, sowing, thrashing, and such like operations. But the Prophet intended to direct the minds of his hearers to higher matters ; for when he discourses about the judgments of God, and shews with what wisdom God governs the world, though wicked men think that everything moves by chance and at random, he intended to lay down and explain a difficult subject, in a plain style, by metaphors drawn from objects which are well known and understood. We often complain that God winks too much at the crimes of wicked men, because he does not immediately punish them agreeably to our wish ; but the Prophet shews that God appoints nothing but what is just and proper.

The design of this preface therefore is, that men may perceive their stupidity in carping at the judgments of God, and putting an unfavourable construction on them, while even in the ordinary course of nature they have a very bright mirror, in which they may see them plainly. There is an implied expostulation with men who shut their eyes amidst so clear light. He shews that they are dull and

[1] " Avec mesme raison et equité ;"—" With the same reason and justice."

stupid in not understanding the works of God which are so manifest, and yet are so rash and daring that they presume to judge and censure what is hidden. In like manner Paul also, when speaking of the resurrection, pronounces that those who do not perceive the power of God in the seeds which are thrown into the earth are madmen. "Thou fool, that which thou sowest does not grow or vegetate till it has rotted." (1 Cor. xv. 36.) Thus Isaiah here declares that those who do not see the wisdom of God in things so obvious are stupid, and, in short, that men are blind and dull in beholding the works of God.

24. *Doth the ploughman plough every day*[1] *to sow?* This passage is commonly explained as if the Lord reproached his people for ingratitude, because he had cultivated the field as a husbandman, and had spent on it all his care and industry, and yet did not reap such fruit as it ought to have yielded. Such is the interpretation given by the Jews, who have been followed also by the Greek and Latin commentators; but Isaiah's meaning was quite different. He connects this doctrine with his former statement, that the destruction of Judea, or of the whole world, had been revealed to him; and therefore he adds, that still God does not always display his hand, or constantly punish the wickedness of men; for he often appears as if he did not see it, and delays the punishment of it for a time. The Lord's forbearance and slowness to punish, which is thus manifested, is abused by wicked men for leading them to greater lengths in wickedness, as Solomon remarks that men are encouraged to commit wickedness by observing that "all things happen alike to the good and to the bad," (Eccles. viii. 14,) that all the worst and basest men enjoy prosperity, while the godly are liable to distresses not less and even greater than those of other men.[2]

[1] "The common version, 'all day,' though it seems to be a literal translation, does not convey the sense of the original expression, which is used both here and elsewhere to mean 'all the time,' or 'always.'" —*Alexander.*

[2] "Et les fideles sont sujets à beaucoup de miseres, voire plus que ne sont pas les reprouvez;"—"And believers are liable to many afflictions, even more than the reprobate are."

In short, when the wicked perceive no difference in outward matters, they think either that there is no God, or that everything is governed by the blind violence of fortune. To such thoughts therefore Isaiah replies, " Do you not know that God has his seasons, and that he knows what he ought to do at the proper time ?" If ploughmen do not " every day" cleave the earth or break the clods, this ought not to be attributed to their want of skill; for, on the contrary, their skill requires them to desist.[1] What would they gain by continually turning over the soil, but to weary themselves to no purpose, and prevent it from yielding any fruit ? Thus God does not act with bustle or confusion, but knows the times and seasons for doing his work.[2]

25. *When he hath levelled its surface.* He now speaks about sowing. The sower will not put into the earth as much as he can, nor will he throw it in at random, but will measure the ground, and give to it as much as is necessary ; for otherwise the superfluous mass would rot, and not a single grain would take root.

Wheat in measure, and barley measured.[3] He will not mix various seeds, but will allot one part of the field for " wheat," another for " vetches," and another for " cummin." He will do this in measure, for that I consider to be the proper interpretation of שׂורה (*sōrāh.*)[4] It does not mean

[1] " Will the ploughman never sow, but always cut the earth by spades and instruments for ploughing ?"—*Jarchi.*

[2] " This apposite simile from the various methods used by the husbandman in preparing his land, and in managing the crop after it is gathered, is addressed to those who might question divine providence, because sentence against the wicked is not executed speedily. God, who teacheth the farmer the proper time and manner of treating his crop, knoweth best when and how to punish sinners : he reduceth them not to dust at once, any more than corn is suffered to lie under pressure till it is rendered unserviceable, but chastiseth in mercy, in order to reclaim them."—*Stock.*

[3] " The principal wheat and the appointed barley. Or, wheat in the appointed place, and barley in the appointed place."—*Eng. Ver.* " The choice wheat and the picked barley."—*Stock.* " The wheat in due measure."—*Lowth.*

[4] " The words שׂורה (*sōrāh*) and נסמן (*nĭmsān*) are by some explained as epithets of the grain ; principal wheat, appointed or sealed barley. Ewald makes them descriptive of the soil ; wheat in the best ground, barley in the rough ground. But the explanation best sustained by usage and analogy is that of Gesenius, who takes נסמן (*nĭmsān*) in the sense of

excellent or good; for he is speaking about measurement. Similar statements are made about reaping and thrashing; for all kinds of grain are not thrashed in the same manner. Wheat is thrashed with the wheel of a cart or waggon, vetches with a staff, and cummin with a thicker rod. He speaks according to the custom of the country. This mode of thrashing is unknown in any part of France, except Provence.[1] In short, he means that the manner of thrashing which is suitable to the grain does not apply equally to all. Besides, the husbandman is not constantly or incessantly employed in thrashing, but exercises moderation, that he may not bruise the grain.

26. *His God instructeth and teacheth him what is right.* From whom did the husbandman learn these things but from God? If they are so well educated and taught in the smallest matters, what ought we to think of so great a teacher and instructor? Does he not know how to apply a fixed measure and equity to his works? Does he not see the time for executing his judgment; when he ought to cut down the people, and, as we may say, to harrow[2] them; when he ought to thrash; what strokes, what kind of chastisements he ought to inflict; in short, what is most suitable to each time and to each person? Will not he who appointed the universal order of nature regulate these things also by a just proportion? Are men so headstrong that they will venture to remonstrate with him, or to impugn his wisdom? The general meaning is, that we ought not to judge rashly, if God does not immediately punish the wickedness of men.

This shews that we ought to restrain the presumption of men, who, even in the smallest matters, often fall into mistakes. If a person ignorant of agriculture should see a husbandman cutting fields with a plough, making furrows, breaking clods, driving oxen up and down and following

appointed, designated, and שׂורה (*sōrāh*) in that of a row or series."— *Alexander.*

[1] "Car en France on n'escout point le bled sinon avec le fleau, excepté en Provence;"—" For in France corn is not thrashed in any way but with the flail, except in Provence."

[2] "Et comme faire passer la charue et la herse sur les peuples;"— "And, as it were, to pass the waggon and the harrow over the nations."

their footsteps, he would perhaps laugh at it, imagining that it was childish sport; but that man would be justly blamed by the husbandman, and convicted of ignorance and rashness; for every person of great modesty will think that those things are not done idly or at random, though he does not know the reason. When the seed is committed to the ground, does it not appear to be lost? If ignorant men find fault with these things, as ignorance is often rash and presumptuous in judging, will not intelligent men justly blame and pronounce them to have been in the wrong? If this be the case, how shall the Lord deal with us, if we dare to find fault with his works which we do not understand?

Let us therefore learn from this how carefully we ought to avoid this rashness, and with what modesty we ought to restrain ourselves from such thoughts. If we ought to act modestly towards men, and not to condemn rashly what exceeds our understanding or capacity, we ought to exercise much greater modesty towards God. When we consider therefore the various calamities with which the Church is afflicted, let us not complain that loose reins are given to the wicked,[1] and that consequently she is abandoned to her fate, or that all is over with her; but let us believe firmly, that the Lord will apply remedies at the proper time, and let us embrace with our whole heart his righteous judgments.

If any person carefully examining those words shall infer from them that some are punished more speedily and others more slowly, and shall pronounce the meaning to be, that punishment is delayed, such a view is not merely probable, but is fully expressed by the Prophet. We draw from it a delightful consolation, that the Lord regulates his thrashing in such a manner that he does not crush or bruise his people. The wicked are indeed reduced by him to nothing and destroyed; but he chastises his own people, in order that, having been subdued and cleansed, they may be gathered into the barn.

29. *This also hath proceeded from Jehovah of hosts.* This

[1] " Comme si les meschans avoyent la bride sur le col;"—" As if the wicked had the bridle on their neck."

passage is explained by some, as if the Prophet had said that the science of agriculture proceeded from the Lord; but I consider it to be the application of what goes before. Having pointed out the wisdom of God, even in the smallest matters, he bids us, in like manner, raise our eyes to higher subjects, that we may learn to behold with greater reverence his wonderful and hidden judgments. A passing observation on the 26th verse may be made, and indeed ought to be made, that not only agriculture, but likewise all the arts which contribute to the advantage of mankind, are the gifts of God, and that all that belongs to skilful invention has been imparted by him to the minds of men. Men have no right to be proud on this account, or to arrogate to themselves the praise of invention, as we see that the ancients did, who, out of their ingratitude to God, ranked in the number of the gods those whom they considered to be the authors of any ingenious contrivance. Hence arose deification and that prodigious multitude of gods which the heathens framed in their own fancy. Hence arose the great Ceres, and Triptolemus, and Mercury, and innumerable others, celebrated by human tongues and by human writings. The Prophet shews that such arts ought to be ascribed to God, from whom they have been received, who alone is the inventor and teacher of them. If we ought to form such an opinion about agriculture and mechanical arts, what shall we think of the learned and exalted sciences, such as Medicine, Jurisprudence, Astronomy, Geometry, Logic, and such like? Shall we not much more consider them to have proceeded from God? Shall we not in them also behold and acknowledge his goodness, that his praise and glory may be celebrated both in the smallest and in the greatest affairs?

CHAPTER XXIX.

1. Woe to Ariel, to Ariel, the city *where* David dwelt! add ye year to year; let them kill sacrifices.

2. Yet I will distress Ariel, and there shall be heaviness and sorrow: and it shall be unto me as Ariel.

1. Heus Ariel, Ariel, urbs quam incoluit David. Addite annum ad annum, quibus jugulentur agni.

2. Atqui in angustum redigam Ariel, et erit mœror et tristitia, eritque mihi tanquam Ariel.

3. And I will camp against thee round about, and will lay siege against thee with a mount, and I will raise forts against thee.

4. And thou shalt be brought down, *and* shalt speak out of the ground, and thy speech shall be low out of the dust, and thy voice shall be, as of one that hath a familiar spirit, out of the ground, and thy speech shall whisper out of the dust.

5. Moreover, the multitude of thy strangers shall be like small dust, and the multitude of the terrible ones *shall be* as chaff that passeth away ; yea, it shall be at an instant suddenly.

6. Thou shalt be visited of the Lord of hosts with thunder, and with earthquake, and great noise, with storm and tempest, and the flame of devouring fire.

7. And the multitude of all the nations that fight against Ariel, even all that fight against her and her munition, and that distress her, shall be as a dream of a night-vision.

8. It shall even be as when an hungry *man* dreameth, and, behold, he eateth ; but he awaketh, and his soul is empty: or as when a thirsty *man* dreameth, and, behold, he drinketh ; but he awaketh, and, behold, *he is* faint, and his soul hath appetite: so shall the multitude of all the nations be that fight against mount Zion.

9. Stay yourselves, and wonder ; cry ye out, and cry : they are drunken, but not with wine ; they stagger, but not with strong drink.

10. For the Lord hath poured out upon you the spirit of deep sleep, and hath closed your eyes : the prophets and your rulers, the seers hath he covered.

11. And the vision of all is become unto you as the words of a book that is sealed, which *men* deliver to one that is learned, saying, Read this, I pray thee : and he saith, I cannot ; for it *is* sealed :

12. And the book is delivered to

3. Et castrametabor adversum te in circuitu, et oppugnabo te in statione, et erigam contra te aggeres.

4. Tum humiliaberis, e terra loqueris, et e pulvere exibit eloquium tuum, et erit quasi Pythonis e terra vox tua, et e pulvere eloquium tuum mussitabit.

5. Et erit quasi pulvisculus sonitus extraneorum tuorum, et quasi stipula transiens multitudo fortium, et erit ad momentum repente.

6. Ab Iehova exercituum visitaberis, in tonitru, et tumultu, et fragore magno, in turbine, et tempestate, et flamma ignis vorantis.

7. Et erit quasi somnium visionis nocturnæ multitudo omnium gentium pugnantium adversus Ariel ; omnis, inquam, pugnantis, et munitiones erigentis in eam, et constringentium eam.

8. Fiet ergo quemadmodum famelicus somniat, et ecce comedit ; cum autem evigilat, inanis est anima ejus ; et quemadmodum sitiens somniat, et ecce bibit ; cum autem evigilat, lassus est, et anima ejus appetens ; sic erit multitudo omnium gentium pugnantium adversus montem Sion.

9. Immoremini, et admiremini. Excæcati sunt et excæcant ; ebrii sunt, et non vino ; concussi sunt, et non sicera.

10. Quia obtexit super vos Iehova spiritu soporis, obstruxit oculos vestros : Prophetas vestros et præcipuos Videntes caligine obduxit.

11. Itaque facta est vobis omnis visio quasi verba libri obsignati ; quem si tradant scienti literas, ac dicant, Lege, quæso, in eo ; tum dicet, Non possum, quia est obsignatus :

12. Quod si detur ei liber qui

him that is not learned, saying, Read this, I pray thee : and he saith, I am not learned.

13. Wherefore the Lord said, Forasmuch as this people draw near *me* with their mouth, and with their lips do honour me, but have removed their heart far from me, and their fear toward me is taught by the precept of men :

14. Therefore, behold, I will proceed to do a marvellous work among this people, *even* a marvellous work and a wonder; for the wisdom of their wise *men* shall perish, and the understanding of their prudent *men* shall be hid.

15. Woe unto them that seek deep to hide their counsel from the Lord, and their works are in the dark, and they say, Who seeth us? and who knoweth us?

16. Surely your turning of things upside down shall be esteemed as the potter's clay: for shall the work say of him that made it, He made me not? or shall the thing framed say of him that framed it, He had no understanding?

17. *Is* it not yet a very little while, and Lebanon shall be turned into a fruitful field, and the fruitful field shall be esteemed as a forest?

18. And in that day shall the deaf hear the words of the book, and the eyes of the blind shall see out of obscurity, and out of darkness.

19. The meek also shall increase *their* joy in the Lord, and the poor among men shall rejoice in the Holy One of Israel.

20. For the terrible one is brought to nought, and the scorner is consumed, and all that watch for iniquity are cut off:

21. That make a man an offender for a word, and lay a snare for him that reproveth in the gate, and turn aside the just for a thing of nought.

22. Therefore thus saith the Lord, who redeemed Abraham, concerning the house of Jacob, Jacob shall not now be ashamed, neither shall his face now wax pale.

non didicit literas, ac dicatur, Lege, quæso, in eo ; tum dicet, Nescio literas.

13. Ergo dicit Dominus : propterea quod appropinquat populus iste ore suo, et labiis suis honorat me, ac cor suum longè a me removit, et fuit timor eorum erga me præcepto hominum doctus ;

14. Propterea ecce adjicio ut faciam rem mirandam in populo hoc, miraculum, inquam, et portentum ; nam peribit sapientia sapientum ejus, et prudentia prudentum ejus evanescet.

15. Væ latitantibus ab Iehova, ut abscondant consilium ; nam sunt in tenebris opera eorum, ac dicunt, Quis videt nos ? et, Quis scit nos ?

16. Vestra conversio an sicut lutum figuli reputatur ? nempe, dicit opus de auctore suo, Non fecit me ; et figmentum de fictore suo, Non intellexit ?

17. Nonne adhuc paululum, paululum, et redigetur Libanus in Carmelum, et Carmelus in sylvam reputabitur.

18. Et audient in die illa surdi verba libri, et de caligine et tenebris oculi cæcorum videbunt.

19. Tunc repetent humiles in Iehova lætitiam, et pauperes hominum exultabunt in Sancto Israelis.

20. Quoniam in nihilum redactus est violentus, contemptus est derisor ; perierunt qui manè festinabant ad iniquitatem.

21. Facientes hominem peccare in verbo, qui arguentem in porta illaquearunt, et justum flexerunt ad nihilum.

22. Propterea sic dicit Iehova ad domum Iacob, qui redemit Abraham : Non confundetur nunc Iacob, neque pallescet nunc facies ejus.

23. But when he seeth his children, the work of mine hands, in the midst of him, they shall sanctify my name, and sanctify the Holy One of Jacob, and shall fear the God of Israel. 24. They also that erred in spirit shall come to understanding, and they that murmured shall learn doctrine.	23. Nam ubi viderit natos suos, opus manuum mearum, in medio sui, sanctificabunt nomen meum, sanctificabunt Sanctum Iacob, Deum Israel timebunt. 24. Tum errantes spiritu discent intelligentiam; et murmuratores discent doctrinam.

1. THIS appears to be another discourse, in which Isaiah threatens the city of Jerusalem. He calls it "Altar,"[1] because the chief defence of the city was in the "Altar;"[2] for although the citizens relied on other bulwarks, of which they had great abundance, still they placed more reliance on the Temple (Jer. vii. 4) and the altar than on the other defences. While they thought that they were invincible in

---

[1] "Il l'appelle *Ariel*, c'est à dire, autel de Dieu;"—"He calls it *Ariel*, that is, Altar of God."

[2] "Some, with the Chaldee, suppose it to be taken from the hearth of the great altar of burnt-offerings, which Ezekiel plainly calls by the same name; and that Jerusalem is here considered as the seat of the fire of God, אור אל, (*ōr ēl*,) which should issue from thence to consume his enemies. Compare chap. xxxi. 9. Some, according to the common derivation of the word, אל ארי (*ărī ēl*,) the lion of God, or the strong lion, suppose it to signify the strength of the place, by which it was enabled to resist and overcome all its enemies."—*Lowth*. "Jonathan interprets it the altar of the Lord, and Ezekiel also (xliii. 15) gives it this name. It is so called, on account of the fire of God, which couched like ארי, (*ări*,) a lion on the altar. Our Rabbins explain אריאל (*ărīēl*) to denote the temple of Jerusalem, which was narrow behind, and broad in front."—*Jarchi*. "The greater part of interpreters are agreed, that אריאל (*ărīēl*,) compounded of ארי (*ări*) and אל, (*ēl*,) denotes the lion of God, or, as Castalio renders it, The Lion—God. But they differ in explaining the application of this name to Jerusalem."—*Rosenmüller*. "The meaning of the Prophet, in my opinion, is, that 'God will make Jerusalem the hearth of his anger, which shall consume not only the enemies but the obstinate rebellious Jews.' This meaning is elegant and emphatic, and agrees well with the wisdom of the prophet Isaiah. Ariel is here taken, in its true signification, not for the altar, but for the hearth of the altar, as in Ezekiel. The import of the name lies here. The hearth of the altar sustained the symbol of the most holy and pure will of God, by which all the sacrifices offered to God must be tried; and to this applies the justice of God, burning like a fire, and consuming the sinner, if no atonement be found. Jerusalem would become the theatre of the divine judgments."—*Vitringa*. "Isaiah foresees that the city will, in a short time, be besieged by a very numerous army of the Assyrians, and will be reduced to straits, and yet will not be vanquished by those multitudes, but, like a lion, will rise by divine power out of the severest encounters."—*Doederlein*.

power and resources, they considered their strongest and most invincible fortress to consist in their being defended by the protection of God. They concluded that God was with them, so long as they enjoyed the altar and the sacrifices. Some think that the temple is here called " Ariel," from the resemblance which it bore to the shape of a lion, being broader in front and narrower behind; but I think it better to take it simply as denoting " the Altar," since Ezekiel also (xliii. 15) gives it this name. This prediction is indeed directed against the whole city, but we must look at the design of the Prophet; for he intended to strip the Jews of their foolish confidence in imagining that God would assist them, so long as the altar and the sacrifices could remain, in which they falsely gloried, and thought that they had fully discharged their duty, though their conduct was base and detestable.

The city where David dwelt. He now proceeds to the city, which he dignifies with the commendation of its high rank, on the ground of having been formerly inhabited by David, but intending, by this admission, to scatter the smoke of their vanity. Some understand by it the lesser Jerusalem, that is, the inner city, which also was surrounded by a wall; for there was a sort of two-fold Jerusalem, because it had increased, and had extended its walls beyond where they originally stood; but I think that this passage must be understood to relate to the whole city. He mentions *David*, because they gloried in his name, and boasted that the blessing of God continually dwelt in his palace; for the Lord had promised that "the kingdom of David would be for ever." (2 Sam. vii. 13; Psalm lxxxix. 37.)

Hence we may infer how absurdly the Papists, in the present day, consider the Church to be bound to Peter's chair, as if God could nowhere find a habitation in the whole world but in the See of Rome. We do not now dispute whether Peter was Bishop of the Church of Rome or not; but though we should admit that this is fully proved, was any promise made to Rome such as was made to Jerusalem? "This is my rest for ever: here will I dwell, for I have chosen it." (Psalm cxxxii. 14.) And if even this were granted, do not we see what Isaiah declares about Jerusalem? That God is driven from it, when there is no room for doctrine, when the worship of God is corrupted. What then shall be said of Rome, which has no testimony? Can she boast of anything in preference to Jerusalem? If God pronounces a curse on the most holy city, which he had chosen in an especial manner, what must we say of the rest, who have overturned his holy laws and all godly institutions.

Add year to year. This was added by the Prophet, because the Jews thought that they had escaped punishment, when any delay was granted to them. Wicked men think that God has made a truce with them, when they see no destruction close at hand; and therefore they promise to themselves unceasing prosperity, so long as the Lord permits them to enjoy peace and quietness. In opposition to this assurance of their safety the Prophet threatens that, though they continue to "offer sacrifices,"[1] and though they renew them year by year, still the Lord will execute his vengeance. We ought to learn from this, that, when the Lord delays to punish and to take vengeance, we ought not, on that account, to seize the occasion for delaying our repentance; for although he spares and bears with us for a time, our sin is not therefore blotted out, nor have we any reason to promise that we shall make a truce with him. Let us not then abuse his patience, but let us be more eager to obtain pardon.

2. *But I will bring Ariel into distress.* I think that ו (*vau*) should here be taken for a disjunctive conjunction: "And yet I will execute my judgments and take vengeance, though, by delaying them for a time, it may seem as if I had forgiven." He next threatens that he will give them *grief and mourning,* instead of the joy of the festivals. אניה (*ănīăh*) is viewed by some as an adjective,[2] but impro-

---

[1] Instead of "Let them kill sacrifices," Vitringa's rendering, in which he has been followed by Lowth, Stock, and Alexander, is, "Let the feasts revolve."—*Ed.*

[2] Symmachus, on whom Montfaucon bestows the exaggerated commendation of having adhered closely to the Hebrew text, wherever it differed from the Septuagint, renders the clause, καὶ ἔσται κατώδυνος καὶ

perly; for it is used in the same manner by Jeremiah.[1] (Lam. ii. 5.) He declares that the Lord will reduce that city to straits, that the Jews might know that they had to contend with God, and not with men, and that, though the war was carried on by the Assyrians, still they might perceive that God was their leader.

And it shall be to me as Ariel. This clause would not apply to the Temple alone; for he means that everything shall be made bloody by the slaughter which shall take place at Jerusalem;[2] and therefore he compares it to an "Altar," on which victims of all kinds are slain, in the same manner as wicked men destined for slaughter are frequently compared to a sacrifice. In short, by alluding here to the word "Altar," he says, that the whole city shall be "as Ariel," because it shall overflow with the blood of the slain. Hence it is evident that the outward profession of worship, ceremonies, and the outward demonstrations of the favour of God, are of no avail, unless we sincerely obey him. By an ironical expression he tells hypocrites, (who with an impure heart present sacrifices of beasts to God, as if they were the offerings fitted to appease his anger,) that their labour is fruitless, and that, since they had profaned the Temple and the Altar, it was impossible to offer a proper sacrifice to God without slaying victims throughout the whole city, as if he had said, "There will be carnage in every part." He makes use of the word "Sacrifice" figuratively, to denote the violent slaughter of those who refused to offer themselves willingly to God.

3. *And I will camp against thee round about.* By the

ὀδυνωμένη, which has been closely followed by Jerome's version, " Et erit tristis ac moerens;"—" And she shall be sad and sorrowful."—*Ed.*

[1] In both cases there are two synonyms, תאניה ואניה (*thăănīāh văănīāh,*) which are derived from the same root. This peculiarity is imitated by the version of Symmachus quoted above, κατώδυνος καὶ ὀδυνωμένη, and by that of Vitringa, (" mœstitia et mœror,") who remarks: " It is somewhat unusual to bring together words of the same termination and derived from the same root; but in this instance it produces an agreeable echo, which convinces me that it must have been frequently employed in poetical writings."—*Ed.*

[2] " Que les ennemis feront en Jerusalem;"—" Which the enemies shall make in Jerusalem."

word כדור (kăddūr[1]) he alludes to the roundness of a ball; and the expression corresponds to one commonly used, ("Je l'environneray,") "I shall surround it." Thus he shews that all means of escape will be cut off.

And will lay siege against thee. This alludes to another method of invading the city; for either attacks are made at various points, or there is a regular siege. He confirms the doctrine of the former verse, and shews that this war will be carried on under God's direction, and that the Assyrians, though they are hurried on by their passions and by the lust of power, will undertake nothing but by the command of God. He reckoned it to be of great importance to carry full conviction to the minds of the Jews, that all the evils which befell them were sent by God, that they might thus be led to enter into an examination of their crimes. As this doctrine is often found in the Scriptures, it ought to be the more carefully impressed on our minds; for it is not without good reason that it is so frequently repeated and inculcated by the Holy Spirit.

4. *Then shalt thou be laid low.* He describes scornfully that arrogance which led the Jews to despise all threatenings and admonitions, so long as they enjoyed prosperity, as is customary with all hypocrites. He says therefore, that, when their pride has been laid aside, they will afterwards be more submissive; not that they will change their dispositions, but because shame will restrain that wantonness in which they formerly indulged. We ought therefore to supply here an implied contrast. He addresses those who were puffed up by ambition, carried their heads high, and despised every one, as if they had not even been subject to God; for they ventured to curse and insult God himself, and to mock at his holy word. "This pride," says Isaiah, "shall be laid low, and this arrogance shall cease."

And thy voice shall be out of the ground.[2] What he had formerly said he expresses more fully by a metaphor, that

---

[1] "Like a circle of tents. כדור, (kăddūr,) like a *Dowar*; so the Arabs call a circular village of tents, such as they still live in."—*Stock.*
[2] "Qu'ils parleront bas, et comme du creux de la terre;"—"That they will speak low, and as out of the heart of the earth."

they will utter a low and confused noise as out of caverns.[1] The voice of those who formerly were so haughty and fierce is compared by him to the speech *of soothsayers*, who, in giving forth their oracles out of some deep and dark cave under ground, uttered some sort of confused muttering; for they did not speak articulately, but whispered. He declares that these boasters (ἀλάζονες) shall resemble them. Some interpret this expression as if the Prophet meant that they will derive no benefit from the chastisement; but the words do not convey this meaning, and he afterwards says that the Jews will be brought to repentance. Yet he first strikes terror, in order to repress their insolence; for they arrogantly and rebelliously scorned all the threatenings of the Prophet. By their being "brought down," therefore, he means nothing else than that they shall be covered with disgrace, so that they will not dare to utter, as from a lofty place, their proud and idle boastings.

5. *And as the small dust.*[2] I shall first state the opinions of others, and afterwards I shall bring forward what I consider to be more probable. Almost all the commentators think that this expression denotes the enemies of the Jews; for they consider "foreigners" to mean "enemies," and allege that the multitude of those who shall oppress the Jews shall be "like dust;" that is, it shall be innumerable. But when I examine closely the whole passage, I am more disposed to adopt a contrary opinion. I think that the Prophet speaks contemptuously of the garrisons on which the Jews foolishly relied, for they had in their pay foreign soldiers who were strong men.

The multitude of the mighty ones. Such is the interpretation which I give to עָרִיצִים (*gnārītzīm*), which is also its literal meaning; and I see no reason why some of the Jews

[1] "And from the dust thou shalt chirp thy words, or, utter a feeble, stridulous sound, such as the vulgar supposed to be the voice of a ghost. This sound was imitated by necromancers, who had also the art of pitching their voice in such a manner as to make it appear to proceed out of the ground, or from what place they chose."—*Stock.*

[2] The Septuagint renders it, καὶ ἔσται ὡς κονιορτὸς ἀπὸ τροχοῦ ὁ πλοῦτος τῶν ἀσιβῶν, "and as the small dust from the wheel shall be the multitude of the wicked." Here it is necessary to attend to the distinction between τρόχος and τροχός—*Ed.*

should suppose it to mean ungodly or wicked persons. Since, therefore, the Jews brought various garrisons from a distance, they thought that they were well defended, and dreaded no danger. The Prophet threatens that their subsidiary troops, though they were a vast multitude, shall in vain create a disturbance, for they shall be like " dust" or " chaff," that is, useless refuse, for they shall produce no effect.[1] Hence we ought to infer, that our wealth and resources, however great they are, shall be reduced to nothing, as soon as the Lord shall determine to deal with us as he has a right to do. The assistance of men lasts indeed for a time; but when the Lord shall lift up his hand in earnest, their strength must crumble down, and they must become like chaff.

And it shall be in a moment suddenly. Some explain the concluding clause of this verse to mean, that the noise of the enemies' attack shall spring up suddenly, and, as it were, in a moment. But I consider והיה, *(vĕhāyāh,) and it shall be,* to relate to the time of duration, which he declares will be momentary; that is, those military aids shall not last long, but shall quickly vanish away.[2] In vain do men boast of them, for God is their enemy.

6. *From Jehovah of hosts shalt thou be visited.* He next assigns the reason why all this multitude of garrisons shall be " like chaff;" and he expresses this by an opposite metaphor, for with those soldiers he contrasts the anger and " visitation of the Lord." What is " chaff" to the flame of " a devouring fire?" What is " dust" to the force and violence of a " whirlwind?" He shews that the vengeance of God will be such as all their preparations shall be unable to resist. This meaning, in my opinion, makes the passage to flow easily, and the clauses will not be so well adjusted, if we follow a different interpretation.

[1] " The military forces of Sennacherib, which shall be fuel for the fire, and shall be reduced to powder."—*Jarchi.*

[2] " They shall be destroyed by the pestilential blast *Simoom*, whose effects are instantaneous. Thevenot describes this wind with all the circumstances here enumerated, with thunder and lightning, insufferable heat, and a whirlwind of sand. By such an ' angel of Jehovah,' as it is called below, (Isa. xxxvii. 36,) was the host of Assyria destroyed."—*Stock.*

Hence we learn that those who assail us can do no more than what the Lord permits them to do. If therefore the Lord determine to save us, the enemies will accomplish nothing, though they raise up the whole world against us. On the other hand, if he determine to chastise us, we shall not be able to ward off his wrath by any forces or bulwarks, which shall quickly be thrown down as by a "whirlwind," and shall even be consumed as by "a flame."

7. *As a dream of a night-vision.* This verse also I interpret differently from others; for they think that the Prophet intended to bring consolation to the godly. There is undoubtedly great plausibility in this view, and it contains an excellent doctrine, namely, that the enemies of the Church resemble "dreamers" in this respect, that the Lord disappoints their hopes, even when they think that they have almost gained their object.[1] But this interpretation does not appear to me to agree well with the text. Sometimes it happens that, when a sentence is beautiful, it attracts us to it, and causes us to steal away from the true meaning, so that we do not adhere closely to the context, or spend much time in investigating the author's meaning. Let us therefore inquire if this be the true meaning of the Prophet.

Since he afterwards proceeds again to utter threatenings, I have no doubt that here he follows out the same subject, which otherwise would be improperly broken off by the present statement. He censures the Jews, and rebukes them for their obstinacy, in boldly despising God and all his threatenings. In short, by a most appropriate metaphor, he reproves them for their false confidence and presumption, when he threatens that the enemies shall arrive suddenly and unexpectedly, while the Jews shall imagine that they are enjoying profound peace, and are very far from all danger; and that the event shall be so sudden and unexpected, that it will appear to be "a dream." "Although then," says he, "thou indulgest the hope of uninterrupted repose, the

---

[1] "As a dream, when one thinks that he sees, and yet does not in reality see, so shall be the multitude of nations; they will indeed think that they are subduing the city of Jerusalem, but they shall be disappointed of that hope, they shall not succeed in it."—*Jarchi.*

Lord will quickly awake thee, and will drive away thy presumption."

The Prophet says wittily, that the Jews are "dreaming," because, in consequence of being drowned in their pleasures, they neither see nor feel anything, but, amidst the dizzy whirl, stupidly fancy that they are happy. Hence he infers that the enemies will come, as in "a dream," to strike terror into those who are asleep, as it frequently happens that a pleasant and delightful sleep is disturbed by frightful dreams. It follows from this, that the pleasures which have lulled them to sleep will be of no advantage to them; for, though they do not at all think of it, yet a tumult will arise suddenly. This might still have been somewhat obscure, if he had not explained the subject more fully in the following verse.

8. *It shall be therefore as when a hungry man dreameth.* He compares the Jews to "hungry men," who are indeed asleep, but whose empty stomach craves for food; for it is natural for men to dream about food and entertainments when they are in want of them. Thus, while the Jews watched, they were like "hungry men." The Lord continually warned them by his prophets, and invited them to the divine feasts of the word; but they despised those feasts, and chose rather to take refuge wholly in their vices, and to fall asleep in them, than to partake fully of those sacred feasts. Accordingly, while they quieted their consciences, they imagined that they had abundance of all things, and that they were free from every inconvenience. Isaiah declares that they greatly resemble this "dream" and airy "vision;" for, when they have been aroused by a sudden calamity, they shall feel how empty and unsubstantial those "dreams and visions" were, and how false and delusive was the opinion which they had formed that they enjoyed abundance. As "hungry men," who have had such dreams, are rendered more feeble by them, so the people, who had been falsely persuaded that everything was going on well with them, will endure much greater uneasiness than if they had never cherished in their minds such a thought, but, on the contrary, had been aware of their poverty and nakedness.

So shall be the multitude. At first sight, the expression appears to be harsh, when he says, "The multitude of those who fight against Ariel shall be as a dream;" but it ought to be explained in this manner:—"When the Jews, through false hope, shall promise to themselves deliverance, as if the enemies would be driven far away, they shall quickly feel that they had been deceived; in the same manner as a person whom hunger leads to dream that he is feasting luxuriously, as soon as he awakes, feels that his hunger is keener than before." I see nothing here, therefore, that is fitted to yield consolation, for the Prophet pursues the same subject, and exclaims against the scorn and rebellion of the Jews, on whom the Prophet could make no impression by exhortation or threatenings.[1]

9. *Tarry and wonder.* Isaiah follows out the same subject, and attacks more keenly the gross stupidity of the people. Instead of "tarry," some render the term, "Be amazed;" but the view which I prefer may be thus expressed: "Though they dwell much and long on this thought, yet it will end in nothing else than that, by long continued thought, their minds shall be amazed." In short, he means that the judgment of God will so completely overwhelm their minds, that though they torture themselves by thinking and reflecting, still they will be unable to find any outlet or conclusion.

They are drunken, and not with wine. He now assigns the reason why fixed thought does not aid them in conquering their slowness of apprehension. It is, because they resemble *drunkards.* When, therefore, they neither see nor understand anything in the works of God, he shews that this is owing to their indolence and stupidity. A proof of

[1] " The comparison is elegant and beautiful in the highest degree, well wrought up, and perfectly suited to the end proposed: the image is extremely natural, but not obvious; it appeals to our inward feelings, not to our outward senses, and is applied to an event in its concomitant circumstances exactly similar, but in its nature totally different. For beauty and ingenuity it may fairly come in competition with one of the most elegant of Virgil, (greatly improved from Homer, Iliad, xxii. 199,) where he has applied to a different purpose, but not so happily, the same image of the ineffectual working of imagination in a dream. Virg. Æn. xii. 908. Lucretius expresses the very same image with Isaiah, (iv. 1091.)"—*Lowth.*

this is given daily in many persons; for spiritual "drunkenness" engrosses and stupifies all their senses to such a degree, that they are blind to the plainest subjects; and, when God shews the brightest light of justice and equity, they are so completely dazzled, that their dim vision bewilders them more and more. This stupidity is a just punishment which the Lord inflicts on them on account of their unbelief.

In order that we may apply this statement of the Prophet for our own use, it is proper to observe, that these words of the Prophet must not be understood to be commands, as if he enjoined them to stop and think longer; but, on the contrary, he mocks and reproves their stupidity, as we have already said. (Pensez y tant que vous voudrez, vous n'y entendrez rien)—"Think as much as you please about it, you will not at all understand it."

They are blinded, and they blind.[1] He means, that they are destitute of judgment and understanding, and that consequently it is useless for them to contemplate these works of God; for as the brightness of the sun is of no avail to the toad, so a blinded understanding in vain does its utmost to comprehend the majestic works of God. When he says that "they are blinded," he means that by nature we are created so as to be endued with reason and understanding for contemplating the works of God; that our being "blinded" is, so to speak, an accidental fault, and that the drunkenness does not naturally belong to us, for it is owing to the ingratitude of men, which the Lord justly censures.

They stagger. This "staggering" of the mind is contrasted by him with a calm and quiet exercise of reason; for he means that violence of the passions which agitates the mind, and causes it to waver and reel.

10. *Because Jehovah hath overpowered you with the spirit of slumber.* For the purpose of shewing more clearly the source of this blindness, he attributes it to the judgment of God, who determined to punish in this manner the wicked-

[1] " Cry ye out, and cry, *or*, Take your pleasure and riot."—Eng. Ver. " Turn yourselves and stare around."—*Stock.* Lowth's rendering resembles this, but is somewhat paraphrastic, " They stare with a look of stupid surprise." Professor Alexander's comes nearer that of CALVIN, " Be merry and blind!"—*Ed.*

ness of the people. As it belongs to him to give eyes to see, and to enlighten minds by the spirit of judgment and understanding, so he alone deprives us of all light, when he sees that by a wicked and depraved hatred of the truth we of our own accord wish for darkness. Accordingly, when men are blind, and especially in things so plain and obvious, we perceive his righteous judgment.

Your prophets and principal seers.[1] He adds, that the people are deprived of those aids and helps which ought to have imparted light to the understanding and given direction to others.[2] Such was the office of the prophets, whom he describes by both of these names, נביאים, (*nĕbīīm,*) and חזים, (*chōzīm,*) "prophets" and "seers." In short, he means not only that men who are endued with reason and understanding will be deprived of common sense, but that their teachers also, whose duty it was to enlighten others, will be altogether senseless so as not to know the road, and, being covered with the darkness of ignorance, will shamefully go astray, and will be so far from directing others that they will not even be able to guide themselves.

11. *Therefore every vision hath become to you.* The Prophet expresses still more clearly what he had formerly said, that the blindness of the Jews will be so great that, though the Lord enlightens them by the clearest light of his word, they will understand nothing. Nor does he mean that this will happen to the common people alone, but even to the rulers and teachers, who ought to have been wiser than others, and to have held out an example to them.[2] In short, he means that this stupidity will pervade all ranks; for both "learned and unlearned," he declares, will be so dull and stupid as to be altogether dazzled by the word of God, and to see no more in it than in a "sealed letter." He makes the same statement, but in different words, which he had made in the former chapter, that the Lord will be to them

---

[1] "Your prophets, and your rulers (Heb. heads)."—Eng. Ver. Our translators very correctly state that the literal meaning of ראשיכם (*rāshēchĕm*) is, "your heads." CALVIN treats it as an adjective, "your principal seers."—*Ed.*

[2] "Et monstrer le chemin aux autres;"—"And point out the way to others."

as " precept upon precept, line upon line ;" for they will always remain in the first rudiments, and will never arrive at solid doctrine. (Isaiah xxviii. 13.)

In the same sense he now shews that, from the highest to the lowest, they will derive no benefit from the word of God. He does not say that doctrine will be taken away, but that, though it be in their possession, they will not have reason and understanding. In two ways the Lord punishes the wickedness of men ; for sometimes he takes away entirely the use of the word, and sometimes, when he leaves it, he takes away understanding, and blinds the minds of men, so that "seeing they do not see." (Isaiah vi. 9.) First, therefore, he deprives them of reading, either by taking away the books through the tyranny of wicked men, as frequently happens, or by a false conviction of men, which leads them to think that the books were not delivered to be read universally by all. Secondly, although he allows them to handle and read the books, yet, because men abuse them, and are ungrateful, and do not look straight to the glory of God, they are blinded, and see no more than if not a single ray of the word had shone upon them. We must not boast, therefore, of the outward preaching of the word ; for it will be of no avail unless it produce its fruit by enlightening our minds. It is as if he had said, " On account of that covenant which he made with your fathers, the Lord will leave to you the tables of that covenant ; but they shall be to you ' a sealed letter,' for you shall learn nothing from them." (Deut. iv. 20, 37, and vii. 6.)

When we see that these things happened to the Jews, as Isaiah threatened, and when we take into view the condition of that people, which God had adopted and separated, it is impossible that we should not altogether tremble at such dreadful vengeance. Though they had been instructed both by the law and by the prophets, and had been enlightened by a light of surpassing brightness, yet they fell into frightful superstitions and shocking impiety ; the worship of God was corrupted, all religion was scattered and overthrown, and they were rent and divided into various and monstrous sects. At length, when the Sadducees, the most wicked of them all, held the chief power, when all faith and all hope of a resurrection, and even of immortality, had been taken away, what, I ask, could they resemble but cattle or swine? for what is left to man if the hope of a blessed and eternal life be taken from him?

And yet the Evangelists (Matt. xxii. 23; Mark xii. 18; Luke xx. 27; Acts xxiii. 8) plainly tell us that there were such persons when Christ came; for at that time these things were actually fulfilled, as they had been foretold by the Prophet, that we may know that these threatenings were not thrown out at random or by chance, and that they did not fail of accomplishment, because at that time they were obstinately and rebelliously despised and scorned by wicked men. At that time, therefore, both their unbelief and their folly were clearly seen, when the true light was revealed to the whole world, that is, Christ, the only light of truth, the soul of the law, the end of all the prophets. At that time, I say, there was, in an especial manner, placed before the eyes of the Jews "that vail which was shadowed out in Moses," (Ex. xxxiv. 30,) whom they could not look at on account of his excessive brightness; and it was actually fulfilled in Christ, to whom it belonged, as Paul tells us, to take away and destroy that vail. (2 Cor. iii. 16.) Till now, therefore, the vail lies on their hearts when they read Moses; for they reject Christ, to whom Moses ought to be viewed as related. In that passage "Moses" must be viewed as denoting the law; and if it be referred to its end, that is, to Christ, that vail will be taken away.

While we contemplate these judgments of God, let us also acknowledge, that he who was formerly the Judge is still the Judge, and that the same vengeance is prepared for those who shall refuse to lend their ear to his most holy warnings. When he expressly names the "learned and unlearned,"[1] it ought to be observed, that we do not understand spiritual doc-

---

[1] "The common version, *I am not learned*, is too comprehensive and definite. A man might read a letter without being learned, at least in the modern sense, although the word was once the opposite of illiterate or wholly ignorant. In this case it is necessary, to the full effect of the comparison, that the phrase should be distinctly understood to mean, *I cannot read.*"—*Alexander.*

trine, in consequence of possessing an acute understanding, or having received a superior education in the schools. Learning did not prevent them from being blinded. We ought, therefore, to embrace the word sincerely and earnestly, if we wish to escape this vengeance, which is threatened not only against the ignorant but also against the "learned."

13. *Therefore the Lord saith.* The Prophet shews that the Lord, in acting with such severity towards his people, will proceed on the most righteous grounds; though it was a severe and dreadful chastisement that their minds should be stupified by the hand of God.[1] Now, since men are so fool-hardy and obstinate, that they do not hesitate to contend with him, as if he were unjustly severe, the Prophet shews that God has acted the part of a righteous judge, and that the blame lies wholly on men, who have provoked him by their baseness and wickedness.

Because this people draweth near with their mouth. He shews that the people have deserved this punishment chiefly on account of their hypocrisy and superstitions. When he says that "they draw near with the *mouth* and the *lips,*" he describes their hypocrisy. This is the interpretation which I give to נגש, (*nāgăsh,*) and it appears to me to be the more probable reading, though some are of a different opinion. Some translate it, "to be compelled," and others, "to magnify themselves;" but the word contrasted with it, *to remove,*[2] which he afterwards employs, shews plainly that the true reading is that which is most generally received.

And their fear toward me hath been taught by the precept of men. By these words he reproves their superstitious and idolatrous practices. These two things are almost always joined together; and not only so, but hypocrisy is never free from ungodliness or superstition; and, on the other hand, ungodliness or superstition is never free from hypocrisy. By the *mouth* and *lips* he means an outward profession, which belongs equally to the good and the bad; but they differ in this respect, that bad men have nothing but idle ostentation, and think that they have done all that is

[1] "Par le jugement de Dieu;"—"By the judgment of God."
[2] "Retirer."

required, if they open their lips in honour of God; but good men, out of the deepest feeling of the heart, present themselves before God, and, while they yield their obedience, confess and acknowledge how far they are from a perfect discharge of their duty.

Thus he makes use of a figure of speech, very frequent in Scripture, by which one part or class denotes the whole. He has selected a class exceedingly appropriate and suitable to the present subject, for it is chiefly by the tongue and the mouth that the appearance of piety is assumed. Isaiah therefore includes, also, the other parts by which hypocrites counterfeit and deceive, for in every way they are inclined to lies and falsehood. We ought not to seek a better expositor than Christ himself, who, in speaking of the washing of the hands, which the Pharisees regarded as a manifestation of holiness, and which they blamed the disciples for neglecting, in order to convict them of hypocrisy, says, "Well hath Isaiah prophesied of you, This people honoureth me with the lips, but their heart is far from me." (Matt. xv. 7, 8.) With the "lips" and "mouth," therefore, the Prophet contrasts the "heart," the sincerity of which God enjoins and demands from us. If this be wanting, all our works, whatever brilliancy they possess, are rejected by him; for "he is a Spirit," and therefore chooses to be "worshipped" and adored by us "with the spirit" and the heart. (John iv. 24.) If we do not begin with this, all that men profess by outward gestures and attitudes will be empty display. We may easily conclude from this what value ought to be set on that worship which Papists think that they render to God, when they worship God by useless ringing of bells, mumbling, wax candles, incense, splendid dresses, and a thousand trifles of the same sort; for we see that God not only rejects them, but even holds them in abhorrence.

On the second point, when God is worshipped by inventions of men, he condemns this "fear" as superstitious, though men endeavour to cloak it under a plausible pretence of religion, or devotion, or reverence. He assigns the reason, that it "hath been taught by men." I consider

מלמדה (mĕlŭmmādāh)[1] to have a passive signification; for he means, that to make "the commandments of men," and not the word of God, the rule of worshipping him, is a subversion of all order.[2] But it is the will of the Lord, that our "fear," and the reverence with which we worship him, shall be regulated by the rule of his word; and he demands nothing so much as simple obedience, by which we shall conform ourselves and all our actions to the rule of the word, and not turn aside to the right hand or to the left.

Hence it is sufficiently evident, that those who learn from "the inventions of men" how they should worship God, not only are manifestly foolish, but wear themselves out by destructive toil, because they do nothing else than provoke God's anger; for he could not testify more plainly than by the tremendous severity of this chastisement, how great is the abhorrence with which he regards false worship. The flesh reckons it to be improper that God should not only reckon as worthless, but even punish severely, the efforts of those who, through ignorance and error, weary themselves in attempts to appease God; but we ought not to wonder if he thus maintains his authority. Christ himself explains this passage, saying, "In vain do they worship me, teaching doctrines, the commandments of men." (Matt. xv. 9.) Some have chosen to add a conjunction, "teaching doctrines *and* commandments of men," as if the meaning had not been sufficiently clear. But he evidently means something different, namely, that we act absurdly when we follow "the commandments of men" for our doctrine and rule of life.

14. *Therefore, behold, I add to do.*[3] He threatens that he will punish by blinding not only the ignorant or the ordinary ranks, but those wise men who were held in admiration by the people. From this vengeance we may easily learn how hateful a vice hypocrisy is, and how greatly it is abhorred by God, as the Prophet spoke a little before about human inventions; for what kind of punishment is more dreadful than blindness of mind and stupidity? This in-

---

[1] " Qui signifie enseigné;"—" Which signifies taught."
[2] " Qu'on renverse tout ordre."
[3] " I will proceed to do. (Heb. I will add)."—Eng. Ver.

deed is not commonly perceived by men, nor are they aware of the greatness of this evil; but it is the greatest and most wretched of all.

For the wisdom of their wise men shall perish. He does not speak of the common herd of men, but of their very leaders, who ought to have been like eyes. The common people in themselves are blind, like the other members of the body; and when the eyes are blinded, what shall become of the rest of the body? "If the light be darkness," as Christ says, "how great shall be the darkness!" This is added in order to place that vengeance in a more striking light.

Hence also, we may infer how vain and foolish is the boasting of the Papists, who think that they have shut the mouths of all men, when they have brought forward the name of Bishops, or other titles of the same kind, such as Doctors, or Pastors, or the Apostolical See. They have perhaps a different kind of wisdom from that which was possessed by the Jews; but whence did they derive it? They pretend that it came from God; but we see that the Prophet does not speak of the wise men of the Chaldeans or Egyptians, but of the order of priesthood which God had appointed, of the teachers, and chief rulers, and ensign-bearers, of the chosen people and of the only Church; for under this term "wise men," he includes all superior excellence and authority among the people.

15. *Wo to them that conceal themselves from Jehovah.* The Prophet again exclaims against those wicked, and profane despisers of God, whom he formerly called לֵצִים, (*lētzīm,*) "scorners," who think that they have no other way of being wise than to be skilful in mocking God. They regard religion as foolish simplicity, and hide themselves in their cunning, as in a labyrinth; and on this account they mock at warnings and threatenings, and, in short, at the whole doctrine of godliness. From this verse it is sufficiently evident that the pestilence, which afterwards spread more widely, prevailed even at that time in the world, namely, that hypocrites delighted in mocking inwardly at God, and in despising prophecies. The Prophet therefore exclaims against them, and

calls them מַעֲמִיקִים, (*măgnămīkīm*,) that is, "diggers,"[1] as if they "dug" for themselves concealments and lurking-places, that by means of them they might deceive God.

That they may hide counsel. This clause is added for the sake of exposition. Some interpret the beginning of this verse, as if the Prophet condemned that excessive curiosity by which some men, with excess of hardihood, search into the secret judgments of God. But that interpretation cannot be admitted; and the Prophet plainly shews to whom he refers, when he immediately adds the mockeries of those who thought that their wickedness was committed in a manner so secret and concealed, that they could not be detected. The "hiding of counsel" means nothing else than hardihood in wickedness, by which wicked men surround themselves with clouds, and obscure the light, that their inward baseness may not be seen. Hence arises that daring question—

Who seeth us? For, although they professed to be worshippers of God, yet they thought that, by their sophistry, they had succeeded not only in refuting the prophets, but in overturning the judgment of God; not openly, indeed, for even wicked men wish to retain some semblance of religion, that they may more effectually deceive, but in their heart they acknowledge no God but the god which they have contrived. This craftiness, therefore, in which wicked men delight and flatter themselves, is compared by Isaiah to a hiding-place, or to coverings. They think that they are covered with a veil, so that not even God himself can see and punish their wickedness. As rulers are principally chargeable with this vice, it is chiefly to them, in my opinion, that the Prophet's reproof is directed; for they do not think that they have sufficient acuteness or dexterity, if they do not scoff at God, and despise his doctrine, and, in short, believe no more than what they choose. They do not venture to reject it altogether, or rather, they are constrained, against their will, to hold by some religion; but they do so only as far as they think that they can promote their own convenience, and are not moved by any fear of the true God.

At the present day this wickedness has been abundantly

[1] " C'est à dire, Fonisseurs."

manifested, and especially since the gospel was revealed. Under Popery men found it easy to transact with God, because the Pope had contrived a god who changed himself so as to suit the disposition of every individual. Every person had a different method of washing away his sins, and many kinds of worship for appeasing his deity. Consequently, none ought to wonder that wickedness was not seen at that time, for it was concealed by coverings of that sort; and when these had been taken away, men declared openly what they had formerly been. Yet not less common in our age is the disease which Isaiah bewailed in his nation; for men think that they can conceal themselves from God, when they have interposed their ingenious contrivances, as if "all things were not naked and open to his eyes," (Heb. iv. 13,) or as if any man could deceive or be concealed from him. For this reason he says, by way of explanation—

For their works are in darkness. He assigns this as the cause of that foolish confidence by which ungodly men are intoxicated. Though they are surrounded by light, they are so slow of perception, that when they do not see it, they endeavour to flee from the presence of God. They even promise to themselves full escape from punishment, and commit sin with as much freedom as if they had been protected and fortified on all sides against God. Such is the import of their question, *Who seeth us?* Not that wicked men ventured openly to utter these words, as we have said, but because they thus spoke or thus thought in their hearts, which was manifested by their presumption and vain confidence. They abandoned themselves to all wickedness, and despised all warnings, in such a manner as if there would never be a judgment of God. The Prophet, therefore, had to do with ungodly men, who in appearance and name professed to have some knowledge of God, but in reality denied him, and were very bitter enemies of pure doctrine. Now, this is nothing else than to affirm that God is not a Judge, and to cast him down from his seat and tribunal; for God cannot be acknowledged without doctrine; and where that is set aside and rejected, God himself must be set aside and rejected.

16. *Is your turning reckoned like potter's clay!* There are

various ways of explaining this verse, and, indeed, there is some difficulty on account of the two particles, אִם (*ĭm*) and כִּי (*kī*). אִם (*ĭm*) is often used in putting a question, and sometimes in making an affirmation ; and therefore some translate it *truly.* The word הַפְכְּ (*hăphăch*) is considered by some to mean " turning upside down,"[1] as if he had said, " Shall your turning upside down be reckoned like clay ?" Others render it " turning," that is, the purposes which are formed in the heart. But the most generally received rendering is, "turning upside down" or " destruction." As if he had said, " I would care no more about destroying you, than the potter would care about turning the clay ; for you are like clay, because I have created you with my hand."

But as the Prophet appears to contrast those two particles אִם (*ĭm*) and כִּי (*kī*), I am more inclined to a different opinion, though I do not object to the former exposition, which contains a doctrine in other respects useful. My view of it therefore is this, " Shall your turning, that is, the purposes which you ponder in your heart, be like potter's clay ? Is it not as if the vessel said to the potter, Thou hast not formed me? Your pride is astonishing ; for you act as if you had created yourselves, and as if you had everything in your own power. I had a right to appoint whatever I thought fit. When you dare to assume such power and authority, you are too little acquainted with your condition, and you do not know that you are men."[2]

This diversity of expositions makes no difference as to the Prophet's meaning, who had no other object in view than to confirm the doctrine taught in the preceding verse ; for he still exclaims against proud men, who claim so much power to themselves that they cannot endure the authority of God, and entertain a false opinion about themselves, which

---

[1] This corresponds with the English version.—*Ed.*

[2] In almost all the ancient versions הָפְכְּכֶם, (*hŏphchĕchĕm*,) generally rendered " your turning," is construed as the nominative to the verb " shall be." Modern critics treat it as a separate clause, and exclamation. " Perverse as ye are !"—*Lowth.* " Perverseness of yours !" —*Stock.* " Your perversion !"—*Alexander.* The same meaning had been brought out by Luther, though in a paraphrastic form, Wie seyd ihr so verkehrt ! " How are you so perverse !"—*Ed.*

leads them to despise all exhortations, as if they had been gods. Thus do they deny that God has created them; for whatever men claim for themselves, they take from God, and deprive him of the honour which is due to him.

Only in the first clause would the meaning at all differ; for those who interpret אם (*im*) affirmatively, consider this verse to mean, "*Truly*, I will destroy you as a potter would break the pot which he had made." But as the Prophet had to do with proud men, who sought out lurking-places in order to deceive God, I rather view it as a question, "Are you so able workmen that the revolutions of your brain can make this or that, as a potter, by turning the wheel, frames vessels at his pleasure?" Let every person adopt his own opinion: I follow that which I consider to be probable.

17. *Is it not yet a little while?* The Lord now declares that he will make those wicked men to know who they are; as if he had said, "You are now asleep in your pride, but I shall speedily awake you." Men indulge themselves, till they feel the powerful hand of God; and therefore the Prophet threatens that the judgment of God will overtake such profound indifference.

And Lebanon shall be turned into Carmel.[1] Under the names "Lebanon" and "Carmel" he intended to express a renovation of the world and a change of affairs. But as to the object of the allusion, commentators differ widely from each other. As Mount "Lebanon" was clothed with trees and forests, and "Carmel" had fruitful and fertile fields. Many think that the Jews are compared to "Carmel," be-

---

[1] This rendering is followed by Lowth and Stock. "Ere Lebanon beams like Carmel. A mashal, or proverbial saying, expressing any great revolution of things, and, when respecting two subjects, an entire reciprocal change."—*Lowth*. "And Lebanon shall be turned into a Carmel. That which is now desert shall become a fruitful field, and the reverse. Or, to quit the figure, the poor and illiterate shall change conditions with the great ones and the wise of this world, with respect to happiness, when the gospel shall be promulgated."—*Stock*. Jarchi, on the other hand, views "Carmel" as meaning "a fruitful field," and Alexander regards this point as decided by the use of the article. "That הכרמל (*hăkkărmĕl*) is not the proper name of the mountain, may be inferred from the article, which is not prefixed to 'Lebanon.'" "The mention of the latter," he adds, "no doubt suggested that of the ambiguous term *Carmel*, which is both a proper name and an appellative."—*Ed.*

cause they will be barren, and Christians to "Lebanon," because they will yield a great abundance of fruits. That opinion is certainly plausible, as men are usually gratified by everything that is ingenious; but a parallel passage, which we shall afterwards see, (Isaiah xxxii. 15), will shew that the Prophet here employs the comparison for the purpose of magnifying the grace of God; for, when he shall again begin to bless his people, the vast abundance of all blessings will take away from "Carmel" the celebrity which it possessed. He therefore threatens that he will turn "Lebanon" into "Carmel," that is, a forest will become a cultivated field, and will produce corn, and the cultivated fields shall yield so great an abundance of fruits that, if their present and future conditions be compared, they may now be pronounced to be unfruitful and barren. This mode of expression will be more fully explained when we come to consider Isaiah xxxii. 15.

Others view "Carmel" as an appellative, but I prefer to regard it as a proper name; for it means that those fruitful fields may now be reckoned uncultivated and barren, in comparison of the new and unwonted fertility. Others explain it allegorically, and take "Lebanon" as denoting proud men, and "Carmel" as denoting mean and ordinary persons. This may be thought to be acute and ingenious, but I choose rather to follow that more simple interpretation which I have already stated. That the godly may not be discouraged, he passes from threatenings to proclaim grace, and declares that when, by enduring for a little the cross laid on them, they shall have given evidence of the obedience of their faith, a sudden renovation is at hand to fill them with joy. And yet, by shutting out the ungodly from this hope, he intimates that, when they are at ease, and promise to themselves peace or a truce, destruction is very near at hand; for, "when they shall say, Peace and Safety," as Paul tells us, "then sudden destruction will overtake them." (1 Thess. v. 3.)

18. *And in that day shall the deaf hear.* He promises that the Church of God, as we have said, shall still be preserved amidst those calamities. Though the world be shaken by innumerable tempests, and tossed up and down, and though heaven and earth shall mingle, yet the Lord will preserve

the multitude of the godly, and will raise up his Church, as it were, out of the midst of death. This ought to strengthen in no ordinary manner the faith of the godly; for it is an extraordinary miracle of God that, amidst the numerous and extensive ruins of empires and monarchies, which happen here and there, the seed of the godly is preserved, among whom the same religion, the same worship of God, the same faith, and the same method of salvation, are continued.

And the eyes of the blind shall see. But Isaiah appears here to contradict himself; for formerly he foretold that among the people of God there would be so great stupidity that nobody would understand, and now he says that even "the deaf" shall understand, and "the blind shall see." He therefore means that the Church must first be chastised and purified, and that not in a common and ordinary way, but in a way so unusual that it will appear to have altogether perished. He therefore says, *in that day,* that is, after having punished the wicked and purified his Church, not only will he enrich the earth with an abundance of fruits, but, by renewing the face of it, he will at the same time restore "hearing to the deaf" and "sight to the blind," that they may receive his doctrine. Men have no ears and no eyes, so long as this dreadful punishment lasts; the minds of all are stupified and confounded, and do not understand anything. When the plagues and distresses shall have come to an end, the Lord will open his eyes, that they may behold and embrace his goodness and compassion.

This is the true method of restoring the Church, when it gives sight to the blind and hearing to the deaf, which we see that Christ also did, not only to the bodies but also to the souls. (John ix. 7, 39.) We too have experienced this in our own time, when we have been brought out of the darkness of ignorance, in which we were enveloped, and have been restored to the true light; and eyes have been restored to see, and ears to hear it, which formerly were shut and closed; for the Lord "pierced them," (Psalm xl. 6,) that he might bring us to obey him. The blessing which he promised in the renovation of the earth was indeed a kind of proof of reconciliation; but far more excellent is that illumination of which he now speaks, without which all God's benefits not only are lost, but are turned to our destruction. Justly does God claim for himself a work so glorious and excellent; because there is nothing for which there is less ground of hope than that the blind should recover sight, and that the deaf should recover hearing, by their own strength. This is evidently promised, in a peculiar manner, to the elect alone; for the greater part of men always continue in their darkness.

19. *Then shall the humble again take joy in Jehovah.* Such is my translation of this passage, while others render it, " They shall add," or " continue to rejoice;" for the Prophet describes not a "joy" which is continued but rather a "joy" which is new. As if he had said, " Though they are now distressed and sorrowful, yet I will give them occasion of gladness, so that they shall again be filled with "joy." He speaks of the " humble;" and hence it ought to be observed that our afflictions prepare us for receiving the grace of God; for the Lord casts us down and afflicts us, that he may afterwards raise us up. Thus, when the Lord corrects his people, we ought not to lose heart, but should recall to remembrance those statements, that we may always hope for better things, and may believe that, after such calamities and distresses, he will at length bring joy to his Church. Yet we again learn from it what I briefly mentioned a little before, that the grace of illumination does not belong indiscriminately to all; for, although all have been chastened together, yet not all have had their hearts subdued by affliction, so as truly to become " poor in spirit," or " meek." (Matt. v. 3, 5.)

20. *For the violent man is brought to nought.* He states more clearly what we have already mentioned in the former verse, namely, that the restoration of the Church consists in this, that the Lord raises up those who are cast down, and has compassion on the poor. But that purification of the Church, of which we have already spoken, is first necessary; for so long as the Lord does not execute his judgment against the wicked, and the bad are mixed with the good, so as even to hold the highest place in the Church, everything is soiled and corrupted, God is not worshipped or feared, and even

godliness is trampled under feet. When therefore the ungodly are removed or subdued, the Church is restored to its splendour, and the godly, freed from distresses and calamities, leap for joy.

First, he calls them עָרִיצִים, (*gnărītzīm,*) "violent." There are various interpretations of this word; but I think that the Prophet distinguishes between those who are openly wicked, and have no shame,[1] and those who have some appearance of goodness, and yet are not better than others, for they mock at God in their hearts. But perhaps by the two adjectives, "violent" and "scorners," he describes the same persons; because, like robbers among men, they seize, oppress, treat with cruelty, and commit every kind of outrage, and yet are not withheld by any fear of God, because they regard religion as a fable.

And they who hastened early to iniquity.[2] Under this class he includes other crimes. He speaks not of the Chaldeans or Assyrians, but of those who wished to be reckoned in the number of the godly, and boasted of being the seed of Abraham.

21. *That make a man an offender for a word.* We have formerly stated who were the persons with whom the Prophet had to do, namely, with hypocrites and profane scorners, who set at nought all the reproofs and threatenings of the Prophets, and who wished to frame a God according to their own fancy. Such persons, desiring to have unbounded license, that they might indulge freely in their pleasures and their crimes, bore very impatiently the keen reproofs of the prophets, and did not calmly submit to be restrained. On this account they carefully observed and watched for their words, that they might take them by surprise, or give a false construction. I have no doubt that he reproves wicked men, who complained of the liberty used by the prophets, and of the keenness of their reproofs, as if they had intended to attack the people, and the nobles, and the

---

[1] " Ceux qui n'ont point honte de commettre leurs meschancetez devant tous ;"—" Those who are not ashamed to commit their acts of wickedness in presence of all."

[2] " Ceux qui se levoyent de matin pour mal faire ;"—" They who rose early to do evil."

priests; for hence arise the calumnies and false accusations which are brought even against the faithful servants of God. Hence arise those doubtful and ensnaring questions which are spread out as snares and nets, that they may either bring a righteous man into danger of his life, or may practise some kind of deceit upon him. We see that the Pharisees and Sadducees did so to Christ himself. (Matt. xxi. 23, and xxii. 17; John viii. 6.)

Who have laid a snare for him that reproveth in the gate. This latter clause, which is added for the sake of exposition, does not allow us to interpret the verse as referring generally to calumnies, and other arts by which cunning men entrap the unwary; for now the Prophet condemns more openly those wicked contrivances by which ungodly men endeavour to escape all censure and reproof. As it was "in the gates" that public assemblies and courts of justice were held, and great crowds assembled there, the prophets publicly reproved all, and did not spare even the judges; for at that time the government was in the hands of men whom it was necessary to admonish and reprove sharply. Instead of repenting, as they ought to have done when they were warned, they became worse, and were enraged against the prophets, and laid snares for them; for "they hated," as Amos says, "him that reproveth in the gate, and abhorred him that speaketh uprightly." (Amos v. 10.) This relates to all, but principally to judges, and those who hold the reins of government, who take it worse, and are more highly displeased that they should receive such reproofs; for they wish to be distinguished from the rank of other men, and to be reckoned the most excellent of all, even though they be the most wicked.

Who have laid snares. Commentators differ as to the meaning of the word יְקֹשׁוּן, (*yĕkōshūn;*) for some render it "have reproved," and others "have reproached," as if the Prophet censured the obstinacy of those who resort to slanders, in order to drive reprovers far away from them. But I trust that my readers will approve of the meaning which I have followed.

And have turned aside the righteous man for nothing, that

is, when there is no cause.[1] By wicked and deceitful contrivances, they endeavour to cause the righteous to be hated and abhorred by all men, and to be reckoned the most wicked of all; but, after having thus sported with the world, they will at length perish. Such is the consolation which the Lord gives, that he will not suffer the wickedness of the ungodly to pass unpunished, though they give way to mirth and wantonness for a time, but will at length restrain them. Yet " we have need of patience, that we may wait for the fulfilment of these promises." (Heb. x. 36.)

22. *Therefore thus saith Jehovah.* This is the conclusion of the former statement; for he comforts the people, that they may not despair in that wretched and miserable condition to which they shall be reduced. We ought to observe the time to which those things must relate, that is, when the people have been brought into a state of slavery, the temple overturned, the sacrifices taken away, and when it might be thought that all religion had fallen down, and that there was no hope of deliverance. The minds of believers must therefore have been supported by this prediction, that, when they were shipwrecked, they might still have this plank left, which they might seize firmly, and by which they might be brought into the harbour. We too ought to take hold of these promises, even in the most desperate circumstances, and to rely on them with our whole heart.

To the house of Jacob. The address made to them should lead us to remark, that the power of the word of God is perpetual, and is so efficacious that it exerts its power, so long as there is a people that fears and worships him. There are always some whom the Lord reserves for himself, and he does not allow the seed of the godly to perish. Since the Lord hath spoken, if we believe his word, we shall undoubtedly derive benefit from it. His truth is firm, and therefore, if we rely on him, we shall never want consolation.

Who redeemed Abraham. Not without good reason does he add, that he who now declares that he will be kind to

---

[1] " Il dit aussi que le juste est renversé sans raison;"—" He says also, that the righteous man is overthrown without any good reason."

the children of Jacob is the same God "who redeemed Abraham." He recalls the attention of the people to the very beginning of the Church, that they may behold the power of God, which had formerly been made known by proofs so numerous and so striking that it ought no longer to be doubted. If they gloried in the name of Abraham, they ought to consider whence it was that the Lord first delivered him, that is, from the service of idols, which both he and his fathers had worshipped. (Gen. xi. 31, and xii. 1; Josh. xxiv. 2.) But on many other occasions he "redeemed" him; when he was in danger in Egypt on account of his wife, (Gen. xii. 17,) and again in Gerar, (Gen. xx. 14,) and again when he subdued kings, (Gen. xiv. 16,) and likewise when he received offspring after being past having children. (Gen. xxi. 2, 5.) Although the Prophet has chiefly in view the adoption of God, when the Lord commanded him to leave "his father's house," (Gen. xii. 1,) yet under the word "redeemed" he includes likewise all blessings; for we see that Abraham was "redeemed" on more than one occasion, that is, he was rescued from very great dangers and from the risk of his life.

Now, if the Lord raised up from Abraham alone, and at a time when he had no children, a Church which he should afterwards preserve, will he not protect it for ever, even when men shall think that it has perished? What happened? When Christ came, how wretched was the dispersion, and how numerous and powerful were the enemies that opposed him! Yet, in spite of them all, his kingdom was raised up and established, the Church flourished, and drew universal admiration. No one therefore ought to doubt that the Lord exerts his power whenever it is necessary, and defends his Church against enemies, and restores her.

Jacob shall not now be ashamed. He means that it often happens that good men are constrained by shame to hang down their heads, as Jeremiah declares in these words, "I will lay my mouth in the dust." (Lam. iii. 29.) Micah also says, "It is time that wise men should hide their mouth in the dust." (Mic. vii. 16.)[1] For when the Lord chastises

---

[1] Both of the above quotations are made inaccurately. The words of Jeremiah are, "He putteth his mouth in the dust," and of Micah, "They

his people so severely, good men must be "ashamed." Now, the Prophet declares that this state of things will not always last. We ought not to despair therefore in adversity. Though wicked men jeer and cast upon us every kind of reproaches, yet the Lord will at length free us from shame and disgrace. At the same time, however, the Prophet gives warning that this favour does not belong to proud or obstinate persons who refuse to bend their neck to God's chastisements, but only to the humble, whom shame constrains to hang down their heads, and to walk sorrowful and downcast.

It may be asked, Why does he say, "Jacob shall not be ashamed?" For "Jacob" had been long dead, and it might be thought that he ascribed feeling to the dead, and supposed them to be capable of knowing our affairs.[1] Hence also the Papists think that the dead are spectators of our actions. But the present instance is a personification, such as we frequently find in Scripture. In the same manner also Jeremiah says, "In Ramah was heard the voice of Rachel bewailing her children, and refusing to be comforted, because they are not;" for he describes the defeat of the tribe of Benjamin by the wailing of "Rachel," who was their remote ancestor. (Jer. xxxi. 15.)

Isaiah introduces Jacob as moved with shame on account of the enormous crimes of his posterity; for Solomon tells us that "a wise son is the glory of his father, and a foolish son brings grief and sorrow to his mother." (Prov. x. 1.) Though mothers bear much, still they blush on account of the wicked actions of their children. What then shall be the case with fathers, whose affection for their children is less accompanied by foolish indulgence, and aims chiefly at training them to good and upright conduct? Do they not on that account feel keener anguish, when their children act wickedly and disgracefully? But here the Prophet intended to pierce the hearts of the people and wound them to the quick, by holding out to them their own patriarch, on whom

shall lay their hand upon their mouth." But while the Author, quoting from memory, has altered the words, the passages are exceedingly apposite to his purpose.—*Ed.*

[1] "Qu'ils peuvent savoir ce que nous faisons au monde;"—"That they can know what we are doing in the world."

God bestowed blessings so numerous and so great, but who is now dishonoured by his posterity; so that if he had been present, he would have been compelled to blush deeply on their account. He therefore accuses the people of ingratitude, in bringing disgrace on their fathers whom they ought to have honoured.

23. *Because, when he shall see his children.* The particle כִּי (*kī*) is here used in its natural and original meaning of *for* or *because.* The Prophet assigns the reason why the disgrace of Israel shall be taken away. It is, because he will have children, and those who were thought to have perished will be still alive.

The work of my hands in the midst of him. By giving them this name, he intended, I have no doubt, to describe the astonishing work of redemption; for those whom God adopts to be his children, and receives into fellowship with himself, are made by him, as it were, new men, agreeably to that saying, " And the people which shall be created shall praise the Lord." (Psalm cii. 18.) In that passage the Psalmist describes in a similar manner the renewal of the Church; for this description, as we have repeatedly stated on former occasions, does not relate to the general creation which extends to all, but leads us to acknowledge his power, that we may not judge of the salvation of the Church by the present appearances of things. And here we ought to observe various contrasts; first, between the ruinous condition of the Church and her surpassing beauty, between her shame and her glory; secondly, between the people of God and other nations; thirdly, between " the works of God's hands" and the works of men, (for by God's hand alone can the Church be restored;) and fourthly, between her flourishing condition and the ruinous and desolate state to which she had formerly been reduced. By the phrase, " in the midst of him," is meant a perfect restoration, by which the people shall be united and joined together in such a manner as to occupy not only the extremities, but the very heart and the chief places of the country.

They shall hallow my name. Last of all, he points out the end of redemption. We were all created, that the goodness of God might be celebrated among us. But as the greater part of mankind have revolted from their original condition, God hath chosen a Church in which his praises should resound and dwell, as the Psalmist says, "Praise waiteth for thee in Zion." (Psalm lxv. 1.) Now, since many even of the flock have degenerated, the Prophet assigns this office to believers, whom God had miraculously preserved.

They shall fear the God of Israel. Because hypocrites, as we have formerly seen, honour God with their lips, but are far removed from him in their heart, after speaking of the ascriptions of praise, he next mentions *fear;* thus meaning that our praises are reckoned of no value, unless we honestly and sincerely obey God, and unless our whole life testify that we do not hypocritically utter the name of God.

24. *Then shall the erring in spirit learn wisdom.* He again repeats that promise which he formerly noticed briefly; for so long as the understandings of men shall be struck with ignorance and blindness, even though they enjoy abundance of every kind of blessings, yet they are always surrounded and besieged by ruin. In making preparation for the restoration of the Church, the Lord therefore enlightens by his word, and illuminates by the light of understanding, his own people, who formerly wandered astray in darkness. He does this by the secret influence of the Spirit; for it would be of little value to be taught by the external word, if he did not also instruct our hearts inwardly.

And the murmurers shall learn doctrine. Some commentators translate רוֹגְנִים (*rōgĕnīm*) "whisperers," and others, "wanderers." But it means that those who formerly murmured against the prophets, and could not endure their warnings, would be obedient and submissive; and therefore I have chosen to render it *murmurers.* Hence we see how wonderful is the mercy of God, who brings back into the path those who were highly unworthy, and makes them partakers of so great blessings. Let us carefully ponder this subject in private. Is there any one of us that has not sometimes "murmured" against God, and despised pure doctrine? Nay, more, if God had not softened the obstinate, and brought them mildly to obey, nearly the whole human race would have perished in their madness.

CHAPTER XXX.

1. Woe to the rebellious children, saith the Lord, that take counsel, but not of me; and that cover with a covering, but not of my Spirit, that they may add sin to sin:

2. That walk to go down into Egypt, and have not asked at my mouth; to strengthen themselves in the strength of Pharaoh, and to trust in the shadow of Egypt!

3. Therefore shall the strength of Pharaoh be your shame, and the trust in the shadow of Egypt *your* confusion.

4. For his princes were at Zoan, and his ambassadors came to Hanes.

5. They were all ashamed of a people *that* could not profit them, nor be an help nor profit, but a shame, and also a reproach.

6. The burden of the beasts of the south: into the land of trouble and anguish, from whence *come* the young and old lion, the viper and fiery flying serpent, they will carry their riches upon the shoulders of young asses, and their treasures upon the bunches of camels, to a people *that* shall not profit *them*.

7. For the Egyptians shall help in vain, and to no purpose: therefore have I cried concerning this, Their strength *is* to sit still.

8. Now go, write it before them in a table, and note it in a book, that it may be for the time to come for ever and ever;

9. That this *is* a rebellious people, lying children, children *that* will not hear the law of the Lord:

1. Væ filiis contumacibus, (*vel, perversis*) dicit Iehova, ut capiant consilium, et non ex me; ut operiant arcanum, (*vel, fundant fusionem,*) et non ex spiritu meo; ut peccatum addant peccato.

2. Proficiscuntur ut descendant in Ægyptum, et os meum non interrogaverunt, roborantes se robore Pharaonis, et sperantes in umbra Ægypti.

3. Erit autem vobis fortitudo Pharaonis in pudorem, et fiducia in umbra Ægypti in ignominiam.

4. Fuerunt enim principes ejus in Zoan et legati ejus in Hanes venerunt.

5. Omnes pudefient in populo qui eis non proderit, neque auxilio erit, neque commodum afferet; sed erit in pudorem, atque etiam in opprobrium.

6. Onus jumentorum Austri. In terra afflictionis et angustiæ, leo, et leo major ab illis, vipera et prester volans, dum portabunt super humerum pullorum divitias suas, et super gibbos camelorum thesauros suos ad populum qui non proderit.

7. Certe Ægyptii vanitas, et frustra auxiliabuntur. Propterea clamavi ad illam: Robur illorum quiescere.

8. Nunc vade, et scribe hanc visionem in tabula coram ipsis, et in libro insculpe eam; ut sit in diem novissimum, in perpetuum usque in secula.

9. Quod populus hic rebellis sit, filii mendaces, filii qui recusant audire legem Iehovæ.

10. Which say to the seers, See not; and to the prophets, Prophesy not unto us right things, speak unto us smooth things, prophesy deceits:

11. Get you out of the way, turn aside out of the path, cause the Holy One of Israel to cease from before us.

12. Wherefore thus saith the Holy One of Israel, Because ye despise this word, and trust in oppression and perverseness, and stay thereon:

13. Therefore this iniquity shall be to you as a breach ready to fall, swelling out in a high wall, whose breaking cometh suddenly at an instant.

14. And he shall break it as the breaking of the potter's vessel that is broken in pieces; he shall not spare: so that there shall not be found in the bursting of it a sherd to take fire from the hearth, or to take water *withal* out of the pit.

15. For thus saith the Lord God, the Holy One of Israel, In returning and rest shall ye be saved; in quietness and in confidence shall be your strength; and ye would not.

16. But ye said, No; for we will flee upon horses; therefore shall ye flee: and, We will ride upon the swift; therefore shall they that pursue you be swift.

17. One thousand *shall flee* at the rebuke of one; at the rebuke of five shall ye flee: till ye be left as a beacon upon the top of a mountain, and as an ensign on an hill.

18. And therefore will the Lord wait, that he may be gracious unto you; and therefore will he be exalted, that he may have mercy upon you: for the Lord *is* a God of judgment: blessed *are* all they that wait for him.

19. For the people shall dwell in Zion at Jerusalem: thou shalt weep no more: he will be very gracious unto thee at the voice of thy cry; when he shall hear it, he will answer thee.

20. And *though* the Lord give you the bread of adversity, and the water

10. Qui dicunt videntibus, ne videatis, et prospicientibus, ne prospiciatis nobis recta; loquimini nobis blanditias, videte errores.

11. Recedite a via, declinate a semita; facite ut a facie nostra facessat Sanctus Israel.

12. Propterea sic dicit Sanctus Israel: quia respuistis verbum hoc, et confisi estis in violentia et pravitate, et innixi estis in eam;

13. Ideo erit vobis iniquitas hæc quasi ruptura cadens, tumor in alto muro, cujus repente et subito venit fractura.

14. Et contritio ejus quasi contritio vasis figulorum, quod absque misericordia comminuitur; nec in ejus fractura invenitur testa ad ignem e foco ferendum, vel aquam e puteo hauriendum.

15. Quoniam sic dixit Dominus Iehova Sanctus Israel: In requie et quiete salvi eritis; in tranquillitate et fiducia erit fortitudo vestra, sed noluistis.

16. Et dixistis, Non, sed equis effugiemus; propterea fugietis; super celerem conscendemus; propterea celeriores erunt qui vos persequentur.

17. Mille unus a facie increpationis unius a facie increpationis quinque fugietis, donec relicti fueritis sicut malus navis in vertice montis, et sicut vexillum in colle.

18. Propterea expectabit vos Iehova, ut misereatur vestri; et propterea exaltabitur, ut propitius sit vobis; quia Deus judicii Iehova. Beati omnes qui expectant eum.

19. Certe populus in Sion habitabit in Ierusalem; flendo non flebis; miserendo miserebitur tui; ad vocem clamoris tui, simulac audierit, respondebit tibi.

20. Ubi dederit vobis Dominus panem angoris et aquam afflictionis,

of affliction, yet shall not thy teachers be removed into a corner any more, but thine eyes shall see thy teachers:

21. And thine ears shall hear a word behind thee, saying, This *is* the way, walk ye in it, when ye turn to the right hand, and when ye turn to the left.

22. Ye shall defile also the covering of thy graven images of silver, and the ornament of thy molten images of gold: thou shalt cast them away as a menstruous cloth; thou shalt say unto it, Get thee hence.

23. Then shall he give the rain of thy seed, that thou shalt sow the ground withal; and bread of the increase of the earth, and it shall be fat and plenteous: in that day shall thy cattle feed in large pastures.

24. The oxen likewise, and the young asses that ear the ground, shall eat clean provender, which hath been winnowed with the shovel and with the fan.

25. And there shall be upon every high mountain, and upon every high hill, rivers *and* streams of waters in the day of the great slaughter, when the towers fall.

26. Moreover, the light of the moon shall be as the light of the sun, and the light of the sun shall be seven-fold, as the light of seven days, in the day that the Lord bindeth up the breach of his people, and healeth the stroke of their wound.

27. Behold, the name of the Lord cometh from far, burning *with* his anger, and the burden *thereof is* heavy: his lips are full of indignation, and his tongue as a devouring fire:

28. And his breath, as an overflowing stream, shall reach to the midst of the neck, to sift the nations with the sieve of vanity: and *there shall be* a bridle in the jaws of the people, causing *them* to err.

29. Ye shall have a song, as in the night, *when* a holy solemnity is kept; and gladness of heart, as when one goeth with a pipe to come into the mountain of the Lord, to the mighty One of Israel.

non arcebitur pluvia tua, et oculi tui videbunt pluviam tuam.

21. Tum aures tuæ audient verbum a tergo tuo, dicendo: Hæc via, ambulate in ea, sive ad dextram sive ad sinistram eatis.

22. Tum profanabitis tectorium sculptilium argenti tui, et operimentum conflatilis auri tui, separabisque ea tanquam pannum menstruo infectum, dicesque illi: Egredere (*vel, Apage.*)

23. Tum dabit pluviam semini tuo, cum seminaveris terram, et panem proventus terræ; et erit uber et pinguis, et pascentur pecora tua in die illo in amplis pascuis.

24. Boves etiam tui, et pulli asinorum colentes terram, pabulum purum comedent, quod in pala ventilatum erit et in vanno.

25. Et accidet, ut super omnem montem excelsum, et super omnem collem elevatum, sint rivi, rivi aquarum in die cædis magnæ cum turres corruerint.

26. Et erit lux lunæ sicut lux solis, et lux solis septuplo major, quasi lux septem dierum, in die quo alligaverit Iehova fracturam populi sui, et perfossionem plagæ ejus sanaverit.

27. Ecce nomen Iehovæ venit e loco remoto; ardens facies ejus, et grave onus; labia ejus plena sunt indignatione; et lingua ejus quasi ignis devorans.

28. Et spiritus ejus quasi torrens inundans, usque ad collum dividet; ad ventilandas gentes in cribro inutili, et fræenum errare faciens in maxillis populorum.

29. Canticum erit vobis, quemadmodum in nocte dum celebratur dies festus, et lætitia cordis quasi ejus qui ad tibiam incedit, ut veniat ad montem Iehovæ, ad Fortem Israelis.

30. And the Lord shall cause his glorious voice to be heard, and shall shew the lighting down of his arm, with the indignation of *his* anger, and *with* the flame of a devouring fire, *with* scattering, and tempest, and hailstones.
31. For through the voice of the Lord shall the Assyrian be beaten down, *which* smote with a rod.
32. And *in* every place where the grounded staff shall pass, which the Lord shall lay upon him, *it* shall be with tabrets and harps: and in battles of shaking will he fight with it.
33. For Tophet *is* ordained of old; yea, for the king it is prepared: he hath made *it* deep *and* large; the pile thereof *is* fire and much wood; the breath of the Lord, like a stream of brimstone, doth kindle it.

30. Et audiri faciet Iehova potentiam vocis suæ, et descensionem brachii sui videri faciet, cum furore vultus et flamma ignis vorantis, dissipatione, inundatione, et lapide grandinis.
31. Sane a voce Iehovæ conteretur Assur, qui virga percussit.
32. Et erit in omni transitu baculus fundatus, quam infliget Iehova super eum cum tympanis, et citharis, et præliis elevationis pugnabit contra eam.
33. Quoniam ordinata est ab hesterno Tophet: etiam Regi præparata est: quam in profundum posuit et dilatavit. Pyra ejus ignis, et ligna multa; flatus Iehovæ quasi torrens sulphuris succendit eam.

1. *Wo to the rebellious children.* The Prophet exclaims against the Jews, because, when they were unable to bear the burden, when they were hard pressed by the Assyrians and other enemies, they fled to Egypt for help. This reproof might appear to be excessively severe, were we merely to consider that weak and miserable men, especially when they are unjustly oppressed, have a right to ask assistance even from wicked persons; for it is a principle implanted in us by nature, that all human beings should willingly, and of their own accord, endeavour to assist each other. But when we come to the very sources, we shall find that no ordinary or inconsiderable guilt had been contracted by the people.

First, it is no light offence, but wicked obstinacy, to disregard and even despise God's government, and follow their own inclinations. But God had strictly forbidden them to enter into any alliance or league with the Egyptians. (Exod. xiii. 17; Deut. xvii. 16.) There were chiefly two causes of this prohibition. One was general, and related to alliances and leagues with other nations; for God did not wish that his people should be corrupted by the superstitions of the Gentiles. (Exod. xxiii. 32, and xxxiv. 15; Deut. vii. 2.) We are gradually infected, I know not how, by the vices of those with whom we have intercourse and familiarity; and as we are more prone by nature to copy vices than virtues, we easily become accustomed to corruptions, and, in short, the infection rapidly spreads from one person to another. This has happened to our own country, France, in consequence of having intercourse with many nations, which leads her too eagerly to imitate their vices, and has covered her with frightful pollution. This immoderate desire of forming alliances unlocked Asia to the Mahometans, and next laid Europe open to them; and though they still retain their moderation in eating and drinking, all that has been subdued by their arms has contracted nothing but filth and debasement. This is what we Frenchmen have also derived from our intercourse with other nations.

The second reason was special and peculiar to this nation; for, since the Lord had delivered the Jews out of Egypt, and commanded them to remember so remarkable a benefit, he forbade them to have any intercourse with the Egyptians. And if they had entered into an alliance with the Egyptians, the remembrance of that benefit might easily have been obliterated; for they would not have been at liberty to celebrate it in such a manner as had been commanded. (Exod. xiii. 3, 8, 14.) It was excessively base to disregard the glory of God for the purpose of cultivating friendship with an irreligious and wicked nation. Since God intended also to testify to his people that he alone was more than sufficient to secure their safety, they ought to have valued that promise so highly as to exclude themselves willingly from other assistance. It was a very heinous crime to endeavour to gain the favour of heathen nations on all sides, and to deprive God of the honour due to him; for if they had been satisfied with having God's protection alone, they would not have been in such haste to run down to Egypt. Their noisy eagerness convicted them of infidelity.

Yet I have no doubt that the Prophet directed his indignation against that sacrilege, because, by labouring earnestly to obtain the assistance of the nations around them, they withheld from God the praise of almighty power. Hence also the Spirit elsewhere compares that ardour to the extravagances of love, and even to licentious courses. (Jer. v. 8.) Ezekiel shews that, by joining the Egyptians, they acted as if a woman, shamefully transgressing the bounds of decency, not only ran furiously after adulterers, but even desired to associate with horses and asses. (Ezekiel xvi. 26.) And yet here he does not absolutely condemn all leagues that are made with idolaters, but has especially in view that prohibition by which the law forbade them to enter into alliance with the Egyptians. It is chiefly on account of the prohibition that he kindles into such rage; for it was not without pouring grievous contempt on God that they ran trembling into Egypt. For this reason he calls them סוררים, (sōrĕrīm,) obstinate and rebellious. We have explained this word at the first chapter.[1] It denotes men of hardened wickedness, who knowingly and willingly revolt from God, or whose obstinacy renders them objects of disgust, so that no integrity or sincerity is left in them. At first he reproves that vice on this ground, that they neglected the word of God, and were devoted to their own counsels.

That they may cover the secret. The words לנסך מסכה, (lĭnsōch măssēchāh,) are explained by some commentators to mean, "to pour out the pouring out." Though this is not at variance with the Prophet's meaning, yet it is more correctly, in my opinion, translated by others, "that they may cover a covering." I have followed that version, because the words relate to counsels held secretly and by stealth, by which they cunningly endeavoured to deceive the prophets, and, as it were, to escape from the eyes of God. Another rendering, "that they may hide themselves by a covering," is absurd; for although it was for the sake of protection that they sought the Egyptians, yet he rather alludes to that craftiness of which I have spoken. Both expositions amount to the same thing.[2]

---

[1] See *Commentary on Isaiah*, vol. i. p. 75.

[2] "The phrase לנסך מסכה (lĭnsōch măssēchāh) has been variously explained. The Peshito makes it mean to pour out libations, probably with reference to some ancient mode of ratifying covenants; and the Septuagint accordingly translates it ἐποιήσατε συνθήκας, 'you made covenants.' Cocceius applies it to the casting of molten images, (ad fundendum fusile,) De Dieu to the moulding of designs or plots. Kimchi and Calvin

By three modes of expression he makes nearly the same statement; that they "cover their counsels," that is, keep them apart from God; that they do not ask at "the mouth of the Lord;" and that they do not suffer themselves to be governed by "his Spirit." They who are guided by their own views turn aside to cunning contrivances, that they may conceal their unbelief and rebellion; and because they have resolved not to obey the word of God, neither do they ask his Spirit. Hence arises that miserable and shameful result. Wretchedly and ruinously must those deliberations and purposes end, over which the Lord does not preside. There is no wisdom that is not obtained from "his mouth;" and if we "ask at his mouth," that is, if we consult his word, we shall also be guided by his Spirit, from whom all prudence and wisdom proceeds.

Let it be observed that two things are here connected, the word and the Spirit of God, in opposition to fanatics, who aim at oracles and hidden revelations without the word; for they wish to come to God, while they neglect and forsake the word, and thus they do nothing else than attempt, as the saying is, to fly without wings. First of all, let it be held as a settled principle, that whatever we undertake or attempt, without the word of God, must be improper and wicked, because we ought to depend wholly on his mouth. And indeed, if we remember what feebleness of understanding, or rather, what lack of understanding, is found in all mankind, we shall acknowledge that they are excessively foolish who claim for themselves so much wisdom, that they do not even deign to ask at the mouth of God.

If it be objected, that the Scriptures do not contain everything, and that they do not give special answers on those points of which we are in doubt, I reply, that everything

derive the words from the root to *cover*, and suppose the idea here expressed to be that of concealment. Ewald follows J. D. Michaelis in making the phrase mean to *weave a web*, which agrees well with the context, and is favoured by the similar use of the same verb and noun in chap. xxv. 7. Knobel's objection, that this figure is suited only to a case of treachery, has no force, as the act of seeking foreign aid was treasonable under the theocracy, and the design appears to have been formed and executed secretly. (Compare chap. xxix. 15, where the reference may be to the same transaction.)"—*Alexander*.

that relates to the guidance of our life is contained in them abundantly. If, therefore, we have resolved to allow ourselves to be directed by the word of God, and always seek in it the rule of life, God will never suffer us to remain in doubt, but in all transactions and difficulties will point out to us the conclusion. Sometimes, perhaps, we shall have to wait long, but at length the Lord will rescue and deliver us, if we are ready to obey him. Although, therefore, we are careful and diligent in the use of means, as they are called, yet we ought always to attend to this consideration, not to undertake anything but what we know to be pleasing and acceptable to God.

The Prophet condemns the presumption of those who attempt unlawful methods, and think that they will succeed in them, when they labour, right or wrong, to secure their safety, as if it could be done contrary to the will of God. It is certain that this proceeds from unbelief and distrust, because they do not think that God alone is able to protect them, unless they call in foreign though forbidden assistance. Hence come unlawful leagues, hence come tricks and cheating, by which men fully believe that their affairs will be better conducted than if they acted towards each other with candour and fairness. There are innumerable instances of this unbelief in every department of human life; for men think that they will be undone, if they are satisfied with the blessing of God, and transact all their affairs with truth and uprightness. But we ought to consider that we are forsaken, rejected, and cursed by God, whenever we have recourse to forbidden methods and unlawful ways. In all our undertakings, deliberations, and attempts, therefore, we ought to be regulated by the will of God. We ought always to consider what he forbids or commands, so as to be fully disposed to obey his laws, and to submit ourselves to be guided by his Spirit, otherwise our rashness will succeed very ill.

That they may add sin to sin. The Prophet says this, because the Jews, by those useless defences which they supposed to fortify them strongly, did nothing else than stumble again on the same stone, and double their criminality, which already was very great. Our guilt is increased, and becomes far heavier, when we endeavour, by unlawful methods, to escape the wrath of God. But we ought especially to consider this expression as applicable to the Jews, because, after having brought the Assyrians into Judea, (for they had called them to their assistance against Israel and Syria,) they wished to drive them out by the help of the Egyptians. (2 Kings xvi. 7, and xvii. 4, and xviii. 21.) The Jews were hard pressed by the Assyrians, and were justly punished for their unbelief, because they resorted to men, and not to God, for aid; and we see that this happened to many nations who called the Turk to their assistance. So far were the Jews from repenting of their conduct, and acknowledging that they had been justly punished, that they even added evil to evil, as if crime could be washed out by crime. On this account they are more severely threatened; for they who persevere in their wickedness, and rush with furious eagerness against God, and do not allow themselves to be brought back to the right path by any warnings or chastisements, deserve to be more sharply and heavily punished.

2. *They walk that they may go down into Egypt.* The reason why the Prophet condemns this "going down" has been already explained;[1] but as their guilt was aggravated by open and heinous obstinacy, he again repeats that they did this without asking at the mouth of God, and even in the face of his prohibition.

Strengthening themselves with the strength of Pharaoh. He again draws their attention to the source of the evil, when he says that it was done for the purpose of acquiring strength, because they placed confidence in the forces of the Egyptians. Hence arose that lawless desire of entering into a league. In this way they shewed that they cared little about the power of God, and did not greatly trust in him; and they openly displayed their unbelief.

It might be objected, that men are the servants of God, and that it is lawful for any one to make use of their services, whenever they are needed. I reply, that while we make use of the labours and services of men, it ought to be

[1] See page 345.

in such a manner as to depend on God alone. But there was another reason peculiar to the Jews, for they knew that God had forbidden them to call the Egyptians to their assistance, and, by doing so, they withheld from God all that they ascribed to Pharaoh and to his forces. Thus it is not without good reason that Isaiah contrasts Pharaoh with God; for the creatures are opposed to God, and enter, as it were, into contest with him when they rise up against God, or whenever men abuse them, or place their hearts and confidence in them, or desire them more than is lawful.

3. *But to you shall the strength of Pharaoh be shame.* He now shews what shall be the end of the wicked, who despise God and his word, and follow those schemes which are most agreeable to their own views. All that they undertake shall tend to their ruin. He threatens not only that they shall be disappointed of their hope, but also that they are seeking with great toil, destruction and ruin, from which they will gain nothing but sorrow and disgrace. To all wicked men it must unavoidably happen that, although for a time they appear to gain their object, and though everything succeeds to their wish, yet in the end all shall be ruinous to them. It is the just reward of their rashness, when they go beyond the limits of the word; for nothing that has been acquired by wicked and unlawful methods can be of advantage to any person.

By way of admission he calls it "the strength of Pharaoh," as if he had said, "You think that you gain much protection from Pharaoh, but it will yield you reproach and disgrace. *The shadow of Egypt*, by which you hoped to be covered, will make you blush for shame." Accordingly, both expressions, "shame" and "disgrace," have the same meaning; and as חרפה, (*chĕrpāh,*)[1] *reproach*, is a stronger expression than "shame," it is afterwards added for the purpose of bringing out the meaning more fully.

4. *For his princes were in Zoan.* The Prophet not only says that the aid of the Egyptians was sought, and that they were invited to assist, but expresses something more, namely, that the Jews obtained it with great labour and

[1] The allusion is to the concluding clause of the fifth verse.—*Ed.*

expense. They had to perform long and painful journeys, to endure much toil, and to expend vast sums of money, in order to arrive, loaded with presents, at the most distant cities of Egypt, which are here named by the Prophet. On this embassy were sent, not persons of mean or ordinary rank, but " princes" and nobles ; and therefore the censure was more severe, because they slavishly solicited an alliance with Egypt, and wandered like suppliants through various countries. It is proper also to bear in mind the contrast which we have already pointed out. They did not need to go far to seek God ; they did not need to endure much toil, or spend large sums of money, in calling on him. He invited them by his promise, " This is my rest," and assured them that in that place they would not call upon him in vain. (Psalm cxxxii. 14 ; Isaiah xxviii. 12.) But those wretched persons despised God, and chose rather to torment themselves, and to run to the very ends of the world, than to receive the assistance which was offered to them.

5. *They shall all be ashamed.* He confirms the former statement ; for it was very difficult to convince ungodly men that all that they undertook without the word of God would be ruinous to them. In order to punish them more severely, God sometimes bestows on them prosperity, that they may be more and more deceived, and may throw themselves down headlong ; for by the righteous judgment of God it is brought about, that Satan draws them by these allurements, and drives them into his nets. Yet the final result is, that not only are they deprived of the assistance which they expected, but they are likewise severely punished both for their presumption and for their unbelief.

Of a people that will not profit them. He threatens not only that the Egyptians will prove false, as wicked men often forsake at the utmost need, or even treacherously ruin, those whom they have fed with empty promises, but that even though they endeavour to the utmost to fulfil the promises which they have made, still they will be of no use. Whatever may be the earnestness with which men endeavour to help us, yet, as events are in the hand of God, they will " profit nothing" without his blessing. It was difficult to believe when the Prophet spoke, that a nation so powerful could yield no assistance; but we ought always to hold it as a principle fully settled, that all the advantage that dazzles us in the world will vanish away, except in so far as God is gracious and kind, and makes it sure for our advantage.

6. *The burden of the beasts of the south.* After having spoken loudly against the consultations of the Jews about asking assistance from the Egyptians, he ridicules the enormous cost and the prodigious inconveniences which they endured on that account; for at so high a price did they purchase their destruction; and he threatens the same curse as formerly, because unhappily they acted in opposition to the word of God. He mentions "the south," because they journeyed through a southern region, Egypt being situated to "the south" of Judea. He therefore calls them "beasts of burden" on account of the journey, and addresses them in order to pour contempt on men, because it was in vain to speak to them, and they were deaf to all exhortations. Accordingly, he threatens that the effect of this prediction shall reach the very "beasts of burden," though men do not understand it.

In the land of trouble and distress. The people having proudly disregarded the threatenings, the Prophet seasonably turns to the horses and camels; and declares that, although they are void of reason, yet they shall perceive that God hath not spoken in vain, and that, though the people imagined that there was uninterrupted prosperity in Egypt, it would be a land of anguish and affliction even to the brute animals. The journey was laborious and difficult, and yet they shrunk from no exertion in order to satisfy their mad desire; and to such a pitch of madness was their ardour carried, that they were not discouraged by the tediousness of the journey.

The young lion and the strong lion. In addition to the inconveniences already mentioned, Isaiah threatens the special vengeance of God, that they shall encounter "lions" and beasts of prey. There was nothing new or uncommon in this to persons who travelled from Judea into Egypt;

but here he threatens something extraordinary and more dangerous. In addition to the inconveniences and toils, and to the sums of money which they shall expend, God will also send disastrous occurrences, and at length they shall be miserably ruined.

This doctrine ought to be applied to us, who are chargeable with a fault exceedingly similar; for in dangers we fly to unlawful remedies, and think that they will profit us, though God disapproves of them. We must therefore experience the same result and fall into the same dangers, if we do not restrain our unbelief and wickedness by the word of God. We ought also to observe and guard against that madness which hurries us along to spare no expense and to shrink from no toil, while we obey with excessive ardour our foolish desire and wish. We had abundant experience of this in Popery, when we were held captives by it, running about in all directions, and wearying ourselves with long and toilsome pilgrimages to various saints; yet the greatest possible annoyances were reckoned by us to be light and trivial. But now, when we are commanded to obey God and to endure "the light yoke" of Christ, (Matt. xi. 30,) we find that we cannot endure it.

7. *Surely the Egyptians are vanity.*[1] This verse contains the explanation of the former statement; for he repeats and threatens the same thing, that the Egyptians, after having worn out the Jews by various annoyances and by prodigious expense, will be of no service to them. "The strength of Egypt" will do them no good, even though he be earnest in assisting them, and employ all his forces. Thus shall the Jews be disappointed of their hope, and deceive themselves to their great vexation. The particle ו ($\bar{u}$) signifies here either *for* or *surely*, as I have translated it.

Therefore have I cried to her. He now shews that the Jews have no excuse for fleeing with such haste into Egypt, and that they are willingly foolish and unworthy of any pardon, because they do not repent when they are warned. When he says that he "cried" to Jerusalem, I consider this to refer to God himself, who complains that his distinct

[1] "For the Egyptians shall help in vain."—Eng. Ver.

warnings and instructions produced no effect, and that his exhortation to them *to sit still* was not without foundation, but was intended to meet the troubles and calamities which he foresaw. Whence came that restlessness, but because they refused to believe the words of the Lord? In a word, he shews that it is mere obstinacy that drives them to flee into Egypt; for by "sitting still" they might provide for their safety.

By the word "cry" he means that he not only warned them by words, but likewise chastised them; and this makes it evident that their obstinacy and rebellion were greater. "To sit still" means here "to remain and to stay at home," though he will afterwards shew (verse 15) that they ought to have peaceable dispositions. The cause of their alarm and impassioned exertions was, that they were terrified and struck with dismay, and did not think that God's protection was sufficient, if they had not also the Egyptians on their side. Thus, they who do not give sufficient honour to God have their hearts agitated by unbelief, so that they tremble and never find peace.

8. *Now go, and write this vision on a tablet.* After having convicted the Jews of manifest unbelief, he means that it should be attested and sealed by permanent records, that posterity may know how obstinate and rebellious that nation was, and how justly the Lord punished them. We have said that it was customary with the prophets to draw up an abridgment of their discourses and attach it to the gates of the temple, and that, after having allowed full time to all to see and read it, the ministers took it down, and preserved it among the records of the temple; and thus the book of the prophets was collected and compiled.[1] But when any prediction was remarkable and peculiarly worthy of being remembered, then the Lord commanded that it should be written in larger characters, that the people might be induced to read it, and to examine it more attentively. (Isaiah viii. 1; Hab. ii. 2.) The Lord now commands that this should be done, in order to intimate that this was no ordinary affair, that the whole ought to be carefully written, and deserved the closest attention, and that it ought not only to

---

[1] See *Commentary on Isaiah*, vol. i. p. 32.

be read, but to be engraven on the remembrance of men in such a manner that no lapse of time can efface it.

Yet there can be no doubt that Isaiah, by this prediction, drew upon himself the intense hatred of all ranks, because he intended to expose and hold them up for abhorrence, not only among the men of his own age, but also among posterity. There is nothing which men resent more strongly than to have their crimes made publicly known and fastened on the remembrance of men; they reckon it ignominious and disgraceful, and abhor it above all things. But the Prophet must obey God, though he should become the object of men's hatred, and though his life should be in imminent danger. Here we ought to observe his steadfastness in dreading nothing, that he might obey God and fulfil his calling. He despised hatred, dislike, commotions, threatenings, false alarms, and immediate dangers, that he might boldly and fearlessly discharge the duties of his office. Copying his example, we ought to do this, if we wish to hear and follow God who calls us.

Before them. אִתָּם (*ittām*) is translated by some, "with them," but it is better to translate it "before them," or, "in their sight;" for it was proper that he should openly irritate the Jews, to whom he presented this prediction written "on a tablet." Hence we ought to infer, that wicked men, though they cannot bear reproof and are filled with rage, ought nevertheless to be reproved sharply and openly; and that threatenings and reproofs, though they be of no advantage to them, will yet serve for an example to others, when those men shall be stamped with perpetual infamy. In them will be fulfilled what is written elsewhere, "The sin of Judah is written with a pen of iron, and with the point of a diamond engraven on their hearts." (Jer. xvii. 1.) They must not think that they have escaped, when they have despised the prophets and shut their ears against them; for their wickedness shall be manifest to men and to angels. But as they never repent willingly or are ashamed of their crimes, God commands that a record of their shame shall be prepared, that it may be placed continually before the eyes of men. As victories and illustrious actions were commonly engraved on tables of brass, so God commands that the disgrace which the Jews brought upon themselves by their transgressions, shall be inscribed on public tablets.

That it may be till the last day. It was very extraordinary, as I remarked a little before, that the Prophet was charged by a solemn injunction to pronounce infamy on his countrymen. For this reason he adds "till the last day," either that they may be held up to abhorrence through an uninterrupted succession of ages, or because, at the appearance of the Judge, the crimes of the wicked shall be fully laid open when he shall "ascend his judgment seat, and the books shall be opened;" for those things which formerly were hidden and wrapped in darkness will then be revealed. (Dan. vii. 10; Rev. xx. 12.)

Here it ought to be carefully observed, that prophecies were not written merely for the men of a single age, but that their children and all posterity ought to be instructed by them, that they may know that they ought not to imitate their fathers. "Harden not your hearts as your fathers did." (Psalm xcv. 8.) What Paul affirms as to the whole of Scripture is applicable to prophecy, that it "is profitable for warning, for consolation, and for instruction," (2 Tim. iii. 16;) and this is proper and necessary in every age. We must therefore reject the fancies of fanatics and wicked men, who say that this doctrine was adapted to those times, but affirm that it is not adapted to our times. Away with such blasphemies from the ears of the godly; for, when Isaiah died, his doctrine must flourish and yield fruit.

9. *For this is a rebellious people.* The word *for* or *because* points to the explanation of what has been already said; for the Prophet explains what the Lord intends to declare to posterity, namely, that the perverseness of this nation is desperate, because they cannot submit to be restrained by any doctrine. That the honourable appellation of the "people" wounded to the quick the hearts both of the ordinary ranks and of the nobles, may be inferred from their loud vaunting; for they boasted that they were the holy and elect seed of Abraham; as if God's adoption had been a veil to cover the grossest crimes. But God commands that

their crimes shall nevertheless be brought to light and openly proclaimed.

Who refuse to hear the law of Jehovah. By accusing them of this, he points out the source of all evils, namely, contempt of the word, which discovers their wickedness and their contempt of God himself; for it is idle to pretend that they worship God, when they are disobedient to his word. Isaiah likewise aggravates their guilt, by saying that they reject the remedy which doctrine offers for curing their diseases. On this account he calls them not only " rebellious," and untameable or abandoned, but *liars* or treacherous persons; for they who refuse to obey the word of God, openly revolt from him, as if they could not endure his authority ; and at the same time, they shew that they are given up to vanity and the delusions of Satan, so that they take no pleasure in sincerity.

10. *Who say to the seers, See not.* He now describes more clearly, and shews, as it were, to the life, the contempt of God and obstinacy which he formerly mentioned ; for wicked men not only pour ridicule on doctrine, but furiously drive it away, and would even wish to have it utterly crushed and buried. This is what Isaiah intended to express. Not only do they turn away their ears, and eyes, and all their senses, from doctrine, but they would even wish that it were destroyed and taken out of the way ; for wickedness is invariably attended by such rage as would lead them to wish the destruction of that which they cannot endure. The power and efficacy of the word wounds and enrages them to such a degree, that they give vent to their fierceness and cruelty like wild and savage beasts. They would gladly escape, but whether they will or not, they are constrained to hear God speaking, and to tremble at his majesty. This bitterness is followed by hatred of the prophets, snares, alarms, persecutions, banishments, tortures, and deaths, by which they think that they can overturn and root out both the doctrine and the teachers ; for men are more desirous to have dreams and fabulous tales told them than to be faithfully instructed.

See not, prophesy not to us right things. The Prophet does not relate the words of wicked men, as if they openly made use of these words, but he describes the state of the fact and their actual dispositions; for he had not to do with men who were such fools as to make an intentional discovery of their wickedness. They were singularly cunning hypocrites, who boasted of worshipping God, and complained that they were unjustly reproached by the prophets. Isaiah tears off the mask by which they concealed themselves, and discovers what they are, because they refused to give place to the truth; for whence came the murmurs against the prophets, but because they could not bear to hear God speaking?

The prophets were called *seers*, because the Lord revealed to them what would afterwards be made known to others. They were stationed, as it were, in a lofty place, that they might behold from on high, and as if from " a watch-tower," (Hab. ii. 1,) the prosperous or adverse events which were approaching. The people wished that nothing of an adverse nature should be told them; and therefore they hated the prophets, because, while they censured and sharply reproved the vices of the people, they at the same time were witnesses of the approaching judgment of God. Such is the import of those words, " Do not see, do not prophesy right things." Not that they spoke in this manner, as we have already said, but because such was the state of their feelings, and because they desired that the prophets should speak with mildness, and could not patiently bear the sharpness of their reproofs. Not one of them was so impudent as to say that he wished to be deceived, and that he abhorred the truth; for they declared that they sought it with the greatest eagerness, as all our adversaries boast of doing at the present day; but they denied that what Isaiah and the other prophets told them was the word of God. In like manner they plainly told Jeremiah that he was " a liar," (Jer. xliii. 2,) and threatened him more insolently, " Thou shalt not prophesy in the name of the Lord, lest thou die by our hand." (Jer. xi. 21.) To them the truth was intolerable; and when they departed from it, they could find nothing but falsehood, and thus they willingly chose to be deceived and to have falsehood told them.

Speak to us smooth things. When he says that they desire "smooth things,"[1] he points out the very source; for they were ready to receive flatterers with unbounded applause, and would willingly have allowed their ears to be tickled in the name of God. And this is the reason why the world is not only liable to be carried away by delusions, but earnestly desires them; for almost all wish to have their vices treated with forbearance and encouragement. But it is impossible that the servants of God, when they endeavour faithfully to discharge their duty, should be chargeable with being severe reprovers; and hence it follows that it is an idle and childish evasion, when wicked men pretend that they would willingly be God's disciples, provided that he were not rigorous. It is as if they bargained that, for their sake, he should change his nature and deny himself; as Micah also says, that no prophets were acceptable to the Jews, but such as "prophesied of wine and strong drink." (Micah ii. 11.)

11. *Depart from the way.* The amount of what is stated is, that when the prophets are set aside, the Lord is also rejected and set aside, and no regard is paid to him. Wicked men pretend the contrary, for they are ashamed to acknowledge so great wickedness. But they gain nothing by it; for God wishes that we should listen to him by means of those to whom he gave injunctions to declare his will to us, and to administer the doctrine of the word. If therefore it is our duty to listen to God, if we are bound to pay him any homage, we ought to shew it by embracing his word, as it is contained in the writings of the prophets and evangelists. This ought to be carefully observed in commendation of the word; for they who set it aside act as if they denied that he is God.

Cause the Holy One of Israel to depart. Here he again points out the cause of so great wickedness, which doubles their guilt; namely, that God does not spare or flatter their vices, but acts the part of a good and skilful physician. Men desire to be flattered, and cannot patiently endure that God should threaten them. Hence it comes that men hate and

[1] "Disant qu'ils demandent d'estre flattez;"—"When he says that they ask to be flattered."

reject the word. Hence proceeds the furious attack on the prophets, whose reproofs and threatenings they cannot endure; for there is no reason why men should revolt from the government of God, but because they take delight in what is wrong and crooked, and abhor the right way. Appropriately, therefore, does the Prophet join these two things, dislike of heavenly doctrine and hatred of uprightness.

12. *Because you have disdained this word.* He next declares the punishment of ungodliness, threatening that they shall not pass unpunished for refusing to hear God speaking; and he expresses their contempt more strongly by the word "disdain." He calls it "this word," making use of the demonstrative; for men would willingly contrive some word adapted to their manner of life, but refuse to listen to God when he speaks.

And trusted in violence and wickedness. God's gentle invitation, and his exhortation to quiet rest, are here contrasted with their disorderly pursuits. The Hebrew word עשׁק (*gnōshĕk*) denotes "robbery," and "seizing property which belongs to another." Others render it "ill-gotten wealth." Those who render it "calumny," do not sufficiently express the Prophet's meaning. For my own part, I do not view it as referring to riches gained by unlawful methods, but rather to that rebelliousness in which that nation insolently indulged.

The word "wickedness,"[1] which is added, ought not to be limited to decisions of courts of law; for, in my opinion, it has a more extensive signification; and by these two words he intended to express the presumption of wicked men, by which they fiercely and wantonly rose up against God, because they always dared to follow their own lawless desires, and to do what was forbidden. And as the poets feign that the giants made war with God,[2] so those men resisted God's threatenings, and thought that they would

---

[1] נלוז (*nālōz*) seems to denote perverseness or moral obliquity in general. It is rendered in a strong idiomatic form by Hitzig, (verschmitztheit, craftiness,) and Ewald, (querwege, crossway.)—*Alexander.* Luther's term, (muthwillen, wantonness,) conveys the same general idea.—*Ed.*

[2] See *Commentary on John's Gospel,* vol. i. p. 223. n. 1.

speedily overcome his power by their fierceness and presumption.

13. *Therefore shall your iniquity be like a breach falling.* This is a threatening of punishment, and Isaiah expresses it by a very appropriate metaphor. He compares wicked men to a wall that is rent, or that bulges out. As the "swelling out" of a wall threatens the ruin of it, because it cannot stand unless all the parts of it adhere closely to each other, so the haughtiness and insolence of wicked men are a sign and very sure proof of their approaching ruin; because the more they are puffed up and swelled without any solid value,[1] the more readily do they throw themselves down headlong, and it is impossible for them not to fall speedily by their own weight. "Rise up," says he, "and act insolently against God; he will quickly put down your presumption and insolence, for it is but an empty swelling." Hence we learn that nothing is better for us than to submit wholly to God, and to keep charge of all our senses, so as to remain chained and bound by his authority; for they who raise themselves by shaking off all humility, destroy themselves by collecting much wind. For a time, indeed, the Lord permits wicked men to swell and utter their big words, that at length, by their "swelling" and idle boasting, they may bring upon themselves ruin and destruction.

14. *And the breaking of it shall be.* When a wall has fallen, some traces of the ruin are still to be seen, and the stones of it may be applied to use, and to some extent the wall may even be rebuilt. But here the Prophet threatens that they who are puffed up with obstinacy against God shall perish in such a manner that they cannot be restored, and all that is left of them shall be utterly useless. Accordingly, he employs the metaphor of a potter's vessel, the broken fragments of which cannot be repaired or put together. These threatenings ought to make a deep impression upon us, that we may embrace with reverence the word of God, when we learn that punishments so severe are prepared for those who despise it; for the Prophet threatens that they shall be utterly destroyed and ruined, and takes away all

[1] "Estans pleins de vent;"—"Being full of wind."

hope of their being restored. Nor is the threatening groundless; for we see how they that despise God, when they have been twice and three times cast down, still do not cease to raise their crests; for nothing is more difficult than to root out the false confidence from their hearts.[1]

15. *For thus saith the Lord.* Here he describes one kind of contempt of God; for when warnings are addressed to hypocrites in general terms, they commonly produce little effect. In addition to the general doctrine, therefore, the prophets specify particular instances, which they specially accommodate to the conduct of those with whom they have to do, so as always to aim at a definite object. They might have wrangled and urged, "Why do you accuse us of so great impiety, as if we rejected the word of the Lord?" He therefore brings forward this class, in order to strike their consciences and cut short their idle sophistry. "Was it not the word of the Lord, In hope and silence shall be your strength? why did you not rely on God? why did you raise a commotion?" Thus the Prophet holds them to be convicted, so that they cannot cavil without the grossest impudence, or, if they do so, will derive no advantage.

The Holy One of Israel. He makes use of this appellation, in order to reproach them the more for their ingratitude, that they may know how great protection they would have found in God : for God wished to be their protector and guardian. When they had forsaken him, their distrust carried them away to solicit the aid of the Egyptians, which was very great and intolerable wickedness. This title contains a bitter complaint, that they shut out God from entering, when he drew near to them.

In rest and quietness shall you be safe. Some render

[1] Here the Author departs from his usual manner, by omitting all mention of the concluding and highly expressive clause of the verse. "For גֵּבֶה, (*gĕbĕh,*) the English version has 'pit,' Lowth, 'cistern,' and most other writers 'well;' but in Ezek. xlvii. 11, it denotes a 'marsh' or 'pool.' Ewald supposes a particular allusion to the breaking of a poor man's earthen pitcher, an idea which had been suggested long before by Gill : ' as poor people are wont to do, to take fire from the hearth, and water out of a well in a piece of broken pitcher.' "—*Alexander.* All must admit, that when one cannot find a "sherd" fit for the meanest purpose, the vessel is broken in pieces.—*Ed.*

שׁוּבָה (*shūbāh*) "repentance." Others render it "rest,"[1] and I am more disposed to adopt that rendering; for I think that the Prophet intended frequently to impress upon the people, that the Lord demands more from them than to rely fully upon him. Nor is the repetition of the statement by two words superfluous; for he expressly intended to bring together the words "rest and quietness," in order to reprove the people the more sharply for their distrust and unbelief.

This verse consists of two clauses, a command and a promise. He enjoins the people to be of a quiet disposition, and next promises that their salvation shall be certain. The people do not believe this promise, and consequently they do not obey the command; for how would they render obedience to God, whom they do not believe, and on whose promises they do not rely? We need not wonder, therefore, that they do not enjoy peace and repose; for these cannot exist without faith, and faith cannot exist without the promises, and as soon as the promises have been embraced, souls that were restless and uneasy are made calm. Thus, unbelief alone produces that uneasiness; and therefore the Prophet justly reproves it, and shews that it is the source of the whole evil.

Though our condition be not entirely the same with that of the Jews, yet God commands us to wait for his assistance with quiet dispositions, not to murmur, or be troubled or perplexed, or to distrust his promises. This doctrine must belong equally to all believers; for the whole object of Satan's contrivances is to distress them, and to cast them down from their condition. In like manner had Moses long before addressed them, "You shall be silent, and the Lord will fight for you." (Exod. xiv. 14.) Not that he wished them to sleep or to be idle, but he enjoined them to have this peace in their hearts. If we have it, we shall feel that it yields

---

[1] Jarchi says, that in this passage שׁוּבָה (*shūbāh*) "signifies rest and quietness," and adduces as a parallel passage one in which the word is commonly viewed as the imperative of שׁוּב, (*shūb*,) with He paragogic. "Give rest, O Lord, to the many thousands of Israel." (Numb. x. 36.) Breithaupt supports that interpretation, and derives the word from יָשַׁב, (*yāshăb*,) "to sit, to rest."—*Ed.*

us sufficient protection; and if not, we shall be punished for our levity and rashness.

16. *We will flee on horses; therefore shall you flee.* He shews how they refused to wait calmly for the salvation of the Lord; for they chose rather to "flee" to the Egyptians. This is a very beautiful instance of ($ἀντανάκλασις$) throwing back an expression, by which he causes their words, so full of confidence, to recoil on themselves. In the first of these clauses, "to flee" means "to escape," and in the second it means "to take flight." The Jews said that it would be better for them, if they adopted timely measures for guarding against the danger which was close at hand, and consequently, that they would best provide for their safety by calling in the aid of the Egyptians. "You shall certainly flee," says Isaiah, "not to find a place of refuge, but to turn your back and to be pursued by horses swifter than yours."

We now perceive more clearly what is the fault which Isaiah describes. By the distinct reply, *No*, he shews how obstinately they refused to comply with the advice which was given to them by the prophets, and chose rather to provide for their safety in another manner. Thus, by despising God, they gave a preference to a groundless appearance of safety, which they had allowed themselves to imagine. We ought, therefore, to turn away our minds from looking at present appearances and outward assistance, that they may be wholly fixed on God; for it is only when we are destitute of outward aid that we rely fully on him. It is lawful for us to use the things of this world for our assistance, but we altogether abuse them by our wickedness in forsaking God.

It is proper also to observe how unhappy is the end of those who rely more on outward aids than on God; for everything must be unsuccessful and contrary to their expectation; as we see that these men, in their attempts to find safety, are constrained to undertake a flight which is highly disgraceful, and from which they obtain no advantage. At first there is some appearance of prosperity; but the only effect is, that the change of condition makes the final result more bitter and distressing. And yet Isaiah does not affirm that they will receive no assistance from Egypt, but forewarns them that the Lord will find new methods of thwarting that assistance, so that they will not be able to escape his hand; for, although all men agree together, yet they will not succeed in opposition to God and to his purposes.

17. *A thousand, as one, shall flee at the rebuke of one.* Because the Jews, on account of their vast numbers, relied on their forces, as men are wont to do when they possess any power, therefore the Prophet threatens that all the protection which they have at home will be of no more avail to them than foreign aid, because the Lord will break and take away their courage, so that they shall not be able to make use of their forces. For what avail arms and a vast multitude of men? What avail fortresses and bulwarks, when men's hearts fail and are dismayed? It is therefore impossible for us to be strong and powerful, unless the Lord strengthen and uphold us by his Spirit. This statement occurs frequently in the law, that when they should revolt from God, a vast number of them would be put to flight by a very small number of enemies. But there is this difference between the law and the prophets, that the prophets apply to a particular subject what Moses announced in general terms, as we have formerly explained.[1]

Here two observations must be made. First, we shall have just as much courage as the Lord shall give us; for we immediately lose heart, if he do not support us by his power. Secondly, it is the result of the righteous vengeance of God, that we are terrified by men, when he could not prevail upon us to fear him; that, when we have despised God's word and warnings, we fall down in terror at the words and threatenings of men. But we must also add, thirdly, God needs not extensive preparations to chastise us; for, if he lift up but a finger against us, we are undone. A small and feeble army will be sufficient to destroy us, even though we be well prepared, and have great numbers on our side. Next, he threatens that there will be no end to these calamities till they have been reduced to the last extremity,

[1] See *Commentary on Isaiah*, vol. i. p. xxix.

and until, amidst the frightful desolation of the earth, but few tokens of God's compassion are left.

As the mast of a ship on the top of a mountain. This may be explained in two ways. Some consider the metaphor to be taken from trees which have been cut down; for, when a forest is cut down, lofty trees are left which may be of use for building ships. But הר, (hār,) "a mountain," probably denotes also a rock or promontory, against which ships are dashed, and to which they adhere, and on which a "mast," the emblem of shipwreck, is afterwards seen.[1]

As a banner on a hill. Another metaphor is now added, borrowed from trophies erected to commemorate the defeat of enemies. In short, the Prophet declares that they will be so few that all that remains shall be an indication of very great ruin. As if he had said, "This great multitude which you now have dazzles your eyes; but there will be such ruin and decrease that you shall no longer have the face of a people." We are thus reminded how humbly and modestly we ought to conduct ourselves, even though we have great wealth and numerous forces; for if our mind be puffed up, God will speedily beat down our pride, and render us more feeble and cowardly than women and children, so that we shall not be able to bear the sight even of a single enemy, and all our strength shall melt away like snow.

18. *Therefore will Jehovah wait.* The Prophet now adds consolation; for hitherto he threatened to such an extent that almost all the godly might be thrown into despair. He intended therefore to soothe their minds, and encourage them to hope for better things, that they might embrace the mercy of God in the midst of those miseries, and might thus nourish their souls by his word. He contrasts this "waiting" with the excessive haste against which he spoke loudly at the beginning of the chapter, where he reproved the people

---

[1] "תרן (tōrĕn) is taken as the name of a tree by Augusti (Tannenbaum, the fir-tree) and Rosenmüller, (pinus, the pine-tree,) by Gesenius and Ewald as a signal or a signal-pole. In the only two cases where it occurs elsewhere, it has the specific meaning of a *mast*. The allusion may be simply to the similar appearance of a lofty and solitary tree, or the common idea may be that of a flag-staff, which might be found in either situation. The word 'Beacon,' here employed by Gataker and Barnes, is consistent neither with the Hebrew nor the English usage."—*Alexander.*

for noisy haste, and condemned them for unbelief; but now, on the contrary, he reproaches them by saying that the Lord will not render like for like in consequence of the contempt with which they have treated him, and will not in that manner hasten to punish them. Others explain it, " He commands you to wait," or " he will cause you to wait." But the meaning which I have brought forward appears to me to be more appropriate.

For Jehovah is a God of judgment. To make the former statement more plain, we must lay down this principle, that God exercises moderation in inflicting punishment, because he is inclined to mercy. This is what he means by the word "judgment;" for it denotes not only punishment, but also the moderation which is exercised in chastening. In like manner, Jeremiah says, " Chasten me, O Lord, but in judgment, not in thy wrath, lest thou crush me." (Jer. x. 24.) And again, I will not consume thee, but will chastise thee in judgment.[1] (Jer. xxx. 11.) "Judgment" is thus contrasted with severity, when the Lord observes a limit in punishing believers, that he may not ruin those whose salvation he always promotes; and, accordingly, as Habakkuk says, " in the midst of wrath he remembers his mercy." (Hab. iii. 2.) He is not like us, therefore; he does not act with bustling or hurry, otherwise at every moment we must perish, but he calmly waits. Nor is it a slight confirmation of this when he adds, that God gives a proof of his glory by pardoning his people.

And therefore will he be exalted, that he may be gracious to you. Others translate the words, " till he be gracious to you;" but I think that the former translation is more appropriate, and it agrees better with the meaning of the particle ל (*lamed.*) The Lord appears to lie still or to sleep, so long as he permits his Church to be assailed by the outrages of wicked men; and the customary language of Scripture is to say that he sits, or lies unemployed, when he does not

---

[1] The latter quotation may appear to be inaccurate, for in the English version it runs thus, " I will correct thee in measure;" but CALVIN adheres closely to the Hebrew original, which employs in both passages the word מִשְׁפָּט (*mishpāt*) "*judgment.*"—*Ed.*

defend his Church. It might be thought that he lay still when he gave loose reins to the Chaldeans to oppress the Jews ; and therefore the Prophet says, that the Lord will arise and ascend his judgment-seat. Why ? " That he may be gracious to you."

Blessed are all that wait for him. This is an inference from the former statement, in which he called Jehovah " a God of judgment." While he thus restrains himself, he draws from it an exhortation to patience and " waiting," and makes use of a part of the same verb, " wait," which he had formerly used. They were chargeable with distrust, and were distressed by strange uneasiness and restlessness of mind ; for they were fearfully harassed by their unbelief, so that they could not " wait" for God calmly. To cure this vice, he enjoins them to " wait," that is, to hope. Now, hope is nothing else than steadfastness of faith, that is, when we wait calmly till the Lord fulfil what he has promised. When he says that they who shall patiently " wait" for him will be " blessed," he declares, on the other hand, that they who allow themselves to be hurried away by impatience, and do not repent of their crimes and their wickedness, are wretched and miserable, and will at length perish ; for without hope in God there can be no salvation or happiness.

19. *Surely the people in Zion shall dwell in Jerusalem.* He confirms the former statement, that the people will indeed be afflicted, but will at length return to " Zion." Now, this might be thought incredible after the desolation of the city and of the whole country, for it seemed as if the whole nation had perished ; yet Isaiah promises that the Church shall be preserved. He begins with Mount " Zion," on which the temple was built, and says that there men will henceforth call on the Lord. He likewise adds, " in Jerusalem," by which he means that the Church shall be enlarged and increased, and that all that had formerly been laid waste shall be restored. Yet he intimates that " Jerusalem" shall again be populous, because God had chosen it to be his sanctuary.

Weeping thou shalt not weep.[1] The meaning is, that this

---

[1] " Thou shalt weep no more."—Eng. Ver.

mourning shall not be perpetual. The Church, that is, all believers, while they were in this wretched and distressed condition, must have been exceedingly sorrowful; but he says that those tears shall come to an end. To the same purport is it said by the Psalmist, "They who sow in tears shall reap in joy." (Psalm cxxvi. 5.) The Lord permits us indeed to be afflicted with great anguish; but at length he cheers us, and gives us reason for gladness, when he restores his Church; for that is the true joy of believers. Besides, as it is difficult to taste any consolation when the mind is overwhelmed by a conviction of God's vengeance, he holds out a ground of consolation in the mercy of God, because, when he is appeased, there is no reason to dread that joy and peace shall not immediately return. But, as the Prophet Habakkuk says in the passage already quoted, "in his wrath the Lord remembers mercy;" and he never punishes believers with such severity as not to restrain and moderate his strokes, and put a limit to his chastisements. (Hab. iii. 2.)

At the voice of thy cry. The Prophet points out the manner of obtaining pardon, in order to arouse believers to pray earnestly, and to supplicate with earnest groanings; for if there be no repentance, if we do not ask pardon from God, we are altogether unworthy of his mercy. If, therefore, we wish that the Church should be gathered together, and rescued from destruction by a kind of resurrection, let us cry to God to listen to our sighs and groanings; and if there be no sorrow of heart that excites us to prayer, we have no right to expect any alleviation.

He will answer thee. This means nothing else than that he will give evidence of his kindness and aid; for the Lord "answers," not by word, but by deed. Yet let us not think that he will instantly comply with our wishes, which are often hasty and unseasonable. He will undoubtedly assist us when the proper time arrives, so that we shall know that he had in view our salvation.

20. *When the Lord shall have given you.* He continues the same subject, and strengthens believers, that they may not faint; for patience springs from the hope of a more prosperous issue. Accordingly, he prepares them for endur-

ing future chastisement, for the wrath of God will press hard on them for a time; but he immediately promises that a joyful issue awaits them, when they shall have endured those calamities and distresses; for God will restrain his severity. Thus, I consider ו (*vau*) to mean "When" or "After;" as if he had said, "*When* you shall have endured those troubles, then will the Lord bless you; for he will change your condition for the better."

Thy rain shall no longer be restrained.[1] The word מורה (*mōrĕh*) is viewed by some commentators as meaning "a teacher." But this does not agree with the context; for, although the chief fruit of our reconciliation to God is to have faithful "teachers," yet, as the ignorant multitude was more deeply affected by the want of food, Isaiah accommodates his language to their ignorance, and gives them a taste of God's fatherly kindness under the emblem of abundance of food.

By the words "bread" and "water," he means extreme want and scarcity of all things, and therefore he calls it "bread of anguish and water of affliction."[2] Instead of this famine, he says that he will send them plenty and abundance. This is what he means by the word *rain;* for he describes the cause instead of the effect, as if he had said, "The earth shall yield fruit in abundance." This had a literal and special reference to a country, the fertility of which depended entirely on heaven; for it was not watered by rivers or fountains, but by rains. "The land whither ye go to possess it," says Moses, "is a land of hills and valleys, and drinketh water of the rain of heaven." (Deut. xi. 11.) He declares that the fruits of the earth, which the Lord took away or

---

[1] "Yet shall not thy teachers be removed."—Eng. Ver.

[2] "Though ye find yourselves reduced to extremities usual in long sieges, though ye be stinted to a short allowance of 'bread and water,' and are forced to undergo a great many other inconveniences, yet use not my prophets ill, make them not run into corners to hide themselves from the violence of an impatient multitude; but be glad to see them among you, and let their examples encourage you to bear up handsomely under the short afflictions which shall then be upon you. This is the plain meaning of the words, without running to the whimsical expositions of some who by 'Panis Angustiæ,' as the Vulgate renders לחם צר, (*lĕchĕm tzār,*) make the prophet mean the compendious doctrine of the gospel, or Christ himself, or the eucharist, and like dreams."—*Samuel White.*

diminished by barrenness, will return; because, in consequence of the copious "rains,"[1] there will be large and abundant produce. Thus, when the Lord shall punish us, let us comfort our hearts with these statements and promises.

21. *Then shall thine ears hear.* It was indeed no despicable promise which he made of an abundant produce of the fruits of the earth, but the chief ground of gladness and joy is, when God restores to us pure and sound doctrine; for no scarcity of wheat ought to terrify and alarm us so much as a scarcity of the word; and indeed, in proportion as the soul is more excellent than the body, so much the more ought we to dread this kind of famine, as another prophet also reminds us. (Amos viii. 11.) Isaiah promises this to the Jews as the most valuable of all blessings, that they shall be fed with the word, by the want of which they had formerly been heavily afflicted. The false prophets also boast of the word, and in a more haughty and disdainful manner than godly teachers: they wish to be reckoned and declared to be the best guides; but they lead men into error, and at length plunge them into destruction. But the word which points out the right path comes from God alone, though it would be of little service to us, if he did not also promise that he would give us ears; for otherwise he would speak to the deaf, and we should hear nothing but a confused sound.

A word behind thee. These words must be extended so far as to mean that he will not permit what he speaks to us to be useless, but will inwardly move our understandings and hearts, so as to train them to true obedience; for by nature we are not willing to learn, and must be altogether formed anew by his Spirit. The word *hear* is very emphatic. He compares God to a schoolmaster, who places the children before his eyes, that he may more effectually train and direct them; by which he expresses the wonderful

[1] "Kimchi's explanation of the word, (מורה, *mōrĕh*, or rather מורים, *mōrīm*,) as meaning the early rain, (which sense it has in Joel ii. 23, and perhaps also in Psalm lxxxiv. 6,) has been retained only by Calvin and Lowth. The great majority of writers adhere not only to the sense of 'teacher,' but to the plural import of the form, (מורים with 2 Sing. Affix.,) and understand the word as a designation or description of the prophets, with particular reference, as some suppose, to their reappearance after a period of severe persecution or oppression."—*Alexander.*

affection and care manifested towards us by God, who does not reckon it enough to go before us, but also " with his eye upon us gives us direction." (Psalm xxxii. 8.) But the Prophet declares that they who follow God as their guide will be in no danger of going astray.

Walk ye in it. This is an exhortation to cheerful progress, so that their journey may not be retarded, as frequently happens, by any uncertainty. What he adds, about *the right hand* and *the left,* might be thought absurd; for when Moses pointed out to the people the way in which they should walk, he at the same time charged them "not to turn aside to the right hand or to the left." (Deut. v. 32, and xvii. 20.) The road is straight, and we ought not to seek any departures from it.

What then does the Prophet mean? I reply, he uses the words " Right" and " Left" in a different sense; for he means by them every kind of transactions which we must undertake to perform. These are various, as there are also various modes of living; and every person meets with difficulties of many kinds, and is under the necessity of deliberating about them. By the "right and left hand," therefore, he means all the actions of human life, whatever they are, so that, in all that we undertake, we may have God for our guide, and may always regulate our transactions by his authority, whether we must go " to the right hand or to the left." And hence we derive very great consolation, that the Lord will favour our undertakings, and will direct our steps, to whatever hand we turn, provided only that we do not turn aside from the path which he points out to us.

22. *Then shall you profane the covering.* This shews that the heavenly direction will not be without effect; for they will bid adieu to their errors, and devote their minds to the pure worship of God; and the Prophet expressly mentions the outward profession of true godliness, by which they will openly proclaim that they have renounced idolatry. For, since statues and images are instruments of idolatry and superstition, they who are truly converted to God detest and abhor them, and, as far as lies in their power, profane them as we read that Jehu did, who profaned the altars of

Baal, and turned his temple into a common sewer. (2 Kings x. 27.) The example given by him and by others of the same class ought to be followed by godly princes and magistrates, if they wish to give a genuine proof of their repentance; for, although repentance is seated in the heart, and has God for a witness, it is shewn by its fruits. Isaiah has mentioned one class of them instead of the whole; for in general he shews that the proof of true repentance is, when men make it appear that they hold in abhorrence everything that is opposed to the worship of God. When he says that the idols are profaned, he does not mean that they were formerly sacred; for how could anything be sacred that dishonours God, and defiles men by its pollution? But, as men falsely imagine that they possess some sacredness, that is the reason why he says that they are "profaned," and that they ought to be despised and rejected as things of no value and altogether unclean.

The covering[1] *of the graven images of thy silver.* When he speaks of the "silver" and "gold" of the graven images, he means that no loss or damage prevents believers from abhorring the worship of idols. Such considerations restrain many from casting away idols altogether, because they see that "gold" or "silver" or something else is lost, and they choose rather to keep their idols than to sustain the smallest loss. Covetousness holds them in its net, so that they are more willing to sin of their own accord, and to pollute themselves with these abominations, than to lose this or that. But we ought to prefer the worship of God to everything else, to set little value on gold, to cast away pearls, and to loathe everything that is accounted precious, rather than defile ourselves with such crimes. In short, nothing can be so valuable that it ought not to be despised and reckoned worthless by us, when it comes into competition

---

[1] "The ephods of your molten images,—short cassocks, without sleeves, with which the heathens adorned their idols."—*Stock*. Cicero tells a story about Dionysius, who found in the temple of Jupiter Olympius a golden cloak of great weight, with which the statue of Jupiter had been ornamented by Gelo out of the spoils of the Carthaginians, and, after making the witty observation that it was too heavy for summer and too cold for winter, carried it off, and threw around the statue a woollen mantle, which, he said, was adapted to every season of the year. (Cic. de Nat. Deor. l. iii)—*Ed*.

with overturning the kingdom of Satan and restoring the worship of God. In this manner we actually shew whether the love of God and of religion dwells in our hearts, when a sincere abhorrence of our wicked ignorance drives us to throw away all that is polluted.

23. *Then will he give rain to thy seed.* From the fruit he again shews how desirable it is to be converted to God; for the fruit of repentance is, that he receives converted persons into favour, and bestows his blessing on them, so that they are in want of nothing, but, on the contrary, are loaded with every kind of blessings. As troubles and distresses proceed from the wrath of God, whom we provoke by our crimes, so, when he is pacified, everything goes on prosperously with us, and we obtain every sort of kindness, as the Law more fully testifies. (Lev. xxvi. 3-13; Deut. xxviii. 3-14.) A little before, he had spoken of "rain," from which they were led to expect an abundant supply of food; but because he had not observed order in beginning with earthly and fading blessings, he therefore now adds to doctrine, which is spiritual nourishment, those things which belong to the use of this corruptible life; for, although godliness has the promise of the present life as well as "of that which is to come," (1 Tim. iv. 8,) yet first of all it aims at heaven. (Matt. vi. 33.)

Hence also let us learn that it is in vain for men to toil in cultivating their fields, if the Lord do not send rain from heaven. Our labours must be watered by him, and he must "give the increase;" otherwise they will be of no service. Yet we must not expect rain but from the blessing of God; and if we receive abundant produce, we ought to give to him the glory. Hence learn also that we shall be in want of nothing, and shall obtain very abundant fruits of our labours, if we are converted to God, and that it is our own fault that we often suffer poverty and want, because by our wickedness we drive away from us the blessing of God. Let us not therefore ascribe barrenness and famine to any other causes than to our own fault; for it is impossible that there should be so great a multitude of men as to be incapable of deriving support and nourishment from the earth; but by our iniquities and transgressions we shut the bosom of the earth, which would otherwise be laid open to us, and would abundantly yield fruits of every description, that we might lead a prosperous and happy life.

And thy cattle shall feed. What he now adds about the "cattle" tends greatly to magnify the grace of God; for if his kindness overflows even on the dumb cattle, (Psalm xxxvi. 6,) how much more on men whom "he created after his image." (Gen. i. 27.) But we need not wonder if brute beasts, which were created for the use of men, suffer hunger along with their masters, and that they have a share in the bestowal of favour when God is reconciled to men.

24. *Thine oxen also.* When he promises that the oxen and the asses shall eat abundant and clean provender, this is a repetition and confirmation of what was stated in the preceding verse. This passage is taken from the Law, (Deut. xxviii. 11,) and is gladly and frequently quoted by the prophets, in order that we may learn to discern in the sickness and death of cattle the indignation of God, and to desire more earnestly to be reconciled to him, that our houses may be filled with his goodness.

25. *And it shall come to pass.* When the prophets describe the kingdom of Christ, they commonly draw metaphors from the ordinary life of men; for the true happiness of the children of God cannot be described in any other way than by holding out an image of those things which fall under our bodily senses, and from which men form their ideas of a happy and prosperous condition. It amounts therefore to this, that they who obey God, and submit to Christ as their king, shall be blessed. Now, we must not judge of this happiness from abundance and plenty of outward blessings, of which believers often endure scarcity, and yet do not on that account cease to be blessed. But those expressions are allegorical, and are accommodated by the Prophet to our ignorance, that we may know, by means of those things which are perceived by our senses, those blessings which have so great and surpassing excellence that our minds cannot comprehend them.

And on every high hill there shall be streams. When he says that "on the mountains" there shall be "streams and rivulets," he gives a still more striking view of that plenty and abundance with which the Lord will enrich his people. Water is not plentiful on the peaks of the mountains, which are exceedingly dry; the valleys are indeed well moistened, and abound in water; but it is very uncommon for water to flow abundantly on the tops of the mountains. Yet the Lord promises that it shall be so, though it appear to be impossible; but by this mode of expression he foretells that, under the reign of Christ, we shall be happy in every respect, and that there will be no place in which there shall not be an abundant supply of blessings of every description; that nothing will be so barren as not to be rendered fruitful by his kindness, so that everywhere we may be happy. This is what we should actually experience, if we were fully under the authority of Christ. We should plainly see his blessing on all sides, if we sincerely and honestly obeyed him; everything would go on to our wish; and the whole world and everything in it would contribute to our comfort; but, because we are very far from yielding that obedience, we have only a slight taste of those blessings, and enjoy them so far as we have advanced in newness of life.

By the day of slaughter, is denoted another mark of the divine favour, that God will keep his people safe and sound against the violence of enemies; and in this way the Prophet gives credibility to the former prediction; for otherwise it would have been difficult to believe that captives and exiles would enjoy such prosperity. Here he speaks therefore of the slaughter of the wicked; as if he had said, "The Lord will not only do you good, but will also drive out your enemies." It is generally thought that the Prophet now speaks of the defeat which befell the wicked king Sennacherib when he besieged Jerusalem. (2 Kings xix. 35; Isaiah xxxvii. 36.) But when I examine it more closely, I am more disposed to view this passage as referring to the destruction of Babylon; for although a vast multitude of persons was slain, when Sennacherib was shamefully put to flight, yet still the people were not delivered. This reminds us that we ought not to despair, even though our enemies be very numerous, and have abundance of garrisons, troops, and fortifications ; for the Lord can easily put them to flight and defend his Church. Let us not be terrified at their power or rage, or be discouraged because we are few in number ; for neither their troops, nor their bulwarks, nor their rage and insolence, will hinder them from falling into the hands of God.

26. *And the light of the moon shall be.* The Prophet was not satisfied with describing an ordinary state of prosperity, without adding something extraordinary; for he says that the Lord will go beyond the course of nature in this kindness and liberality. It never happened that the brightness of "the sun" was increased, unless when "the sun" stood still in the days of Joshua, in order to give time for pursuing the enemies, (Jos. x. 12, 13,) and when, for the sake of Hezekiah, the dial went backward. (2 Kings xx. 11 ; Isaiah xxxviii. 8.) But on this occasion nothing is said about those miracles.[1] Besides, the Prophet does not speak about prolonging the course of "the sun" above our horizon, but about increasing its brightness *sevenfold.* He shews what will be the condition of the godly under the reign of Christ ; for in other respects the Lord " maketh his sun to shine on the bad as well as on the good." (Matt. v. 45.) But here he speaks of happiness in which ungodly men can have no share. There is one kind of liberality which is bestowed indiscriminately on all, and another kind which is peculiar to believers alone ; as it is said, " Great is the abundance of thy goodness which thou hast laid up for them that fear thee." (Psalm xxxi. 19.) Isaiah speaks of this special favour,[2] and, in order to describe it, borrows metaphors from well-known objects. Accordingly, he declares that God will enlighten believers with so great brightness that, if " seven" suns were brought together, their brightness would be far inferior to this.

When the Lord shall have bound up the breach of his people. That the weight of afflictions, by which the people were soon afterwards overwhelmed, might not hinder them from believing this statement, he likewise adds another promise, that the Lord will be like a physician to heal their wounds. Hence it follows, that the people must be chastened, and, in

---

[1] " De his." " De ces miracles-là."
[2] " Isaie parle de ceste faveur speciale."

some measure, prepared for repentance by wounds, and must even be crushed and bruised in such a manner as to be reduced almost to nothing.

And healed the stroke of their wound. What he now adds about a "stroke," is intended to shew that this bruising will not be slight; for it resembles a body beaten and wounded by many strokes. If therefore we shall be ready at any time to think that the Lord deals harshly with us, let us call to remembrance those predictions, that the Lord will "bind up our wounds," which otherwise might appear to be mortal. And if any one ask why the Lord chastises his people so severely, I reply, that it produces no good effect on us when he treats us mildly; our vices are deeply rooted, and adhere to our very marrow, and cannot be separated but by a razor which has a sharp and keen edge.

27. *Behold the name of the Lord cometh.* He threatens the destruction of the Assyrians, who were at that time the chief enemies of the Church. From almost all their neighbours, indeed, the Jews received annoyance; but as the Assyrians were greatly superior to others in wealth and power, so the prophets, when they speak of enemies, mention them almost exclusively, and afterwards the Babylonians, who obtained the monarchy; though, as we have already seen, they frequently, by a figure of speech in which a part is taken for the whole, include the Chaldeans under the name of Assyrians. By "the name of God" he unquestionably means God himself; but he makes use of this circumlocution, because the Assyrians and other nations worshipped gods made of gold and silver, and held up the Jews to ridicule, because they did not worship him under any image, or statue, or resemblance; as one who wrote against them says that "they worship the bright clouds and the deity of the sky."[1] Thus wicked and ungodly men always judge of God according to outward appearances; while the prophets, on the other hand, remind believers of "the name of God." "That God who revealed himself to you by his name, whom you do not feel, whom you do not see, will take vengeance on your insults."

[1] "Qui puras nubes, et cœli numen adorant."

From afar. He adds this as if he granted what was said by them; for ungodly men, when they do not perceive the hand of God, think that he is at a great distance, and mock at the confidence of believers as groundless. Accordingly, the Prophet, adapting his language to the views of unbelievers, shews that God, whom they thought to be at a great distance, will come, or rather, has already come, and is at hand. This is what he means by the particle הִנֵּה, (*hinnĕh*,) *behold*, which he contrasts with the word מִמֶּרְחָק, (*mimmĕrhŏk*,) "from afar," directing believers, in this manner, to rise above all obstructions, that by their hope they may arrive at that assistance which he promised.

His face burneth. In order to shew that the celebration of the name of God in Judea is not vain or groundless, the Prophet describes the power of God, that is, the power which he will employ in driving out the enemies of the Church, as dreadful. When he addresses those who believe in him, in order to encourage them to the exercise of faith, he shews himself to be kind, gentle, patient, slow to anger, and merciful; but to the ungodly he holds out nothing but fear and terror. (Exod. xxxiv. 6.) And as the ungodly are terrified when God is mentioned, so believers, drawn by a conviction of his goodness, rely on him, and are not distressed by such fears. This shews us that we ought continually to persevere in the fear of God, that we may not find God to be what he is here described by the Prophet.

His burden is heavy.[1] That is, the Lord will bring with him dreadful calamities, which the ungodly will not be able to endure; for by "burdens" he means the punishments which are inflicted on the ungodly. He expresses the same thing by the words *lips* and *tongue*. But why did he speak of them rather than of the hands? It is, because ungodly men mock at all the threatenings which are uttered by the word of God, and treat as fabulous all that is declared by the prophets. To their own cost, therefore, they shall learn

[1] "And the burden thereof (or, And the grievousness of flame) shall be heavy."—*Eng. Ver.* "And heavy the column of flame."—*Stock.* "And the burning is heavy; for so ought we to translate מַשְׂאָה, (*mǎssāāh*,) in the same sense as in Judges xx. 40, and in other passages, from נָשָׂא, (*nāsā*,) 'to lift up,' because flame and smoke naturally ascend."—*Rosenmüller.*

that the sound which proceedeth from the sacred name of God is not without meaning, and is not idle thunder intended merely to strike the ears, but shall at length know by experience what is the power of that word which they despised.

28. *And his Spirit.*[1] He proceeds with that threatening which he had begun to utter, namely, that the Church will indeed be chastised, but yet that the Assyrians shall utterly perish; for he says that they will be plunged into the deep by the "Spirit" of God, or rather, that the "Spirit" himself is like a deep torrent which shall swallow them up. Others translate רוּחַ, (*rūăch,*)[2] by "blowing," and think that the allusion is to a storm or violent wind.

And with a useless sieve. The next metaphor employed is that of a "sieve," which is very frequent in Scripture. (Matt. iii. 12.) He says that he will shake the Assyrians with a sieve, in order to thrash and scatter them; and therefore he calls it "the sieve of vanity," that is, a useless sieve,[3] intended not to preserve, but to destroy; for, in another sense, the Lord is wont to "sift" his own people also, so as to gather them like good grain into the barn.

And a bridle causing to err.[4] The third metaphor is that of a "bridle," by which the Lord continually restrains the pride and rebelliousness of wicked men, and, in a word, shews that he is their Judge. True, indeed, the Lord commonly restrains and subdues his own people by a "bridle," but it is in order to bring them to obedience; while, on the other hand, he restrains wicked men in such a manner as to cast them down headlong to destruction. This is what he means by the phrase "causing to err." As furious horses are driven about in all directions by their riders, and, the more they kick are more violently struck and beaten; so the ungodly, when they are kept back, rush eagerly in the opposite direction, as it is beautifully described by David. (Psalm xxxii. 9.)

[1] "And his breath."—*Eng. Ver.*

[2] "Grotius renders רוּחַ (*rūăch*) *anger,* Luther and the English version *breath;* but there is no sufficient reason for excluding an allusion to the Holy Spirit as a personal agent."—*Alexander.*

[3] "The sieve of emptiness. A sieve full of holes, that suffers both corn and chaff to pass together to the ground. So shall Jehovah make no distinction among the enemies of Israel."—*Stock.*

[4] "And a misleading bridle."—*Alexander.*

The object of these metaphors is to shew that we must not sport with the Lord; for, although he appear for a time to act differently, we shall at length know by experience the truth of what the Prophet says, that his "breath" alone will be like a torrent to cast down the wicked, that they may be suddenly overwhelmed. Next, when he gives warning that the nations shall be winnowed with "a useless sieve," we ought to fear lest the Lord, if he find in us nothing but chaff, throw us on the dunghill. Lastly, we must observe the difference that exists between the children of God and the reprobate; for the Lord chastises both, but in different ways—the children of God, that they may be purified and preserved—and the reprobate, that they may be cast down headlong and destroyed.

29. *And you shall have a song as in the night.* Here he declares that all the punishments which he threatened against the Assyrians shall tend to the advantage of the Church, because the Lord punishes the outrages committed against his people not less severely than if they had been committed against himself. In this way he testifies his infinite love and kindness towards his own people, when he deigns to take up arms on their behalf. Hence we ought to conclude, that all the threatenings which are found in any part of Scripture tend to the consolation of believers.

When a festival is kept. He says that this "song" will be sacred, and compares it to a "holy solemnity," in order to excite believers to thankfulness, and to shew that their joy should be directed to God; for it is not enough to rejoice, unless our joy look straight towards God, and unless we keep him alone always in our view; otherwise our joy will be fruitless and irreligious, and will not promote our salvation, or be acceptable to God. He calls it "a song *of the night,*" because the Jews began the day at sunset, and, as soon as the evening came, celebrated the festival.

To the mountain. He explains more fully of what nature this joy shall be. They shall not dance, as irreligious men do, but shall raise and fix their eyes on God, whom they acknowledge to be the author of every blessing. By "the mountain" he means the temple which was built "on the mountain." He calls God *The Mighty One of Israel,* because it was by his assistance that they had been redeemed and preserved; and hence he reminds them that in future they will not be safe in any other way than by placing their hope in God alone. And indeed, when we cherish any conviction of our own strength, we rob God of this title, which is truly and sincerely bestowed on him by none but the lowly and humble, who have laid aside all confidence in their own strength.

30. *And Jehovah shall cause to be heard.* He confirms what he formerly said about the judgment of God on the Assyrians, and he describes it figuratively, as is very customary both with himself and with the other prophets. When God delays, and does not immediately punish the wicked, we think that he is either asleep or not powerful, and are distracted by doubt and uncertainty. And if we behold some of his judgments, yet such is our natural stupidity, or rather our ingratitude, that we keep before us those masks which hinder us from perceiving the glory of God; for we ascribe it to fortune, or to the plans and contrivances and strength of men, and never, unless when we are compelled, acknowledge that we owe anything to God.

The power of his voice.[1] For the reasons now stated, the Prophet was not satisfied with having once foretold the vengeance of God against the Assyrians; but he likewise describes it in a lively manner, and repeats it with great earnestness. He declares that the destruction shall be such that men will be constrained to hear "the voice of God;" that is, to acknowledge his judgment, and to confess that this calamity hath proceeded from him, as if he had spoken openly. The matter, therefore, may be thus summed up. The event will be so manifest, that there shall be no one who does not understand that this calamity proceeded from "the mouth," that is, from the decree of God.

And the descent of his arm shall he cause to be seen. He begins with "the voice of God," that we may know that he directs by his authority everything that is done on the earth.

[1] "His glorious voice. (Heb. The glory of his voice.)"—Eng. Ver. "The majesty of his voice."—*Stock.*

Yet at the same time he applauds the power of his doctrine, on which it was necessary that his people should rely, in order that the effect might be openly displayed at the proper time. But as the work quickly follows the decree and " voice of God," he adds " the descent of his arm." These two things ought always to be joined together; for we ought not to imagine that God is like men, or that he suddenly undertakes anything, and then leaves it defective or incomplete. Whatever he has decreed he likewise executes, and his hand can never be separated from his mouth. On the other hand, he executes nothing at random, but all must have been previously decreed, so that all the punishments which he inflicts are so many displays of righteous judgment.

With deluge and hailstone. That vengeance is illustrated, in the conclusion of the verse, by figures, in order that its terrific character may lead the Jews more cheerfully to raise their faith on high; for it was highly consolatory to them to know that, though they were heavily afflicted, a far more dreadful judgment would soon fall on their enemies. And yet we must not dream, as the Rabbins do, that the Assyrians were struck by a thunderbolt, for their conjecture is excessively frivolous. On the contrary, the Prophet follows the ordinary custom, and, by means of these comparisons, describes the judgment of God, which our prodigious dulness makes us excessively slow to comprehend. Conflagrations, thunderbolts, inundations, and deluges, are somewhat unusual and monstrous events, and thus produce a stronger impression on our own minds. For this reason, the prophets draw a comparison from them, that men may perceive the dreadful and avenging hand of God against the wicked.

31. *Surely by the voice of Jehovah.* He added this for two reasons; first, to shew why the Assyrian must be bruised; for, since he was cruel and savage to others, it is proper that " the same measure which he meted should be measured to him again." (Matt. vii. 2.) This is the ordinary judgment of God against tyrants, as the Prophet says in a subsequent passage of this book, " Wo to thee that spoilest, for thou shalt be spoiled." (Isaiah xxxiii. 1.) The second reason is,

because the power of the Assyrian king appeared to be so great that he could not fall. Although, therefore, he was fortified on every hand, not only to defend himself, but also to attack others, yet the Prophet says, that " by the voice of God" alone he shall be bruised. Hence we learn how groundless is the confidence of wicked men, who rely on their garrisons and arms, and presumptuously despise God, as if they had not been liable to his judgment. But in order to destroy them, the Lord will have no need of any other arms than his own " voice ;" for by the slightest expression of his will he will lay them low. Nor can it be doubted that the Prophet intends to withdraw the minds of believers from earthly means, that they may not inquire how it shall be done, but may be satisfied with the bare promise of God, who is fully able to execute his word as soon as it has gone forth from him.

32. *And there shall be in every passage.* He means that the Assyrians will in vain try every method of escaping from the hand of God; for wherever they go, whether they attempt to go forward or to turn back, the hand of God shall pursue them. As to the phrase, *fastened staff*,[1] I readily adopt the opinion of those who think that the metaphor is taken from those on whom have been inflicted strokes so heavy, that the marks of the instrument of punishment remain, as if a rod or staff were "fastened" in the wound. It will perhaps be thought preferable to interpret it to mean, that the wound is "fastened"[2] on the Assyrian, as a foun-

[1] CALVIN's phrase, baculus fundatus, is followed by almost all the Latin interpreters, including Vitringa, and appears to have suggested the rendering, grounded staff, which is given in our common version, and has been followed by other translators. Almost all the commentators treat מוסדה (*mūsādāh*) as the participle Hophal of יסד (*yāsăd*); but there are strong reasons for viewing it as an abstract noun, for Rosenmüller has justly remarked that מטה (*măttēh*,) with Tzere instead of Segol, is in the construct state. Availing himself, as it would seem, of this suggestion, Professor Alexander very felicitously renders it "the rod of doom." "The common version, grounded staff," says he, "is almost unintelligible. It is now very generally agreed that מוסדה (*mūsādāh*) denotes the divine determination or decree, and that the whole phrase means the rod appointed by him, or, to put it in a form at once exact and poetical, the rod of destiny or doom." Diodati's Italian version gives " Ed ogni passagio della verga ferma," " and every passage of the firm staff."—*Ed.*

[2] " Que la playe a esté attachee au dos de l'Assyrien ;"—" That the wound has been fastened to the back of the Assyrian."

dation is fixed in the earth; for what is not "fastened" may be moved out of its place and carried away. But he shews that that wound is so deeply fixed that it cannot be shaken off or removed. In like manner, the weight of God's wrath lies on the reprobate, and holds them weighed down to the end. To shew that there is no hope of being able to derive advantage from a change of place, he says *everywhere*, thus declaring that there shall be no retreat. The clause ought to be thus arranged, "wherever the staff shall pass, there it will stick firmly."

With tabrets and harps. He means that the issue of the battle will not be doubtful, as when the combatants meet on equal terms; for he says that the victory will be certain; because, as soon as God determines to go forth to fight, he already holds the victory in his hand. "Tabrets and harps," hands spread out and lifted up, are expressive of the joy of conquerors, when they shout aloud and chant the song of victory.

Shall fight against her. The feminine pronoun בָּהּ (*bāhh*) is viewed by some commentators as referring to the army; but the Prophet undoubtedly intended to express something higher, namely, the head of the army, that is, Babylon, as contrasted with Jerusalem, which also he formerly denoted by a similar pronoun.

From these statements we ought to infer, that the wicked shall at length be destroyed, though they appear to have many means of escape; for wherever they turn, whatever road they take, the "staff" of the Lord shall pursue them, and shall ever remain "fastened" to their back; they shall never escape his hand or get quit of their wounds. We, too, are chastened by the hand of God, but the wounds do not always last; our pains are soothed and abated, and "our grief is turned into joy." (John xvi. 20.) Besides, God carries on war against the reprobate in such a manner that they cannot resist him, or gain anything by their attempts. He joins battle with them, indeed, but it is as a conqueror; he even allows them to obtain some advantages, but represses their insolence whenever he thinks proper. If, therefore, we fight under his banner, let us entertain no doubt of obtaining the victory; for, when we have him as our leader, we shall be safe from all danger, and shall undoubtedly come off conquerors.

33. *For Tophet is ordained.* The Prophet goes on to threaten the vengeance of God, and says that not only a temporary calamity, but also everlasting destruction awaits the wicked; for hell is prepared for them, and not merely for persons of ordinary rank, but likewise for the king himself and the nobles. By "Tophet" he unquestionably means Hell; not that we must fancy to ourselves some place in which the wicked are shut up, as in a prison, after their death, in order to endure the torments which they deserve; but it denotes their miserable condition and excruciating torments. In the book of Kings, it denotes that place where the Jews sacrificed their children to the idol Moloch. (2 Kings xxiii. 10.) It is also mentioned by Jeremiah, (xix. 6;) and that place was destroyed and profaned by Josiah on account of the detestable superstition committed in it. (2 Kings xxiii. 10.) The prophets, I have no doubt, intended to give the name of this place to the punishments and torments of the wicked, in order that the bare mention of it might excite horror in godly persons, and that idolatry might be universally regarded with greater abhorrence. The word "Gehenna"[1] has the same etymology; for "the Valley of Hinnom" was a name given to Hell (Gehenna) on account of the abominable sacrilege practised in it.

Since yesterday.[2] When we see that all goes well with the wicked, and that they have everything to their wish, we think that they will pass unpunished. For this reason the Prophet, on the contrary, exclaims: "Since yesterday, that is, of old since the beginning of the world, the Lord hath determined what punishments he shall inflict on them." Though this decree is still hidden from us, yet it must be certain, and cannot fail. Let us not, therefore, judge of the lot of the wicked according to outward appearances; let us wait for the Lord, who in due time will execute his righteous judgment. Yet let us not be rash, or think that God hath

---

[1] גיא הנום, (*gē hinnōm,*) "the Valley of Hinnom."
[2] "Of old."—Eng. Ver.

forgotten to take vengeance; for he had determined what he should do before it could enter into our mind; nor can we so speedily desire the destruction of the wicked as not to have our thoughts and desires anticipated long before by the Lord, for from the beginning he determined to inflict on them punishments and torments. Some think that it is a parallel passage to that of the Apostle, "Christ yesterday, to-day, and for ever." (Heb. xiii. 8.) But I consider "yesterday" to be here used simply as contrasted with our thoughts, that we may not think that we possess so much wisdom as to be capable of anticipating God: for there is nothing sudden in his purposes, but all were long ago settled and determined by him. He speaks of the punishments of the life to come, as I have already said, that is, of the punishments which the wicked shall endure, in addition to the distresses which they suffer in this life. On this subject it is strange that the Sadducees (Matt. xxii. 23; Acts xxiii. 8) were so dull and stupid as to confine rewards and punishments within the limits of this life, as if the judgment of God did not extend beyond this world; for the modes of expression which immediately follow would not apply to temporal punishments, and the very name "Tophet," taken metaphorically, could denote nothing else than God's highest curse.

Yea, for the king it is prepared. He shews that not even "kings," who are supposed to be entitled, on account of their majesty and power, to enjoy some peculiar privilege, are exempted from this punishment. Their greatness dazzles the eyes of men, but will yield them no defence, so as to prevent the Lord from punishing them as they deserve.

He says that the slaughter of them will be *in a deep place*, that we may know that they cannot escape or be rescued from it; and he calls hell *broad*, that we may know that however numerous they may be, though they all conspire together, they shall likewise perish; for the Lord will not be exhausted by punishing, and he will have a place so large as to contain all his enemies.

The pile of it is fire. He speaks metaphorically concerning the destruction of the reprobate, which otherwise we cannot sufficiently comprehend, in the same manner as we do not understand the blessed and immortal life, unless it be shadowed out by some figures adapted to our capacity. Hence it is evident how foolish and absurd the sophists are, who enter into subtle arguments about the nature and quality of that fire, and torture themselves by giving various explanations of it. Such gross imaginations must be banished, since we know that the Prophet speaks figuratively; and in another passage (Isaiah lxvi. 24) we shall see that "fire" and the "worm" are joined together.

CHAPTER XXXI.

1. Woe to them that go down to Egypt for help, and stay on horses, and trust in chariots, because *they are* many; and in horsemen, because they are very strong: but they look not to the Holy One of Israel, neither seek the Lord!
2. Yet he also *is* wise, and will bring evil, and will not call back his words: but will arise against the house of the evil-doers, and against the help of them that work iniquity.
3. Now the Egyptians *are* men, and not God; and their horses flesh, and not spirit. When the Lord shall stretch out his hand, both he that helpeth shall fall, and he that is holpen shall fall down, and they all shall fail together.
4. For thus hath the Lord spoken unto me, Like as the lion and the young lion roaring on his prey, when a multitude of shepherds is called forth against him, *he* will not be afraid of their voice, nor abase himself for the noise of them: so shall the Lord of hosts come down to fight for mount Zion, and for the hill thereof.
5. As birds flying, so will the Lord of hosts defend Jerusalem; defending also he will deliver *it*; *and* passing over he will preserve *it*.

1. Væ descendentibus in Ægyptum ad auxilium, et qui equis innituntur; et qui curribus confidunt, quia multi sunt; et equitibus, quia prævalidi; et non respexerunt ad Sanctum Israel, nec Iehovam inquisierunt.
2. Atqui ipse quoque sapiens est. Itaque adducet malum, nec verba sua faciet irrita; insurgent, inquam, contra domum malignorum, et contra auxilium opificum vanitatis.
3. Et certe Ægyptius homo est, non Deus; et equi eorum caro, et non spiritus. Itaque simulac extenderit Iehova manum suam, ruet auxiliator, et cadet adjutus, omnesque simul deficient.
4. Quoniam sic dixit Iehova ad me: Ut leo rugit et catulus leonis ad prædam suam, contra quem si convocetur coetus pastorum, a clamore eorum non commovebitur, neque ob eorum tumultum humiliabitur; sic descendet Iehova exercituum ad præliandum pro monte Sion, et pro colle ejus.
5. Sicut aves quæ volant, ita proteget Iehova exercituum Ierusalem; protegens liberabit, transiliens servabit.

6. Turn ye unto *him from* whom the children of Israel have deeply revolted.
7. For in that day every man shall cast away his idols of silver, and his idols of gold, which your own hands have made unto you *for* a sin.
8. Then shall the Assyrian fall with the sword, not of a mighty man; and the sword, not of a mean man, shall devour him: but he shall flee from the sword, and his young men shall be discomfited.
9. And he shall pass over to his strong hold for fear, and his princes shall be afraid of the ensign, saith the Lord, whose fire *is* in Zion, and his furnace in Jerusalem.

6. Revertimini ut profundam fecistis defectionem, filii Israel.
7. Quoniam in die illa abjicit homo idola argenti sui, et idola auri sui, quæ fecerunt vobis manus vestræ peccatum.
8. Tum cadet Assur per gladium, non viri; et gladius non hominis devorabit eum; et fuga sibi consulet a facie gladii, et juvenes ejus in liquefactionem erunt.
9. In arcem suam præ formidine transibit, et pavebunt Principes ejus a vexillo, dicit Iehova, cui ignis est (*vel, qui ignis illi est*) in Sion, et cui fornax in Ierusalem.

1. *Wo to them that go down to Egypt.* He again returns to the subject which he had handled at the beginning of the former chapter; for he still cries loudly against the Jews, whose ordinary custom it was, in seasons of danger, to resort, not to the Lord, but to the Egyptians. We have formerly explained why this was so highly displeasing to God. To state the matter briefly, there are two reasons why the Prophet reproves this crime so severely. The first is, because it is impossible for us to place confidence for our salvation in creatures, and at the same time in God; for our eyes must be withdrawn from him as soon as they are directed to them. The second reason is, God had expressly forbidden them to enter into alliance with the Egyptians. (Deut. xvii. 16.) To sinful confidence was added rebelliousness, as if they had resolved to provide for their safety by despising God, and by disobeying his will.

We must therefore look at the source of this evil, if we wish to understand fully the Prophet's meaning. There was also a peculiar reason, as we have formerly remarked, why the Lord wished the Jews to have no intercourse with the Egyptians. It was, lest that wicked alliance should obliterate the remembrance of the redemption from Egypt, and lest they should be corrupted by the superstitions and sinful idolatry of the Egyptians. Yet these arguments were regarded by them as of no weight; and, though God had forbidden it, this did not hinder them from continually applying to them for assistance, and imagining that their assistance was a shield which defended them against the arm of God. Consequently, there are good reasons why the Prophet exclaims so earnestly against such madness. Even on the ground that God had forbidden it, their "going down into Egypt" deserved to be severely blamed; but it was still more intolerably criminal, that by false confidence they bestowed on mortal men the glory which was due to God. In order to make it still more clear that in this manner they defraud God of his right, he not only accuses them of having relied on the Egyptians, but likewise brings a charge against them, on the other hand, that

They have not looked to the Holy One of Israel. Here appears more clearly the reason why that treachery of the Jews is so sharply reproved by Isaiah; for in other respects God does not disapprove of our using lawful remedies, just as we eat bread and other kinds of food which were intended for our use. Thus if any person, placed in danger, employ means which were not forbidden, but which are customary and lawful, provided that he do not at all deny the power of God, he certainly ought not to be blamed; but if we are so strongly attached to outward means, that we do not at the same time seek God, and if, through distrust of his promises, we resort to unlawful methods, this is worthy of condemnation and abhorrence.

The word *look* is frequently employed in Scripture to denote this confidence; for we commonly turn our eyes towards that quarter from which we expect assistance. In a word, we are here taught that we ought to place our trust for salvation in none other than in God alone, that, relying on his promises, we may boldly ask from him whatever is desirable. He undoubtedly permits us to use all things which he intended for our use, but in such a manner that our minds must be entirely fixed on him.

When he calls God "the Holy One of Israel," he presents in a striking light the wickedness and ingratitude of the people, who, after having been taken under God's protection and guardianship, despised such a protector and guardian of their salvation, and ran eagerly after their own lusts. By immediately adding, *neither have they sought Jehovah,* he shews that neither the power, nor the goodness, nor the fatherly kindness of God, could keep them in the discharge of their duty. In the present day, since he invites us not less kindly to come to him, we offer a grievous insult to him if we look to any other, and do not resolve to trust in him alone; and everything that shall turn away and withdraw our minds from God will be to us like "Egypt."

2. *Yet he also is wise.* By calling God "wise," he does not merely bestow on him the honour of an attribute which always belongs to him, but censures the craftiness of those whom he saw to be too much delighted with their own wisdom. He said a little before, (Isaiah xxix. 15,) that they "dug caves for themselves," when they thought that, by hidden plans and secret contrivances, they avoided and deceived the eyes of God. He now pours witty ridicule on this madness, by affirming that, on the other hand, wisdom belongs also to God; indirectly bringing against them the charge of believing that they could shut God's mouth as not knowing their affairs. As if he had said, "What shall become of your wisdom?" Will the effect of it be that God shall cease to be "wise?" On the contrary, by reproving your vanity, he will give practical demonstration that "he taketh the wise in their own craftiness." (Job v. 13; 1 Cor. iii. 19.)

We may draw from this a general doctrine, that they who shelter themselves under craftiness and secret contrivances, gain nothing but to provoke still more the wrath of God. A bad conscience always flees from the judgment of God, and seeks lurking-places to conceal itself. Wicked men contrive various methods of guarding and fortifying themselves against God, and think that they are wise and circumspect, even though they be covered only with empty masks; while others, blinded by their elevated rank, despise God and his threatenings. Thus, by declaring that "God is also wise," the Prophet wounds them painfully and sharply, that they may not lay claim to so great craftiness as to be capable of imposing on God by their delusions.

He will arise against the house of the evil-doers. As they did not deserve that he should reason with them, he threatens that they shall feel that God has his arguments at his command, for ensnaring transgressors. First, they did not think that God has sufficient foresight, because he did not, according to the ordinary practice of the world, provide for their safety amidst so great dangers, and because they considered all threatenings to be empty bugbears, as if they had it in their power by some means to guard against them. Hence arises their eagerness to make every exertion, and their hardihood to plot contrivances. He therefore threatens that God will take revenge on so gross an insult, and that he has at his command the means of executing what he has promised; and that no schemes, inventions, or craftiness can overthrow the word of God.

Of the workers of vanity.[1] He gives them this appellation, because they wished to fortify themselves against the hand of God by a useless defence; that is, by the unlawful aid of the Egyptians. Formerly, it might be thought that he silently admitted their claim to the appellation of "wise men," by contrasting them with the wisdom of God; but now he scatters the smoke, and openly displays their shame and disgrace. This teaches us that there is nothing better than to renounce our own judgment, and to submit entirely to God; because all that earnest caution by which wicked men torture themselves has no solidity, but, on the contrary, as if on purpose, provokes the wrath of God by the deceitful contrivances of the flesh.

3. *And surely the Egyptian is a man, and not God.* It may be thought that Isaiah here brings forward nothing but what is common and beyond all doubt; for who ever imagined that the Egyptians were not "men," and must be put in the place of "God?" There is indeed no debate on this point, and it is openly acknowledged; but when it is found necessary to reduce it to practice, men are altogether dull of apprehension, or remain uncertain about that which they formerly appeared to know and firmly to believe. They exalt themselves as highly, and claim as much for themselves, as if they did not believe that they are men, and did not think that they ought to obey God. This is the reason why Scripture

[1] "Of them that work iniquity."—Eng. Ver.

so frequently warns "not to trust in men, than whom nothing can be more vain." (Psalm cxlvi. 3.) " Cursed is he who trusteth in man, and relieth on an arm of flesh." (Jer. xvii. 5.)

Yet we see both princes and men of ordinary rank contrive and resolve in such a manner as if they could establish for a hundred years all that they contrived, and could subject heaven, sea, and earth, and could regulate and dispose everything according to their will. When we perceive in men such pride and arrogance, we need not wonder that the Prophet exclaims that "the Egyptians are men, and not God;" for the Jews ascribed to them what ought to be ascribed to God, the defence and preservation of the Church, which God claims for himself alone, and does not allow to be given to another. Isaiah therefore indirectly censures that contempt of God and wicked confidence by which they are swelled with pride.

Here we see how great a difference there is between God and men; for men have no power in themselves but what God has granted to them. If we were reasoning about the nature and excellence of man, we might bring forward the singular gifts which he has received from God; but when he is contrasted with God, he must be reduced to nothing; for nothing can be ascribed to man without taking it from God. And this is the reason why we cannot agree with the Papists, when we argue about the cause of salvation, freewill, the value of works, and merits; for since on this subject God is contrasted with man, we must take from God whatever is attributed to man. But they make a division between man and God, so as to assign one part to God, and another part to man; while we say, that the whole and undivided cause of salvation must be ascribed to God, and that no part of it can be attributed to another without detestable sacrilege. In a word, let us learn that in such a contrast nothing worthy of praise can be left for man.

And their horses are flesh and not spirit. By the word flesh he means weakness and frailty; for what is there in "flesh" but corruption? He speaks of "horses," but to the Egyptians also belongs a weakness of the same or of a kindred nature; as if he had said that they, and all their forces, have nothing that is solid or permanent. Although the Egyptians had a soul as well as a body, yet, so far as they were creatures, and dwelt in a frail tabernacle, they must hold an inferior rank; as if he had said, that they do not possess heavenly or spiritual power; as it is said also in the Psalm, "Do not trust in princes; for their breath shall go out, and they shall return to their earth." (Psalm cxlvi. 3.) So far as relates to "horses," the word "flesh" applies to them with greater propriety; but it is not wonderful that men are sent to learn from rottenness how frail they are.

As soon as Jehovah shall stretch out his arm. From this threatening we may draw a universal doctrine, that this wickedness shall not pass unpunished; for the Lord will not suffer men with impunity to give to creatures the honour due to him, or to rely on the assistance of men with that confidence which ought to be placed on him alone. He therefore threatens those who shall yield assistance and give occasion to false confidence, as well as those who shall make use of their assistance and rely on it for their safety. And if the Lord cannot endure this wicked confidence, where nothing more than temporal safety is concerned, how much less will he endure those who, in order to obtain eternal salvation, contrive various aids according to their own fancy, and thus elevate the power of men, so as to ascribe to it the place and authority of God.

4. *For thus hath Jehovah said to me.* The Prophet adds this verse, that it may not be thought that the Lord leaves us destitute of necessary means; for if, while he forbids us to place our confidence in creatures, he did not promise us any assistance, we might complain that he gave ground for despair, and not for consolation; as we saw, a little before, that men are more careful and attentive than they ought to be, because they think that they will be deficient in thoughtfulness, if they rest satisfied with God alone, and abstain from forbidden means. He therefore takes away every excuse, when he promises that he will be a faithful guardian to us; for what pretence can be left, if we despise the salvation which he offers to us of his own accord? It is therefore as if he had said, "The Lord assists, and will

assist ; he forbids you to ask assistance from the Egyptians." By comparing himself to *a lion*, a very powerful animal and keenly bent on prey, he employs a very appropriate comparison, to shew that he is in the highest degree both able and willing to defend us.

In the second part of the comparison, the Prophet dwells largely on the great eagerness with which the Lord takes hold of his people, keeps them near himself, preserves them from being carried off, and defends them against all dangers; while he also points out that strength and power which no arms and no forces can resist. Now, it is impossible that comparisons should hold on every point, nor is it necessary, but they ought to be suitable to the subject which is handled. Since therefore we know that the Lord loves us so much and takes such care of us, must we not be worse than mad if we despise him, and seek other aids, which will not only be useless but destructive to us?

5. *As birds that fly.* This is the second comparison, by which the Prophet shews how great care the Lord takes of us, and how earnestly he is bent on making us happy. It is taken from *birds*, which are prompted by astonishing eagerness to preserve their young ; for they almost kill themselves with hunger, and shrink from no danger, that they may defend and preserve their young. Moses makes use of the same comparison when, reproaching the people for their ingratitude, he compares the Lord to an eagle "laying her nest, spreading her wings, and fluttering over her young." (Deut. xxxii. 11.) Christ also remonstrates with Jerusalem, " How often would I have gathered thy children together, as a hen gathereth her chickens, and ye would not !" (Matt. xxiii. 37.)

The sum of this passage is, that the Lord will be sufficiently powerful to defend his people, for whom he has a special love and a peculiar care. What Moses relates that God did, Isaiah promises that he will always do ; for he will never forsake those whom he has once received into his favour. Lest any one therefore should imagine that this statement related only to the men of a single age, hê expressly declares that God will spread his wings to defend Jerusalem. Nor is it unnecessarily that he mentions not only *Mount Zion* but *its hill;* for on that "hill" was built the temple in which God desired that men should call upon him. Wherever therefore the worship of God is pure, let us know that salvation will be certain; for men cannot call upon him in vain. "Let us be his people, and, on the other hand, he will be our God." (Lev. xxvi. 12.)

6. *Return.* This verse is explained in various ways; for the Hebrew commentators explain it thus, "Return to the Lord, for you have multiplied revolts." But, in my opinion, the meaning is more simple: "Return according as you have made a deep revolt;"[1] for לאשר (*lăăshĕr*) is, I think, employed in the same sense as כאשר (*kăăshĕr*), "according as."[2] He means that the aggravated nature of their wickedness does not shut the door against them from returning to God, if they repent; that, although they have been sunk into the deepest wickedness, still God will pardon them. Yet, at the same time, he makes use of this spur to stimulate them to earnest grief and hatred of their sins, that they may not carelessly and lightly, as frequently happens, aim at a half repentance. He therefore bids them consider attentively with what fearful destruction they have cast themselves down to hell, that they may abhor themselves on account of their aggravated transgressions.

---

[1] "Return to him against whom you have entertained deep thoughts; in the same manner as you revolted, and have still revolted, from him, return now to him."—*Jarchi.* Among the commentators who belonged to the Hebrew nation, or wrote in the Hebrew language, Jarchi was probably held, on the ground of the first part of his paraphrase, to support that view which our Author condemns; but the second part of it, beginning with "in the same manner as," approaches very closely to the Reformer's own words.—*Ed.*

[2] Piscator and others construe לאשר (*lăăshĕr*) as equivalent to אליו אשר ממנו, (*ēlāiv ăshĕr mĭmmĕnnū,*) "to him from whom." Vitringa does not reject this exposition, which he acknowledges to be supported by an analogous use of מאשר, (*mēăshĕr,*) in Ruth ii. 9; but he pronounces the rendering, "according as," to be more elegant and probably more correct. Modern critics, however, approve of the meaning given in our common version. "The syntax may be solved either by supposing 'to him' to be understood, and giving לאשר (*lăăshĕr*) the sense of 'with respect to whom,' or by assuming that, as both these ideas could be expressed by this one phrase, it was put but once in order to avoid the tautology."—*Alexander.* The other mode of resolving the syntax, by bringing out the sense, "to him from whom," appears to adhere more closely to the usage of the Hebrew language.—*Ed.*

It ought first to be observed, that the Prophet does not lessen the guilt of the people. They who need to be brought back to the Lord must first be made to have a deep and painful conviction of their guilt; for they who flatter themselves in their iniquities are very far from obtaining pardon, and therefore there is nothing better than to lay open the alarming nature of the disease, when a remedy must be applied. Yet, that their hearts may not be led to despair, they must be encouraged and comforted by holding out to them the mercy of God; for Satan aims at nothing else than to cut us off from all hope of pardon. Accordingly, Isaiah declares that, although by their wickedness they have sunk down to hell, God is ready to forgive; for not in vain does the Lord invite us to repentance, but he likewise offers pardon. Hence also, to such exhortations the Scripture always adds promises of grace, that, whenever we are called to repentance, we may know that the hope of pardon is also held out to us.

As you have made a deep revolt. Instead of this rendering, the word עמק, (*gnāmăk,*) which signifies to be deep, is explained by some as meaning to multiply and the metaphor is supposed to be borrowed from heaps, "As you have heaped up your sins, so return now." But I prefer the former exposition. סרה (*sārāh*) signifies "revolt." Others explain it to mean here "depravity," but the word "revolt" is more appropriate. The Prophet therefore invites them to return to the Lord.[1]

O children of Israel. In calling them by this name, he does not intend to shew them respect, but reproaches them for their ingratitude; for they were degenerate sons[2] who had revolted from the faith and obedience of their fathers, and therefore this title contains an indirect reproach. Yet he means that the Lord had not forgotten the covenant which he made with their fathers, though they had departed widely from him by their treachery; for he declares, that he

---

[1] העמיקו סרה (*hĕgnĕmīkū sārāh*) literally signifies, "they have deepened revolt;" and Professor Alexander justly remarks that the substitution of the second person for the third, in the ancient versions, and in Barnes, (ye have revolted), is wholly arbitrary.—*Ed.*

[2] "Enfans rebelles;"—"Rebellious children."

will acknowledge them to be "the children of Israel," and will fulfil all that he promised to Abraham and the other patriarchs, if they return to him with all their heart.

7. *For in that day.* He continues the subject which he began in the former verse. Yet there is this difference, that in the former verse he exhorted to repentance, but now he points out the fruits of repentance, which, we know, is the customary way of teaching in Scripture; for, since repentance is concealed within us, and has its root in the heart, it must be made known by the practical result, and by works, as "a tree shews by its fruits" (Matt. vii. 17) its inherent goodness; and therefore he points out repentance by works which are the fruit of it.[1]

Shall cast away the idols. When he speaks of "idols" only, it is by a figure of speech frequently employed in Scripture, in which a part is taken for the whole; for the Prophet undoubtedly intended to speak of the whole of man's conversion, but, as it would have been tedious to enumerate all the kinds, under one of them he includes all the rest. Now, the beginning of repentance is the change of the heart; and next we must come to outward fruits, that is, to works. Above all, we must observe the object which the Prophet had in view in discoursing about repentance. It was because the Lord had promised salvation near at hand; and, that they might be capable of it, he exhorts them to repentance. Hence it ought to be observed that, when we persevere in being wicked, we resist God by our wickedness, and thus restrain his grace from assisting us; and, therefore, that the way may be open for God's assistance, he demands that we shall repent.

He calls them *The idols of his silver and the idols of his gold,* because, as we have formerly seen,[2] they who sincerely repent are affected by deep grief for their sin, so that the traces of their superstitions, which are stamped with the highest dishonour of God, cannot be beheld by them without the greatest horror. On this account they abhor them, and

---

[1] "Et pourtant il marque la repentance par les fruits;"—"And therefore he points out repentance by the fruits."
[2] See *Commentary on Isaiah,* vol. i. p. 118.

do not dread the loss of " gold or silver," to testify their conversion and their faith ; for he who has sincerely renounced superstitions does not spare any expense in order to possess the pure worship of God. This is what the Prophet intended to express by calling them " gold and silver" rather than wood and stone. However excellent anything may be, the loss of it is a happy event when we are cleansed from such base and abominable pollutions. Those who retain them, though they profess to be Christians, shew that they are still involved in the remains of superstition ; and hence it is evident that their hearts are not truly or completely reformed. In this matter we must listen to none of the excuses which we frequently hear from the lips of hypocrites, who cannot absolutely renounce idolatry, " What could I do ? How could I live ? I am aware that this revenue, this ' gold,' is detestable in the sight of God, because it arises from idolatry ; but in some way or other my life must be supported." Away with such fooleries ! say I ; for where the conversion of the heart is real, that which cannot be retained without insulting or dishonouring God is instantly thrown away.

Which your own hands have made. The Prophet urges them to make a more full acknowledgment of their sin ; for, when men are accused, they generally throw the blame on some other person, and do not willingly allow it to fall on themselves, or acknowledge that it is chargeable upon them ; in like manner as the common people willingly accuse the priests, but no man is willing to acknowledge his own guilt. The Prophet therefore bids them look to "their own hands," that they may know that they have committed so great a crime. He reminds them, at the same time, how grossly they have been deceived by their unbelief in making gods to themselves ; and hence we ought to conclude that God rejects everything that is of our contrivance, and that he cannot accept as good that worship which has originated with ourselves.

I consider חטא, (*chēt*,) *sin*, to be a noun ;[1] as if he had

---

[1] That is, he does not follow the ancient versions. by viewing it as an adjective, qualifying the word " hands,"—" your sinful hands."—*Ed.*

said, "Whenever you behold idols, behold your guilt; acknowledge the proofs of your treachery and revolt; and if you are truly converted to God, shew it practically, that is, by throwing away idols and bidding adieu to superstitions; for this is the true fruit of conversion."

8. *Then the Assyrian.* The copulative ו (*vau*) is better translated as an adverb of time: "*Then* the Assyrian shall fall down;" that is, "When you shall have turned to the Lord, and when your life shall testify a sincere repentance, *then* the enemy shall fall down;" for, as the Lord raised up the Assyrian to punish the Jews for their crimes, and especially for idolatry, so he promises that the Assyrians shall be brought down, when they shall have ceased to sin and worship idols. Hence he informs us, that our obstinacy is the reason why the Lord adds evil to evil, and doubles his strokes, and pursues us more and more; for we continually supply fresh materials to inflame his vengeance against us more and more. If therefore we wish that God's chastisements should be less severe, if we wish that the enemies should fall to the ground and perish, let us endeavour to be reconciled to him by repentance; for he will speedily put an end to the chastisement, and will take away from enemies strength and power to injure us.

By the sword not of a man.[1] The Prophet means that the deliverance of the Church is God's own work, that the Jews may know that, although no earthly power is visible, God's secret power is sufficient to deliver them. If therefore enemies are subdued, if their rage is restrained, let us know that it proceedeth from the Lord. By various methods, indeed, he represses the force and violence of wicked men, but by his own hand alone he delivers his Church; for, while the Lord makes use of human means, he preserves his

---

[1] " לא איש, (*lō īsh,*) not of a man, that is, of one who is totally different from a man. The word לא (*lō*) often unites with a substantive, so as to form one word, which shall bear a quite different and even opposite meaning; as תהו לא דרך (*tōhū lō dĕrĕch*) 'desolation not-a-way,' that is, 'an impassable way.' Psalm cvii. 40; and לא שם לו, (*lō shēm lō,*) 'he shall have not-a-name,' that is, 'he shall have public disgrace.' (Job xviii. 17.)"—*Rosenmüller.* "An Hebrew idiom; of one far different from a man, viz., an angel."—*Stock.*

own people miraculously and by extraordinary methods, which may be seen to have happened since the beginning of the world, and which we may even now behold, if we are not blind. And yet this does not hinder the Lord from employing his servants to deliver the Church; but he employs them in such a manner that his own hand is peculiarly and illustriously displayed in it.

We know that this prediction of Isaiah was fulfilled when the Assyrian army was destroyed, and Sennacherib was put to flight; for "not by the arm of man" was he destroyed, but the Lord displayed his power, that it might be known that he alone is the deliverer of his Church. (2 Kings xix. 35; Isaiah xxxvii. 36.) By delivering Jerusalem at that time from the siege, God thus exhibited, as in a picture, spiritual redemption. He alone, therefore, will destroy our spiritual enemies. In vain shall we resort to other aids or remedies, or rely on our own strength, which is nothing; but let us have the direction and assistance of God, and we shall come off victorious.

And his young men shall melt away.[1] He means that the power of the Lord displayed against the Assyrians will be so great that the hearts of young men, who in other circumstances are wont to be fierce, shall be altogether softened and melt like wax; for young men, having less experience than old men, are on that account more fierce and impetuous. God will easily restrain such fierceness, when he shall determine to deliver his people from the hands of their enemies. For this reason Isaiah has especially mentioned "young men;" as if he had said, "the very flower or strength."

9. *He shall pass to his stronghold for fear.*[2] He now speaks of Sennacherib himself, who, trembling, shall betake himself in base and shameful flight to his "stronghold" or fortress, Nineveh, as to his nest. (2 Kings xix. 36.) The Prophet adds that "his princes," or military officers, whose

---

[1] "And his young men shall be discomfited. (Heb. for melting or tribute.)"—Eng. Ver.
[2] "And he shall pass over to his stronghold (or, his strength) for fear. (Heb. his rock shall pass away for fear.)"—Eng. Ver.

duty it is to encourage the rest of the soldiers, will be so timid that they shall not venture to join the ranks or await the battle, but shall "flee away from the standard."

Saith Jehovah, who hath a fire in Zion. At length he declares that he is God's herald in making this proclamation, that the Jews may not, as they are accustomed to do, dispute or hesitate as to the accomplishment of it, or afterwards forget so great a blessing, and ascribe it to fortune. If we read, as some do, Whose fire is in Zion, the meaning will be, that God has abundance of fiery power to consume his enemies. But I think that the relative אשר (*ăshĕr*) is redundant, or that it should be rendered in the nominative case, "*Who* shall be to him a fire;" for God is justly called "a fire," in reference to the Assyrians, whom he will consume.

When the Prophet calls him "a fire," some consider it to refer to sacrifices; but such an interpretation appears to me to be feeble and unnatural. I have no doubt that he says either that "the Lord has a fire" to consume the Assyrian, or that "God himself is a fire," and that he thus makes an implied comparison of the Assyrian to straw or chaff. He says that this "fire" is kindled and kept alive "in Zion and Jerusalem," that is, in the midst of his people, in order to intimate that the persecution of the Church of God by wicked men shall not pass unpunished; for they shall one day feel that he is their Judge, and shall know by experience that he assists his people, who thought that they had been left without all assistance.

In a word, against wicked men, who have maintained unceasing hostility against the Church, vengeance is prepared; and the Lord will not only avenge himself, but will also avenge his people. Let us therefore enjoy this consolation; and though it may appear as if we were defenceless and exposed to every danger, yet let us be fully convinced that the Lord will be "a fire" to our adversaries.

CHAPTER XXXII.

1. Behold, a king shall reign in righteousness, and princes shall rule in judgment.
2. And a man shall be as an hiding-place from the wind, and a covert from the tempest; as rivers of water in a dry place; as the shadow of a great rock in a weary land.
3. And the eyes of them that see shall not be dim; and the ears of them that hear shall hearken.
4. The heart also of the rash shall understand knowledge, and the tongue of the stammerers shall be ready to speak plainly.
5. The vile person shall be no more called liberal, nor the churl said *to be* bountiful.
6. For the vile person will speak villany, and his heart will work iniquity, to practise hypocrisy, and to utter error against the Lord, to make empty the soul of the hungry; and he will cause the drink of the thirsty to fail.
7. The instruments also of the churl *are* evil: he deviseth wicked devices to destroy the poor with lying words, even when the needy speaketh right.
8. But the liberal deviseth liberal things; and by liberal things shall he stand.
9. Rise up, ye women that are at ease; hear my voice, ye careless daughters; give ear unto my speech.
10. Many days and years shall ye be troubled, ye careless women: for the vintage shall fail, the gathering shall not come.
11. Tremble, ye women that are at ease; be troubled, ye careless ones; strip you, and make you bare, and gird *sackcloth* upon *your* loins.
12. They shall lament for the teats, for the pleasant fields, for the fruitful vine.
13. Upon the land of my people shall come up thorns *and* briars;

1. Ecce in justitia regnabit rex, et principes in judicio præerunt.
2. Et erit ille vir velut latibulum a vento, receptus ab imbre, rivi aquarum in terra arida, umbra magnæ rupis in terra laboriosa.
3. Tunc non oblinentur oculi videntium, et aures audientium auscultabunt.
4. Et cor stultorum intentum erit ad scientiam, et lingua balborum expedita erit ad loquendum diserte.
5. Non vocabitur amplius sordidus liberalis, neque parcus dicetur largus.
6. Quoniam sordidus loquetur sordes, et cor ejus machinabitur iniquitatem, ad designandam pravitatem, ut proferat subsannationem contra Iehovam, exinaniat animam famelicam, et potum sitienti subtrahat.
7. Avari arma sunt mala, (*vel, mensuræ sunt malæ:*) ipse pravitates excogitat, ut circumveniat simplices verbis mendacibus, et loquatur contra pauperem in judicio.
8. At liberalis liberalia agitabit, et liberaliter agendo progredietur.
9. Mulieres quietæ, surgite; audite vocem meam, filiæ confidentes; auscultate sermonem meum.
10. Dies super annum expavescetis, confidentes; quia deficiet vindemia, et collectio non veniet.
11. Contremiscite, quietæ; trepidate, confidentes; spoliate, nudate, accingite lumbos.
12. Super ubera plangentes, super agros desideratos, super vitem frugiferam.
13. Super terram populi mei ascendet spina et vepris; etiam super

yea, upon all the houses of joy *in* the joyous city:

14. Because the palaces shall be forsaken; the multitude of the city shall be left; the forts and towers shall be for dens for ever, a joy of wild asses, a pasture of flocks;

15. Until the Spirit be poured upon us from on high, and the wilderness be a fruitful field, and the fruitful field be counted for a forest.

16. Then judgment shall dwell in the wilderness, and righteousness remain in the fruitful field.

17. And the work of righteousness shall be peace; and the effect of righteousness, quietness and assurance for ever.

18. And my people shall dwell in a peaceable habitation, and in sure dwellings, and in quiet resting-places,

19. When it shall hail, coming down on the forest: and the city shall be low in a low place.

20. Blessed *are* ye that sow beside all waters, that send forth *thither* the feet of the ox and the ass.

omnes domos lætitiæ in urbe exultationis.

14. Quoniam palatium desertum, strepitus urbis relictus, turris et propugnaculum redigentur in speluncas in perpetuum, ubi gaudeant onagri, et pascantur greges.

15. Donec super nos effundatur Spiritus ex alto, et ponatur desertum in agrum cultum, et ager cultus instar sylvæ reputetur.

16. Et habitabit in deserto judicium, et justitia in agro culto sedebit.

17. Et erit opus justitiæ pax; effectus, inquam, justitiæ, securitas et quies in perpetuum.

18. Et sedebit populus meus in tabernaculo pacis, et in mansionibus securis, et in refrigeriis quiei s.

19. Et grando in sylvam descensu divertet, et in loco humili consideret civitas.

20. Beati vos qui seritis super omnes aquas, qui immittitis pedem bovis et asini.

1. *Behold, a king shall reign.* He means that God will still be gracious to his Church, so as to restore her entirely; and the best method of restoring her is, when good government is maintained, and when the whole administration of it is conducted with propriety, and with good order. This prediction undoubtedly relates to Hezekiah and his reign, under which the Church was reformed and restored to its former splendour; for formerly it was in a wretched and ruinous condition. Ahaz, who was a wicked and disgraceful hypocrite, had corrupted everything according to his own wicked dispositions, and had overturned the whole condition of civil government and of religion. (2 Kings xvi. 2, 3.) He therefore promises another king, namely, Hezekiah, whose power and righteousness shall restore the state of affairs which is thus wretched and desperate. In a word, he presents to us in this passage a lively picture of the prosperous condition of the Church; and as this cannot be attained without Christ, this description undoubtedly refers to Christ,

of whom Hezekiah was a type, and whose kingdom he foreshadowed.

In righteousness and judgment. Here he follows the ordinary usage of Scripture, which employs those expressions to denote good government; for by righteousness is meant equity and good government, and by judgment is meant that part of equity which upholds good men, and defends them from the assaults of the wicked. It is undoubtedly true that the duty of a good prince embraces a wider extent than "righteousness and judgment;" for his great aim ought to be to defend the honour of God and religion. But the ordinary usage of Scripture is, to describe the whole observation of the law by the works of the second table; for, if we refrain from acts of injustice, if we aid, as far as lies in our power, those who are oppressed by others, and, in a word, if we maintain brotherly kindness, we give evidence of the fear of God, from which such fruits spring and grow. From a part, therefore, the Prophet has described the whole.

And princes shall rule. It is not without good reason that he likewise mentions nobles;[1] for it would not be enough to be a good prince, if he were not supported by upright ministers and counsellors. Frequently has the condition of the people, under good princes, been very bad; as we read of Nerva,[2] under whose reign every kind of conduct was tolerated, so that many persons were far less favourably situated under his reign than under Nero; for the carelessness and indolence of a single individual gave freedom of action to

---

[1] In our Author's version, from which the heading of this paragraph is taken, he makes use of the word *principes*, which commonly means "rulers," but sometimes also (as in the phrases, "facile princeps, femina princeps,") denotes persons of high rank, or those who in any respect are highly distinguished. But here he employs the word *proceres*, "nobles;" and he does so evidently for the purpose of removing ambiguity, and of stating clearly that view which is contained in the conclusion of this sentence.—*Ed.*

[2] The singular mildness of the Roman Emperor Nerva, which made him personally beloved, was carried to such excess as to impair the efficiency of his government, and compelled him to resign the throne to the able and excellent Trajan. On the other hand, Nero, whose name cannot be mentioned without awakening the remembrance of his monstrous cruelty, held the reins with a firmer hand, and prevented the repetition of many disorders which had been committed under the reign of his amiable predecessor Nerva.—*Ed.*

many wicked men. It is therefore necessary that a king shall have good governors, who shall supply the place of eyes and hands, and aid him in the righteous exercise of his authority. If this be not the case, a good king cannot advance a step without being more or less retarded by other men; and unless rulers move with a harmony resembling that which we find in musical instruments, the government of a state cannot be carried on with advantage.

On this subject, men ought to listen to the advice of Jethro, Moses' father-in-law, to unite with him "able men fearing God, men of truth, and hating covetousness, and to appoint such men to be rulers of thousands, rulers of hundreds, rulers of fifties, and rulers of tens." (Exod. xviii. 21.) But at the present day, those who aid, or pander to their lusts, and who favour and flatter them, are promoted by kings to honours and high rank, which are bestowed on them as the just reward of their flattery or base servility. Nor ought we to wonder if we see, almost throughout the whole world, states thrown into confusion, ranks overturned, and all good government despised and set aside; for this is the just punishment of our iniquities, and we deserve to have such governors, since we do not allow God to rule over us. How shall this extraordinary kindness of God be enjoyed by men who are openly rebellious and profane, or by wicked hypocrites who cast God behind them, and cannot bear the yoke of Christ, through whom this prosperity and restoration of a declining Church is promised?

2. *And that man shall be.* How great is the importance of well-regulated government the Prophet shews plainly by these words, when he calls that king *a hiding-place from the wind, and a covert from the rain;* for mankind can never be so happy as when every one voluntarily abstains from every kind of violence and injustice, and when they conduct themselves peaceably and without restraint. Since, therefore, most men are urged and driven by their furious passions to acts of injustice, men would be embroiled in incessant quarrelling if a remedy were not provided in the laws and courts of justice; but as many rulers, by a tyrannical exercise of power, raise more troubles than they allay, it is not

without good reason that the good king is honoured by this peculiar commendation. If this was said with truth concerning Hezekiah, much more may it be said concerning Christ, in whom we have our best, or rather, our only refuge in those storms by which we must be tossed about as long as we dwell in this world. Whenever, therefore, we are scorched by oppressive heat, let us learn to retire under his shadow; whenever we are tossed about by tempests, and think that we are overwhelmed by the violence of the waves, let us learn to betake ourselves to him as our safest harbour; he will speedily bring every storm to a calm, and will completely restore what was ruined and decayed.

3 and 4. *Then the eyes of them that see.* Hence we see more clearly that, while the Prophet describes the reign of Hezekiah, he intends to lead us farther; for here he discourses concerning the restoration of the Church, which indeed was shadowed out by Hezekiah, but has been actually fulfilled in Christ. We know that the Church is never in a healthy condition, unless she be internally ruled by righteous and wise governors. Now, this cannot be, unless Christ reign; and here, therefore, Christ and his reign are specially recommended to us. This promise is contrasted with the dreadful threatening which he had uttered in a former chapter, (Isaiah xxix. 10,) that he would blind the Jews; for here, on the other hand, he promises the true light, that they who were formerly blind may be enlightened, that "the deaf may begin to hear, that fools may understand, and that stammerers may speak."

He calls them *seeing* and *hearing* who ought to have seen and heard when the word of God was exhibited to them; but they chose to be blind and deaf, and turned away their thoughts and hearts from doctrine. The Lord promises that he will restore to these persons eyes, ears, a tongue, and understanding. Now, it is certain that nothing is here promised which does not proceed from the grace of God; for he does not merely declare what men will do, but what God himself will do in men. These are extraordinary gifts of God; as, on the contrary, when he blinds, when he takes away understanding and the right use of speech, when he suffers ignorance and barbarism to prevail, these are dreadful punishments by which he takes vengeance on men for their ingratitude and for their contempt of the word. He promises that, at length, in compassion towards his people, the Lord will restore what he had justly taken away from them; and it must have been through the kindness of Christ that a tongue to speak, a mind to understand, and ears to hear, are restored to us; for formerly we were dull of apprehension, and were struck with frightful stupidity.

Let us therefore know that out of Christ there is no spiritual life in the world, because here they are declared to be destitute of sight, hearing, sound understanding, and the proper use of speech, "till they be united in one body, of which he is the head."[1] (Eph. iv. 15, 16.) Hence it follows that, when the kingdom of Christ is overthrown, these blessings are also taken away. It ought also to be observed, that the blessings which are here recommended are above all others excellent and desirable; for riches, and possessions, and everything else in which men commonly judge the happiness of life to consist, ought to be reckoned of no value in comparison of these blessings. Amidst the abundance of all things we shall be miserable, unless the Lord restore those spiritual blessings of which the Prophet speaks in this passage; and therefore, when they are taken away, let us know that Christ also is at a distance from us, and that we are strangers to him, seeing that it is from him alone, as Paul informs us, that all spiritual blessings flow. (Eph. i. 3.) When we see that those blessings which had been taken away for a long period are now restored to us, let us be ashamed of our ingratitude in not rendering to Christ that glory which was due to him, and in not employing the understanding which he gave to us in spreading his kingdom and promoting his worship; for we plainly shew that he has no dominion over us.

And the heart of fools.[2] As fools are commonly hasty

---

[1] "Duquel il soit le chef."
[2] "The heart also of the rash. (Heb. hasty.)"—Eng. Ver. "The heart also of the hasty."—*Stock.*

and rash, so the Hebrew writers take the word *haste*[1] as denoting *folly;* for wise men are usually cautious.

5. *No longer shall the base person be called.* The Prophet means that everything will be restored to good order, so that vices will not, as formerly, be reckoned virtues; for, when the public government is wicked, covetous persons are in power, and are honoured and esteemed, because men judge of virtue by wealth and power; a poor man is everywhere despised, though he be truly upright and bountiful to the full extent of his ability; and, in a word, in such a state of things there is nothing but disorder and confusion. But good government quickly detects such pretences and masks; for, where virtue is esteemed, vices are immediately exposed. Good men also have greater freedom allowed them in restraining the wantonness of those who formerly trod under their feet all that is just and lawful.

When the Prophet speaks here about the condition and reformation of the Church, which is a spiritual government, we ought to raise our minds somewhat higher, so as to view all this as relating to Christ, to whom it specially and peculiarly belongs to expose hidden vices, and to remove those vails and coverings by which the appearance of vices is changed, so that they are praised as if they were virtues. He does this by means of the gospel, by which he drags into light the disgraceful actions which were formerly concealed, and openly shews what they really are, so that no man, unless he choose it, can be deceived by their outward appearance. And this is the reason why the gospel is so much hated by the world; for no man can patiently endure to have his "hidden thoughts" and concealed baseness "revealed." (Luke ii. 35.) Philosophers indeed reason admirably about covetousness and liberality, and in some degree explain what is the difference between them; but they never penetrate into the hearts, so as to search them and actually distinguish between the covetous man and the bountiful. This can only be done by Christ's light, when he shines by

[1] This observation is founded on the Hebrew word נמהרים, (*nimharim,*) which our Author translates Fools, and which literally means Hasty. —*Ed.*

means of the gospel, and, by exploring the deepest corners of the human heart, brings us to spiritual and inward obedience. In this passage, therefore, we are brought to the judgment-seat of Christ, who alone, by exposing hypocrisy, reveals whether we are covetous or bountiful.

6. *For the vile person will speak vileness.* We might also render it, "The wicked man will speak wickedly;" for נבלה (*nĕbâlâh*) denotes "baseness" or any wickedness, such as is meant by the French word *laschetè*, or by the English words, "lewdness" or "baseness." It might also be rendered, "The fool will speak wickedly;" and thus there would be an allusion to the words נבל (*nâbâl*) and נבלה, (*nĕbâlâh*,)[1] though the meaning would be considerably different; but, since he employed this word in the former verse, when speaking of "vile" persons, I willingly adopt that interpretation.

And his heart will contrive iniquity. I consider און (*âvĕn*) to denote "wickedness;" for he speaks of giving themselves up continually to sin and do wickedly, as is plainly shewn by what follows; for his earnest remonstrances are directed against wicked men, who abandon themselves to all that is vile, and are not moved by any feeling of conscience, who laugh at all warnings, and ridicule God and his servants. Christ also drags them into the light, and exposes what lay concealed under coverings; for to him, as we have said, it peculiarly belongs to "pierce, by the sword of the gospel, the hidden feelings of the heart, that they may answer to the judgment of God." (Heb. iv. 12.) Isaiah therefore continues the same subject which he had formerly begun to explain.

Others explain it differently, but, as I think, in an unsuitable manner; for they think that it is a kind of proverbial saying, and render it in the present tense, "The vile person speaketh vileness." But I think that the Prophet means something higher, namely, that Christ is the Judge of the world, and therefore, when he shall ascend the judgment-seat, he will shew what is the disposition of every person; for, so long as he does not exercise the office of a judge,

[1] The allusion would be better brought out by rendering it, "The fool will speak folly."—*Ed.*

everything remains in confusion, the wicked are applauded, because they have the appearance of piety, and the most excellent men are despised. But Christ will openly display the life of every person, so that what formerly, under some pretence, bore a fair reputation, will be manifested to be wickedness; and on this account he is said to "have in his hand a sieve for separating the wheat from the chaff." (Matt. iii. 12.) Now, this sieve is the gospel, by which, as a Judge, he brings malefactors to trial, and draws forth, in spite of their efforts, the exposure of their transgressions and crimes.

We have the experience of this more and more every day, when an exposure is made of that wickedness which had been concealed under the mask of Popery and the strange folds of superstitions. Who would ever have thought, amidst that darkness, that there were concealed in the hearts of men such dreadful monsters as are brought forward at the present day? To such a height has the contempt of God arisen, that many discover themselves to be more like beasts than men. Yet the Papists slander us, as if by our doctrine we gave loose reins to men, and exhorted them to despise God and follow wickedness without fear or shame. But let them listen to Isaiah, who replies that, when the truth of God shall be made known, vile persons will speak vileness, and wicked persons will speak baseness and wickedness; and, indeed, Christ would not be a spiritual judge if he did not "reveal the secret thoughts of the heart, and bring every hidden thing to light." (Luke ii. 35.)

To make empty the hungry soul. In addition to those mockeries which the reprobate cast against God, cruelty is next mentioned. The Prophet thus gives an exact enumeration of those actions which are contrary to the second table. Wicked men begin with despising God, then rush to outward crimes, and practise cruelty of every sort against their neighbours. Now, the worst and most flagrant of all cruelty is, to "snatch food from the hungry soul and drink from the thirsty;" for mere natural feeling prompts us to mercy and ($συμπάθειαν$)[1] compassion. When men are so brutalized that

---
[1] $Συμπάθεια$, a more extensive term than the English word "sympathy,"

they are not affected by the misery of others, and lay aside every feeling of humanity, they must be worse than the beasts themselves, who have some sort of pity for the wants of their own kind.

7. *The instruments of the covetous man are evil.* We must always keep by the future tense; for he does not inquire what wicked men are, but declares that they shall be revealed under the reign of Christ, that they may no longer deceive or impose upon any one. He speaks of the heavenly light which would arise, as we have already said, to expose hidden wickedness. Christ therefore shews what covetous men are, and how destructive are the means which they employ. If it be thought better that כלי (*kĕlē*) should be translated "measures," I have no objection; but the word "instrument" is more appropriate and extensive, for it includes "instruments" of every description. It means therefore every kind of means, tricks, and cunning devices, by which "covetous men" put simple persons off their guard, and draw them into their nets.

To deceive the simple by lying words. He now assigns the reason. It is, because they do not cease to contrive some injury.[1] It is certain that this is a description of the practices of bad men, who think of nothing but their own convenience and gain, and are always bent on cheating and "deceiving." Christ brings to light those persons, and their tricks and contrivances.

To speak against the poor in judgment.[2] Various circumstances are brought forward, to present in a more striking light the shamefulness of this wickedness. First, "to deceive the simple," who cannot take care of themselves, is more shameful and flagrant than to deceive sharpers and veterans in crime. It is shameful, secondly, to make use of deceitful blandishments under the pretence of friendship; thirdly, to deceive "the poor," whose poverty we ought rather to have

literally denotes "fellow-feeling," and is frequently employed by our Author to express that kind of feeling which every man ought to cherish towards his fellow-men.—*Ed.*

[1] "Quelque trahison;"—"Some treachery."
[2] "Even when the needy speaketh right;" or, "when he speaketh against the poor in judgment."—*Eng. Ver.*

relieved; fourthly, to lay snares in the very court of justice. This is more highly criminal than if a man were attacked by open violence; for the court of justice ought to be a refuge for the poor, and what shall become of them, if it be a den of robbers or thieves? If the roads are beset by robbers, and if snares are laid, there may be some way of avoiding them; but there is no possibility of guarding against the frauds committed in courts of justice. These circumstances, therefore, ought to be carefully remarked.

8. *But the liberal shall devise liberal things.* We have already said that these statements of the Prophet have a deeper meaning than is commonly supposed; for he does not speak in the ordinary sense of the words, but treats of the reformation of the Church. This relates therefore to the regenerate, over whom Christ reigns; for, although all are called by the voice of the gospel, yet there are few who suffer themselves to be placed under his yoke. The Lord makes them truly kind and bountiful, so that they no longer seek their own convenience, but are ready to give assistance to the poor, and not only do this once or oftener, but every day advance more and more in kindness and generosity.

In acting liberally he shall make progress. This passage is commonly explained in a different manner, namely, that the liberal advance themselves, and become great by doing good; because God rewards them, and bestows on them greater blessings. This view pleases at first sight; but the Prophet, on the contrary, shews that the liberal will never cease to perform acts of generosity, for they will daily make greater progress, and will pursue the same designs and adhere firmly to their intention, as it is said by the Psalmist, " He hath dispersed, he hath given to the poor; his righteousness endureth for ever." (Psalm cxii. 9 ; 2 Cor. ix. 9.) This is added, because it is easy to counterfeit liberality for a time; many even think that they are sincerely bountiful because they have performed an act of beneficence, but quickly cease and change their purpose. But true liberality is not momentary or of short duration. They who possess that virtue persevere steadily, and do not exhaust themselves in a sudden and feeble flame, of which they quickly afterwards repent.

This is what the Prophet intended to express by the word קוּם, (*kūm,*) which signifies to "arise" and "grow." There are indeed many occurrences which retard the progress of our liberality. We find in men strange ingratitude, so that what we give appears to be ill bestowed. Many are too greedy, and, like horse-leeches, suck the blood of others. But let us remember this saying, and listen to Paul's exhortation " not to be weary in well-doing ;" for the Lord exhorts us not to momentary liberality, but to that which shall endure during the whole course of our life. (Gal. vi. 9.)

9. *Ye women at ease, arise.* These words appear not to be connected with what goes before ; for formerly he spoke about restoring the Church, but now he threatens that the judgment of God is ready to strike a people carelessly reposing amidst riches and pleasures ; and therefore it is probable that here Isaiah begins a new and distinct subject. Yet there will be no absurdity in connecting this with the former prediction, for the Prophets commonly observe this order. After having promised the grace of God to believers, they next direct their discourse to hypocrites, to declare that the mercy which the Lord promises to believers will be of no avail to hypocrites, and that notwithstanding they shall be punished for their sins.

As to *women* being chiefly addressed, the Hebrew commentators, agreeably to the frequent usage of their language, suppose "cities"[1] to be meant ; but I think that the language here is not figurative, and I rather adhere to the simple meaning of the words. He addresses "women" rather than men, in order to shew the extent of that calamity ; for in ordinary circumstances women and children are spared, because they are unfit for war, and have no power to defend themselves. He says that the destruction will be so cruel that none shall be spared.

He expressly addresses them also as " women *at ease,*" who are usually more delicate than others, and, enjoying the advantages of wealth, have some means of providing for

[1] " Ye provinces that dwell at ease."—*Jarchi.*

their safety and of rescuing themselves from calamities, even when persons of ordinary rank are suffering grievous hardships. But to them especially Isaiah makes the intimation, that they must "arise" and "tremble;" and he contrasts this trembling with the ease and luxury which they peacefully enjoyed. He bids them *arise*, that they may know that this is not the time for repose, and that the Lord will arouse them from their ease and indifference.

Hear my voice, ye careless daughters.[1] In the same manner as before, the word daughters is interpreted by the rabbins to mean "villages" or "smaller cities;" but I think, as I have already said, that it ought to be taken in its literal meaning. He shews them whence shall arise this terror, whence shall arise that violence which shall compel them to "arise" and "tremble." It is from the judgment of God. But he mentions "a voice," that they may know that this prophecy shall not fail of its accomplishment; because he proclaims war against them by the command of God. "How efficacious this speech shall be, and what power it shall have to arouse you, one day you shall actually feel." So frequently does he reproach them for indolence, carelessness, and luxury, not only because it is harder for those who live at ease to be harshly aroused, but because the corruption and depravity of human nature make it scarcely possible for the world to enjoy ease and prosperity without becoming indolent. Next, falling gradually into slothfulness, it will deceive itself by a false imagination, and drive far away from it all fear, and, relying on this confidence, will insolently rise up against God.

10. *Days above a year.*[2] By these words he declares that the calamity will be of long duration; for it is no slight consolation in adversity, when the distresses which must otherwise have been endured by us with grief and sorrow pass quickly away. But when no end and no mitigation of

---

[1] "Ye cities that dwell carelessly."—*Jarchi.* In this, as well as in the former case, he refers to Jonathan's Targum.—*Ed.*

[2] "Many days and years; (Heb. days above a year.)"—Eng. Ver. "In a year and more."—*Alexander.* "Shortly after a year; Heb. days upon a year: that is, the time will soon come after the expiration of one year, when ye shall be troubled with a dearth."—*Stock.*

sorrows, no comfort or hope of deliverance is held out to us, what can be left but despair? He therefore threatens not only that they shall endure them for one year, but that afterwards they must look for new afflictions.

You shall tremble. By this word he indirectly stings their slothfulness, by declaring that they who grudged to listen to calm instruction shall be dragged forth with trembling and alarm. As the Jews were excessively anxious about earthly blessings and perishing food, he addresses their senses by threatening a scarcity of wine and wheat. If they had been more thoroughly purified from grovelling desires, he would rather have threatened what Jeremiah deplores in his Lamentations, that "the sacrifices and festivals had ceased, and that the holy assemblies were discontinued." (Lam. i. 7.) But, because they were sunk in their pleasures, and had not made such proficiency as to know the value of spiritual blessings, the Prophet accommodates himself to their ignorance, and addresses their bellies rather than their understandings. He speaks of the desolation of the fields, which would be the necessary consequence of that calamity; for abundance and plenty commonly give rise to ease and indifference. "The Lord will therefore," says he, "deprive you of all food, and shake off your slothfulness, and take away all ground of confidence." Accordingly, we are here reminded that we ought not to sleep in the midst of prosperity, nor imagine that we are safe, as if we could expect uninterrupted prosperity in the world. But we ought to use with moderation the gifts of God, if we do not wish to be suddenly aroused, and to be overwhelmed when we are off our guard, and to feel the heavier distress because we did not look for a change of our affairs.

11. *Tremble.* This repetition is not unnecessary, but states more fully what he formerly said; for when men are asleep, they are not easily aroused by the voice of the prophets, and therefore it is needful to cry aloud and reprove them continually. And thus, by adding one threatening to another, or by repeating the same threatenings, he shews how great is the stupidity of men, when they have once been blinded by prosperity; for they can scarcely endure any longer to

hear the warnings which God addresses to them. Men are undoubtedly more in danger from prosperity than from adversity; for when matters go smoothly with them, they flatter themselves, and are intoxicated by their success; and therefore it was necessary to deal more sharply with the Jews, in order to shake off that slothfulness. This exhortation of the Prophet ought to be explained in the future tense; as if he had said, "You shall at length tremble, for the rest which you now enjoy will not be perpetual."

By bidding them *make themselves bare, and gird sackcloth on their loins*, he describes the manner and dress of mourners. Whenever they were visited by deep adversity, they put on sackcloth, made bare the other parts of their body, and by dress, and attitude, and every method, manifested their grief. He desires women to put on sackcloth and other expressions of mourning, instead of the luxuries and pleasures in which they eagerly indulged.

12. *Mourning over the breasts.* This verse is explained in various ways. Some understand it to mean simply, that there will be so great a scarcity of provisions, that women will lose their milk, and thus the children will "mourn over dry breasts;" which we see sometimes happen, when a very great scarcity of provisions occasions leanness. But the more generally received and more appropriate interpretation is, to view the word "breasts" as figuratively denoting fields and vineyards, as the Prophet himself declares; for they are justly compared to the breasts of mothers, because, by deriving nourishment from them, we suck the milk or blood of the earth. He therefore means that there will be a want of food and nourishment, because the Lord will curse the earth, so that it shall yield no fruits. Thus shall men sigh over that scarcity, as if over their mother's "breasts," from which they formerly received delicious nourishment. This appears to me to be a more natural meaning, and to agree best with the context; for it serves to explain what afterwards follows, about "rich fields and the fruitful vine."[1]

---

[1] "It may be better translated, striking your breasts, because of the pleasant fields and fruitful vines, which should be destroyed

13. *There shall grow up the brier and the thorn.* He confirms the former verse, and explains the cause of barrenness and famine, which is, that the fields, which formerly used to be fat and fertile, will be uncultivated, desolate, and barren. This was a frightful change of affairs; for we know that that country yielded corn and fruits more plentifully than other countries, not so much by nature as by the blessing of God; for he had said, "I will give you a land flowing with milk and honey." (Exod. iii. 8, 17, and xiii. 5, and xxxiii. 3.) This was the cause of the abundance and fertility.

On the land of my people. By giving it this name, he meets an objection which they might otherwise have brought, that there was no reason to fear that the land which God had chosen would not produce fruits every year; because, although the kindness of God extends to all mankind, yet he was in a peculiar manner the Father and supporter of that nation. It was therefore incredible that this land, which had been set apart for the children of God, would be covered with "briers and thorns;" and thus the Prophet reproves the Jews more sharply, because they not only made void the blessing of God by their wickedness, but drew down his wrath, so as to spoil and deface the beauty of the land.

Even on all the houses of joy. The particle כִּי (*ki*) signifies *even*, though some think that it means "for" or "because," "Because there is joy in their houses."[1] But that interpretation cannot be admitted, because בָּתֵּי, (*bāttē*,) "houses of," is in the construct state. This appears to me therefore to be an enlargement of what he had now said, and to mean that this desolation will be, not only in the utmost corners of the land, but "*even* in the houses of joy," that is, in the splendid and magnificent houses, which formerly were the abodes of the most refined luxury. When the Prophet said this, he was undoubtedly ridiculed by the men of that age;

by the Assyrians. It was a common gesture used on all mournful occasions, to strike the breasts; though others think teats may be taken metaphorically for the pleasant fields and fruitful vine by which they subsisted, as infants by the mother's paps."—*Samuel White.*

[1] "For all that desolation shall be on all joyful houses."—*Jarchi.*

men certainly did not listen to him amidst those luxuries by which they were blinded. Besides, they grew insolent on account of the promises of God, and thought that they would never be in want of anything. Yet all that Isaiah foretold came to pass. From this example let us learn to be moderate in our use of prosperity, and to depend on the blessing of God, so as to obey his word with a good conscience.

14. *For the palace shall be forsaken.* Here also he describes more fully the desolation of the country; for, having mentioned in the former verse magnificent houses, he now likewise adds palaces and cities, so as to shew that there is nothing, however splendid and illustrious, that is exempted from that calamity. We see that men are dazzled by their own splendour, till they lift up their eyes to heaven; and the consequence is, that they are soothed to sleep in the midst of their wealth, and dread nothing. He therefore declares that all that was splendid, magnificent, and lofty, in Judea, cities, palaces, bulwarks, fortresses, all will be brought to nothing. When he says *for ever*, he again gives warning, as he formerly did, that this calamity will not last only for a single day, but that, as they had been long hardened in their vices, so it will be of long duration; for, if they had been punished only for a short time, being obstinate and intractable, they would quickly have relapsed into their natural disposition.

15. *Till the Spirit be poured out upon you.* Because the Prophet speaks of the Jews among whom God had determined to plant his Church, it was therefore necessary to leave to them some hope of salvation, that they might not faint amidst so great afflictions; for, while the Lord is severe towards wicked men who falsely shelter themselves under his name, yet in some manner he preserves his Church. The Prophet therefore adds this promise, that they might know that, whatever be the severity with which he punishes his people, still he is always mindful of his covenant; for he never threatens in such a manner as not to leave some ground for consolation, so as to cheer and comfort the hearts of believers, even when their affairs are utterly desperate.

Besides, in order that they may fully enjoy the comfort which is offered to them, he raises their eyes to the very Author of life; and indeed we see that, when a favourable change takes place, the greater part of men fill themselves to excess with bread and wine, and, when they are pressed by famine, they neglect God and solicit the earth.

With good reason, therefore, does Isaiah say that "the Spirit" will come *from on high* to refresh and fertilize the earth; and he alludes, I have no doubt, to that saying of David, "Send forth thy Spirit, and they shall be created, and thou wilt renew the face of the earth." (Ps. civ. 30.) Holding out this as an evidence that God is reconciled, he at the same time declares that the restoration of the Church proceeds solely from the grace of God, who can remove its barrenness as soon as he has imparted strength from heaven; for he who created all things out of nothing, as if they had formerly existed, is able to renew it in a moment.

And the wilderness become a Carmel.[1] In explaining this comparison of "the wilderness" to "Carmel," commentators are sadly at a loss; but, as I remarked on a former passage, (Isaiah xxix. 17,) where a similar phrase occurred,[2] the Prophet merely, in my opinion, points out the happy effect of that restoration, namely, that the abundance and plenty of all things will prove that God is actually reconciled to his people. He says that places which formerly were "wildernesses" shall be like "Carmel," which was a rich and fertile spot, and on that account receives its name; and that "Carmel" shall be like "a wilderness," that is, it shall be so fertile, that if we compare what it now is with what it shall afterwards be, it may seem like "a wilderness." It is an enlarged representation of that unwonted fertility. "Fields now barren and uncultivated shall be fertile, and cultivated and fertile fields shall yield such abundant fruit that their present fertility is poverty and barrenness, in comparison of the large produce which they shall afterwards yield; just as if we should compare the fields of Savoy with those of Sicily

---

[1] "And the wilderness become a fruitful field." Such is the Author's own translation of the clause, which corresponds to our authorized version. —*Ed.*

[2] See our Author's Commentary on that passage.—*Ed.*

and Calabria, and pronounce them to be a "wilderness." In a word, he describes unparalleled fertility, which believers shall enjoy, when they have been reconciled to God, in order that they may know his favour by his acts of kindness.

While Isaiah thus prophesies concerning the reign of Hezekiah, all this is declared by him to relate to the kingdom of Christ as its end and accomplishment; and therefore, when we come to Christ, we must explain all this spiritually, so as to understand that we are renewed as soon as the Lord has sent down the Spirit from heaven, that we who were "wildernesses" may become cultivated and fertile fields. Ere the Spirit of God has breathed into us, we are justly compared to wildernesses or a dry soil; for we produce nothing but "thorns and briers," and are by nature unfit for yielding fruits. Accordingly, they who were barren and unfruitful, when they have been renewed by the Spirit of God, begin to yield plentiful fruits; and they whose natural dispositions had some appearance of goodness, being renewed by the same Spirit, will afterwards be so fruitful, that they will appear as if they had formerly been a "wilderness;" for all that men possess is but a wild forest, till they have been renewed by Christ. Whenever, therefore, the Church is afflicted, and when her condition appears to be desperate, let us raise our eyes to heaven, and depend fully on these promises.

16. *And judgment shall dwell in the wilderness.* The Prophet shews what is the actual condition of the Church, that is, when justice and judgment prevail; for men ought not to be like cattle, which seek nothing but plenty of food and abundance of outward things. And hence it is plain enough that the Jews were not confined to transitory enjoyments, so as to have their hope fixed exclusively on earthly blessings, as some fanatics imagine. They were enjoined to attend to that which was of the greatest importance, that justice and judgment should prevail; and undoubtedly they knew that true happiness consists in it. It is therefore our duty to look chiefly to this, that we should not, like hogs in a sty, judge of the happiness of life by abundance of bread and wine; for this is the end of all

the blessings which the Lord bestows upon us, this is the object of our deliverance, "that we should serve him," as Zacharias says, "in holiness and righteousness." (Luke i. 74, 75.)

Under the terms "justice" and "judgment," as we have already seen, he includes all that belongs to uprightness; for although these two words relate strictly to that equity which ought to be mutually cultivated among us, yet, since it is customary to describe the observation of the whole law by the duties of the second table, here the Prophet, by a figure of speech in which a part is taken for the whole, embraces also piety and the worship of God. The Prophets are accustomed to notice the chief duties of brotherly kindness, and those which belong to the second table, because by these, more than by any others, we manifest the real state of our feelings towards God.

When he declares that justice and judgment have their abode in the wilderness, as well as in the cultivated fields, this shews more clearly that the abundance of blessings promised a little before was so great that, when men saw it, they would consider that those fields which they formerly looked upon as very excellent had been comparatively barren.

17. *And the work of righteousness shall be peace.* A little before, he censured severely that peace which made the Jews drowsy and slothful; he now promises a different kind of repose, which will be a striking proof of the love of God, who has received them into favour, and will faithfully guard them. We ought therefore to observe the implied contrast between that brutal repose which the reprobate think that they obtain by their presumption in committing every kind of wickedness, and in which they also fall asleep, and that different kind of repose, on the other hand, which the children of God obtain by a religious and holy life, and which Isaiah exhorts us to desire, shewing that we ought fearlessly to believe that a blessed and joyful peace awaits us when we have been reconciled to God.

In this way he recommends to them to follow uprightness, that they may obtain assured peace; for, as Peter declares, there is no better way of procuring favour, that no man may do us injury, than to abstain from all evil-doing. (1 Peter iii. 13.) But the Prophet leads them higher, to aim at a religious and holy life by the grace of God; for nothing is more unreasonable than that wicked men should desire to have peace, while they are continually fighting against God. That wish is indeed common; for hardly one person in a hundred shall be found who does not loudly extol peace, while at the same time every man raises up enemies to himself in the earth, and all in vast crowds disturb heaven and earth by their crimes. Now, the latter repose, being perpetual, is compared by him to the former, which is slight and momentary.

The effect of righteousness. When peace receives this designation, let us learn that, as wars proceed from the wrath of God, which we provoke by our wickedness, so peace springs from his blessing. When, therefore, we see enemies enraged to battle, and rising furiously against us, let us seek no other remedy than repentance; for the Lord will easily allay commotions when we have returned to him. He it is, as the Psalmist says, who "maketh wars to cease to the ends of the earth, who breaketh the bow, and cutteth the spear in pieces, and burneth the chariots in the fire." (Psalm xlvi. 9.) We have already said that these things do not relate exclusively to Hezekiah, but must be referred to Christ.

18. *And my people shall dwell.* As we have said that spiritual righteousness is that which has its seat in the hearts of men, we must say the same thing about peace, which is the fruit of it. Accordingly, when *quiet habitations* and *resting-places* are here mentioned, let us remember the saying of Paul, "justified by faith, we have peace with God." (Rom. v. 1.) When Christ says that he "leaves" this peace to the disciples, (John xiv. 27,) he affirms that "it cannot be given by the world;" and we ought not to wonder at this, for, as the same Apostle Paul informs us in another passage, "this peace surpasses all understanding." (Philip. iv. 7.) Having obtained this righteousness, we are no longer restless or alarmed within, as when we feel in the

gnawings of conscience the wrath of God. A bad conscience is always alarmed, and harassed by wretched uneasiness.

Wicked men must therefore be uneasy, and distressed by a variety of terrors; for where righteousness is banished that peace cannot be found; and where Christ reigns, there alone do we find true peace. Assured peace, therefore, is enjoyed by none but believers, who appeal to the heavenly tribunal, not only by their piety, but by their reliance on the mercy of God. Hence we infer that Christ does not yet reign where consciences are uneasy, and tossed by the various waves of doubts, as must be the case with Papists and all others who are not built on the sacrifice of Christ and the atonement obtained through him.

19. *And the hail.* We have already said that the prophets are accustomed frequently to describe under figures the reign of Christ; for they borrow their metaphors from an earthly kingdom, because our ignorance would make it almost impossible for us to comprehend, in any other way, the unspeakable treasure of blessings. The meaning is, " The Lord will remove from his people distresses and annoyances, and will make them fall on others;" because here we are liable to various storms and tempests, and must endure rain, hail, showers, winds, and tempests. He says that God, by his wonderful providence, will prevent all distresses from doing any injury to believers, because he will drive their violence in another direction.

By *forests* he means unfrequented and desert places, where there are no crowds of men. Hence we learn that, when we are under the guardianship of Christ, we are protected from inconveniences and dangers, but that, at the same time, various storms and tempests are ready to burst on our heads. But the Lord is our deliverer, who turns away in another direction the evils that are approaching, or rescues us when we are in danger.

And the city shall be situated in a low place.[1] In order to confirm what he had said about peace, he says, that " cities," which shall be situated on level ground, will be

[1] " And the city shall be low in a low place;" or, " And the city shall be utterly abased."—Eng. Ver.

out of danger; for at that time it was customary to build on high and elevated places, that the access to them might be more difficult. "Such," says he, "will be God's protection of his people, that they will not need the ordinary fortifications, because the city may be safely set down in valleys; and even although it be liable to the attacks of enemies, it will sustain no inconvenience, for the hand of the Lord will protect it." We must not therefore seek safety by relying on our defences, lest we be immediately driven from our nest; but since our heavenly Father deigns to provide for our safety, let us be satisfied with having him for our protector and guardian.[1]

20. *Blessed are ye.* He shews how great will be the change, when Christ shall begin to reign; for he had formerly said that so great would be the desolation, that "thorns and briers" would overspread the holy land, costly houses would be thrown down, and cities and palaces would be levelled with the earth. This would happen, when the incessant attacks of enemies should lay that country desolate. But now he says that they shall be *blessed*, because God will give them abundant produce of all fruits. That fertility which might have been described in simple language, he illustrates by figures, that they shall "sow in marshes," and shall "send forth their cattle" into the fields without dread of losing them.

By *waters* some understand a rich and fertile soil; but the universal particle כֹּל, (*chōl,*) *all*, leads me to take a different view; as if he had said, "Places which were overrun with waters shall be fit for sowing, and there will be no reason to fear that the water shall spoil our fields." We are accustomed also to drive away oxen, and asses, and other animals, from fields, and especially from sown fields, that they

[1] "Some by the Forest understand Nineveh, some Babylon, some Jerusalem, and some the Assyrian army; but Gataker, and Vatablus before him, think the words may be rendered, he shall hail with hail on the forest, and cities shall be built in low places; as if he had said, God shall preserve the fruits of the earth from the injuries of unseasonable weather, and, when he sends a storm of hail, cause it to fall on the woods and deserts; and he shall give them so great security, that for the future they shall build their cities in low grounds, to shew that they are under no apprehensions of being overrun any more by an enemy."—*White.*

may not eat the corn. But here he says that the corn will grow so thick and plentifully, that it shall be necessary to send oxen and asses to crop the early blade, as is commonly done when the corn is luxuriant.[1]

He calls them *blessed,* in accordance with the usage of the Hebrew language, because their labour will never be unprofitable. If it be objected that, under the reign of Christ, such fertility has never been seen, I acknowledge that, even when God has shewn the highest kindness to his people, still there have always been visible marks of the curse, which was entailed on mankind by the fall and revolt of Adam. (Gen. iii. 17.) But since Christ has restored to believers the inheritance of the world, with good reason do the prophets assert that he would renew the earth, so as to remove its filthiness and restore that beauty which it had lost. They who complain that it is not yet fulfilled, ought to consider whether or not they themselves are purified from every stain of sin. And if they are still at a great distance from spiritual righteousness, let them be satisfied with enjoying the blessing of God according to the measure of regeneration, the full enjoyment of which we must not expect to obtain, till, freed from the pollutions of the flesh, we shall bear the perfect image of God.

[1] "Happy ye who shall enjoy as great fertility as if all your lands lay on the side of a running stream. Your corn shall grow so thick and fast that ye shall be forced to let your cattle crop the luxuriant ears; a practice still in use among our husbandmen."—*White.*

A TRANSLATION

OF

CALVIN'S VERSION

OF

THE PROPHECIES OF ISAIAH.

CHAPTERS I.—XXXII.

CHAPTER I.

1 The vision of Isaiah, the son of Amoz, which he saw concerning Judah and Jerusalem, in the days of Uzziah, Jotham, Ahaz, and Hezekiah, kings of Judah.
2 Hear, O heavens,
And hearken, O earth,
For thus the Lord speaketh:
I have nourished and brought up children;
Yet they have acted wickedly towards me.[1]
3 The ox knoweth his owner,
And the ass his master's crib;
Israel doth not know;
My people doth not understand.
4 O sinful nation, a people laden with iniquity,
Seed of evil-doers, degenerate children!
They have forsaken Jehovah,
They have despised[2] the Holy One of Israel,
They are estranged backwards.

5 Why should I strike you any more?
Ye will add faithlessness.
The whole head is sickness,
And the whole heart is faintness.

[1] Or, Have rebelled against me; or, Have revolted against me.
[2] Or, Have provoked to anger.

6 From the sole of the foot even to the head
  There is no soundness in it;
  A wound, a swelling, and a putrifying sore;
  And they have not been plastered, nor bound up,
  Nor softened with ointment.
7 Your country is desolation;
  Your cities are burnt with fire;
  Your land do strangers devour in your presence,
  It is reduced to solitude, like the destruction of foreigners.
8 And the daughter of Zion shall be left,
  As a cottage in a vineyard,
  As a lodge in a garden of cucumbers,
  As a city laid waste.
9 Unless the Lord of hosts had left us a very small remnant,
  We should have been as Sodom,
  And like Gomorrah.

10 Hear the word of the Lord, ye princes of Sodom!
   Give ear to the law of our God, ye people of Gomorrah!
   Of what value to me is the multitude of your sacrifices?
   Saith the Lord.
11 I am full of the burnt-offerings of rams,
   And of the fat of fed beasts;
   And in the blood of oxen, or of sheep, or of he-goats,
   I delight not.
12 When you come that you may appear before my face,
   Who hath required this at your hand?
   Even to tread my courts.
13 Do not continue to bring an offering of vanity.
   Incense is an abomination to me.
   The new-moon, and the sabbath, and the yearly assemblies,
   I cannot endure,
   (It is a vain thing.)
   Nor the assembly.
14 Your new-moons and your yearly festivals
   My soul hateth;
   They have been a burden to me;
   I am weary of bearing them.
15 When ye spread forth your hands,
   I will hide mine eyes from you.
   Even though you multiply prayer,
   I will not hear.
   Your hands are full of blood.
16 Wash you, make you clean;
   Take away the wickedness of your practices from before mine
     eyes;
   Cease to do evil;
17 Learn to do well:

Seek judgment, restore[1] the oppressed;
Plead for the orphan, defend the widow.
18 Come now, and let us reason together,
Hath the Lord said:
If your sins be as scarlet,
They shall be white as snow;
If they be red like purple,
They shall be as wool.
19 If ye shall be willing and shall hearken,
Ye shall eat the good of the land.
20 But if ye shall refuse and rebel,
Ye shall be consumed by the sword;
For the mouth of the Lord hath spoken it.

21 How is the faithful city become a harlot!
She was full of judgment,
And righteousness lodged by night[2] in her;
But now murderers.
22 Thy silver is become dross,
And thy wine is mixed with water.
23 Thy princes are rebellious,
And are companions of thieves;
Every one loveth a gift,
And seeketh eagerly for rewards.
They judge not the cause of the fatherless,
Nor doth the cause of the widow come to them.

24 Therefore saith the Lord,[3] Jehovah of hosts,
The mighty One of Israel;
Alas! I will take consolation on mine adversaries,
I will be avenged of mine enemies.
25 I will turn my hand upon thee;
I will purely purge away thy dross,
And I will take away all thy tin.
26 And I will restore thy judges as at the first,
And thy counsellors as at the beginning.
Then shall it be said of thee,
The city of righteousness,
The faithful city.
27 Zion shall be redeemed with judgment,
And they who shall be brought back to her with righteousness.
28 And the destruction of the transgressors and of the sinners shall be together,
And they who have revolted from the Lord shall be consumed.
29 Yea, they shall be ashamed
Of the trees which ye have desired,

[1] Or, Guide. [2] Or, Dwelt. [3] Or, The Governor.

And they shall be covered with disgrace
By the groves which ye have chosen.
30 Ye shall surely be as a tree whose leaf fadeth,
And as a grove that hath no water.
31 And your strong man[1] shall be as tow,
And the maker of it as a spark;
And they shall both be burnt,
And there shall be none to quench them.

CHAPTER II.

1 The word which Isaiah, the son of Amoz, saw concerning Judah and Jerusalem.
2 And it shall come to pass in the last of the days,
That the mountain of the house of Jehovah
Shall be established on the top of the mountains,
And shall be exalted above the hills;
And all nations shall flow to it.
3 And many peoples shall come, and shall say,
Come, and we shall go up
To the mountain of Jehovah,
To the house of the God of Jacob;
And he will teach us in his ways,
And we shall walk in his paths;
For out of Zion shall go forth the law,
And the word of the Lord from Jerusalem.
4 And he will judge among the nations,
And will rebuke many peoples :
And they shall beat their swords into spades,
And their spears into pruning-hooks;
And nation shall not lift up sword against nation,
Neither shall they practise war any more.

5 O house of Jacob, come ye,
And we shall walk in the light of the Lord.
6 Verily thou hast forsaken thy people, the house of Jacob;
Because they are filled with the east,[2]
And with soothsayers, like the Philistines;
And they have delighted in the children of foreigners.
7 Their land is full of silver and gold,
And there is no end to their treasures.
Their land is also full of horses,
And there is no end to their chariots.
8 Their land is also full of idols,

---

[1] Otherwise, Your god. [2] Or, With antiquity.

And they have bowed down
Before the work of their own hands,
Before that which their fingers have made.
9 And the man of low degree boweth down,
And the man of rank humbleth himself;
Therefore do not thou forgive them.[1]

10 Enter into the rock,
Hide thee in the dust,
From before the fear of the Lord
And the glory of his majesty.
11 The loftiness of the eyes of men shall be humbled,
And the haughtiness of men shall be bowed down;
And Jehovah alone shall be exalted in that day.
12 For the day of Jehovah of hosts shall be
On every one that is proud and lofty,
And on all that is lifted up,
And it shall be brought low.
13 Even on all the cedars of Lebanon high and lifted up,
On all the oaks of Bashan,
14 And on all the lofty mountains,
And on all the high hills,
15 And on every lofty tower,
And on every fortified wall;
16 On all the ships of Tarshish,
And on delightful pictures.
17 And the loftiness of man shall be bowed down,
And the haughtiness of men shall be humbled;
And Jehovah alone shall be exalted on that day.
18 And he will utterly abolish the idols.
19 And they shall enter into caverns of the rocks,
And into clefts of the earth,
From the presence of the terror of Jehovah,
And from the glory of his majesty,
When he shall arise to shake the earth.
20 In that day shall a man cast away
His idols of silver,
And his idols of gold,
Which they made for him to worship,
Into the cavern of the moles and of the bats;
21 And they shall enter into the clefts of the rocks,
And into the tops of the ragged rocks,
From before the fear of the Lord,
And from the glory of his majesty,
When he shall arise to shake the earth.
22 Cease then from man,

[1] Or, Thou wilt not forgive them.

Whose breath is in his nostrils;
For in what respect[1] is he valued?

CHAPTER III.

1 For, behold, the Governor, Jehovah of hosts,
  Will take away from Jerusalem and Judah
  The stay and the strength;
  The whole stay of bread;
  The whole stay of water;
2 The strong man and the man of war,
  The judge and the prophet,
  And the diviner and the elder;
3 The captain of fifty, and the man of rank,
  The senator, and the skilful artificer, and the eloquent.[2]
4 And I will appoint boys to be their rulers,
  And babes shall rule over them.
5 The people shall violently oppress each other,
  A man his neighbour;
  The youth shall behave insolently towards the old man,
  The despicable towards the honourable.
6 When every man shall take hold of his brother
  Of the family of his father, saying,
  Thou hast raiment;
  Be thou our ruler;
  Let this ruin be under thy hand;
7 He shall swear in that day, saying,
  I will not be a healer;
  For in my house is neither bread nor raiment;
  Therefore make me not a ruler of the people.
8 Verily Jerusalem is ruined,
  And Judah is fallen;
  Because their tongue and their practices are against Jehovah,
  To provoke the eyes of his glory.
9 The proof of their countenance answereth in them;[3]
  They have declared their sin, as Sodom,
  And have not hid it.
  Wo to their soul!
  For they have brought evil on them.
10 Say ye to the righteous man,
   It shall be well;
   For they shall eat the fruit of their hands.
11 Wo to the wicked man!
   It shall be ill;

[1] Or, To what? or, How much?
[2] Or, Skilled in mysterious style.
[3] Or, Against them.

For according to the works of his hands
Shall it be rewarded to him.
12 Of my people children are oppressors,
And women rule over them.
O my people!
They who govern thee lead thee astray,
And pervert the way of thy paths.

13 Jehovah standeth to plead,
And standeth up to judge the people.
14 Jehovah will enter into judgment
With the elders of his people,
And with their rulers;
And ye have destroyed the vineyard,
And the spoil of the poor is in your houses.
15 What mean ye that ye crush my people,
And grind the faces of the poor?
Saith the Lord Jehovah of hosts.

16 Jehovah also saith,
Because the daughters of Zion are haughty,
And walk with stretched-forth neck,
And with wandering eyes,
And walk and mince as they go,
And make a tinkling with their feet.
17 Therefore will the Lord make bald
The crown of the head of the daughters of Zion,
And the Lord will expose their shame.
18 In that day will the Lord take away
Ornaments that tinkled, or were made of net-work, or like a half-moon,
19 Perfumes, bracelets, and head-bands;
20 Bonnets, ornaments of the legs,
Chaplets, neck-amulets, and ear-rings;
21 Rings and nose-jewels,
22 Changeable dresses, mantles,
Upper garments, and hair-ties,
23 Mirrors and fine linens,
Hoods and veils.
24 And instead of a sweet odour there shall be rottenness,
And instead of a girdle, a rent,
And instead of curled locks, baldness;
Instead of a belt, a girdle of sackcloth,
Instead of beauty, burning.
25 Thy men shall fall by the sword,
And thy might in the battle.
26 Her gates shall lament and mourn,
And she, desolate, shall sit on the ground.

CHAPTER IV.

1 In that day, therefore, shall seven women
 Take hold of one man, saying,
 We will eat our own bread,
 We will wear our own raiment;
 Only let thy name be called on us,[1]
 And take thou away our reproach.

2 In that day shall the branch of Jehovah
 Be for beauty and glory,
 And the fruit of the earth
 Be for excellence and comeliness,
 To the escaped of Israel.
3 And it shall come to pass
 That he who shall be left in Zion,
 And shall remain in Jerusalem,
 Shall be called holy,
 And all shall be enrolled
 Among the living[2] at Jerusalem.
4 When the Lord shall have washed away
 The filth of the daughter of Zion,
 And shall have cleansed the blood of Jerusalem
 From the midst of her,
 Both by the Spirit of judgment,
 And by the Spirit of burning.
5 And Jehovah will create
 On every dwelling-place of Mount Zion,
 And on all her assemblies,
 A cloud and darkness by day,
 And the brightness of a flaming fire by night;
 For on all the glory shall be a defence.
6 And a covering shall be by day
 For a shadow from the heat, and for refuge,
 And for a covert from storm and from rain.

CHAPTER V.

1 Come, I will sing for my beloved
 A song of my beloved to his vineyard.
 My beloved had a vineyard
 On a hill, the son of oil.
2 He fenced it, and gathered out the stones,
 And planted it as a choice vine;

---

[1] Or, Let us be called by thy name.   [2] Or, To life.

He reared a tower in the midst of it,
And built a wine-press in it:
He therefore hoped that it would yield grapes,
And it yieldeth wild grapes.
3 Now then, O inhabitant of Jerusalem,
And man of Judah,
Judge ye between me and my vineyard.
4 What more ought to have been done to my vineyard,
Which I have not done to it?
How did I look that it should yield grapes,
And yet it hath yielded wild grapes?
5 And now come, I will shew to you
What I will do to my vineyard.
I will take away its hedge, that it may become pasture;
I will break down its wall, that it may be trodden down.
6 I will lay it waste;
It shall not be pruned nor digged;
And the brier and thorn shall grow up.
Yea, I will command the clouds
That they do not rain on it.
7 Verily the vineyard of Jehovah of hosts is the house of Israel,
And the men of Judah his pleasant plant.
Hence he looked for judgment, and behold oppression;
For righteousness, and behold a cry.

8 Wo to them that join house to house,
And add field to field,
Till there be no place;
That you may be placed alone
In the midst of the earth.
9 This is in the ears of Jehovah of hosts,
If many houses be not laid desolate,
Great and fair, without inhabitant.
10 Yea, ten acres of vineyard shall produce one bath,
And the seed of a homer shall yield an ephah.
11 Wo to them that rise early
To follow drunkenness,
And who prolong the time till night,
While wine inflameth them.
12 And the harp, the lyre, the tabret, and the pipe, and wine
Are in their entertainments;
But they do not regard the work of Jehovah,
Nor consider the operation of his hands.

13 Therefore my people are gone into captivity,
Because they have no knowledge;
And their glory are men famished,
And their multitude are dried up with thirst.

14 Therefore hell hath enlarged his soul,
   And opened his mouth without measure;
   And his glory and his multitude hath descended,
   And his wealth, and he that rejoiced in her.
15 And the man of low degree shall be bowed down,
   And the man of rank shall be humbled;
   Yea, the eyes of the haughty shall be humbled.
16 And Jehovah of hosts shall be exalted in judgment,
   And God, who is holy, shall be sanctified in righteousness.
17 And the lambs shall feed after their manner,
   And the waste places of the fat ones shall strangers eat.

18 Wo to them that draw iniquity with cords of vanity,
   And sin as with cart-ropes.
19 Who say, Let him make speed, and hasten his work,
   That we may see it;
   Let the counsel of the Holy One of Israel draw near and come,
   That we may know it.
20 Wo to them that call evil good,
   And good evil;
   That put darkness for light,
   And light for darkness;
   That turn bitter into sweet,
   And sweet into bitter.
21 Wo to them that are wise in their own eyes,
   And are prudent in their own sight.
22 Wo to them that are powerful to drink wine,
   And powerful men to mingle strong drink;
23 Who justify the wicked for reward,
   And take away the righteousness of the righteous from him.

24 Therefore, as the tongue of fire devoureth the stubble,
   And the chaff is consumed by the flame;
   So their root shall be as rottenness,
   And their blossom shall pass away as dust;
   Because they have cast away the law of Jehovah of hosts,
   And have loathed the word of the Holy One of Israel.
25 Therefore the anger of Jehovah
   Hath been kindled against his people,
   And, stretching forth his hand against them,
   He hath smitten them;
   And the mountains trembled,
   And their torn carcase was thrown into the midst of the streets;
     And for all these things his anger hath not been turned away,
     But his hand is stretched out still.

26 And he will lift up an ensign to the nations from afar;
   He will hiss to the nation from the end of the earth;

And lo, it will come speedy and swift.
27 None shall be weary nor stumble among them;
None shall slumber nor sleep;
None shall have the girdle of their loins loosed,
Nor shall the latchet of their shoes be broken.
28 Their arrows will be sharp,
And all their bows bent.
The hoofs of their horses shall be counted as flint,
And their wheels as a whirlwind.
29 Their roaring shall be like that of a lion;
They shall roar like young lions;
They shall gnash and seize the prey;
They shall carry away the spoils,
And none shall deliver.
30 He shall roar against them in that day, as the roaring of the sea;
Then shall he look to the earth,
And behold! the darkness of tribulation;
And the light shall be darkened in the heavens.

CHAPTER VI.

1 In the year that King Uzziah died, I saw the Lord sitting on a throne high and lifted up, and his remotest parts filled the temple.
2 And seraphim stood above it;
Each had six wings;
With two they covered their face,
With two they covered their feet,
And with two did they fly.
3 And one cried to another, saying,
Holy, holy, holy, is Jehovah of hosts;
The whole earth is full of his glory.
4 And the posts of the doors were moved by the voice of him
5 that cried, and the house was filled with smoke. Then I said,
Wo to me, for I am undone;[1]
Because I am a man of polluted lips,
And I dwell amidst a people having polluted lips;
And yet mine eyes have seen the king, Jehovah of hosts.
6 And one of the seraphim flew to me, having in his hand a
7 live coal, snatched with a fork from the altar. And laying it on my mouth, he said,
Lo, this hath touched thy lips,
And thy sin shall be expiated.
8 Afterwards I heard the voice of the Lord, saying, Whom shall I send? And who shall go for us? Then I said, Here am
9 I, send me. Then he said,

[1] Or, Reduced to silence.

Go and tell this people :
Hearing hear, and do not understand;
Seeing see, and do not know.
10 Harden the heart of this people,
And make heavy their ears,
And close up their eyes;
Lest they see with their eyes,
And hear with their ears,
And their heart understand,
And when they have been converted, they be healed.
11 And I said, how long, O Lord? And he said,
Till the houses be laid waste without inhabitant,
And the houses be emptied of men,
And the land be reduced to solitude;
12 Till God have removed men far away,
And till there be great desolation in the midst of the land;
13 Till a tenth shall return,
And be destroyed like a teil and an oak,
Whose substance is in them, when they cast their leaves;
So in it shall the substance be the holy seed.

CHAPTER VII.

1 It came to pass, in the days of Ahaz, the son of Jotham, the son of Uzziah, king of Judah, that Rezin, the king of Syria, and Pekah, the son of Remaliah, king of Israel, went up against Jerusalem, to besiege it, but could not overcome it.
2 And it was told the house of David, saying, Syria is allied with Ephraim; and his heart was moved, as when the trees of the
3 forest are moved by the wind. Then said Jehovah to Isaiah, Go out to meet Ahaz, thou and Shearjashub, thy son, at the end of the conduit of the upper pool, at the road of the fuller's
4 field. And thou shalt say to him :
Take heed, and be quiet;
Fear not, and let not thy heart be soft,
For the two tails of those smoking firebrands,
For the fierceness of the anger of Rezin the Syrian,
And of the son of Remaliah.
5 Because the Syrian hath taken wicked counsel against thee
With Ephraim, and the son of Remaliah, saying :
6 Let us go up against Judah, and harass it,
And let us open it for us;
And let us appoint a king in the midst of it,
The son of Tabeal.
7 Thus hath the Lord Jehovah said,
It shall not stand, and shall not be.

8   For the head of Syria is Damascus,
    And the head of Damascus is Rezin;
    And within sixty-five years shall be broken
    Ephraim, that it be not a people.
9   Yet the head of Ephraim is Samaria,
    And the head of Samaria is the son of Remaliah.
    If ye do not believe,
    Surely ye shall not stand.

10   And Jehovah added to speak to Ahaz, saying:
11 Ask thee a sign from Jehovah thy God,
    By asking in the deep,
    Or in the height above.
12   And Ahaz said, I will not ask, and I will not tempt the Lord.
13 And he said,
    Hear now, O house of David!
    Is it a small thing for you to weary men,
    If ye do not also weary my God?
14 Therefore will the Lord himself give you a sign:
    Behold, a virgin shall conceive, and bear a son,
    And shall call his name Immanuel.
15 Butter and honey shall he eat,
    Till he know to refuse the evil,
    And to choose the good.
16 And before the child shall know
    To refuse the evil and choose the good,
    Forsaken shall be the land which thou hatest
    By both her kings.
17 Jehovah will bring upon thee,
    And on thy people, and on thy father's house,
    Days which have not come
    Since the day of the revolt of Ephraim from Judah,
    The king of Assyria.
18 It shall be in that day, Jehovah shall hiss
    For the fly, which is in the extremity of the rivers of Egypt,
    And for the bee which is in the land of Assyria.
19 And they shall all of them come and rest
    In the desolate valleys, and in the caverns of the rocks,
    And on all thorns, and on all bushes.
20 In that day shall Jehovah shave with a hired razor,
    By those who are beyond the river, by the king of Assyria,
    The head and the hair of the feet;
    And shall also take away the beard.

21 And it shall be in that day, that a man shall nourish
    A young cow and two sheep.
22 And it shall come to pass,
    That, on account of the abundance of milk which they shall yield,

He shall eat butter.
Yea, butter and honey shall every one eat
That shall be left in the midst of the land.
23 It shall also be in that day,
That, wherever there are a thousand vines,
They shall be sold for a thousand pieces of silver,
On account of thorns and briers.
24 With arrows and bow shall they come thither,
Because thorns and briers shall be throughout all the land.
25 And on all the mountains which are dug with the hoe
Thither shall not come the dread of thorns and briers;
But they shall be laid out for pasture to the cattle,
And shall be trodden by the flocks.

CHAPTER VIII.

1 And Jehovah said to me: Take thee a large roll, and write in it with an ordinary pen:[1] Make speed to spoil, hasten to
2 the prey. And I took unto me faithful witnesses, Uriah the
3 priest, and Zechariah the son of Jeberechiah. And I approached the prophetess, who conceived and bare a son. And Jehovah spake to me:
Call his name,
Make speed to spoil,
Hasten to the prey.
4 Verily before the child shall know
To cry, My father and my mother,
The riches of Damascus and the spoil of Samaria
Shall be taken away before the king of Assyria.

5 Moreover, Jehovah spake unto me, saying again:
6 Because this people hath refused
The waters of Shiloah, which flow softly,
And hath rejoiced in Rezin and the son of Remaliah:
7 Therefore, behold, the Lord bringeth upon them
The waters of the river, rapid and strong,
The king of Assyria and all his force;
And he shall come up over all his channels,
And shall pass over all his banks.
8 And, crossing over into Judah,
He shall overflow and pass over;
He shall reach even to the neck;
And the stretching out of his wings shall fill
The breadth of thy land, O Immanuel.

9 Associate yourselves, ye peoples,

[1] Or, With the pen of a man.

And ye shall be broken in pieces;
Give ear, all ye that are from a distant land.
Gird yourselves, and ye shall be broken in pieces;
Gird yourselves, and ye shall be broken in pieces.
10 Take counsel together, and it shall be disannulled;
Decree a decree, and it shall not stand;
For God is with us.[1]
11 For thus did Jehovah speak to me, as if seizing[2] my hand,
And taught me not to go in the way of this people, saying,
12 Say ye not, A confederacy,
In all things in which this people saith, A confederacy;
And fear not their fear,
Nor be ye afraid.
13 Sanctify Jehovah of hosts himself;
And let him be your fear,
And let him be your dread.
14 Then shall he be for a sanctuary;
A stone of stumbling and rock of destruction
To the two houses of Israel;
A net and a snare
To the inhabitants of Jerusalem.
15 And many among them shall stumble, and fall,
And shall be bruised, snared, and taken.
16 Bind up the testimony;
Seal the law among my disciples.
17 Therefore will I wait for Jehovah,
Who hideth his face from the house of Jacob,
And I will look for him.
18 Behold I, and the children whom Jehovah hath given me,
Are for signs and wonders in Israel,
From Jehovah of hosts,
Who dwelleth in Mount Zion.

19 And if they shall say to you,
Inquire at soothsayers and diviners,
Who whisper and mutter;
Should not a people ask counsel of their God?
From the living to the dead?
20 To the law and to the testimony:
If they have not spoken according to this word,
It is because there is no light in them.
21 Then shall they pass through this land distressed and hungry,
And it shall happen that, when they are hungry, they shall fret,
And shall curse their king and their God, looking upward.
22 And when they shall look to the earth,

[1] (Hebrew,) Immanuel.
[2] Or, Strengthening.

Lo, trouble and darkness, dimness and distress,
And they shall be driven to gloominess.

CHAPTER IX.

1 Yet the darkness shall not be
According to the affliction which happened to her,
When they first lightly afflicted
The land of Zebulun and the land of Naphtali;
Nor when they afterwards did more grievously afflict
By the way of the sea beyond Jordan,
In Galilee of the nations.
2 The people walking in darkness
Hath seen a great light.
They who dwelt in the land of the shadow of death,
Light hath shined on them.
3 By multiplying the nation thou hast not increased the joy;
They have rejoiced before thee according to the joy of harvest,
As men shout in dividing the spoils.
4 For his burdensome yoke,
And the staff of his shoulder,
The sceptre of his oppressor
Hast thou broken, as in the day of Midian.
5 Although every battle of the warrior is made
With noise and rolling of the vesture in blood,
This shall be for burning,
For fuel of fire.
6 For to us a child is born;
To us a son is given;
And the government hath been laid upon his shoulder;
And his name shall be called, Wonderful, Counsellor,
The mighty God, The Father of the age, The Prince of Peace.
7 To the increase of the government and to peace
There shall be no end;
On the throne of David and on his kingdom,
To order and establish it
In judgment and justice,
Henceforth, even for ever.
The zeal of Jehovah of hosts will do this.

8 The Lord sent a word against Jacob,
And it hath fallen on Israel.
9 And all the people shall know,
Ephraim, and the inhabitants of Samaria,
Who say in the pride and haughtiness of their heart,
10 The bricks are fallen down, and we will build with hewn stones;
The sycamores are cut down, and we will substitute cedars.

11 But Jehovah will strengthen the enemies of Rezin against him,
And will aid his adversaries.
12 Syria before, and the Philistines behind;
And they shall devour Israel with open mouth.
And for all this his anger is not turned away,
But his hand is stretched out still.

13 But the people have not turned to him that smote them,
And have not sought Jehovah of hosts.
14 Therefore will Jehovah cut off from Israel
The head and the tail,
The branch and the reed,
In one day.
15 The elder and the honourable, he is the head;
And the prophet who teacheth falsehood, he is the tail.
16 For the governors of this people are seducers,
And they who are guided by them are destroyed.
17 Therefore the Lord will not rejoice over their young men,
And will not have compassion on the orphans and widows;
For all are hypocrites and evil-doers,
And every mouth speaketh villany.
For all this his anger is not turned away,
But his hand is stretched out still.

18 For wickedness burneth as the fire;
It shall devour the briers and thorns;
Afterwards it shall kindle into the thickets of the forest,
And the smoke of that which ascendeth shall go up.
19 Through the wrath of Jehovah of hosts
Shall the land be darkened,
And the people shall be as the fuel of fire:
No man shall spare his brother.
20 Every one shall snatch on the right hand, and be hungry;
He shall eat on the left hand, and shall not be satisfied;
Every one shall devour the flesh of his own arm:
21 Manasseh, Ephraim;
And Ephraim, Manasseh;
They together shall be against Judah.
And yet for all this his anger is not turned away,
But his hand is stretched out still.

CHAPTER X.

1 Wo to them that decree unrighteous decrees,
And who prescribing prescribe injustice:
2 To keep back the poor from judgment,
And to take away the right from the poor of my people,

>   To defraud the widows,
>   And to plunder the orphans.
> 3 And what will ye do in the day of visitation?
>   And when the desolation shall come from afar,
>   To whom will ye flee for aid?
>   And where will ye deposit[1] your glory?
> 4 Unless[2] they shall stumble among the vanquished,
>   And shall fall down among the slain.
>   For all this his anger shall not be turned away,
>   And his hand is stretched out still.
>
> 5 O Assyrian! the rod of mine anger!
>   And the very staff in their hand is my wrath.
> 6 Against a hypocritical nation will I send him,
>   And against the people of my indignation will I command him,
>   To seize the prey,
>   To carry off the spoils,
>   And to tread him down as the mire of the streets.
> 7 Yet will he not so intend,
>   Nor will his heart think so;
>   For it will be in his heart to destroy,
>   And to cut off nations not a few.
> 8 For he saith, Are not my princes also kings?
> 9 Is not Calno as Carchemish?
>   Is not Hamath as Arpad?
>   Is not Samaria as Damascus?
> 10 As my hand hath found the kingdoms of the idols,
>   For their graven images excelled Jerusalem and Samaria.
> 11 As I have done to Samaria and her idols,
>   Shall I not do so to Jerusalem and her idols?
> 12 But it shall come to pass,
>   When the Lord shall have performed his whole work
>   In mount Zion and Jerusalem,
>   I will punish the fruit of the haughtiness of the heart of the king of Assyria,
>   And the glory of the loftiness of his eyes.
> 13 For he saith, By the strength of my hand have I done it;
>   And by my wisdom; for I am sagacious;
>   And therefore have I removed the boundaries of the peoples,
>   And have plundered their treasures,
>   And have brought down the inhabitants, like a mighty man.
> 14 And my hand hath found as a nest the riches of the peoples;
>   And as eggs which have been left are gathered,
>   So have also I gathered the whole earth;
>   And there was none that moved the wing,
>   Or opened the mouth, or chirped.

---

[1] Or, Secure.   [2] Or, Without me they shall stumble.

15 Shall the axe boast against him that heweth with it?
   Shall the saw magnify itself against him that moveth it?
   Like the rising up of a rod against him that raiseth it,
   Like the risings up of a staff, as if it were not wood.
16 Therefore will the Governor, Jehovah of hosts, send
   Against his fat ones leanness,
   And under his glory will kindle
   A burning, like the burning of a fire.
17 And the light of Israel shall become a fire,
   And his Holy One shall become a flame;
   And it shall burn and devour
   His briers and thorns in one day.
18 The glory of his forest and of his fruitful field,
   From the soul even to the flesh, will he consume;
   And it shall be as the fainting of a standard-bearer.
19 And the remains of the wood of his forest
   Shall become a number,
   Such that a child may count them.

20 It shall be in that day,
   The remnant of Israel,
   And they that are left of the house of Jacob,
   Shall not add to rely on him that smote them;
   For they shall rely on Jehovah,
   The Holy One of Israel, in truth.
21 The remnant shall return, the remnant of Jacob,
   To the mighty God.
22 For if thy people Israel be as the sand of the sea,
   A remnant of it shall return.
   The consumption decreed overfloweth righteousness.[1]
23 For a consumption and consummation
   Doth the Lord Jehovah of hosts make
   In the midst of all the land.

24 Therefore thus saith Jehovah of hosts:
   O my people, the inhabitants of Zion,
   Fear not the Assyrian.
   He will smite thee with a rod,
   And will lift up his staff against thee,
   After the pattern of Egypt.
25 But yet a little while,
   And my rage and indignation
   Shall be discharged in their destruction.
26 And Jehovah of hosts will stir up a scourge against him,
   According to the slaughter of Midian on the rock Oreb;
   And his rod shall be on the sea,

[1] Or, With righteousness.

    And he will lift it up after the pattern of Egypt.
27 And it shall come to pass in that day,
  That his burden shall be removed from thy shoulder,
  And his yoke from thy neck;
  And the yoke shall be destroyed
  From the face of the anointing.

28 He is come to Aiath; he hath passed to Migron;
  At Michmash he will lay up thy baggage.
29 They have crossed the ford; they have lodged by night at Geba;
  Ramah is terrified; Gibeah of Saul hath fled.
30 Neigh with thy voice, O daughter of Gallim!
  Cause it to be heard at Laish, O poor Anathoth.
31 Madmenah is removed;
  The inhabitants of Gebim have gathered themselves.
32 Yet a day, when he shall remain at Nob,
  He will lift up his hand
  Against the mount of the daughter of Zion,
  The hill of Jerusalem.

33 Behold! The Lord Jehovah of hosts
  Will cut off the branch with terror;[1]
  And the lofty of stature shall be cut down,
  And the haughty shall be brought low.
34 And he will cut down the thickets of the forest with iron,
  And Lebanon shall fall violently.

CHAPTER XI.

1 But a branch shall spring from the stock of Jesse,
  And a sprout from his roots shall yield fruit.
2 And the Spirit of Jehovah shall rest upon him,
  The Spirit of wisdom and understanding,
  The Spirit of counsel and strength,
  The Spirit of knowledge and of the fear of Jehovah;
3 And will make him sagacious in the fear of Jehovah;
  Not according to the sight of his eyes shall he judge,
  Nor according to the hearing of his ears shall he reprove.
4 For in righteousness he shall judge the poor,
  And in equity shall he reprove for the meek of the earth;
  And he shall smite the earth with the rod of his mouth,
  And with the breath of his lips shall he slay the wicked.
5 And righteousness shall be the belt of his loins,
  And faithfulness the belt of his reins.

[1] Or, Powerfully.

6 The wolf shall dwell with the lamb,
  And the leopard shall lie down with the kid;
  The calf, and the lion, and the fatling together;
  And a little child shall lead them.
7 The cow and the bear shall feed;
  Their young ones shall lie down together;
  And the lion shall eat straw like the ox.
8 And the child shall play on the hole of the asp,
  And on the den of the basilisk shall the weaned child lay his hand.
9 They shall not hurt, nor do injury,
  In all the mountain of my holiness;
  For the earth shall be full of the knowledge of Jehovah,
  As with waters that cover the sea.

10 And it shall be in that day, The root of Jesse,
   Which shall stand for an ensign of the peoples,
   Shall be sought by the nations;
   And his rest shall be glory.
11 And it shall be in that day,
   The Lord will again apply his hand
   To recover the remnant of his people, which shall be left,
   From Assyria, and from Egypt, from Parthia,
   From Arabia, from Ethiopia, from Persia,
   From Chaldea, from Hamath, and from the islands of the sea.
12 And he shall lift up an ensign to the nations,
   And shall gather the outcasts of Israel,
   And shall gather the dispersed of Judah,
   From the four corners of the earth.
13 And the envy of Ephraim shall depart,
   And the adversaries of Judah shall be cut off.
   Ephraim shall not envy Judah,
   And Judah shall not vex Ephraim.
14 But they shall fly on the shoulders of the Philistines to the west;
   They shall plunder together the children of the east;
   Edom and Moab shall be the stretching out of their hands,
   And the children of Ammon shall be their obedience.
15 And Jehovah shall utterly destroy
   The tongue of the Egyptian sea;
   And he shall lift up his hand on the river
   By the might of his wind;
   And he shall smite it in the seven streams,
   And shall make them to be shod with shoes.
16 And there shall be a path for the remnant of his people,
   Which shall be left from Assyria,
   As there was to Israel,
   In the day when he came up out of the land of Egypt.

CHAPTER XII.

1 And in that day thou shalt say:
   I will sing to thee, O Jehovah;
   Though thou wast angry with me,
   Thine anger is turned away, and thou hast comforted me.
2 Behold! God is my salvation;
   I will trust, and not be afraid;
   For God Jehovah is my strength and song;
   And he hath become[1] my salvation.
3 Ye shall draw waters with joy
   From the fountains of the Saviour.[2]
4 And in that day shall ye say:
   Sing to Jehovah; call upon his name;
   Make known his works among the peoples;
   Proclaim that his name is exalted.
5 Sing to Jehovah;
   For he hath done glorious things;
   And this hath been made known throughout all the earth.
6 Shout and sing,
   O inhabitress of Zion!
   For great in the midst of thee
   Is the Holy One of Israel.

CHAPTER XIII.

1 The burden of Babylon, which Isaiah, the son of Amoz, saw.
2 On a lofty mountain lift up a banner;
   Raise the voice to them; shake the hand;
   That they may enter into the gates of the nobles.
3 I have commanded my sanctified ones;
   And for mine anger have I also called my mighty ones,
   Who rejoice in my glory.
4 The noise of a multitude in the mountains,
   As of a great people;
   The noise of the sound of kingdoms,
   Of nations gathered together;
   Jehovah of hosts mustereth the host of the battle.
5 Coming from a distant land,
   From the end of heaven,
   Jehovah and the vessels of his anger,
   To destroy the whole land.

6 Howl ye, for the day of Jehovah is at hand;

---

[1] Or, Will be.   [2] Or, Of salvation.

      As destruction from the Strong One[1] shall it come.
7 Therefore shall all hands be weakened,
    And every heart of man shall melt.
8 And they shall be afraid;
    Pangs and sorrows shall take hold of them;
    They shall be in pain like a woman in labour;
    Every one shall be amazed at his neighbour;
    Their faces shall be faces of flames.
9 Behold! the day of Jehovah shall come cruel;
    Even indignation and the burning of anger,
    To lay the land desolate,
    And to destroy the sinners thereof out of it.
10 Therefore the stars of heaven, and the constellations,
     Shall not give their light;
     The sun shall be darkened in his going forth,
     And the moon shall not give forth her brightness.
11 And I will visit upon the world wickedness,
     And upon the wicked their iniquity;
     And I will cause the arrogance of the proud to cease,
     And I will lay low the loftiness of tyrants.
12 I will make a mortal more precious than fine gold,
     And a man than the weight of the gold of Ophir.
13 Therefore I will shake the heavens,
     And the earth shall be moved out of its place,
     In the indignation of Jehovah of hosts,
     And in the day of the fierceness of his anger.
14 And it shall be as a chased roe,
     And a sheep which no man taketh up;
     Every one shall look to his own people,
     And every one shall flee to his own land.
15 Every one that is found shall be pierced through,
     And every one that is joined to them shall fall by the sword.
16 Their infants shall be dashed in pieces before their eyes;
     Their houses shall be plundered,
     And their wives shall be ravished.

17 Behold! I raise up against you the Medes,
     Who shall not think of silver,
     And shall not desire even gold.
18 And with their bows shall they dash in pieces the children;
     They shall not pity the fruit of the womb,
     Nor shall their eye spare children.
19 And Babylon, the glory of kingdoms,
     And the ornament of the brightness of the Chaldeans,
     Shall be like God's overthrowing of Sodom and Gomorrah.
20 Never shall it be inhabited any more,

---

[1] Or, From a strong destroyer.

Nor shall it be dwelt in from generation to generation;
Nor shall the Arabian pitch his tent there,
Nor shall the shepherds make their flocks to lie down there.
21 But the Ziim shall lie down there;
And their houses shall be full of Ohim;
There shall the daughters of the ostrich dwell,
And there shall the satyrs dance.
22 And Iim shall cry in their splendid houses,
And dragons in their delightful palaces;
And her time is near at hand,
And her days shall not be prolonged.

CHAPTER XIV.

1 Jehovah will now pity Jacob,
And will yet choose Israel,
And will cause them to rest in their own land;
And the stranger shall be joined to them;
They shall be allied to the house of Jacob.
2 And the peoples shall take them,
And shall bring them to their own place,
And in the land of Jehovah shall the house of Israel
Possess them for servants and for handmaids;
And they shall take them whose captives they were,
And shall rule over their oppressors.

3 And it shall be in the day
When Jehovah shall have given thee rest
From thy labour,
And from thy trembling,
And from the hard bondage which had been laid on thee.
4 Then against the king of Babylon
Shalt thou take up this proverb, and shalt say,
How hath the oppressor ceased!
How hath the city covetous of gold ceased!
5 Jehovah hath broken the staff of the wicked,
The sceptre of the rulers,
6 Which smote the nations in anger
With an incurable wound;
Which ruled over the nations with anger;
If any one suffered persecution,
He did not hinder it.
7 The whole earth is at rest, and is quiet;
They have sung praise.
8 Yea, the fir-trees rejoice over thee,
And the cedars of Lebanon:
Since thou art laid down,

No feller hath come up against us.
9 Hell from beneath is moved on account of thee;
To meet thy coming
He hath stirred up the dead for thee,
And hath made to rise from their thrones
All the leaders of the earth,
All the kings of the nations.
10 All shall speak, and say to thee:
Art thou also become weak as we?
And art thou become like to us?
11 In the grave is laid thy splendour,
And the noise of thine instruments of music;
The worm is spread under thee,
And reptiles cover thee.
12 How art thou fallen from heaven,
O Lucifer, son of the dawn!
How art thou thrown down to the earth,
That didst cast the lot upon the nations![1]
13 But thou saidst in thy heart,
I will ascend to heaven;
In high places near the stars of God
Will I place my throne,
And will sit on the mountain of the testimony,
On the sides of the north.
14 I will ascend above the heights of the clouds,
And will be like the Most High.
15 But thou art brought down to the grave,
To the sides of the pit.
16 They that see thee shall bend forward,
And shall view thee attentively.
Is this the man that made the earth to tremble?
That shook the kingdoms?
17 That made the world as a wilderness;
That destroyed its cities?
That opened not the house to his prisoners?
18 All the kings of the nations, all of them,
Lie in glory, each in his own house.
19 But thou art cast out of thy grave,
As an abominable branch,
As the garments of the slain
Who were killed with the sword,
Who go down to the pit;
As a carcase trodden under foot.
20 Thou shalt not be joined with them in burial;
Because thou hast laid waste thy land,
Thou hast slain thy people;
The seed of wicked men shall not be continually remembered.

[1] Or, That didst weaken the nations.

21 Prepare slaughter for his children,
   For the iniquity of their fathers;
   That they may not rise, and possess the land,
   And fill the face of the world with cities.
22 For I will rise up against them, saith Jehovah of hosts,
   And the name and the remnant,
   The son and the grandson,
   Will I cut off, saith Jehovah.
23 And I will make it to be a possession of the hedgehog,
   And pools of water;
   And I will sweep it with a besom, emptying it,
   Saith Jehovah of hosts.
24 Jehovah of hosts hath sworn, saying,
   If it hath not been as I thought,
   And if it shall not stand as I purposed,
25 That in my land I will crush the Assyrian,
   And on my mountains will tread him under foot;
   And that his yoke shall depart from them,
   And his burden be removed from their shoulder.
26 This is the purpose which is purposed on the whole earth;
   And this hand is stretched out on all the nations.
27 For Jehovah of hosts hath decreed, and who shall disannul it?
   His hand is stretched out, and who shall turn it back?

28   In the year in which Ahaz the king died, was this burden.
29 Rejoice not, thou whole Palestina,
   Because the rod of him that smote thee is broken;
   For from the root of the adder shall spring a cockatrice,
   And his fruit shall be a fiery serpent.
30 And the first-born of the poor shall feed,
   And the needy shall lie down in safety;
   And I will cause thy root to die with famine,
   And he shall slay thy remnant.
31 Howl, O gate! cry, O city!
   Thou whole Palestina art dissolved;
   For smoke cometh from the north;
   And no one shall be alone in his appointed day.
32 And what shall be answered to the messengers of the nations?
   That Jehovah hath founded Zion,
   And the poor of his people shall have confidence in her.

CHAPTER XV.

1   The burden of Moab.
   Because in the night Ar of Moab
   Is laid waste, and brought to silence;
   Surely in the night Kir of Moab

Is laid waste, and brought to silence.
2 He shall go up into the house, and to the high places of Dibon,
   to weep;
Over Nebo, and over Medeba, shall Moab howl.
On all his heads shall be baldness,
And every beard shall be shaved.
3 In his cross-roads shall they be girded with sackcloth;
On his roofs, and in his streets,
Shall every one howl, and go down to weep.
4 Heshbon and Elealeh shall cry aloud;
As far as Jahaz shall their voice be heard;
Therefore shall the armed men of Moab howl;
The soul of each man shall howl to itself.
5 My heart shall cry aloud for Moab;
Her fugitives to Zoar, a heifer of three years old;
By the going up of Luhith shall they go up with weeping,
By the way of Horonaim shall they raise the cry of sorrow.
6 The waters of Nimrim are cut off;
The grass is withered,
The herbage hath failed,
No verdure is left.
7 Therefore what every one hath left, and his riches,
They shall carry to the brook of the willows.[1]
8 The cry hath gone round the borders of Moab;
Even to Eglaim is his howling.
And even to Beer-Elim is his howling.
9 Because the waters of Dimon shall be full of blood;
For I will lay additions upon Dimon,
Lions to them that are escaped of Moab,
And to the remnant of the land.

CHAPTER XVI.

1 Send ye the lamb to the governor of the land,
From the rock of the desert
To the mountain of the daughter of Zion.
2 And it shall be as a bird let loose, wandering from its nest,
So shall the daughters of Moab be at the fords of Arnon.
3 Assemble a council; execute judgment;
Make thy shadow as the night in the midst of noon-day;
Hide the banished;
Betray not the fugitive.
4 Let mine outcasts dwell with thee.
Moab, be thou a place of concealment
From the face of the destroyer;

[1] Or, To the Arabians.

> For the extortioner hath ceased;
> The destroyer hath failed;
> He that trod us under foot hath been consumed out of the land.
> 5 And in mercy shall the throne be prepared;
> And he shall sit upon it in steadfastness,
> To judge in the tabernacle of David,
> And to seek judgment,
> And to hasten righteousness.
>
> 6 We have heard of the pride of Ahab, (he is very proud,)
> His pride, his haughtiness, and his insolence;[1]
> But his lies shall not be successful.
> 7 Therefore shall Moab howl to Moab, all shall howl,
> On account of the foundations of Kirhareseth;
> You will groan, being only smitten.
> 8 For the vines of Heshbon are cut down,
> The vine of Sibmah.
> The lords of the nations have trodden down her choicest roots,[2]
> Which reached even to Jazer,
> Which wandered even to the wilderness;
> Her noble plants have been thrown down,
> Which crossed the sea.
> 9 Therefore will I bewail with the weeping of Jazer the vine of Sibmah;
> I will water thee with my tears, O Heshbon and Elealeh!
> Because on thy summer fruits, and on thy harvest,
> A shouting shall break forth.[3]
> 10 Joy and rejoicing have been taken away from the fruitful field;
> In the vineyards shall there be no rejoicing nor shouting.
> The treader shall not tread wine in the presses;
> I have made the shouting to cease.
> 11 Therefore my bowels shall sound like a harp for Moab,
> And my inward parts for Kirharesh.
> 12 And it shall be, when it shall be seen
> That Moab hath been wearied on the high places,
> Then shall he come to the sanctuary to pray,
> And shall not profit by it.
>
> 13 This is the word which Jehovah uttered concerning Moab
> 14 since that time. Now, I say, Jehovah hath spoken, saying—
> Three years, as the years of a hireling;
> And the glory of Moab,
> With all her multitude, however great,
> Shall be turned into disgrace;
> And her remnant shall be few, small, and feeble.

[1] Or, His indignation. [2] Or, Her choicest branches.
[3] Or, Shall fall.

CHAPTER XVII.

1 The burden of Damascus.
   Behold, Damascus is taken away, that it be not a city;
   For it shall be a heap of ruins.
2 The cities of Aroer are forsaken;
   They shall be changed into sheepfolds;
   They shall lie down,
   And there shall be none to terrify them.
3 And the fortress shall cease from Ephraim,
   And the kingdom from Damascus;
   And the remnant of Syria shall be
   As the glory of the children of Israel,
   Saith Jehovah of hosts.
4 And it shall be in that day,
   The glory of Jacob shall be diminished,
   And the fatness of his flesh shall become lean.

5 And it shall be as he who gathereth the harvest of the corn,
   Who reapeth the ears with his arm,
   Like as one gleaneth grapes in the valley of Rephaim.
6 And in thee shall be left a gleaning, as the shaking of an olive-tree;
   There two or three berries remain on the top of the highest branch,
   Four or five on the spreading branches of its fruit,
   Saith Jehovah, the God of Israel.
7 In that day shall a man look to his Maker,
   And his eyes shall be fixed on the Holy One of Israel.
8 And he shall not look to the altars, the work of his own hands,
   Nor view the things which his fingers have made,
   Nor the groves,
   Nor the graven images.

9 In that day the cities of his strength shall be
   As the forsaking of a thicket and of a branch,
   In like manner as they left before the children of Israel;
   And there shall be desolation.
10 Because thou hast forgotten the God of thy salvation,
   And hast not been mindful of the God of thy strength;
   Therefore shalt thou plant pleasant plants,
   And thou shalt ingraft a foreign shoot.
11 In the day of thy plantation shalt thou make it to grow,
   And in the morning thou shalt make thy seed to sprout;
   But in the day of enjoying shall the harvest fail,
   And the grief shall be desperate.
12 Alas! the multitude of many peoples;

   Like the sound of many peoples shall they sound,
   And like the noise of nations;
   Like the noise of mighty waters shall they rush.
13 Like the noise of mighty waters
   Shall the peoples make a noise,
   And he will rebuke them,
   And will drive them far away;
   They shall be chased
   As the chaff of the mountains before the wind,
   And as a rolling thing before the whirlwind.
14 In the evening time, behold! trouble:
   Ere it be morning, it shall not at all be.
   This is the portion of them that tread us down,
   And the lot of them that plunder us.

CHAPTER XVIII.

1 Alas! the land shadowing with wings,
  Which is beyond the rivers of Ethiopia.
2 Sending ambassadors by the sea,
  In ships of reeds on the waters.
  Go, ye swift messengers,
  To a nation scattered and plundered,
  To a people terrible from that time and till now,
  To a nation trodden down on every side,
  Whose land the rivers have plundered.
3 All ye inhabitants of the world,
  And dwellers on the earth,
  When he shall set up a standard on the mountains, you shall see it;
  When he shall sound a trumpet, you shall hear it.
4 Thus also hath Jehovah said to me,
  I will rest, and will look in my tabernacle,
  As the heat that drieth up the rain,
  And as a cloud of dew in the heat of harvest.
5 For when the harvest shall be at hand,
  The bud shall be perfect,
  And the ripening fruit shall go out of the flower;
  Then will he prune the twigs with pruning-hooks,
  And cut down and take away the branches.
6 They shall be left together to the fowls of the mountains,
  And to the beasts of the earth.
  The fowls shall spend the summer upon them,
  And all the beasts of the earth shall spend the winter upon them.

7 At that time shall a present be brought to Jehovah of hosts,

A people torn and plundered,
And from a people terrible from the beginning hitherto;
From a nation trodden down on every side,
Whose land the rivers have plundered,
To the place of the name of Jehovah of hosts,
To Mount Zion.

CHAPTER XIX.

1 The burden of Egypt.
Behold, Jehovah rideth on a swift cloud,
And will come into Egypt;
And the idols of Egypt shall be moved before his face,
And the heart of Egypt shall melt in the midst of her.
2 And I will set the Egyptians against the Egyptians;
Then shall they fight every one against his brother,
Every one against his neighbour;
City against city,
And kingdom against kingdom.
3 And the spoil of Egypt shall be emptied in the midst of her,
And I will destroy her counsel,
Even though they seek to the idols, to the magicians,
To the soothsayers, to the diviners.
4 And I will deliver the Egyptians into the hand of a cruel master,
And a powerful king shall rule over them,
Saith the Lord, Jehovah of hosts.
5 Then shall the waters fail from the sea,
And the flood shall be wasted and dried up.
6 The rivers shall be turned aside;
The brooks of defence shall be emptied and dried up;
The reed and the flag shall wither.
7 The herbs at the brook, and on the mouth of the brook,
And all the seed of the river,
Shall wither, and be driven away, that it may be no more.
8 And the fishers shall mourn,
And all who cast a hook into the brook shall lament;
They who spread a net on the face of the waters shall languish.
9 They who work in the finest flax shall blush,
And they who weave perforated[1] meshes.
10 For their nets shall be broken,
And all that make a net shall be sad in their heart.

11 Surely the princes of Zoan are fools;

---

[1] Or, Transparent.

The counsel of the wise counsellors of Pharaoh is foolish.
How say ye to Pharaoh,
I am the son of the wise,
And the son of ancient kings?
12 Where are now thy wise men?
That they may declare to thee,
Or that they may even know,
What Jehovah of hosts hath decreed concerning Egypt.
13 The princes of Zoan are become infatuated,
The princes of Noph are deceived;
Egypt hath been led astray
By a corner of her tribes.
14 Jehovah hath mingled a spirit of perverseness in the midst of her;
And they have misled Egypt in all her work,
As a drunken man staggereth in his vomit.
15 Neither shall Egypt have any work to do,
The head or the tail,
The branch or the rush.
16 In that day shall Egypt be like women;
For it shall shudder and tremble,
From before the shaking of the hand of Jehovah of hosts,
Which he shall shake over it.
17 And to the Egyptians shall the land of Judah be a terror.
Every one that shall mention it
Shall tremble on account of her,
Because of the purpose of Jehovah of hosts,
Which he hath decreed concerning her.

18 In that day shall there be five cities in the land of Egypt,
Speaking with the lip of Canaan,
And swearing by Jehovah of hosts.
One shall be called, The city of desolation.
19 In that day shall there be
An altar to Jehovah in the midst of the land of Egypt,
And a statue to Jehovah near its border.
20 And it shall be for a sign and for a witness
To Jehovah of hosts, in the land of Egypt;
For they shall cry to Jehovah because of the oppressors,
And he will send to them a saviour,
And a ruler, that he may deliver them.
21 And Jehovah shall be known by the Egyptians;
The Egyptians shall know Jehovah in that day,
And shall make sacrifice and oblation,
And shall vow vows to Jehovah, and perform them.
22 Therefore will the Lord smite Egypt,
Smiting and healing;
For they shall be turned to Jehovah,

And he will be entreated by them,
And will heal them.

23 In that day shall there be a way from Egypt into Assyria;
The Assyrians shall go into Egypt,
And the Egyptians into Assyria;
And the Egyptians shall serve the Assyrians.[1]
24 In that day shall Israel be,
With Egypt and with Assyria,
The third blessing in the midst of the land.
25 For Jehovah of hosts will bless him, saying,
Blessed be the Egyptian, my people,
And the Assyrian, the work of my hands,
And Israel, my inheritance.

CHAPTER XX.

1 In the year that Tartan came to Ashdod, (when Sargon, the king of Assyria, sent him,) and attacked Ashdod, and took
2 it. At that time Jehovah spake by the hand of Isaiah, the son of Amoz, saying,
Go and loose the sackcloth from thy loins,
And put off thy shoe from thy foot.
3 And he did so, walking naked and barefooted. And Jehovah said:
As my servant Isaiah for three years
Hath walked naked and barefooted,
A sign and a wonder
Concerning Egypt and concerning Ethiopia;
4 So will the king of Assyria lead away the captivity of Egypt,
And the removal of Ethiopia,
Of the young and of the old,
Naked and barefooted,
And with their hinder parts uncovered,
To the disgrace of Egypt.
5 And they shall be afraid and ashamed
Of Ethiopia their expectation,
And of Egypt their glory.[2]
6 And in that day shall the inhabitant of this island say,
Behold! what is become of our expectation,
To which we fled for aid,
That we might be delivered from the face of the king of Assyria;
And how shall we escape?

---

[1] Or, Shall serve with the Assyrians.   [2] Or, Their beauty.

CHAPTER XXI.

1 The burden of the desert of the sea.
As storms that pass from a southerly direction,
It will come from the wilderness,
From a terrible land.
2 A harsh vision hath been declared to me,
The transgressor to the transgressor,
And the plunderer to the plunderer.
Go up, O Persian! Besiege, O Mede!
All his groaning have I made to cease.
3 Therefore are my loins filled with pain;
Pangs have seized me, as the pangs of a woman in labour;
I am bowed down at hearing,
And am dismayed at seeing.
4 My heart is shaken;
Terror hath overwhelmed me;
The night of my pleasures
He hath changed to terror.
5 Prepare the table;
Watch in the watch-tower;
Eat, drink;
Arise, ye princes, and anoint the shield.
6 For thus hath the Lord said to me:
Go, appoint a watchman,
That he may declare what he seeth.
7 And he saw a chariot of a couple of horsemen,
A chariot of an ass, and a chariot of a camel;
Next, he looked attentively,
And watched eagerly.
8 Then he cried, A lion.
On my watch-tower, my lord, I continually stand by day,
And in my ward am I stationed whole nights.
9 And behold, here cometh a chariot of a man,
A couple of horsemen.
And he spake, and said,
Babylon is fallen, is fallen!
And all the graven images of her gods
Hath he broken to the ground.
10 O my thrashing, and the corn of my floor!
I have related to you what I have heard
From Jehovah of hosts, the God of Israel.

11 The burden of Dumah.
He calleth to me out of Seir:
Watchman, what of the night?
Watchman, what of the night?

12 The watchman said:
   The morning cometh, afterwards the night.
   If ye will inquire, inquire ye.
   Return, come.

13   The burden in Arabia.
   In the forest in Arabia shall ye lodge,
   In the ways of Dedanim.
14 To meet the thirsty bring waters,
   O inhabitants of the land of Tema!
   Relieve the fugitive with thy bread.
15 For they flee from the face of the swords,
   From the face of the drawn sword,
   From the face of the bent bow,
   From the face of the grievousness of war.
16 For thus hath the Lord said to me:
   Yet a year, according to the years of a hireling,
   Then shall all the glory of Kedar fail;
17 And then shall be diminished the number of the archers,
   Which shall be reckoned among the mighty sons of Kedar;
   For Jehovah, the God of Israel, hath spoken it.

CHAPTER XXII.

1   The burden of the valley of vision.
   What hast thou here,[1]
   That thou art entirely gone up upon the roofs?
2 Full of miseries,
   Tumultuous city, joyful city;
   Thy slain men are not slain by the sword,
   And are not dead in battle.
3 All thy rulers have fled;
   Together have they been made prisoners by the archers;
   All that were found in thee have been made prisoners together,
   Who have fled from afar.
4 Therefore I said, Let me alone;
   I will be bitter in my weeping;
   Labour not to comfort me
   Because of the plundering of the daughters of my people.
5 For it is a day of trouble, and of treading down, and of perplexity,
   From the Lord Jehovah of hosts, in the valley of vision,
   Demolishing the city,
   And crying to the mountain.

[1] Or, What hast thou now?

6 Yet Elam beareth the quiver
   In a chariot of men and horsemen,
   And Kir uncovereth the shield.
7 And the choice of thy valleys was filled with chariots,
   And horsemen set themselves in array at the gate.
8 And he took away the covering of Judah;
   And thou didst look in that day
   To the armory of the house of the forest.
9 And ye have seen the breaches of the city of David, which were many;
   And ye collected the waters of the lower pool.
10 And the houses of Jerusalem have ye numbered,
    And ye have thrown down houses to fortify the wall.
11 For the waters of the old pool
    Have ye also made a ditch between the walls;
    And ye have not looked to him that made it,
    And have not seen him that formed it in ancient times.[1]

12 And in that day the Lord, Jehovah of hosts,
    Called to weeping and to lamentation,
    To baldness and girding with sackcloth;
13 And, behold! joy and gladness,
    Slaying oxen, killing sheep,
    Eating flesh, and drinking wine,
    Eating and drinking;
    For to-morrow we shall die!
14 It was revealed in my ears by Jehovah of hosts,
    If this iniquity shall be forgiven you till ye die,
    Saith the Lord Jehovah of hosts.

15 Thus saith the Lord Jehovah of hosts,
    Go, approach to that abettor,
    To Shebna, the ruler of the house.
16 What hast thou here? and whom hast thou here?
    That thou hast hewed out here for thyself a sepulchre,
    As he who heweth out his sepulchre on high,
    Or who cutteth out a habitation for himself in the rock.
17 Behold, Jehovah will carry thee away with a remarkable carrying away,
    And covering will cover thee.
18 Whirling he will turn thee with whirling,
    As a ball with the hands, into a distant country;
    There shalt thou die;
    And there the chariot of thy glory
    Shall be the disgrace of the house of thy lord.
19 And I will drive thee from thy post,
    And from thy abode shall he cast thee out.

[1] Or, From a distance.

20 And it shall be in that day, I will call my servant,
   Eliakim, the son of Hilkiah.
21 And I will clothe him with thy raiment,
   And will strengthen him with thy girdle,
   And will deliver thy power into his hand;
   And he shall be a father of the inhabitant of Jerusalem,
   And of the house of Judah.
22 And I will lay the key of the house of David upon his shoulder;
   He will open, and none shall shut;
   He will shut, and none shall open.
23 And I will fasten him as a nail in a sure place,
   And to the house of his father he shall become a throne of glory.
24 And all the glory of his father's house,
   Grandchildren and great-grandchildren,
   All smaller vessels,
   From vessels of cups to all vessels of musical instruments,
   They shall hang upon him.
25 In that day, saith Jehovah of hosts,
   The nail fixed in a sure place shall be removed,
   And shall be cut down, and shall fall;
   And the burden which was upon it shall be cut off;
   For Jehovah hath spoken it.

CHAPTER XXIII.

1 The burden of Tyre.
  Howl, ye ships of Tarshish;
  For desolation has been made,
  So that there is no house,
  That there is no entering in from the land of Chittim.
  This was revealed to them.
2 Be silent, ye inhabitants of the islands,
  The merchant of Sidon; they that crossed the sea;
  Who supplied thee.
3 By great waters was the seed of the Nile;
  Her fruits were the harvest of the river;
  And she was a mart of nations.
4 Be ashamed, O Sidon;
  For the sea hath spoken,
  The strength of the sea, saying,
  I have not conceived nor brought forth,
  And I have not brought up young men,
  And have not reared virgins.
5 As soon as the report shall reach the Egyptians,
  They shall be grieved according to the report of Tyre.

6 Pass ye over to Tarshish;

Howl, ye inhabitants of the islands.
7 Is this your exulting city?
From ancient days is her antiquity.
Her feet shall carry her,
To travel into a distant country.
8 Who hath consulted this concerning crowning Tyre,
Whose merchants are princes,
Whose traders are the nobles of the land?
9 Thus hath Jehovah of hosts decreed,
To profane the pride of all that are illustrious,
To bring into contempt all the renowned of the land.
10 Cross over from thy land, like a river,
To the daughter of Tarshish;
For there is no longer any girdle.
11 He laid his hand upon the sea,
He shook kingdoms.
Jehovah hath commanded concerning Canaan,
To weaken her strength.
12 And he saith, O virgin daughter of Sidon,
When thou shalt be oppressed,
Thou shalt not add any more to rejoice.
Arise, that thou mayest pass over into Chittim;
Yet even there thou shalt not have rest.
13 Behold, the land of the Chaldeans;
This was not a people;
Assyria founded it for the inhabitants of the wilderness;
They have reared its fortresses;
They have built its palaces;
He hath reduced it to desolation.
14 Howl, ye ships of Tarshish;
For your strength is laid waste.

15 It shall come to pass in that day,
That Tyre shall be forgotten seventy years,
According to the days of one king;
At the end of seventy years
Shall Tyre have a song like that of a harlot.
16 Take a harp, go about the city,
O harlot, devoted to forgetfulness!
Make sweet melody, multiply song,
That thou mayest be kept in remembrance.
17 It shall then be at the end of seventy years,
That Jehovah will visit Tyre;
And then shall she return to her hire,
And shall commit fornication
With all the kingdoms of the earth
Which are upon the earth.
18 Yet her merchandise and her hire

Shall be holy to Jehovah;
It shall not be treasured nor laid up;
But her merchandise shall be
For them that dwell before Jehovah,
That they may eat sufficiently,
And may have a thick covering.

CHAPTER XXIV.

1 Behold, Jehovah emptieth the earth,
  Maketh it bare,
  Overturneth its face,
  And scattereth its inhabitants.
2 And it shall be, as the people, so the priest;
  As the servant, so his master;
  As the maid, so her mistress;
  As the buyer, so the seller;
  As the lender, so the borrower;
  As the usurer, so he that giveth usury.[1]
3 By emptying shall the earth be emptied,
  And by plundering shall it be plundered;
  For Jehovah hath spoken this word.
4 The earth hath lamented, and hath fallen;
  The world hath languished, and hath fallen;
  They who were the lofty people of the earth have languished.
5 And the earth hath been deceitful under its inhabitants;
  Because they have transgressed the laws,
  They have changed the ordinance,
  They have broken the covenant of eternity.

6 Therefore hath the curse consumed the earth,
  And its inhabitants are made desolate;
  Therefore are the inhabitants of the earth burned,
  And few men have been left.
7 The wine hath failed;
  The vine hath languished;
  All who were of joyful heart have groaned.
8 The joy of tabrets hath ceased,
  The noise of them that exult is ended,
  The mirth of the harp is silent.
9 They shall not drink wine with a song;
  Strong drink shall be bitter to them that drink it.
10 The city of vanity is broken down;
   Every house is shut up, that none may enter.
11 There is a cry about wine in the streets;

---

[1] Or, As the creditor, so the debtor.

　　　　All joy is darkened;
　　　　The mirth of the land hath departed.
　　12 Desolation is left in the city,
　　　　And the gate is smitten with desolation.

　　13 For in the midst of the land,
　　　　In the midst of the peoples,
　　　　Thus shall it be as the shaking of an olive-tree,
　　　　And as the shaking of the grapes, when the vintage is ended.
　　14 They shall lift up their voice;
　　　　They shall shout for the majesty of the Lord;
　　　　They shall cry aloud from the sea.
　　15 Therefore glorify ye Jehovah in the valleys,
　　　　The name of Jehovah, the God of Israel, in the isles of the sea.
　　16 From the uttermost part of the earth have we heard songs,
　　　　Glory to the Righteous One!

　　　　And I said, I have leanness! I have leanness! Wo to me!
　　　　The treacherous dealers have dealt treacherously;
　　　　With treachery have the treacherous dealers dealt treacherously.
　　17 Fear, and the pit, and the snare
　　　　Are upon thee, O inhabitant of the earth!
　　18 And it shall come to pass,
　　　　That he who fleeth from the voice of fear
　　　　Shall fall into the pit,
　　　　And he who goeth up out of the midst of the pit
　　　　Shall be taken in the snare;
　　　　For the windows from on high are opened,
　　　　And the foundations of the earth are shaken.
　　19 By bruising is the earth bruised;
　　　　By breaking down is the earth broken down;
　　　　By shaking is the earth shaken.
　　20 With reeling doth the earth reel, like a drunkard;
　　　　And it shall be removed, like a tabernacle;
　　　　And its transgression shall be heavy upon it;
　　　　And it shall fall, and shall not add to rise again.

　　21 And it shall be in that day,
　　　　Jehovah will visit
　　　　Upon the high army on high,
　　　　And upon the kings of the earth on the earth.
　　22 And with gathering together shall they be gathered together
　　　　Like prisoners in a dungeon;
　　　　And they shall be shut up in a prison;
　　　　Afterwards at the end of many days shall they be visited.
　　23 The moon shall be confounded,
　　　　And the sun shall be ashamed,

When Jehovah of hosts shall reign
In Mount Zion, and in Jerusalem;
And before his elders glory.

CHAPTER XXV.

1 O Jehovah, thou art my God;
I will exalt thee;
I will praise thy name;
For thou hast done a wonderful thing;
Counsels which have been already decreed of old;
Firm truth.
2 For thou hast made of a city a heap;
A fortified city to be a ruin;
A palace of foreigners, that it may not be a city,
That it may never be built.
3 Therefore shall the mighty people glorify thee;
The city of the powerful nations shall fear thee.
4 For thou hast been strength to the poor;
Strength to the needy in his affliction;
A refuge from the flood,
A shadow from the heat;
For the breath of the strong[1] ones
Was as a storm[2] against the wall.
5 As the heat in a dry place,
Thou wilt lay low the noise of foreigners,
As the heat by the shadow of a cloud;
The shouting[3] of the strong ones wilt thou lay low.

6 And Jehovah of hosts will make
For all people in that mountain
A feast of fat things,
A feast of liquids purified,
Of fat things full of marrow,
Of liquids purified.
7 And he will destroy in that mountain
The face of the covering with which all nations were covered,
And the veil which was spread over all nations.
8 He hath destroyed death eternally.
And the Lord Jehovah will wipe away tears from all faces,
And will take away the disgrace of his people from all the earth;
For Jehovah hath spoken it.
9 And it shall be said in that day:
Lo, this is our God;

---

[1] Or, Of the violent ones. [2] Or, As a flood.
[3] Or, The singing; or, The cutting off.

>   We have waited for him,
>   And he will save us;
>   This is Jehovah;
>   We have waited for him;
>   We will rejoice and be glad in his salvation.
> 10 For the hand of Jehovah shall rest on that mountain;
>   And Moab shall be trodden down under him,
>   As straw is trodden down on the dunghill.
> 11 And he will spread out his hand under the midst of them,
>   As a swimmer spreadeth forth his hands to swim;
>   And he will lay low their pride,
>   With the arms of their hands.
> 12 And the fortress of the loftiness of thy walls
>   He will bring down,
>   He will lay low,
>   And he will cast down to the ground,
>   To the dust.

CHAPTER XXVI.

> 1 In that day shall a song be sung in the land of Judah;
>   We have a city of strength;
>   He hath made salvation to be walls and a rampart.
> 2 Open ye the gates,
>   And the righteous nation shall enter,
>   Which keepeth the truth.
> 3 The thought is fixed;
>   Thou wilt keep peace, peace;
>   For they have trusted in thee.
> 4 Hope ye in Jehovah for ever;
>   For in Jah Jehovah is the strength of ages.
>
> 5 For he will bow down the inhabitants of loftiness;
>   He will lay low the elevated city;
>   He will lay it low to the ground;
>   He will bring it to the dust.
> 6 The foot shall tread it down;
>   The feet of the poor,
>   The steps of the needy.
> 7 Straightnesses are the path of the righteous man;
>   The straight way of the righteous man thou wilt weigh.[1]
> 8 Even in the way of thy judgments, O Jehovah,
>   We have waited for thee;
>   To thy name,

---

[1] Or, Thou, who art upright, wilt weigh (or, wilt direct) the path of the righteous man.

And to the remembrance of thee,
Is the desire of the soul.
9 My soul hath desired thee in the night;
Yea, with my spirit within me I will seek thee in the morning;[1]
For so soon as thy judgments shall be in the earth,
The inhabitants of the earth shall learn righteousness.
10 The wicked man will obtain favour,
And will not learn righteousness;
In the land of upright actions he will deal unjustly,
And will not behold the majesty of Jehovah.
11 Jehovah, though thy hand is lifted up,
They will not see;
They shall see, and be ashamed,
Through their envy of the people;
Yea, the fire of thine enemies shall devour them.

12 O Jehovah, thou wilt ordain peace for us;
For thou also hast wrought all our works for us.
13 O Jehovah our God,
Lords besides thee have had dominion over us;
By thee only will we call thy name to remembrance.
14 The dead shall not live;
The slain shall not rise again;
Therefore thou hast visited and driven them away,
And hast destroyed all remembrance of them.
15 Thou hast added to the nation, O Jehovah!
Thou hast added to the nation;
Thou art glorified;
Thou hast enlarged all the boundaries of the earth.
16 O Jehovah, in trouble have they visited thee;
They poured out a prayer, when thy chastening was upon them.
17 As a woman with child, who draweth near to her delivery,
Is in pain, and crieth out in her pains;
So have we been before thy face, O Jehovah.
18 We have been in labour,
We have had pain,
As if we had brought forth wind;
Salvation hath not been wrought for the earth,
And the inhabitants of the world have not fallen.

19 Thy dead men shall live;
My dead body, they shall arise;
Awake and sing, ye inhabitants of the dust;
For thy dew is the dew of herbs;

[1] Or, Earnestly.

And the earth shall cast out the dead.[1]
20 Come, O my people;
Enter thou into thy chambers;
Shut the door behind thee;
Hide thyself a little for a moment,
Till the indignation pass over.
21 For, behold, Jehovah cometh out of his place,
To visit the iniquity of the inhabitant of the earth against him;
And the earth shall disclose her blood,
And shall no longer cover her slain.

CHAPTER XXVII.

1 In that day will Jehovah visit
With his hard, and great, and strong sword,
On leviathan the piercing serpent,
And on leviathan the crooked serpent;
And he will slay the dragon that is in the sea.

2 In that day sing ye to the vineyard of redness.
3 I Jehovah keep it;
Every moment will I water it;
That (the enemy) may not visit it,
I will keep it night and day.
4 Fury doth not dwell in me.
Who shall engage me in battle with the brier and thorn?[2]
I will pass through it in a hostile manner,
I will utterly burn it up.
5 Will she take hold of my strength,
That she may make peace with me?
Yea, that she may make peace with me?
6 Afterwards shall Jacob put forth roots;
Israel shall bud and blossom;
And the face of the world shall be filled with fruit.

7 Hath he smitten him according to the stroke of him that smote him?
Hath he been slain according to the slaughter of them that slew him?
8 In measure, in her shooting forth,
Thou wilt contend with her;
Even though he blow with his violent wind

[1] Or, Thou wilt overthrow the land of the giants; or, The earth will cause the giants to fall.
[2] Or, Who shall set the brier against the thorn? or, Who shall set me as a brier and thorn?

In the day of the east wind.
9 Therefore in this manner shall the iniquity of Jacob be expiated;
And this is all the fruit,
The taking away of his sin;
When he shall make all the stones of the altar
As lime-stones broken in pieces,
That groves and images may not rise again.
10 Yet the fortified city shall be desolate;
The inhabited place shall be deserted,
And forsaken like a wilderness.
There the calf shall feed,
And there shall lie down,
And shall browse on its tops.
11 When its harvest shall wither, they shall break[1] it;
Women coming shall burn it;
For it is a people that doth not understand;
Therefore their Maker will not have compassion on them,
And he who formed them will not be gracious to them.

12 Yet in that day it shall come to pass
That Jehovah will thrash
From the channel of the river
To the river of Egypt;
And ye shall be gathered one by one,
O children of Israel.
13 It shall also come to pass in that day
That the great trumpet shall be blown;
And they shall come who were perishing in the land of Assyria,
And who had been scattered in the land of Egypt;
And they shall worship Jehovah
In the holy mountain, in Jerusalem.

CHAPTER XXVIII.

1 Wo to the crown of pride of the drunkards of Ephraim;
For the splendour of his glory shall be a fading flower,
Which is on the head of the valley of the fat ones,
Of them that are overcome by wine.
2 Behold, the Lord hath a mighty and strong one;
As a deluge of hail,
A desolating whirlwind;
As the violence of mighty waters overflowing,
Casting down to the earth with the hand.
3 The crown of pride of the drunkards of Ephraim

---

[1] Or, Shall cut it down.

Shall be trodden under feet.
4 And the splendour of his glory shall be a fading flower,
Which is on the head of the valley of the fat ones;
Like the premature fig before the summer,
Which, while he looketh at it,
While it is yet in his hand,
He that seeth it devoureth.

5 In that day will Jehovah of hosts
Become a crown of glory
And a diadem of excellence
To the remnant of his people,
6 And a spirit of judgment to him that sitteth on the judgment-seat,
And strength to them that drive back the battle to the gate.

7 But they also have erred through wine;
Through strong drink they have gone astray.
The priest and the prophet have erred through strong drink;
They have been swallowed up by wine;
They have gone astray through strong drink;
They have erred in vision,
They have stumbled in judgment.
8 For all tables are full of nauseous vomiting,
So that no place is unoccupied.

9 Whom shall he teach knowledge?
And whom shall he make to understand doctrine?
Them that are weaned from the milk?
Them that are withdrawn from the breasts?
10 For precept must be on precept, precept on precept;
Instruction on instruction, instruction on instruction;
Here a little, there a little.
11 For with stammering lips will he speak to this people,
And with a foreign tongue.
12 For he said to them, This is the rest;
Cause the weary to rest;
And this is the refreshing;
And they refused to hear.
13 The word of Jehovah shall therefore be to them
Rule upon rule, rule upon rule;
Instruction upon instruction, instruction upon instruction;
Here a little, there a little;
Therefore they shall go, and shall fall backward,
Shall be broken, and snared, and taken.

14 Therefore hear the word of Jehovah, ye scornful men,
Who govern this people, which is in Jerusalem.

15 Because ye have said,
   We have struck a league with death,
   And with hell have we made a compact;
   When the overflowing scourge shall pass through,
   It shall not come to us;
   For we have made falsehood our refuge,
   And under vanity have we hidden ourselves.
16 Wherefore thus saith the Lord Jehovah:
   Behold, I will lay in Zion a stone, a stone of trial,
   A precious corner-stone, a sure foundation.
   He that believeth shall not make haste.

17 And I will lay judgment to the line,
   And righteousness to the measure.[1]
   The hail shall sweep away the reliance of falsehood,
   And the waters shall overflow the hiding-place.
18 And your compact with death shall be disannulled;
   Your agreement with hell shall not stand;
   When the overflowing scourge shall pass through,
   Then shall ye become a treading down to it.
19 From the time that it shall pass,
   It shall seize you every morning,
   And shall pass every day by day and by night;
   And it shall be that terror[2] alone
   Shall cause them to understand the report.
20 For the bed is short, so that it is not enough;
   The covering shall be narrow for wrapping.
21 For as in Mount Perazim will Jehovah stand up,
   And as in the valley of Gibeon will he be angry;[3]
   To do his work, his strange work;
   To perform his act, his strange act.
22 Now therefore be ye not mockers,
   Lest your chains be more firmly fastened;
   For I have heard from the Lord Jehovah of hosts a consumption,
   And a completion on the whole earth.

23 Listen ye, and hear my voice;
   Hearken, and hear my speech.
24 Doth the ploughman plough every day, that he may sow?
   Doth he open and break the clods of his field?
25 When he hath levelled its surface,
   Will he not then scatter fitches, and sow cummin,
   And allot wheat in measure, and barley measured,
   And spelt in its order?

[1] Or, Plummet.   [2] Or, Agitation of mind.
[3] Or, He will make a noise.

26 His God instructeth him,
   And teacheth him what is right.
27 Certainly vetches shall not be thrashed with a toothed instrument,
   Nor shall the wheel of a cart be turned round on the cummin;
   For vetches are beaten with a staff,
   And cummin with a rod.
28 Though wheat be bruised,
   He doth not bruise it continually,
   Nor always cause the wheel of his cart to grind it,
   Lest he crush it with its teeth.
29 This also hath proceeded from Jehovah of hosts,
   Who is wonderful in counsel,
   And majestic in procedure.

CHAPTER XXIX.

1 Alas! Ariel, Ariel,
  The city which David inhabited,
  Add ye year to year,
  That the lambs may be slain.
2 Yet I will bring Ariel into distress,
  And there shall be grief and sorrow,
  And it shall be to me as Ariel.
3 And I will encamp against thee round about,
  And will attack thee with a military force,
  And will erect ramparts against thee.
4 Then shalt thou be brought low,
  Thou shalt speak out of the earth,
  And thy speech shall come out of the dust,
  And thy voice shall be like that of a sorcerer out of the earth,
  And thy speech shall mutter out of the dust.
5 And the sound of thy foreigners shall be as the small dust,
  And the multitude of thy mighty men as the passing chaff,
  And it shall be in a moment suddenly.
6 Thou shalt be visited by Jehovah of hosts
  With thunder, and earthquake, and great noise,
  With whirlwind and tempest,
  And with the flame of devouring fire.

7 And as a dream of a vision of the night shall be
  The multitude of all the nations that fight against Ariel,
  Of every one that fighteth,
  And that raiseth fortifications against her,
  And that distresseth her.
8 It shall therefore be
  As when a hungry man dreameth, and behold! he eateth,

But when he awaketh, his soul is empty;
And as when a thirsty man dreameth, and behold! he drinketh,
But when he awaketh, he is faint, and his soul hath appetite;
So shall be the multitude of all the nations
That fight against Mount Zion.

9 Tarry and wonder;
They are blinded and they blind;
They are drunken, but not with wine;
They stagger, and not with strong drink.
10 For Jehovah hath overpowered you with the spirit of slumber,
And hath closed your eyes;
Your prophets and principal seers
He hath struck with darkness.
11 Therefore every vision hath become to you
As the words of a sealed book;
Which if they deliver to one who knoweth letters,
And say, Read in it, I pray,
Then shall he say, I cannot,
For it is sealed:
12 And if the book be delivered to one who hath not learned letters,
And it be said, Read in it, I pray,
Then shall he say, I know not letters.

13 Therefore the Lord saith:
Because this people draw near to me with their mouth,
And honour me with their lips,
And have removed their heart far from me,
And their fear toward me hath been taught by the commandment of men;
14 Therefore, behold! I add to do
A wonderful work among this people,
A miracle and a prodigy;
For the wisdom of their wise men shall perish,
And the prudence of their prudent men shall vanish away.
15 Wo to them that conceal themselves from Jehovah,
That they may hide counsel;
For their works are in the dark, and they say,
Who seeth us? and, Who knoweth us?
16 Is your turning reckoned like potter's clay?
Doth a work say of its author, He did not make me?
And doth a thing framed say of its framer, He did not understand?

17 Is it not yet a little, a little,
And Lebanon shall be changed into Carmel,

And Carmel shall be reckoned a forest?
18 And in that day shall the deaf hear
The words of the book,
And the eyes of the blind shall see
Out of obscurity and out of darkness.
19 Then shall the humble again take joy in Jehovah,
And the poor of men shall rejoice in the Holy One of Israel.
20 For the violent man is brought to nought,
The mocker is despised;
And they who hastened early to iniquity are ruined.
21 Who make a man to offend in word,
Who have laid snares for him that reproveth in the gate,
And have turned aside the righteous man for nothing.
22 Therefore Jehovah, who redeemed Abraham,
Speaketh thus to the house of Jacob:
Jacob shall not now be confounded,
Nor shall his face now become pale.
23 For when he shall see in the midst of him
His children, the work of my hands,
They shall sanctify my name,
They shall sanctify the Holy One of Jacob,
They shall fear the God of Israel.
24 Then they that erred in spirit shall learn understanding,
And the murmurers shall learn doctrine.

CHAPTER XXX.

1 Wo to the rebellious[1] children, saith Jehovah,
That they may take counsel, and not from me;
That they may cover a secret,[2] and not from my Spirit;
That they may add sin to sin.
2 Who set out that they may go down into Egypt,
And have not inquired at my mouth;
Strengthening themselves with the strength of Pharaoh,
And trusting in the shadow of Egypt.
3 But the strength of Pharaoh
Shall become to you shame;
And reliance on the shadow of Egypt
Shall become disgrace.
4 For his princes were in Zoan,
And his ambassadors came to Hanes.
5 All shall be ashamed
Of a people that will not profit them,
And will not become a help,
And will not yield advantage,

---

[1] Or, Perverse.   [2] Or, That they may pour out a pouring out.

But will become shame,
And even disgrace.

6 The burden of the beasts of the south.
In the land of trouble and anguish,
The lion and the stronger lion,
The viper and the flying serpent;
While they shall carry their riches
On the shoulders of young asses,
And on the bunches of camels,
To a people that will not profit them.
7 Surely the Egyptians are vanity,
And shall help in vain.
Therefore have I cried to her,
Their strength is to sit still.

8 Now go, and write this vision on a tablet before them,
And engrave it in a book,
That it may be till the last day,
For ever and ever.
9 For this is a rebellious people,
Lying children,
Children who refuse to hear the law of Jehovah.
10 Who say to the seers, Do not see,
And to the foreseers, Do not foresee to us right things;
Speak ye to us flatteries,
See ye errors.
11 Go out of the way;
Turn aside from the path;
Cause the Holy One of Israel
To depart from our presence.
12 Therefore thus saith the Holy One of Israel:
Because ye have disdained this word,
And have trusted in violence and wickedness,
And have rested on it;
13 Therefore shall your iniquity be to you
Like a breach falling,
Like the bulging out in a lofty wall,
The fall of which comes suddenly and unexpectedly.
14 And the breaking of it shall be
As the breaking of a potter's vessel,
Which is broken without mercy;
And in its breaking there is not found a sherd
To carry fire from the hearth,
Or to draw water from a well.
15 For thus saith the Lord Jehovah,
The Holy One of Israel:
In rest and quietness shall you be safe;

In peace and confidence shall be your strength ;
But ye would not.
16 And ye said, No, but we will flee on horses ;
Therefore shall ye flee ;
We will ride on the swift;
Therefore they that shall pursue you shall be more swift.
17 A thousand as one from the face of the rebuke of one,
From the face of the rebuke of five shall ye flee,
Until ye shall be left
As the mast of a ship on the top of a mountain,
And as a banner on a hill.

18 Therefore will Jehovah wait for you,
That he may have compassion on you ;
And therefore will he be exalted,
That he may have compassion on you ;
For Jehovah is a God of judgment :
Blessed are all they that wait for him.
19 Surely the people in Zion shall dwell in Jerusalem :
Weeping thou shalt not weep ;
With compassion will he have compassion on thee ;
At the voice of thy cry, as soon as he shall hear it,
He will answer thee.
20 When the Lord shall have given to you
Bread of anguish
And water of affliction,
Thy rain shall not be withheld,
And thine eyes shall see thy rain.
21 Then shall thine ears hear a word behind thee,
Saying, This is the way ;
Walk ye in it ;
Whether ye go to the right,
Or go to the left.
22 Then shall ye profane
The covering of the graven images of thy silver,
And the covering of thy molten gold ;
And thou shalt put it away from thee as a menstruous cloth,
And shalt say to it, Depart.[1]
23 Then will he give rain to thy seed,
When thou shalt have sowed the ground,
And bread of the produce of the earth ;
And it shall be plentiful and fat ;
And in that day thy cattle
Shall feed in large pastures.
24 Thine oxen also,
And the young asses that labour the ground,

[1] Or, Begone!

Shall eat clean provender,
Which shall be winnowed with the shovel
And with the sieve.
25 And it shall come to pass,
That on every high mountain,
And on every lofty hill,
Shall be streams, streams of waters,
In the day of the great slaughter
When the towers shall have fallen.
26 And the light of the moon shall be as the light of the sun,
And the light of the sun shall be sevenfold,
As the light of seven days,
In the day when Jehovah
Shall have bound up the breach of his people,
And shall have healed the stroke of their wound.

27 Behold! the name of Jehovah cometh
From a distant place:
His face burneth,
And the burden is heavy;
His lips are full of indignation,
And his tongue as a devouring fire.
28 And his breath, as an overflowing torrent,
Shall divide even to the neck;
To sift the nations with a useless sieve;
And on the cheeks of the peoples
There shall be a bridle causing to err.
29 You shall have a song, as in the night
When a festival is kept,
And gladness of heart,
As of him that moveth to a pipe,
That he may come to the mountain of Jehovah,
To the Mighty One of Israel.
30 And Jehovah shall cause to be heard the power of his voice,
And shall cause to be seen the descent of his arm,
With rage of countenance,
And with the flame of devouring fire,
With scattering, with flood, and with hailstones.
31 Verily by the voice of Jehovah shall the Assyrian be crushed,
Who smote with a rod.
32 And in every passage shall be the fastened staff,
Which Jehovah shall lay upon him
With tabrets and harps,
And with battles of lifting up
Shall he fight against her.
33 For Tophet is ordained since yesterday;
Yea, for the king it is prepared:
He hath made it deep and large;

The pile of it is fire, and much wood;
The breath of Jehovah, like a torrent of brimstone,
Doth kindle it.

CHAPTER XXXI.

1 Wo to them that go down into Egypt for help,
And who rely on horses,
And who trust to chariots, because they are numerous,
And to horses, because they are very strong,
And have not looked to the Holy One of Israel,
Nor have sought Jehovah.
2 Yet he also is wise:
Therefore he will bring evil,
And will not make void his words;
He will rise up against the house of the evil-doers,
And against the aid of the workers of vanity.
3 And verily the Egyptian is a man, and not God;
And his horses are flesh, and not spirit.
Therefore, as soon as Jehovah shall stretch out his arm,
The helper shall fall,
And he who is helped shall fall down,
And all shall fail together.
4 For thus hath Jehovah said to me:
As the lion roareth,
And the young lion for his prey,
Against whom, if a multitude of shepherds be gathered together,
He shall not be alarmed by their cry,
And shall not humble himself on account of their noise;
Thus will Jehovah of hosts come down
To fight for Mount Zion,
And for its hill.
5 As birds which fly,
So will Jehovah of hosts defend Jerusalem;
Defending, he will deliver it,
And passing over, he will preserve it.

6 Return ye,
As ye have made a deep revolt,
O children of Israel!
7 For in that day shall a man cast away
The idols of his silver,
And the idols of his gold,
Which your hands have made for you, a sin.

8 Then shall the Assyrian fall by the sword, not of a mighty man;
  And the sword, not of a man, shall devour him;
  And by flight shall he seek safety from the face of the sword,
  And his young men shall melt away.
9 He shall pass to his stronghold through fear,
  And his princes shall tremble at the banner, saith Jehovah,
  Who hath a fire[1] in Zion,
  And who hath a furnace in Jerusalem.

CHAPTER XXXII.

1 Behold! a king shall reign in righteousness,
  And princes shall rule in judgment.
2 And that man shall be
  As a hiding-place from the wind,
  As a covert from the rain,
  As streams of waters on dry ground,
  As the shadow of a great rock in a weary land.
3 Then the eyes of them that see shall not be closed up,
  And the ears of them that hear shall hearken.
4 And the heart of fools shall be eagerly directed to knowledge,
  And the tongue of stammerers shall be ready to speak plainly.
5 No longer shall the base man be called liberal,
  Nor shall the parsimonious man be called bountiful.
6 For the vile person will speak vileness,
  And his heart will contrive iniquity,
  To commit wickedness,
  That he may utter mockery against Jehovah,
  That he may make empty the hungry soul,
  And that he may withhold drink from him that is thirsty.
7 The instruments of the covetous man are evil;[2]
  He contriveth wickednesses,
  That he may deceive the simple by lying words,
  And that he may speak against the poor man in judgment.
8 But the liberal man shall devise liberal things,
  And in acting liberally he shall make progress.

9 Ye women at ease, arise;
  Hear my voice, ye careless daughters;
  Hearken to my speech.
10 Days above a year shall ye tremble, ye careless women;
  For the vintage shall fail,
  And the gathering shall not come.
11 Tremble, ye women that are at ease;

---

[1] Or, Who is to him a fire.   [2] Or, The measures are evil.

Be troubled, ye careless women;
Strip you, make you bare, gird your limbs.
12 Mourning over the udders,
Over the pleasant fields,
Over the fruitful vine.
13 There shall come up the thorn and brier
On the land of my people,
Even on all the houses of gladness in the city of rejoicing.
14 For the palace shall be forsaken;
The noise of the city shall be left;
The tower and the fortress
Shall be reduced to dens for ever,
Where wild asses may delight themselves,
And where flocks may feed.

15 Till the Spirit be poured out upon you from on high,
And the wilderness become a cultivated field,
And the cultivated field be reckoned like a forest.
16 And judgment shall dwell in the wilderness,
And justice shall have its abode in the cultivated field.
17 And the work of righteousness shall be peace;
The effect of righteousness shall be
Safety and quietness for ever.
18 And my people shall dwell in a tabernacle of peace,
And in safe dwellings,
And in quiet resting-places.
19 And in coming down the hail shall turn aside on the forest,
And the city shall be situated in a low place.
20 Blessed are ye who sow on all waters,
Who send forth the feet of the ox and of the ass.